THE NEW AMERICAN POLITICAL SYSTEM

Samuel H. Beer, Fred I. Greenstein,
Hugh Heclo, Samuel C. Patterson,
Martin Shapiro, Austin Ranney,
Jeane J. Kirkpatrick, Richard A. Brody,
Leon D. Epstein, and Anthony King

Edited by Anthony King

 American Enterprise Institute
for Public Policy Research
Washington, D.C.

Library of Congress Cataloging in Publication Data
Main entry under title:

The New American political system.

  (AEI studies ; 213)
  Includes index.
    1. United States—Politics and government—1969–1974
—Addresses, essays, lectures. 2. United States—
Politics and government—1974–1977—Addresses, essays,
lectures. 3. United States—Politics and government—
1977–   —Addresses, essays, lectures. I. King,
Anthony Stephen. II. Series: American Enterprise
Institute for Public Policy Research. AEI studies ; 213.
JK1717.N48   320.9′73′092   78-11849
ISBN 0-8447-3315-6

AEI Studies 213

Second printing, March 1979

Third printing, April 1980

Printed in the United States of America

Teresa D. Egan

THE NEW AMERICAN POLITICAL SYSTEM

Exam —

Discuss the signif of the
... D ... in the Dem of Reg —

CONTENTS

INTRODUCTION

Political scientists, more than many of them realize, are takers of snapshots rather than moving pictures. This is especially true of those political scientists who study political institutions. They identify an institution, they describe how it functions, they explain why it functions in the way that it does, and they then often go on to infer, sometimes explicitly, sometimes implicitly, that it must function in the way that it does and that it could not possibly function in any other way.

Take, for example, the seniority system in the United States Congress, under which the ranking majority member of any congressional committee was the chairman of that committee, irrespective of his personal qualities and the views of the other members of the committee. For many years students of Congress noted that the seniority system had been in existence since about 1910 and noted, too, that all of the various attempts that had been made to change the system had failed. They pointed out that, whatever its defects, the system prevented the deep splits in the majority party that would undoubtedly occur if committee chairmen were elected; it also ensured that committee chairmen were invariably men of great experience. The seniority system in the committees was perpetuated by the pervasiveness of seniority as a norm in Congress, by the ease with which older members of Congress could put down any younger members who dared to criticize the system, and also by the fact that younger members typically accumulated seniority remarkably quickly, so that before very long they, too, had acquired a vested interest in the system.

The trouble with this analysis was that it failed to give an indication of the circumstances in which the seniority system might be

1

successfully challenged. It failed, in other words, to anticipate the events of January 1975, when the Democratic caucus in the House of Representatives denied reelection as chairmen to three senior congressmen who were the ranking majority members of their committees. Suddenly, seniority was not the only criterion for the election of committee chairmen. Everyone was surprised (not only, it must be said, political scientists). Moreover, most students of Congress had also assumed that committee chairmen would continue to be virtually all-powerful on their committees—that they would go on being able to determine when their committees would, and would not, meet, which items of legislation their committees would consider, and in what order, and so on. Yet by the late 1970s committee chairmen, although still very influential people, had lost much of their former power. They felt bound to defer to the other members of the committee; much of the committees' work had been devolved onto subcommittees, often chaired by junior, even freshman, congressmen and senators.

This volume arises out of the puzzlement felt by many political scientists—and by many ordinary Americans—when they contemplate the workings of the American political system in the late 1970s. The old landmarks are still there. The Supreme Court and Congress still meet, the White House still stands, the national nominating conventions still select two presidential candidates every four years. Yet the old landmarks are features of a landscape that has changed in all sorts of ways, some of them dramatic, some more subtle. Were someone to return to the United States today, having been out of the country and out of touch with its politics for the past twenty years, he would be like a man returning after many years to his childhood home. Everything would be familiar and unfamiliar at the same time. The national conventions still select presidential candidates, but they do so in ways, and as the result of processes, that are almost entirely a product of the 1960s and early 1970s. In presidential nominating politics, the year 1960 was closer to 1932, even to 1912, than to 1976. Voters still identify with political parties, but in much smaller numbers than was the case twenty years ago.

No one who lived through the period between the inauguration of John Kennedy and the inauguration of Jimmy Carter needs to be reminded that this was an enormously turbulent period. It was the period of the New Frontier and the Great Society, of the abortive invasion of the Bay of Pigs and the Cuban missile crisis, of riots in the cities and unrest on the campuses, of civil rights and women's rights, of the war in Vietnam, of America's rapprochement with

2

China; a period in which one President was assassinated and another became the first American President ever to be driven from office. The period began with the American economy the strongest in the world and looking as though it would remain that way indefinitely; as it closed, the American economy was still the strongest in the world, but its prospects seemed bleaker than at any time since before the Second World War. The period began optimistically: "we shall pay any price, bear any burden, meet any hardship." It ended on a note that was altogether more subdued: "we have learned that 'more' is not necessarily 'better,' that even our great nation has its recognized limits."

Some of the changes that have taken place in the American political system have been a specific response to the events of the 1960s and 1970s. For example, the new restrictions placed on autonomous presidential involvement in foreign affairs are clearly the result of the Vietnam War and of such episodes as the secret bombing of Cambodia. Others, however, do not so obviously reflect the events of the period, but seem to represent a working out of forces that were already present in the system. For example, a causal connection can be drawn between the Vietnam War and the events at the 1968 Democratic convention in Chicago, and between the 1968 Democratic convention and the McGovern-Fraser commission, whose report led directly (if unintentionally) to the proliferation of primary elections. All the same, it seems probable that, if the Vietnam War and McGovern-Fraser had not led to the proliferation of primaries, something else would have. Primaries are a response not just to the politics of a specific epoch but to ideas and forces at work much deeper inside American political life—television, the jet airplane, the decline in party identification, the idea of direct popular participation.

The contributors to this volume were all set a similar task. Given the particular aspects of the American political system that they were to write about, they were asked to describe any important changes that they thought had taken place between roughly 1960 and the present, to account for the changes, and also to assess their significance. In other words, they were asked the classic questions of political science: "How?", "Why?", and "So what?" Beyond that, there was no formula that the various contributors were expected to adhere to, and each contributor has handled his subject in his own way. This is not another "revisionist" book on American politics; its authors for the most part neither praise nor blame (though their own preferences, inevitably, sometimes emerge). Nor is it a book that seeks to explore in detail the connections between polity and

3

society; its units of analysis are, by and large, the units of analysis of the traditional political science textbook, and social and economic factors are introduced into the analysis only where they are required to explain purely political phenomena.

Some readers may balk at the book's title, *The New American Political System*. Particular features of the system are new, of course; but is the system really new? Such readers are requested most humbly to be patient: the extent to which the system is new will emerge very clearly in the chapters that follow. An attempt to determine whether the system as a whole deserves to be called new will be made in the last chapter.

The focus of this book is, as we have said, on political institutions and political structures. But the workings of political institutions and structures cannot be fully understood without some understanding of the context of ideas within which they have their being. It is therefore with ideas—with the climate of opinion in the 1960s and 1970s—that we begin.

1

In Search of a New Public Philosophy

Samuel H. Beer

In the early 1960s the New Deal finally came to an end. My question is: What, if anything, has taken its place?

By the New Deal I mean here a state of mind, an outlook on politics and government, a public philosophy.[1] For the New Deal consisted not merely of the political and governmental acts constituting the administration of Franklin Roosevelt, but also of a rationale for those acts. In all that furious motion of campaigns, lobbying, and law making, and in the vast and confusing output of statutes, policies, and programs issuing from it, one can discern certain ideas at work. The New Deal had a general character which we recognize by using the term not only as a noun, to refer to a certain period in history, but also as an adjective with broader application, as when we characterize some proposal as "New Dealish" or some candidate as "a New Deal liberal." Certain broad premises gave to the multifarious works of the New Deal a coherence of purpose that made it conceptually not simply a compound of special interests, but also a rationale for the public interest. When I ask, therefore, what has taken the New

---

[1] I am not using the term in the sense given it by Walter Lippmann when he wrote about "the" public philosophy. He meant, in brief, a modernized version of natural law which could be accepted as a set of enduring principles by the nations of the contemporary world generally. *Essays in the Public Philosophy* (Boston: Little, Brown, 1955). I am thinking of something much more limited in time and space. By a public philosophy I mean an outlook on public affairs which is accepted within a nation by a wide coalition and which serves to give definition to problems and direction to government policies dealing with them. While I am concerned in this present discussion with the attitudes of leaders and activists—broadly, members of the political class—my usage fits with that of Everett Ladd who uses the concept in his analysis of public opinion in general. See his *Transformations of the American Party System: Political Coalitions from the New Deal to the 1970s* (New York: Norton, 1975), p. 87 and *passim*.

Deal's place, I mean its place as that crucial element in a democratic polity, a public philosophy.

To say that a public philosophy is crucial to a democratic polity is not to say that its presence will eliminate, or even reduce, political conflict. Quite the contrary. Even when a public philosophy prevails within a nation, its assertions will provoke counterassertions, as the "liberalism" of the 1930s called forth the "conservatism" of the 1940s. Yet such conflict too has its coherence: one side says "yes," the other "no," but both are trying to answer the same question. Very different is the model of conflict which some observers see in contemporary societies in which warring groups, emptied of any vision of the social whole and guided only by the residuum of their private concerns, quarrel over the spoils.

The following discussion will be limited to domestic affairs. To take up attitudes toward foreign policy would unduly complicate the analysis. Moreover, although one can for fairly long periods of time identify important continuities in American approaches to foreign affairs, these approaches often do not depend on or vary in harmony with current approaches to domestic affairs. In its early years, for instance, the New Deal outlook coincided first with an isolationist phase in foreign policy, then with an internationalist one. In accord with this history, the term, in common usage, refers essentially to attitudes toward domestic matters.

The Public Philosophy of the New Deal

If we are to grasp what is new in the meaning of American politics today, we must distinguish it from what went before. Since I identify that earlier outlook with the New Deal, I need first to look at the thought of the thirties. There is no better place to start than the famous first inaugural of Franklin Roosevelt.[2]

One major premise of that statement of purpose was highly articulate: what was to be done would be directed and largely conducted by the federal government. The national idea was as strenuously championed by Franklin as it had been by Theodore Roosevelt, and the address of March 4, 1933, could fittingly have been entitled "the new nationalism." None of the main points can be summarized without reference to the nation: The emergency is national because of "the inter-dependence of the various elements in, and parts of,

[2] "F.D. Roosevelt's First Inaugural Address" in *Documents of American History*, ed. Henry Steele Commager, 7th ed., 2 vols. (New York: Meredith, 1963), vol. 2, no. 476.

the United States." Our purpose must be, first, "the establishment of a sound national economy" and beyond that "the assurance of a rounded and permanent national life." The mode of action must be national, conducted by the federal government and carried out "on a national scale," helped "by national planning." It is "this nation" which "asks for action," as "the people of the United States . . . have registered a mandate." Indeed, it is the nation that will embody and carry out that action as "this great army of our people, dedicated to a disciplined attack upon our common problems." The term "nation," as noun or adjective, is used sixteen times in the speech, appearing in fourteen of the fifty-two paragraphs. No other thematic term faintly rivals it in emphasis. Democracy is mentioned only once; liberty, equality, or the individual, not at all. Next to "nation" the term given most emphasis is, not strangely, "leadership," with five mentions. God received the obligatory reference at the end. But there was no effort to seek spiritual guidance in biblical quotation. On the contrary, "our common difficulties," in Roosevelt's view, concerned "only material things."

Roosevelt's nationalism was a doctrine of federal centralization, and under his administration, in peace as well as war, the balance of the American federal system swung sharply toward Washington. This was a sharp break from the normal expectations of the past, especially for the Democratic party, but also for the whole country. Traditionally, if there had been a party of centralization, it had been the party which had preserved the Union and laid the governmental foundations for the immense economic expansion of the decades following the Civil War. But the Republican conception of federal functions, however advanced over Jacksonian norms, had been limited, calling for the establishment of the infrastructure of a free market economy within the nation and legitimizing intervention on occasion to perfect, but not to supersede that market. Although the Democrats had long attracted support from less well off and especially immigrant groups in northern cities, neither there nor in the South did they encourage their adherents to look to Washington for benefits or remedies. In short, before Roosevelt the issue of national action to sustain and direct the economy did not arise. In Congress the question of "government management of the economy," which in later years would stand out as one of the main issues evoking stable voting alignments, was simply not on the agenda.[3] A major event in the

---

[3] Barbara D. Sinclair, "Party Realignment and the Transformation of the Political Agenda: the House of Representatives 1925–1938," *American Political Science Review*, vol. 71 (September 1977), pp. 940–53.

realignment of the thirties was the emergence of this issue and its division of the national legislature along highly partisan lines. Federal activism, which some have taken as the principal dividing line between the main forces in American politics since the thirties,[4] was introduced by the New Deal.

But as in the first inaugural itself, Roosevelt called not only for a centralization of government, but also for a nationalization of politics. He not only said that the federal government would take the lead; he also urged the people to demand and shape that lead. He exhorted voters and citizens to turn to Washington as the center of power on which to exert their pressures and project their expectations. This was not a norm that was immediately or readily adopted. A principal and reiterated theme of the utterance of his administration was to assure the people that the federal government could solve their problems, would not harm them, was their agent, indeed consisted simply of the people themselves acting in their national capacity.[5]

Economists have doubted that the New Deal was a "social revolution" in the sense of doing much to redistribute income, promote economic growth, or restore full employment.[6] They may well be right. But in creating among Americans the expectation that the federal government could and should deal with the great economic questions and that the nation could and should bear the consequent burdens, the achievement of the New Deal was close to revolutionary.

In accord with this appeal, a new model of political action arose. Roosevelt called for a new kind of mass politics and even took steps toward party government. He identified the Democratic party as "the party of liberalism"—indeed as "the party of militant liberalism."[7] He struck at its old sectional basis with his abolition of the two-thirds rule in the national convention and, by his "purge" of 1938, attempted

---

[4] For example, James L. Sundquist, *Politics and Policy: The Eisenhower, Kennedy, and Johnson Years* (Washington, D.C.: Brookings Institution, 1968), pp. 500-503 and *passim*.

[5] Here I am speaking from personal experience. During 1935–1936 I worked in the Resettlement Administration, my job being to draft articles that appeared under the name of Rexford G. Tugwell, a leading New Dealer. Frequently I also helped Thomas G. Corcoran, then a rising brain-truster, with speeches for President Roosevelt. I vividly recall our preoccupation with persuading people to look to Washington for the solution of problems and our sense of what a great change in public attitudes this involved.

[6] For example, Douglass C. North, "Was the New Deal a Social Revolution?" in *Growth and Welfare in the American Past*, 2d ed. (Englewood Cliffs, N.J.: Prentice-Hall, 1974), pp. 164-69.

[7] Ronald D. Rotunda, "The 'Liberal' Label: Roosevelt's Capture of a Symbol," in *Public Policy*, ed. John D. Montgomery and Albert O. Hirschman, vol. 17 (Cambridge, Mass.: Harvard University Press, 1968), p. 393.

to mold the party in the legislature and the country into greater conformity with his basic aims.

In this time a nationalization of electoral behavior took place as the old rustic and sectional politics gave way to a new urban and class politics. Yet Roosevelt never phrased his appeal in class terms, nor did the resulting divisions become exclusively class based. His rhetoric remained within the imagery of radical democracy which perceives "the people" as fighting against "the special interests." In the first inaugural the source of our afflictions was seen as "the rulers of the exchanges of mankind's goods," "the unscrupulous money changers." Even at the peak of economic and political conflict in the mid-thirties, Roosevelt found the resources of the American tradition sufficient for his abrasive rhetoric. In his acceptance speech of 1936, he declared that just as 1776 had wiped out "political tyranny" so the present task was to bring "economic tyranny" to an end. "[O]ut of this modern civilization," he continued, "economic royalists had carved new dynasties. New kingdoms were built upon concentration of control over material things. . . . Economic royalists complain that we seek to overthrow the institutions of America. What they really complain of is that we seek to take away their power." [8] "Economic royalist": a powerful metaphor, suggesting the character of the contending forces and the proper direction of policy.[9] It became one of the most quoted items in the Rooseveltian demonology. The President himself relished the phrase and rolled it off in great style.

The New Idea of Equality. One principle of the public philosophy of the New Deal was its nationalism. The New Deal stood for the centralization of government authority and the nationalization of political action as ways of furthering national economic and social development. The substance of such development was shaped by a new view of equality and participation. This democratic principle determined purposes of policy as well as modes of action, giving to the New Deal that bias toward "the forgotten man at the bottom of the economic pyramid" whom Roosevelt had promised to remember in his campaign.[10] But how the forgotten man is to be remembered, in what

---

[8] *The Public Papers and Addresses of Franklin D. Roosevelt*, ed. Samuel I. Rosenman, 13 vols. (New York: Random House, 1938–1950), vol. 5, *The People Approve: 1936*, pp. 230-36.

[9] I have examined the relation between Roosevelt's use of this metaphor and the emerging rationale of the New Deal in "Two Models of Public Opinion: Bacon's 'New Logic' and Diotima's 'Tale of Love'" (The Prothero Lecture), *Transactions of the Royal Historical Society*, 5th ser., vol. 24 (1974), pp. 79-96.

[10] James MacGregor Burns, *Roosevelt: The Lion and the Fox* (New York: Harcourt Brace, 1956), p. 133.

way and to what degree equality is to be promoted, are questions to which quite different answers have been given by the governments of modern industrial societies.

The egalitarianism of the New Deal was a response to what was seen as a twofold problem: a maldistribution of income and a concentration of economic power. In other industrialized countries, similar perceptions had given rise to the social democratic and socialist answers of income redistribution and public ownership. In spite of what might seem to be the considerable opportunities presented by the collapse of the economy and of the Republican party in the early 1930s, however, these alternatives, although put forward by some writers and by leaders of minor parties, never achieved currency in American political debate. The social security system, established in 1935 and deliberately modeled upon foreign examples as well as on the few starts already made in some American states, did involve a mild degree of redistribution. The old age insurance scheme, for instance, while based primarily on the private insurance principle of adjusting benefits to individual contributions, also in some respects embodied the "social principle" of adjusting benefits to need. The welfare part of the system, which provided assistance to poor people not covered by insurance, also could be considered redistributive insofar as its transfers derived from progressive income tax revenues. "Security," however, better than "redistribution," denotes the rationale of the new arrangements.

We commonly remember Roosevelt as a "spender" and the New Deal as introducing a new principle of federal largesse. Federal grants to state and local governments in the name of the "emergency" did rise to unprecedented heights. As the economy recovered under the impact of the defense effort, however, these expenditures on federal aid were radically scaled down. Public expenditure by all governments, which had stood at 11 percent of gross national product in 1927, was still no more than 19.4 percent in 1948.[11] The big leap upward came later.

The kind of redistribution that took priority in the public philosophy of the New Deal was not a redistribution of wealth, but a redistribution of power. This rationale—worked out, statute by statute, in a series of hard fought battles during the formative years of the mid-thirties—was manifest in the economic royalist speech. It was not, however, derived by deduction from an ideology or im-

[11] Frederick C. Mosher, *Recent Trends in Governmental Finances in the United States* (Berkeley: Bureau of Public Administration, University of California, 1961), p. 13.

posed through a comprehensive plan. On the contrary, it was not clearly perceived until, twenty years after Roosevelt took power, John Kenneth Galbraith discovered the concept of "countervailing power" as the unifying principle of some of the major achievements of the thirties. According to Galbraith, although it had hitherto gone unrecognized in political and economic theory, the idea of counter-vailing power alone made fully comprehensible much of the domestic legislation of the previous two decades.[12] Taking up specifically the Wagner Act, the Agricultural Adjustment Act, the Wage and Hour Act, and the Securities and Exchange Commission, he argued that all shared the object of increasing the economic power of a numerous and disadvantaged group obliged to deal with a smaller and more advantaged group. He found that increasingly the differences in American politics had come to center on this issue and indeed concluded that in the previous two decades the major peacetime function of the federal government had become the support of countervailing power.

Since it dealt with the central issues of economic conflict at that time, the National Labor Relations Act (Wagner Act) of 1935 can reasonably be considered the most important example of the method of countervailing power.[13] As stated in Section 1, the act was directed at redressing "the inequality of bargaining power between employees who do not possess full freedom of association or actual liberty of contract and employers who are organised in the corporate or other forms of ownership association." To accomplish this object the act created an administrative body, the National Labor Relations Board, and charged it with two main tasks: (1) to protect the right of employees to organize and to bargain collectively through representatives of their own choosing and (2) to conduct elections by which such representatives would be chosen. Utilizing these new rights, a massive organizing effort swept through American industry, trade union membership rising from 4 million in 1935 to 9 million in 1940 and 15.5 million in 1947. In spite of bitter and sometimes bloody resistance, the act did, in the course of time, substantially achieve its objectives, changing not only the practices but also the attitudes of employers and permanently altering the distribution of power in the economy.

In the context of an industrialized America the Wagner Act gave a new expression to the idea of equality. It departed from the method

---

[12] John Kenneth Galbraith, *American Capitalism: The Concept of Countervailing Power* (Boston: Houghton Mifflin, 1952), pp. 141-42 and *passim*.

[13] Commager, *Documents*, no. 500.

of classical liberalism, however, by explicitly concerning itself with the rights of a particular group, namely wage and salary earners. The older view had directed attention to individuals, seeking to give to each the same rights without regard to group or class identity. Abraham Lincoln had made clear this individualistic and universalistic premise in the way in which he perceived the peculiar evil of slavery and in his vision of the special mission of America. In his message to Congress of July 4, 1861, he elaborated his view of the significance of the struggle to preserve the Union in these words:

> On the side of the Union it is a struggle for maintaining in the world that form and substance of government whose leading object is to elevate the condition of men—to lift artificial weights from all shoulders; to clear the paths of laudable pursuit for all; to afford for all an unfettered start, and a fair chance in the race of life.[14]

This is the pure doctrine of equality of opportunity. On this principle, the kind of equality the law seeks to maintain consists in the guarantee of identical liberties to all individuals, especially with regard to their pursuit of economic success. The Wagner Act departed from this principle by creating rights for a special group; yet it retained the essence of the old rationale since, once these rights were guaranteed by law, it was up to the group to utilize them. Its object was an equality of group rights for employees in their relations with their employers. Any equalizing of results that might follow, however— and the act did anticipate that "the purchasing power of wage earners in industry" would be increased—was up to individual and group effort.

Other reforms of economic structure sustained countervailing power in additional ways. The New Deal farm program gave substance to the slogan "equality for agriculture" by the concept of "parity," defined as the reestablishment of "prices to farmers at a level that will give agricultural commodities a purchasing power with respect to articles farmers buy, equivalent to the purchasing power of agricultural commodities in the base period, August, 1909–July, 1914." The Fair Labor Standards (Wage and Hour) Act of 1938 directly intervened in the market to fix a maximum length for the working week and a minimum hourly wage for certain sectors of the economy. In the establishment of the Tennessee Valley Authority, public ownership was utilized for the production and distribution of electric power. Its principal function, however, was to protect consumers

---

[14] Ibid., no. 205.

generally by providing a "yardstick" against which the performance of private utilities could be judged and regulated. On the whole, although American capitalism was subjected to important reforms, the basic structure remained intact, and the new egalitarianism, while constituting the divisive principle of some bitterly contested political and economic encounters, fitted into the old doctrine of equality of opportunity. Apart from the new guarantees of countervailing power, the beneficiary groups and their members were still on their own in what Lincoln had called "the race of life."

When one looks at the New Deal in the light of the American political tradition, certain broad continuities stand out. As Herbert Croly observed, political belief in America has been oriented by two poles, "the principle of nationality" and "the principle of democracy." [15] In American political history, the two principles have often been divided, as contending leaders and forces have identified with one against the other. Such was the case in the contest of Hamilton against Jefferson. At other times, they have been united, as when Lincoln and the Republican party challenged separatism and slavery in the name of nationalism and democracy. During the New Deal, Franklin Roosevelt again joined the national with the democratic idea in an effort to master the new economic and social realities of the American twentieth century. Power was centralized and politics nationalized for the sake of economic stability and a new balance of economic power. Looking back on his achievement, one can see the continuity of the tradition, but also its adaptation in a unique public philosophy.

The New Terminology. The Roosevelt administration posed a new set of questions, offering to them its own distinctive answers, which, although provoking a relevant set of counterassertions, on the whole prevailed in the actual course of policy making during the following years. So much innovation might reasonably be expected to give rise to new words to describe what was happening in the American polity. A new terminology did arise, first the term "liberalism" and then the term "conservatism," to denote the new divisions in politics and over policy.

Clarity about the history of these words can help with two problems. One problem is that these same words also have a long usage

---

[15] Herbert Croly, *The Promise of American Life* (New York: Macmillan, 1909). I have used Croly's ideas to interpret the New Deal and American liberalism in "Liberalism and the National Idea" in *Left, Right and Center: Essays on Liberalism and Conservatism in the United States,* ed. Robert A. Goldwin (Chicago: Rand McNally, 1965), pp. 142-69.

in European politics which, however, has given them a meaning different from, and to a degree even opposite to, the meaning given them by their history in the United States. Second, as we shall see when we come closer to the present time, this political terminology continued to be used with regard to new issues that arose in the sixties and seventies. This later usage can cause confusion if we do not first clarify the meanings given these terms by the public philosophy of the New Deal.

"Liberal" may seem an odd name for an approach to policy that imposed so many new compulsions. In American political debate the term had had virtually no usage before the New Deal. Originating in post-Napoleonic Europe, it had been used to describe the champions of economic and civil liberty against the restrictions of the *ancien régime*. In Great Britain in later years, however, certain philosophers from T. H. Green to L. T. Hobhouse had put forward justifications for positive government and, just before World War I, Liberal Governments gave a new connotation to the term by a burst of social reform. In the United States this expanded meaning made it easy for intellectual advocates of similar measures to adopt the label, as *The New Republic* did almost from its founding in 1916. This recognition of ideological kinship with the British example constituted one reason for Roosevelt's choice.[16]

What he was trying to do also provided reasons for excluding other possible terms. "Progressive" was wrong because its nostalgic hope of holding back the age of organization in business and politics by trust busting and boss busting did not accord with Roosevelt's acceptance of big government and mass politics. Although he accepted the collectivism of the age, "socialism" was in no sense what he aimed at—besides being politically fatal. Richard Hofstadter has spoken of the "social democratic tinge" of the New Deal reforms.[17] But that term would have been rhetorically awkward, and, moreover, it suggested a redistributive purpose that Roosevelt did not entertain. In short, on the merits alone, and apart from political advantage, "liberal" was right as a label for that uniquely American purpose embodied in the great reforms. In his acceptance speech of 1932, Roosevelt spoke of the Democratic party as "the bearer of liberalism and progress," but it was only in the mid-thirties that the term came to be widely used in comment and debate as a verbal symbol for the New Deal.

---

[16] Rotunda, "The 'Liberal' Label," pp. 385, 394-95.
[17] Richard Hofstadter, *The Age of Reform: From Bryan to F.D.R.*, Vintage ed. (New York: Random House, 1955), p. 308.

In the country of its origin, Great Britain, the term "conservatism" had not only an aristocratic but also a paternalistic and etatist connotation. The name, therefore, which had enjoyed hardly more currency than "liberal" in American political history, was not welcomed by the opponents of the New Deal. In the campaign of 1928, Herbert Hoover had identified his cause with "liberalism," deploying the older meaning of the term in resistance to the proposals for government intervention put forward by Governor Smith, and well into the New Deal years, Hoover continued to make the opposing case in the name of what he called "true liberalism."[18] As in the adoption of the term "liberal," "conservative" was taken up favorably first by intellectuals and then, after a time, by practicing politicians. Robert Taft called himself a "liberal" to the end, while the first major politician to embrace the name "conservative" was Barry Goldwater.[19]

Both terms thus came into wide usage in a specific historical context and acquired their meanings from the new issues that characterized that period. They make sense as identifying the political counterpoint inspired by the New Deal. But the liberalism and conservatism that were formed in this manner should be likened to other ideologies and parties in Europe or in the America of an earlier or later time only with great caution and appropriate qualification. Certainly, American liberalism and American conservatism should not be assimilated to the grand perspectives normally associated with these terms in the history of Western philosophy. Edmund Burke can be accommodated to the themes and methods of Franklin Roosevelt and John F. Kennedy just as well as Jeremy Bentham can be to those of Herbert Hoover and Richard Nixon. Countervailing power, although radical in challenge and achievement, adapted to new facts of economic life the American tradition of balancing power against power for the purpose of protecting rights. The New Deal was renewal as well as reform.

The Dual Revolution of the Sixties

In December 1962 President Kennedy said to Walter Heller, the chairman of his Council of Economic Advisers, during the year-end review of economic conditions: "Now, look! I want to go beyond

---

[18] Beer, "Liberalism and the National Idea," p. 148.
[19] Peter P. Witonski, in "A Symposium: What is a Liberal? Who is a Conservative?" *Commentary*, vol. 62, no. 3 (September 1976), p. 108.

the things that have already been accomplished. Give me facts and figures on the things we still have to do. For example, what about the poverty problem in the United States?" [20] If there was any one moment that marked the demise of the New Deal, this was it. The legislation of the first two Kennedy years had derived from the broad premises of the great Rooseveltian initiatives: its concerns were minimum wages, social security, public works, housing, food stamps, regional economic development. In method and purpose, however, the war on poverty broke fundamentally with New Deal precedents. Moreover, its new departures were later embodied in the most characteristic programs of the Great Society.

These new departures were twofold. Daniel Patrick Moynihan has characterized them vividly in describing the origins of the antipoverty program: on the one hand, "the shiny, no nonsense, city-as-a-system, Robert S. McNamara style," and on the other, "the shaggy, inexact, communitarian anarchism of the Paul Goodman variety." [21] The first of these—the technocratic component—is the more evident. Moynihan identified it with a fundamental change in the background of policy making: "the increasing introduction into politics and government of ideas originating in the social sciences which promise to bring about social change through manipulation of what might be termed the hidden processes of society." As a result, he continued, politics was becoming no longer merely "the business of who gets what, when, where, how" but "a process that also deliberately seeks to effect such outcomes as who *thinks* what, who *acts* when, who *lives* where, who *feels* how."[22]

Three points need to be stressed. First, the antipoverty program was not shaped by the demands of pressure groups of the poor— there were none—but by the deliberations of government task forces acting largely on the research-based theories of two sociologists, Professors Lloyd Ohlin and Richard A. Cloward of the Columbia School of Social Work.[23] In the second place, intrinsic to the methodology of applied social science, as Moynihan observes, was the assumption that by controlling certain inputs, one could bring about mass behavioral results. In a sense, therefore, even if the framers of the program had wished, they could not have limited their concern merely to creating new rights. Their method compelled them to consider

---

20 Sundquist, *Politics and Policy*, p. 112.
21 Daniel Patrick Moynihan, *Maximum Feasible Misunderstanding* (New York: Free Press, 1969), p. 42.
22 Ibid., p. xiii.
23 Ibid., pp. 45-46.

probable results. Finally, the processes they sought to affect were mainly psychological: the poor, it was believed, were poor not only because of lack of jobs—that was the New Deal definition of the problem—but also because of their motivation and attitudes and especially their feelings of frustration, hostility, and alienation.

The other novel component in the background of thought that went into the antipoverty program was that diffuse but powerful movement among intellectuals in the early sixties that has been called the counterculture. Among its leaders was Paul Goodman, one of the three most influential intellectuals of the period, along with Herbert Marcuse and Norman O. Brown, according to one historian.[24] In *Growing Up Absurd*, his vastly popular book published in 1960, Goodman concerned himself with juvenile delinquency, a leading problem of urban poverty.[25] Assessing the influence of Goodman's ideas on the poverty program, Moynihan observes that his work "gave structure to a problem that had somehow escaped classification and provided an agenda for public action."[26] His contribution appeared especially in the emphasis on the need for the poor themselves to participate in and indeed control, the local efforts on their behalf. Yet his book did not resemble the usual effort of social research or policy science. On the contrary, it could hardly have been more antiscientific in method and antitechnocratic in spirit. It contained not a single table or figure. Its case for participation rested as much on contempt for expertise as on faith in the poor. Personalistic, egalitarian, participatory in their message, cultural rather than economic in their concerns, Goodman's ideas made the counterculture an influence on the antipoverty program fully comparable to that of technocracy.

I have introduced this discussion of the new approaches to public policy by looking first at the antipoverty program in order to give these new departures a location in time. For the meaning and the content of this shift in political sensibility cannot be studied statically. One must see the development of the two currents of thought, the technocratic and the countercultural. After a positive and indeed euphoric phase, each, so to speak, turned against initiatives that it had itself inspired, giving shape to a wave of distrust that is still powerful among the political class and the general public. Students of our present attitudes toward government and politics often remark

[24] Morris Dickstein, *Gates of Eden: American Culture in the Sixties* (New York: Basic Books, 1977), pp. 69-70.
[25] Paul Goodman, *Growing Up Absurd: Problems of Youth in the Organized System* (New York: Random House, 1960).
[26] Moynihan, *Maximum Feasible Misunderstanding*, p. 18.

on the influence of one or the other. Each approach, however, has its own tactic of alienation.

The Technocratic Takeover. The faith that science can transform society goes back to the beginnings of the modern state. In *The New Atlantis* (1627) Francis Bacon with dazzling prescience sketched the outlines of a technocratic utopia. Similar hopes informed Enlightenment thought and found an especially warm welcome in America, where from the days of Benjamin Franklin the ideals of popular government were joined with great expectations of what science could do in the service of man.[27] This promise of power came into its own during and after World War II. Physicists invented nuclear weapons, transforming defense and foreign policy, and in the late 1950s launched the space program that culminated in the moonshot of 1969. Advances in medicine made possible the development of the National Institutes of Health and the great expansion of federal programs in these fields even under the cautious Eisenhower. In perhaps the greatest novelty of all, the social sciences of psychology, economics, sociology, and even political science seemed to achieve in their "behavioral revolution" the capacity for specific social control necessary to make them the foundation of government action. Social engineering based on the policy sciences gained new prestige.

From the mid-1950s a new professionalism emerged in the public service. Founded on the "professional specialisms" produced by developments in the natural and social sciences, it gave to technically and scientifically trained people in government service a great and growing influence on the initiation and formation of public policy.[28] The expert had always been a presence in modern bureaucracy, and something of a problem to modern democracy. He now gained a greater role in government and new respect from leaders and from the public. John F. Kennedy, preoccupied with the rivalry of America and Russia, saw the power of science as a central, shaping influence on that rivalry. In his speech accepting the Democratic nomination in 1960, he asked:

> Can a nation organized and governed such as ours endure? That is the real question. Have we the nerve and the will? Can we carry through in an age where we will witness not only new break-throughs in weapons of destruction—but

---

[27] Don K. Price, *The Scientific Estate* (Cambridge, Mass.: Harvard University Press, 1965), pp. vii, 87, 88.

[28] Frederick C. Mosher, *Democracy and the Public Service* (New York: Oxford University Press, 1968), p. 105.

also a race for mastery of the sky and the rain, the ocean and the tides, the far side of space and the inside of men's minds . . .[29]

No doubt, the new professionalism displayed its influence on public policy most strikingly in the fields of defense and space. But similar initiating and formative forces also helped produce the domestic programs of the Great Society. In the fields of health, housing, urban renewal, highways, welfare, education, and poverty the new programs drew heavily upon specialized and technical knowledge in and around the federal bureaucracy for conception and execution.[30] The distinctive features of the process are illustrated by the history of the Community Mental Health Facilities Act of 1963.[31] The central figure was Dr. Robert Felix of the National Institute of Mental Health, who from his earliest days as a resident was committed to abolishing the state mental hospital in favor of some form of community care. The compassion of Dr. Felix and his associates, however, would have been ineffectual without the advances in medical technology promoted by the NIMH and its National Advisory Mental Health Council. In Congress these bureaucratic professionals found powerful allies and partners in Senator Lister Hill and Representative John Fogarty, chairmen of the respective subcommittees that handled appropriations for the National Institutes of Health. The cause was promoted before the interested public by a conglomerate of professional organizations, the Joint Commission on Mental Illness and Health. Lobbying of Congress was conducted by the National Committee Against Mental Illness. As the fleeting reference to mental illness in his acceptance speech suggests, Kennedy was a sympathetic listener and his State of the Union Message of 1963 put the measure before Congress. In this process, professionals in the federal service identified a problem, promoted the research necessary for a solution, attracted a coalition united in its goals and successful in its lobbying, and finally administered the resulting program of federal-state cooperation.

---

[29] "Text of Kennedy and Johnson Acceptance Speeches," Supplement to Weekly Report, *Congressional Quarterly*, July 22, 1960, p. 1297.

[30] Under the heading of "the professional bureaucratic complex," I have discussed this subject in more detail in "The Adoption of Revenue Sharing: A Case Study of Public Sector Politics," *Public Policy*, vol. 24, no. 2 (Spring 1976), pp. 158-66.

[31] I have based this summary on Henry Foley, *Community Mental Health Legislation: The Formative Process* (Lexington, Mass.: Lexington Books/D.C. Heath, 1975).

By comparison with the New Deal model of politics, the influence of parties and pressure groups had declined, while that of the expert and professional had risen. Likewise, in policy there were major departures. In their usual design, the new social programs had certain distinctive traits: they depended on government spending, to provide specific services, delivered by professionally trained persons, to certain categories of consumers, for the sake of designated outcomes. And, not least important, they were to be carried out not directly by the federal government but by agencies of state and local governments.

The greater role of government spending can hardly be over-emphasized. In the United States as in other industrialized nations, the tendency of public expenditure to take an increasing share of gross national product began some generations ago. In the American case, comparing totals of government expenditure at all levels, federal, state, and local, one finds that the PE/GNP ratio rose from 6.5 percent in 1902 to 19.1 percent in 1938 and 25.8 percent in 1959, in 1976 reaching 34.2 percent.[32] The advent of the Great Society, however, marked a significant increase in the rate of increase of the PE/GNP ratio. And that increase is even more marked if we leave out defense and look only at domestic expenditure. It was not Vietnam but the Great Society that inaugurated the sharp surge in public expenditure which began in the mid-sixties and continued into the seventies under Republican administrations. Much of the increase in federal expenditure consisted of transfer payments under the social insurance provisions of the Social Security system. But in the late sixties and early seventies, federal aid to state and local governments, consisting largely of professionally shaped categorical programs, grew at an even more rapid rate. In the twelve years from 1960 to 1972, federal aid of this type increased from $7 billion to $34 billion.[33] By 1976 the figure had reached $45 billion, to which was now added $15 billion in less restrictive grants. At the present writing the overall figure for federal aid in 1979 is estimated at $86 billion.[34]

Not all of the money came from the federal government, but the ideas and the thrust behind the new programs did. Those economic reasons for centralization set forth in Roosevelt's first inaugural

---

[32] Samuel H. Beer, "Political Overload and Federalism," *Polity: The Journal of the Northeastern Political Science Association*, vol. 10, no. 1 (Fall 1977), pp. 5-7.
[33] Michael Bell and L. Richard Gabler, "Government Growth: An Intergovernmental Concern," *Intergovernmental Perspective*, vol. 2, no. 4 (Fall 1976), p. 9.
[34] Weekly Report, *Congressional Quarterly*, vol. 36, no. 4 (January 28, 1978), p. 232.

continued to operate. But to them had now been added the further major force of professionalism. Professionalism means the formation of an occupational skill by general concepts. The knowledge of the professional, as of the scientist, is theoretical. That is, it can be applied generally to similar problems wherever and whenever they exist. What the professional brings to government, therefore, is not just an interest in a specific problem at a certain time and place, but rather a preparation to deal with all such problems. The generality of the professional's expertise prepares him and incites him to apply his discipline to the widest possible public. John Stuart Mill put the essential question this way in a letter to Tocqueville in 1835:

> Up to now centralization has been the thing most foreign to the English temperament. Our habits or the nature of our temperament do not in the least draw us toward general ideas; but centralization is based on general ideas; that is, the desire for power to attend, in a uniform and general way, to the present and future needs of society.[35]

A present-day view echoes this same analysis:

> Professionals profess. They profess to know better than others the nature of certain matters, and to know better than their clients what ails them or their affairs. . . . Physicians consider it their prerogative to define the nature of disease and health, and to determine how medical services ought to be distributed and paid for. Social workers are not content to develop a technique for case work; they concern themselves with social legislation. Every profession considers itself the proper body to set the terms in which some aspect of society, life or nature is to be thought of, and to define the general lines, or even the details, of public policy concerning it.[36]

Yet, paradoxically, these centralizing influences also had powerful fragmenting effects. As the amounts spent on federal aid increased, so also did the number of programs. In 1962 there were some 160 separate categorical programs. In the following years, they "proliferated." By 1975 a careful review counted 442 funded categorical grants.[37] As science itself grows by the creation of new fields of special knowledge, professionalism in government seems to expand

---

[35] Quoted by Angus Maude in *Encounter*, vol. 26, no. 2 (February 1966), p. 62.
[36] Everett C. Hughes, "Professions," *Daedalus*, vol. 92 (1963), pp. 656-57.
[37] David B. Walker, "Categorical Grants: Some Clarifications and Continuing Concerns," *Intergovernmental Perspective*, vol. 3, no. 2 (Spring 1977), p. 14.

by the creation of specialized programs. Between different levels of government, common disciplines and subdisciplines promote cooperation within vertical hierarchies. These bureaucratic elements in turn establish cordial relations with specialized legislative committees and with the groups of consumers who benefit from their services. However cooperative these professionals may be with their fellows in the same discipline and program, their dispersion among the many vertical hierarchies leaves them little opportunity or incentive for concerted action toward common national priorities and problems. Policy makers are separated from one another and so are the beneficiary groups. The outcome of the technocratic takeover, as Hugh Heclo shows in greater detail in Chapter 3 of this volume, is to centralize the making of policy, but at the same time to weaken the ability of the political actors to function as a national public.

The Romantic Revolt. The counterculture of the sixties reincarnated the romantic impulse. That impulse is as deeply rooted in modern culture as is the faith in science. Periodically, it bursts forth in literature, the arts, and social life, often with a political message of utopian expectations. It was given its most notable expression by the famous literary and philosophical spokesmen of the romantic movement of the late eighteenth and early nineteenth centuries in Europe: in France, Rousseau, Chateaubriand, Victor Hugo; in Germany, Herder, Schiller, von Schlegel and, at times, Goethe; in England, Blake, Wordsworth, Coleridge, Byron, and Shelley. No one who has listened to the early Bob Dylan can fail to mark the affinity between the counterculture and the romantics when confronted with these lines from Wordsworth:

> One impulse from a vernal wood
>   May teach you more of man
> Of moral evil and of good
>   Than all the sages can.
> Sweet is the lore that Nature brings;
>   Our meddling intellect
> Mis-shapes the beauteous forms of things:
>   We murder to dissect.
> Enough of science and of art;
>   Close up these barren leaves;
> Come forth, and bring with you a heart
>   That watches and receives.
>   (*Lyrical Ballads*, 1798)

That is the message: for guidance in conduct, trust the heart not the head; emotion not reason; spontaneity not calculation; nature not civilization. Subjectivity, moreover, not only controls the mode of conduct, but also dictates its ends. The important thing is not the fruit of experience, but experience itself; not utility, but sentiment; not wealth, power, or any external possession, but feeling. "Feeling is all" in Goethe's words, and from so indefinite a purpose romanticism draws a sense of longing and boundlessness that gives great power of arousal to its poetry, music, and political rhetoric.

The political message is ambiguous. Both the conservative Scott and the radical Hazlitt could respond to the romantic impulse. But overwhelmingly, in that earlier manifestation, the romantic spirit was on the side of equality. "The phrase *equal feeling* is the root of the matter," wrote Crane Brinton when discussing the political ideas of one of the early English romantics. "Man is by nature good. He is by nature the equal of any of his fellow men; that is to say, equality among men is really an equality of goodness."[38] Accordingly, man finds his models not in organized society, but in physical nature—the "vernal wood"—and his teachers not among persons of authority or knowledge, but among those closest to nature—children and the young, the "noble savage" of Rousseau, the simple peasant of Wordsworth's Lake District. The message is a message of liberation from conventional morality, authority, and society in the name of freely rendered mutuality and love. To be sure, the appeal to feeling sometimes had other outcomes, turning sour and dangerous as in the demonic and violently self-centered heroes of Byron.

There was a message not only for the individual, but also for the group. Here again the romantic approach was dominated by subjectivity. The basis of group life was found not in economic need or universal values, but in a common culture, a distinctive way of feeling and acting. In Herder's powerful formulation of this approach, the concept of the *Volksgeist* swept over Europe as a doctrine of cultural nationalism. This doctrine soon took on a political form as the early advocates of nationalism claimed that such a "people's spirit" provided the only legitimate foundation for a state.[39] The romantics

[38] Crane Brinton, *The Political Ideas of the English Romanticists* (New York: Russell and Russell, 1962), p. 25.

[39] The classic history of the rise of nationalism is Friedrich Meinecke, *Cosmopolitanism and the National State*, first pub. in German in 1907, trans. by Robert B. Kimber (Princeton, N.J.: Princeton University Press, 1970). For an overview see Chapter I and Felix Gilbert's perceptive Introduction.

did not create the nationalities of Europe, which had deep historical roots. But in formulating and spreading the ideology of nationalism, they had an impact that was hardly less revolutionary than that of the new ideas of individual equality. Nationalism brought warmth and emotion to the support of the modern state. It justified diversity— the nations were "great historical individualities"—within the framework of universalistic liberal values that was being generally adopted in Western Europe. It also had powerfully disruptive effects. The new view of the rights of the national group supplied the rhetoric of rebellion against the old multi-ethnic regimes, arousing the Irish against the British, the Poles against the Russians, and a host of nationalities against the Austrian and Turkish empires. Moreover, as only too abundantly illustrated in the later history of the nation states arising from these revolutionary efforts, joyful self-liberation could readily turn into belligerent self-assertion.

Since that first great outburst, the romantic impulse and example have often been summoned to the support of rebellion. In the United States during the interwar years, they were deployed in an attack against Puritanism and in favor of self-expression generally and a freer sex life in particular. But on that occasion their effect on politics was inconsequential, and the movement of criticism and reconstruction that took place under the New Deal drew, as we have seen, on other sources of justification. The counterculture of the sixties, however, had a major impact on political attitudes, affecting both the way in which political action was conceived and also the ends of policy that were pursued.

The new cultural style of the sixties, writes Morris Dickstein, "thrust American literature back into the Romantic mainstream."[40] It had immediate predecessors in the fifties, such as Jack Kerouac (*On the Road*, 1957), Robert Lowell (*Life Studies*, 1959), and Norman Mailer (*Advertisements for Myself*, 1959). Its philosophers were Paul Goodman (*Growing Up Absurd*, 1960), Norman O. Brown (*Life against Death*, 1959), and Herbert Marcuse (*One Dimensional Man*, 1964). It produced ideological and polemical works like Charles Reich's *Greening of America* (1970) and Theodore Roszak's *Making of a Counter Culture* (1969). It did not flourish without opposition, as when Susan Sontag (*Against Interpretation*, 1966) depicted the "new sensibility" with ecstatic approval as a redemption of the senses from the mind and Irving Howe ("The New York Intellectuals," 1968) replied, agreeing with the description, but finding the results

---

[40] Dickstein, *Gates of Eden*, p. 16.

"shallow, escapist, and nihilistic—built upon a simplistic faith in innocence and instinct, a 'psychology of unobstructed need'." [41]

These names and titles may recall the tone and temper of the counterculture for those who lived through those times. Its impact is conveyed by Dickstein who, as a young man in the sixties, experienced Paul Goodman "as a pervasive and inescapable *presence*." He writes:

> The immediate subject of *Growing Up Absurd* is the young, mainly those who have dropped out into the Beat subculture and the others whose delinquency has dropped them into the hands of the law. Its real subject is the America of the Eisenhower age, a society which, in Goodman's view, gives its youth no world to grow up in. The world seems "absurd," meaningless; it fails to provide satisfying roles and models. Hence the young do not simply drop out; rather, "they act out a critique of the organized system that everybody in some sense agrees with." Goodman is here applying existential and psychological concepts that are usually excluded from social analysis. He aims to produce an account of youth and of society that is impermissibly inward, novelistic, even subjective. Since his concern, like that of the nineteenth-century English culture critics, is more with the *quality* of life than with material well-being, he needs above all to convey the *feel* of contemporary experience both for himself and for his youthful subjects. [42]

Participatory Democracy. As the names mentioned above suggest, this literary and artistic movement quickly acquired a strong political thrust and its ideas and their advocates were caught up in the fierce struggles of the middle and late sixties over race and war. While some of these later offshoots were extreme and violent, it is important to note that the original political message of the counterculture could be, and was, influential within the normal politics of the time. In the late sixties, a splinter of the Students for a Democratic Society became the Weathermen, who were as incoherent as they were destructive. But the Port Huron Statement in which the founders of SDS had set forth their ideology and program of action in 1962, while radical, was not extreme. Proclaiming the old romantic faith that people have "unrealized potential for self-cultivation, self-direction, self-understanding, and creativity," their manifesto declared that

---

[41] Ibid., p. 9.
[42] Ibid., p. 77.

"the goal of man and society should be human independence: a concern with finding a meaning in life that is personally authentic." In sentiments that could have been taken directly from Goodman, it found that "loneliness, estrangement, isolation describe the vast distance between man and man today," which, moreover, can be overcome only "when love of man overcomes the idolatrous worship of things by man." As a goal for America, SDS, therefore, proposed "a participatory democracy" that would bring people "out of isolation and into community," providing in the economic sphere "incentives worthier than money or survival."[43]

The term "participatory democracy" may well seem redundant: What is a democracy if it is not participatory? In the early sixties, however, the term had a distinct and novel meaning, which, as it won acceptance, added a new dimension to American attitudes toward self-government. The essential and initial meaning was to give power at the level of immediate impact directly to those people most affected by government policy. The first major application was in the Community Action Agencies (CAA) of the war on poverty, which took the "maximum feasible participation" specified in the act to mean "the participation of the program beneficiaries in policy development, planning, and implementation."[44] In the rationale for this innovation in public welfare, technocratic and romantic themes mingled harmoniously. A certain psychological and sociological analysis, identifying the powerlessness of the poor as the principal source of their inability to cope with their surroundings and to break out of "the culture of poverty," prescribed participation in the control of these surroundings as the means for restoring confidence and capability. At the same time, there was, as a CAA board chairman remarked, "a certain kind of naiveté or mysticism which surrounds this doctrine with some people. There is the notion that poor people are more objective about their own predicament, that they are able to make simple, naive pronouncements which are far closer to the truth than their more sophisticated but affluent neighbors. There is the feeling that only the poor people know what is wrong with the poor."[45]

---

43 "The Port Huron Statement" in Paul Jacobs and Saul Landau, The New Radicals: A Report with Documents, Vintage Books (New York: Random House, 1966), pp. 154-62.

44 Sanford Kravitz, "The Community Action Program—Past, Present, and its Future?" in On Fighting Poverty: Perspectives from Experience, ed. James L. Sundquist (New York: Basic Books, 1969), p. 62.

45 Quoted in James L. Sundquist, Making Federalism Work: A Study of Program Coordination at the Community Level (Washington, D.C.: Brookings Institution, 1969), p. 71.

Like the New Deal, this approach to politics called for a redistribution of power, but the function of this redistribution was quite differently conceived. The Wagner Act gave wage earners certain new rights which they then used to achieve objective goals, such as higher wages and better conditions. While the participatory democracy of the antipoverty program enabled its beneficiaries to make changes in their environment, a further and important purpose of the mechanism was to bring about a subjective change in the participants themselves. Asking whether the emphasis of the program was on "poverty (a lack of money)" or on "the culture of poverty (the life style that goes with poverty)," a lawyer, who as a federal official had been close to this aspect of the program in its early years, recalls with nice balance that "the emphasis (and it was only a matter of emphasis) was on attempting to deal with the life style of the poor, but primarily through qualities in the environment—particularly institutions—that affect that life style." [46] In this degree, the approach of participatory democracy to social problems and government action was cultural and, broadly, educational.

American politics will always be disorderly. Yet in a real sense political action during the generation of the New Deal had exemplified the methods of organized mass politics in which parties and pressure groups were the main agents. Such a politics requires some degree of organization, including expertise on the part of leaders and discipline among followers. But in the eyes of many champions of participatory democracy such a politics represented precisely those impersonal, bureaucratic, centralistic tendencies that were dehumanizing American society. In contrast, participatory democracy was taken to mean a decentralization of authority that sometimes seemed to extend down to the lone individual. Political action based on these beliefs, accordingly, had little cohesion or continuity, rarely followed a calculated strategy, and fell victim to endless discussion punctuated by outbursts of direct action.

In this form participatory democracy could not have much future. Yet in a larger sense the participatory idea had, and continues to have, a profound effect on American politics. In qualified form the formula requiring participation was incorporated in many Great Society programs and has become a normal ingredient of program structure. It would be difficult today to find a program involving regulation or delivery of services in such fields as health, education,

---

[46] John G. Wofford, "The Politics of Local Responsibility: Administration of the Community Action Program—1964–1966" in Sundquist, *On Fighting Poverty,* p. 71.

27

welfare, and the environment that does not provide for "community input." In a more diffuse, but more important way, the participatory idea has affected attitudes toward the whole process of representative government. It was a powerful influence on the McGovern reforms of the methods of selecting delegates to the Democratic National Convention. It has legitimized and stimulated the increasingly populistic style of campaigns for public office. Recent reforms of Congress, which also serve to break down cohesion and hierarchy, are in harmony with this outlook. Indeed, the immense new structure of intergovernmental relations based on federal grants, which inserts state and local governments between the central government and the impact of programs, has been presented as forwarding the cause of participation. Many forces, ideal and material, have been reshaping American attitudes toward political action. But the idea of participatory democracy, drawing on old themes of political romanticism, has given a sharp new twist to the democratic values of the American political tradition and to any future public philosophy.

Cultural Equality. The idea of equality which came to occupy a central place in the domestic programs of Kennedy and Johnson embraced not only new political means, but also new ends of policy. But to think of these objectives as concerned simply with "the poor" is to miss the point. Primarily, the new idea of equality meant equality for blacks. In the course of years, other groups suffering similar disadvantages were recognized as deserving similar consideration. But at the turning point in policy as the new egalitarian attitude emerged in the early sixties, it referred overwhelmingly to blacks, and especially to those who populated the slums of the great urban centers swollen by a migration en masse from South to North during and after World War II. The "urban crisis" which came to occupy so much attention was—as it still is—very largely the problem of the living conditions of black people in the central cities of the nation.

Daniel Bell has observed that "equality of result" is "the central value problem of post-industrial society."[47] Equality in its various meanings also provided major themes of political development in the preindustrial and industrial phases of modern society. In the earlier generations the struggle for equality centered on equality before the law. In the nineteenth century, as the franchise was broadened, the issue was political equality, and in the present century

[47] Daniel Bell, "Meritocracy and Equality," *The Public Interest*, no. 29 (Fall 1972), p. 40.

the welfare state introduced programs to equalize economic status.[48]
The American variation on this pattern is significant. Advocacy of
the welfare state in this country has not emphasized redistribution of
income or wealth. American liberalism has never been quite in
harmony with the social democracy of Europe, nor has socialism
managed to establish a significant following among voters. Similarly
in the 1960s, although a new view of Marxism, strongly influenced
by romantic themes, as in Marcuse's work,[49] won many followers in
academic circles, it did not have much effect on the political life of
the country. The idea of equality that arose then, while transcending
New Deal precedents, focused on conditions peculiar to the cultural
and ethnic make-up of American society.

For Kennedy and Johnson, the question was, first of all, civil
rights. This was a task of securing for blacks the legal and political
rights that had been won for whites in earlier generations. But the
problem of civil rights, which was mainly a problem of the South,
quickly merged with the problem of black deprivation, which was
becoming the problem of the northern cities. How this problem was
conceived, and the new meaning it gave to the idea of equality, was
a major development of the sixties.

The antipoverty program was only a few months old when
Johnson opened up this new and expansive dimension of the problem
of equality. In an address on June 4, 1965, to the graduating class of
Howard University, he spoke of moving the civil rights program
"beyond opportunity to achievement." His variation on the Lincolnian
metaphor of "the race of life" conveyed the meaning of the new
egalitarianism:

> You do not take a person who, for years, has been hobbled
> by chains and liberate him, bring him to the starting line
> of a race, and then say you are free to compete with all the
> others, and still just believe that you have been completely
> fair. Thus it is not enough just to open the gates of oppor-
> tunity. All our citizens must have the ability to walk through
> those gates. This is the next and more profound stage of
> the battle for civil rights. We seek not just freedom but
> opportunity. We seek not just legal equity but human ability,

---

[48] T. H. Marshall, *Class, Citizenship, and Social Development* (Garden City, N.Y.:
Anchor Books, 1965).

[49] For example, Marcuse's *Eros and Civilization* (Boston: Beacon Press, 1955),
which Dickstein aptly characterizes as "an attempted synthesis of Marx and
Freud in which the magic word 'Marx' is never mentioned." *Gates of Eden*, p. 68.

not just equality as a right and a theory but equality as a fact and equality as a result.[50]

His theme derived from a recent report by Daniel Patrick Moynihan, then an assistant secretary of labor, who was also one of the principal architects of the speech. Referring to recent legislation relating to manpower training, antipoverty programs, and civil rights, Moynihan pointed out that while these measures could create opportunities, they could not ensure outcomes. Yet, he said, blacks will expect proportionate results as well as proportionate opportunities in comparison with other ethnic groups. "This is what ethnic politics is all about in America." It followed that the principal challenge of the next phase of the "Negro revolution" was to take action to ensure not only equality of rights, but also equality of results. "If we do not, there will be no social peace in America for generations."[51]

What was new in this definition of the problem of equality was not its concern with a group. The Wagner Act, after all, had explicitly recognized "wage earners in industry" as prospective beneficiaries of its provisions. The most evident novelty was rather the emphasis not merely on rights but on results. One can identify various causes for this change: for instance, the pressure from blacks stressed by Moynihan. But in terms of a rationale, the new technocratic attitudes made such a shift not only legitimate, but almost inevitable. The ability to control and to measure social outcomes of government action was at the heart of the promise of the behavioral revolution in the social sciences. As we have seen, this promise had already informed the tactics of the antipoverty program. At the time of the Howard University speech, it was entirely in accord with the rising technocratic approach to public policy that "the product of three decades of social science research" should have been "so central to a major presidential address"[52] and that accordingly a concern for outcomes should have been embodied in the new line of policy it announced.

An even more radical innovation was the recognition of culture as identifying those groups who might make claims on government favor. If culture was the source of disproportionate results, then the group disadvantaged by its culture had a claim to government action

---

[50] Lyndon Baines Johnson, *The Vantage Point: Perspectives of the Presidency 1963–1969* (New York: Holt, Rinehart and Winston, 1971), p. 166.

[51] A summary of Daniel Patrick Moynihan, "The Negro Family: The Case for National Action" in *Congress and the Nation*, vol. 2, 1965–1968 (Washington, D.C., 1969), p. 390. The Moynihan report was issued in March and published in August 1965.

[52] Sundquist, *Politics and Policy*, pp. 283–84.

that would bring the results into balance. This did not mean, however, an equality of results for every individual. The new approach was not socialist or social democratic. The rationale of the new egalitarianism was equality of results for each cultural group. Within each group individuals would still be sorted out by "the race of life."

The new egalitarianism explicitly recognized the rights of groups and, moreover, perceived groups as constituted by their distinctive cultures and life styles. In spite of this recognition of separate group identities, however, its object was national through and through— the integration of disadvantaged groups, above all, blacks, into the national community. This purpose shaped the rhetoric of one of Lyndon Johnson's most fervent declarations, his address on March 15, 1965, to a joint session of Congress introducing the Voting Rights Act. Only a few days before, a civil rights march led by Martin Luther King had been brutally broken up by Alabama state troopers in the full view of national television. Johnson said:

> At times history and fate meet at a single time in a single place to shape a turning point in man's unending search for freedom. So it was at Lexington and Concord. So it was a century ago at Appomattox. So it was last week in Selma, Alabama. . . .
>
> There is no constitutional issue here. The command of the Constitution is plain. There is no moral issue. It is wrong—deadly wrong—to deny any of your fellow Americans the right to vote in this country. . . .
>
> What happened in Selma is part of a far larger movement which reaches into every section and state of America. It is the effort of American Negroes to secure for themselves the full blessings of American life. . . .
>
> Their cause must be our cause too. Because it is not just Negroes, but really it is all of us who must overcome the crippling legacy of bigotry and injustice. And . . . we . . . shall . . . overcome. . . .[53]

For a time in the mid-sixties—rather a longer time than it now seems to have been when one looks back over the disorder of later years from the disorientation of the present—the new professionalism and the new egalitarianism were joined in an approach to politics and policy that enjoyed wide acceptance and seemed to promise solid

---

[53] Johnson, *The Vantage Point*, p. 165.

success. Writing in 1965, Theodore H. White reflected that self-confidence and hope. Expanding on his account of the speech of May 22, 1964, in which Lyndon Johnson had proposed that America "move not only toward the rich society and the powerful society but upward to the Great Society," White commented:

> For Americans live today on the threshold of the greatest hope in the whole story of the human race, in what may be the opening chapter of the post-industrial era. No capital in the world is more exciting than Washington in our time, more full of fancies and dreams and perplexities. For the first time in civilization, man's mastery over things is sufficient to provide food for all, comfort for all, housing for all, even leisure for all. The question thus arises: What, then, is the purpose of man? How shall he conduct himself at a moment when he is being freed from want, yet freed to ask the tormenting questions of who he is and what he seeks and what his soul needs? [54]

Three years later, James Sundquist, writing about politics and government from Eisenhower to Johnson, could still make his theme "the triumphs of responsive government in 1964 and 1965." In his introductory chapter entitled "From Gloom to Euphoria," he wrote:

> In one of the most remarkable outpourings of major legislation in the history of the country, the Congress in 1964 and 1965 had expressed the national purpose in bold and concrete terms—to outlaw discrimination in many of its forms, to improve educational opportunity at every level, to eradicate poverty, to assure health care for old people, to create jobs for the unemployed, to cleanse the rivers and the air and to protect and beautify man's outdoor environment. [55]

Speaker McCormack had termed the session of 1965 "the Congress of realized dreams." The AFL-CIO said it was "the most productive congressional session ever held." The polls showed overwhelming approval of Johnson's presidency and "the highest public approval registered in modern times" for Congress. "Monumental," "unprecedented," "political magic," "a revolution in the making," "a political miracle" were the terms of praise of other observers.

---

[54] Theodore H. White, *The Making of the President 1964* (New York: Atheneum, 1965), pp. 391-92.
[55] Sundquist, *Politics and Policy*, p. 3.

Equilibrium without Purpose

Today the euphoria of the mid-sixties seems very far away. A comprehensive effort to explain how the country, starting from that point, reached its present confused and chastened condition would need to trace a sad and complex narrative, traversing the riots in the black ghettos, the Vietnam War, and Watergate. My concern here must be narrower: to follow the change in attitudes and, without pretending that I am offering a complete explanation, to suggest how the new political approaches of technocracy and romanticism affected the development of the present climate of opinion.

The self-confidence of the mid-sixties suffered from a touch of hubris, to which the new approaches amply contributed. Both technocracy and romanticism foster illusions of perfectibility—in one case, technological perfectibility; in the other, moral perfectibility—that lead respectively to overestimates of human power and underestimates of human perversity. Such misperceptions fed that characteristic attempt of the Great Society to try to do too much with too few resources, moral and material; and so, one may conclude, they bore some responsibility for the failure of these programs fully to match their promise. At the same time, the readiness of many observers today to put down these programs as failures itself continues to reflect the same exaggerated expectations that accompanied their inception. Although often hastily formulated and inadequately funded, the Great Society programs can be seen as achieving numerous successes, when measured by a sober and historical view of human possibility.

Whatever the causes of the disproportion, the performance of the Great Society is generally perceived to have fallen short of the original expectations of its authors and of its many prospective beneficiaries. Curiously, moreover, each of the two approaches, the technocratic and the romantic, which had shaped these initiatives, also contributed to the negative reaction to them. The techniques of behavioral science, for instance, hold out the promise of knowledge sufficient for social control. But these techniques also constitute a method of identifying and measuring the actual consequences of such presumed knowledge when it is applied to government action. When science-based policy has fallen short of its promise of social control, critics have been able to perceive and measure these failures thanks to the methods of behavioralism itself. Indeed, the capacity to demonstrate that programs have not worked sometimes seems far in advance of the capacity to determine what will work. One should not complain of this. It is useful to be able to know for sure that Johnny has not learned to read even though this reveals that we do not really know how to teach him to read. At the same time, the widespread application of the new methods of testing performance, of measuring to what extent objectives have been reached and in what ways side effects have been produced, has contributed to the skepticism, bordering on defeatism, that conditions current expectations of what government can and should do. In this sense, technocratic methods have worked to deflate the technocratic mood.

One example of crucial importance relates to the new egalitarianism. When Kennedy and Johnson made equality the central theme of their social policy, the new programs, following, as we have seen, the current findings of behavioral research, stressed the burdens of cultural disadvantage and sought to relieve them by various means that were, broadly speaking, educational—Head Start, manpower training, compensatory education, school integration, busing, open admissions, and so on. This approach was undermined by the conclusions of the massive and authoritative Coleman Report published in 1966. In this study, conducted by James S. Coleman of Johns Hopkins under a mandate of the Civil Rights Act of 1964 and based on a survey of 4,000 schools and 600,000 students, it was shown that schooling was actually making little difference in the achievement of pupils, which varied rather with the attainments of their parents.[56] Six years later, a comprehensive discussion and reanalysis of the Coleman Report was published under the editorship of Daniel P. Moynihan and Frederick Mosteller of Harvard.[57] Like Coleman, the editors accepted as a national goal "equal educational opportunity defined as approximately equal distributions of achievement . . . for the different ethnic/racial groups." Again like Coleman, however, its authors concluded that this was a goal the nation "does not know how to attain," and for this reason they felt obliged to recommend further "fairly intensive educational experimentation and research."[58] This was not to say that research had been neglected. As we have seen, "three decades of social science research" lay behind Johnson's Howard University speech. Research had not yet shown what would work, although it was quite capable of showing what did not work.

[56] James S. Coleman et al., *Equality of Educational Opportunity*, 2 vols. (Washington, D.C.: Office of Education, Department of Health, Education, and Welfare, 1966).

[57] *On Equality of Educational Opportunity: Papers Deriving from the Harvard University Seminar on the Coleman Report*, Vintage Books (New York: Random House, 1972).

[58] Ibid., p. 45.

As scientific method revealed the inadequacies of applied social science, a momentous shift in the tactics of the new egalitarianism took place. Now the indirect, manipulative approach of social science was supplemented by the direct, imperative approach of "affirmative action."[59] That term had been used by Kennedy and by Johnson, but it did not have much bite until in 1969 Nixon's secretary of labor under the so-called Philadelphia Plan first required federal contractors to move toward hiring a certain number of minority workers on construction projects. In later years this use of numerical hiring goals was broadened to include women, strengthened by more elaborate regulations, and extended to apply to all employers receiving funds from federal contracts. Numerical goals, sometimes amounting to quotas, were also used by legislatures, courts, and universities to favor minorities and women in employment and in education.

In any context, such a tactic would have met with some antagonistic response. But the social context on which it was imposed in the late sixties was especially sensitive. The recognition of cultural groups as proper objects of public policy had itself raised group consciousness among those who benefited—and among those who did not. Perhaps even more important in eliciting the new group sensitivities was the general affirmation of diversity in life styles and tastes by the counterculture. Once again, as in the great age of European nationalism, the romantic message called attention to and legitimated cultural diversity as a basis for social life, literary utterance, and political action. Dickstein is a perceptive guide to these changes in the climate of opinion. He points out that the "dominant impulse toward self-assertion in the sixties" was not confined to individuals but also showed itself in "expressions of group insurgency, outbursts of militant collective consciousness, especially among ethnic groups."[60] In his view "the Jews . . . first discovered how much of their identity and affective life they might have to surrender to the bland uniformity of the melting pot," as Jewish writers in the fifties "showed the way toward a healthy particularism and self-acceptance that would grow and flourish in the sixties." The most striking assertions of group identity, however, came from blacks. He writes:

The resurgence of black writing in the sixties was different from the Jewish flowering in that it ran parallel to a political and social movement, and had deep links to the ongoing

---

[59] The history of "affirmative action" is summarized in *The National Journal,* vol. 5, nos. 38 and 39 (1973), vol. 8, no. 41 (1976), and vol. 9, nos. 38 and 40 (1977).

[60] Dickstein, *Gates of Eden,* p. 154.

social life of the mass of black people. If black leaders and black artists remained a highly self-conscious and sometimes neglected minority, they nevertheless reflected a shift of attitude that ran strong in the black community. The rage and frustration that showed itself in the urban riots of the sixties were the inchoate counterpart of the self-conscious new nationalism and militant separatism that emerged as a challenge to the old civil rights leadership. This new stance, which stressed cultural pride and autonomy over the old integrationist goals, spread quickly among artists, intellectuals, militants, and educated young blacks in general, as if their whole lives had prepared them for it.[61]

In the later sixties "a wave of ethnic feeling" surged over the country and through the cities.[62] The earlier celebration of diversity gave way to conflict, as groups resisted preferential treatment for others or sought it for themselves. In 1963 Glazer and Moynihan foresaw with optimism that ethnicity would continue, as in the past, to contribute to the evolution of American nationality. By the end of the decade they reported with alarm that in the recent politics of New York City "race has exploded to swallow up all other distinctions."[63] Ethnic consideration had always been important in the social and political tensions of the city. What was new was that they now had taken "the center of the stage."

The term "ethnic group" refers to a group based not on class, occupation, or economic interest, but on a distinctive life style and cultural endowment, a normal component of its culture being a belief in common descent. In this nation of immigrants, ethnicity has been an old and fundamental fact of politics. But in the politics of the sixties and seventies "ethnicity," like "the poor," with its derivatives was a relatively new term. It also signified new facts, as working-class and occupational identities, strong from New Deal days, lost in status and respect and ethnicity gained as a ground of action and reaction in politics. "From the mid-sixties," Glazer has observed, ". . . the ethnic identity began to gain on the general American identity. Indeed, the very term 'American' became depreciated in the late 1960s."[64] The romantic élan of joyful self-liberation had turned into an attitude of distrust and abrasive self-assertion.

---

[61] Ibid., p. 155.

[62] Nathan Glazer and Daniel Patrick Moynihan, *Beyond the Melting Pot: The Negroes, Puerto Ricans, Jews, Italians and Irish of New York City*, 2d ed. (Cambridge, Mass.: M.I.T. Press, 1970), p. xxxvi.

[63] Ibid., p. viii.

[64] Nathan Glazer, *Affirmative Discrimination: Ethnic Inequality and Public Policy* (New York: Basic Books, 1975), pp. 177-78.

Standing back and looking at the impact of what I have called the dual revolution of the sixties, one can view it in two ways: in terms of structures and in terms of attitudes. From the structural perspective, one sees a fragmentation of the national community that is itself twofold: on the one hand, a pluralism of consumer groups enjoying benefits from the categorical programs of central technocracies; on the other hand, a pluralism of cultural groups protecting or claiming advantages for their members in relation to government and other groups. This vast array of groups does not form a public. One does not find among its activists and leaders the shared attitudes constituting a public philosophy. Technocratic and romantic attitudes remain strong, and, while they conflict sharply with one another, both tend to produce withdrawal and skepticism rather than identification and trust.

Commenting on the change in the climate of opinion from the early sixties to the later seventies, Theodore White characterized the contrast in mood and behavior. In the sixties, he said, "the dominant theme was invincibility. America was going to the moon. America was going to end poverty. America was going to end discrimination." Then he asked, "What's the mood of the seventies?" and replied: "It's a life-style mood. It's a period when each group and each sect is trying to find its own virtue and trying to tyrannize over the other groups." [65]

Liberalism and Conservatism Today. For a clearer impression of the current confusion in political attitudes, we may review the several meanings that have come to be attached to the terms "liberalism" and "conservatism," which first entered into wide public use a generation ago. The rhetoric of the presidential campaign of 1976 is a convenient field for such a survey. This is not because candidates are likely to bare their inmost thoughts at a time when the pressures of vote-getting overwhelm them. On the contrary, what they say is interesting because, compelled by such pressures to exploit to the utmost their resources of political combat, these experts in political influence reveal what they believe to be effective argumentation. The mode of classification will be historical, or rather geological, as we characterize the various meanings of the terms according to the layer of usage from which they derive. There are three layers, a "paleo," a "meso," and a "neo" layer, dating respectively from the New Deal, the Great Society, and the reaction against the Great Society.

[65] Boston *Globe*, November 24, 1977.

The paleo-conservatism that arose in opposition to the New Deal still colors the rhetoric of some political leaders and activists, especially among Republicans. Barry Goldwater, however, was the last serious candidate for the presidency who adopted—or seemed to adopt—this position, which today would spell danger to almost any candidate espousing it. While criticism of the inefficiency and incompetence of Washington is common among conservatives of any stamp, conservatives normally deploy such criticism in connection with an acceptance of the American welfare state that goes well beyond what we associate with Goldwater or Herbert Hoover. A crucial incident in Ronald Reagan's campaign for the nomination in 1976 will serve to introduce the distinctive features of this more recent brand of conservatism and to illustrate why candidates feel compelled to adopt it.[66]

In September 1975, Reagan gave a speech in Chicago in which he presented his scheme for a massive reduction in the Washington bureaucracy and in federal activity and expenditure. Insofar as it was an attack on government intervention in general and centralized bureaucracy in particular, it did sound rather like paleo-conservative doctrine, and Reagan gave his opponents ample opportunity to hammer home this interpretation by mentioning a figure—$90 billion—by which he proposed to reduce federal outlays. In the following weeks he was attacked by spokesmen for Gerald Ford who sought to pin "the old Goldwater label" on him. Ford's campaign manager, for instance, warned that "the American people will not go back to a system where you don't take care of people in need. The American people don't want elderly people thrown out in the snow."

Whatever Reagan's inmost beliefs may have been, he made his recovery by setting forth a position that escaped the Goldwater label and yet was distinctly different from New Deal or Great Society centralism. His statement was carefully and coherently drafted:

> Very simply, it has concerned me that many programs that Washington administers aren't efficient and don't really help the people they were designed to help. I suggested that we consider them prime candidates for an orderly, phased transfer to state and local governments. This was not a budgetary proposal but one for transfer of control—authority and responsibility—from the federal government to those closer to the people. The people, through their state and

---

[66] I have based my account of this episode on Jules Witcover, "New Hampshire: Reagan's $90-Billion Problem," in *Marathon: The Pursuit of the Presidency 1972–1976* (New York: Viking, 1977).

local governments, would and should decide if they wanted to expand, modify, change, or replace these programs, and how best to do so.

As set forth here, Reagan's conservatism did not imply that the intended beneficiaries of the federal government did not deserve help; nor did it aim at a reduction of overall government expenditure. It was essentially political not fiscal, proposing not that the welfare state be dismantled, but that it be decentralized. And indeed this model of government activity fitted well with Reagan's record as governor of California when, as he boasted to the voters of New Hampshire, he had hired more minority citizens for executive and policy-making positions than any previous governor, had reduced the state mental hospital population from 26,500 to 7,000 by adequately funding county mental health clinics, had increased state support of local public schools to a record figure, and, while reducing the welfare rolls, had increased aid to the genuinely needy. He could have added that under his administration from 1967 to 1974 the state budget more than doubled, rising from $4.6 to $10.2 billion.[67]

This conservatism of the decentralized welfare state consisted of more than a tactical maneuver in a presidential campaign and had an intellectual history originating under Eisenhower and culminating in Nixon's New Federalism. Behind Eisenhower's various efforts to devolve more responsibility and power from Washington to the states lay the conviction that there was, in his words, an "undeniable need" for action by some level of government with regard to many urgent social problems.[68] In the crucial field of intergovernmental finance, general revenue sharing became a major element in this decentralizing thrust, which, by the later years of the Great Society, constituted the principal conservative challenge to the current line of policy. This larger meaning was brought out by a leading Republican when introducing a revenue-sharing proposal into Congress in 1966:

> This proposal seeks to provide for the great public needs of the 1960s and 1970s by equipping State and local governments to meet these needs. It is an alternative to the philosophy of the Great Society which would meet these needs by massive expansion of Federal programs and by further

---

[67] Weekly Report, *Congressional Quarterly*, vol. 33, no. 46 (November 15, 1975), p. 2482.

[68] Address to National Governors' Conference (1957) in *Final Report*, Joint Federal-State Action Committee (Washington, D.C., 1960), p. 42.

proliferation of narrow categorical grant-in-aid programs that end up in administrative confusion, waste and centralized control.[69]

Nixon saw revenue sharing in the same large political framework. When sending his proposal to Congress in August 1969, he called for "the restoration of a rightful balance between the state capitals and the national capital" and, in a climactic contrast with the fiscal austerity of paleo-conservatism, explained how the formula of the bill would "provide the States with some incentive to maintain (and even expand) their efforts to use their own tax resources to meet their needs." [70]

Without an appreciation of this conservative activism—meso-conservative, since it was formulated mainly during the Great Society period—it is hard to understand the prodigious growth in the public sector which, beginning under Lyndon Johnson, continued unchecked for eight years under Republican Presidents.[71] Yet this decentralizing activism did in a fundamental way express enduring conservative values. At its roots, what has come to be called conservatism in America was a defense of liberty against government power. This basic position sets it in opposition to the thrust of the welfare state toward equality. As a defense of liberty, conservative reasoning, when transferred to questions of federal structure, inspired resistance to bureaucratic centralization and support for state and local independence. In the conservatives' defense of localism and states' rights, their liberal opponents often saw merely a disguise for laissez-faire. Conservatives would not reject that comment entirely. But American conservatives also favor the diversity of state and local government for reasons that are not a disguise. In the American conservative conception of distributive justice, liberty is the preeminent value.[72] Merit therefore attaches to self-determination. This may be the self-determination of individuals, as in a free economy, or the self-determination of communities under popular government. In this perspective, self-government—the exercise of political liberty —by state and local jurisdictions expresses an important value and its practice is a contribution to the common good of a free country.

---

[69] Press release by Charles E. Goodell (N.Y.), chairman of the Republican Planning and Research Committee of the House of Representatives, November 27, 1966.

[70] *Public Papers of the Presidents: Richard Nixon 1969* (Washington, D.C., 1971), pp. 667-68.

[71] See above p. 20.

[72] I have discussed this subject under the heading of "Distributive Justice and Federalism" in "The Adoption of General Revenue Sharing," pp. 132-49.

In this sense the new decentralist activism of the conservatism formulated in the sixties derived from the basic concern for liberty, while at the same time breaking sharply with the rugged individualism of paleo-conservative doctrine.

Distinguishable from this decentralizing activism is a line of attack on "big government" which puts its main emphasis on the inefficiency of centralized bureaucracies. Fueled by the technocratic criticism of technocracy in recent years, this current of opinion may be called neo-conservative. In the presidential campaign of 1976, this neo-conservative attack was joined by a neo-liberal attack on "big government." Although these neo-liberals broke with New Deal nationalism, they remained in the liberal camp by reason of their commitment to equality and participation. The premises of their attack on Washington, moreover, did not consist of a technocratic concern for efficiency, but on the contrary of a romantic distrust of power and faith in "the people." The nearest thing to a pure embodiment of these attitudes was Fred Harris. In 1971 he had donned the garments of cultural radicalism in a campaign which, to the delight of college campuses, he conducted under the banner of "No More Bullshit." He was George Wallace without the racism. Stumping the country in the company of his wife, an American Indian, he promised to "take the rich off welfare" and won a warm response from workingmen, black and white, with his folksy, shirtsleeve style. Again in the years before 1976 he attempted what he called a "people's campaign." But, although, as Witcover remarks, he appealed to "the restless young voter radicalized by the Vietnam war and by dislike of the glaring inequities of American society," he appeared to others as "the head of some rag-tag, blue-jeaned cult of the disaffected," and his constituency remained intense but narrow.[73]

If Harris may be called a neo-liberal because of his all-out acceptance of the "new politics" of the sixties, Henry Jackson may properly be termed a paleo-liberal. During twelve years in the House and twenty-two in the Senate, he had been "a loyal workhorse of the New Deal." The coalition that he painstakingly put together included many of the same constituents—organized labor, big city mayors, state party leaders, wealthy Jews—that had produced majorities for Democratic Presidents from Roosevelt to Johnson. He confronted, however, a fundamental issue inherited from the sixties which these leaders had not been obliged to face, and in Boston

---

[73] Witcover, *Marathon*, p. 212. For this account of the presidential campaign I have drawn on Witcover as well as my own recollections.

(which George Wallace actually carried in the primary) he made his choice clear by running full-page ads that read: "I am against forced busing."

The outstanding meso-liberal was Morris Udall. He had supported the Great Society programs and did not recant on his support, so that listening to him set forth his views on the needs of the country during the campaign was rather like listening to an intelligent, witty, and self-deprecatory Lyndon Johnson. His environmentalism made him critical of unchecked economic growth. But he did not join the attack on "big government." On the contrary, while granting the need to restore trust in government, he denied that this could be done "by turning our backs on Washington." "For," he continued, "we must not forget that our federal government remains the only recourse for thousands of otherwise powerless people, like the poor, the indigent, the elderly and the disadvantaged to name but a few." [74] Fearing its McGovernite symbolism, he tried to avoid the "liberal" tag, but on the race question his position was squarely with the Great Society initiatives. He called Wallace a "politician of negativism" and recalled how John F. Kennedy had used the powers of the federal government to "enforce equality by removing George Wallace from that now-famous doorway at the University of Alabama." Udall's attempt to bear the whole inheritance of liberalism lent a certain legitimacy to his urgent and repeated claim to be recognized as the standard bearer of "the progressive mainstream of the Democratic party." If that inheritance had been less divided internally, Udall might have been more successful in winning such recognition.

The man who won the nomination did not do so as the unqualified champion of that "mainstream," but as its critic or—perhaps it is more accurate, although more confusing, to say—as both its supporter and its critic. On such questions as unemployment, tax reform, national health insurance, and welfare reform, while not overly generous with specific proposals, Jimmy Carter took a fairly standard liberal line. Where the issues elicited conflicts within his potential constituency, as in the case of questions raised by neo-liberalism, such as abortion and amnesty, he showed exceptional skill in finding a compromise position that would alienate the least and win the most support. Even on the great question of race, he could combine consistent opposition to "forced busing" with a demonstrated hostility to discrimination that won him the endorsements of Andrew Young and Martin Luther King, Sr. The complexities of his political outlook,

---

[74] Form letter dated February 26, 1976, to Massachusetts voters before the presidential primary of March 2.

however, were not merely the product of tactics. In quite fundamental ways, Carter's political attitudes resonate to the dual revolution of the sixties.

Jimmy Carter is at once a technocrat and a romantic: on the one hand, by education a naval officer and, as he likes to emphasize, a "nuclear engineer," a problem solver who gives numbers to the reasons for and against a decision and then adopts the side with the larger total; on the other hand, by upbringing a southern Baptist who, although given to quoting Reinhold Niebuhr, professes a faith in the goodness of human nature that is Wordsworthian in its naiveté. His assault upon Washington was, accordingly, twofold, pressing both the neo-conservative and neo-liberal lines of attack. Although not calling for major steps of decentralization, his criticism of "the complicated, confusing, overlapping and wasteful Federal Government bureaucracy" was as sharp as Reagan's. He gave even greater emphasis to his populistic stance. Avoiding the vulgarity and bombast of Harris, he elaborated in his standard speech on the theme that what we need is "a government as good as our people," "a government as filled with love as our people." Jimmy Carter does not avoid or reconcile or choose among the inner conflicts of the present climate of opinion; he embodies them.

In his inaugural address, like Roosevelt in 1932, Carter was concerned almost entirely with domestic affairs.[75] His nationalism, moreover, was as pronounced as Roosevelt's, and the references to the "nation" directly or by synonym were even more numerous. But the telling differences appear when we consider that Carter's second most important thematic term was "spirit." While in Roosevelt's speech, references to the economy or material conditions identified the problem, in Carter's what was called for and heralded was "a new spirit." He was not entirely unmindful of material problems and remarked on the need to provide "productive work for those able to perform it." He also wished to strengthen "the American family." His overwhelming concern, however, was with "a new national spirit of unity and trust." He sought to forward "human rights" and "equality of opportunity" so that in the future it could be said that, while he was President, "our nation . . . had torn down the barriers that separated those of different race and region and religion, and where there had been mistrust, built unity, with a respect for diversity."

For Roosevelt, the instrument for achieving his ends was the nation, acting as a "great army" with "discipline" under his "leader-

---

[75] For the text see Weekly Report, *Congressional Quarterly*, vol. 35, no. 4 (January 22, 1977), p. 106.

ship." For Carter, while a "President may sense and proclaim" the "new spirit," "only a people can provide it." He therefore recognized before them his "great responsibility—to stay close to you, to be worthy of you, and to exemplify what you are." "Your strength," he said, "can compensate for my weakness, and your wisdom can minimize my mistakes."

For Roosevelt "the only thing we have to fear is fear itself." What was needed, above all, was "action, and action now." Carter, on the other hand, reminded his listeners that "we have learned that 'more' is not necessarily 'better', that even our great nation has its recognized limits, and that we can neither answer all questions nor solve all problems."

Conclusion. In the early sixties the New Deal came to an end. As a public philosophy, it had for a generation oriented the prevailing approaches to domestic policy, at the same time provoking a fruitful and coherent opposition. Today certain familiar issues will from time to time call forth the old rhetoric and revive the old coalition, as when a vote in Congress on unemployment compensation rallies all Democrats outside the South against all Republicans. But with regard to many fundamental questions, such as those relating to race, the New Deal outlook offers only confused and partial answers and exercises only feeble powers of aggregation. During that brief middle period of the Great Society, it did look as if new attitudes, technocratic and romantic, were being fused in an outlook that would supplement or supplant the old liberalism. These attitudes survive powerfully, but with nothing in common except their negativism.

One should not exaggerate. We do not enjoy a public philosophy. But there is such a thing as equilibrium without purpose. The balance of social forces today tends toward a kind of peace. Moreover, a great hinterland of common belief, the American political tradition, helps to hold conflicts within manageable limits and to enable exchange, economic and political, to flourish. The question is whether the nation will be able to elicit from this body of belief the forces of renewal constituting a new public philosophy.

2
Change and Continuity in the Modern Presidency

Fred I. Greenstein

Although my main concern here is change in the American presidency since 1960, it is necessary to begin with an extended prefatory account of the evolution of the presidency from Franklin D. Roosevelt's inauguration through the end of the Eisenhower administration. This is because the most striking changes in the institution occurred during the first three modern presidencies, and many of those that have occurred since Kennedy took office appear to have been oscillations in patterns that began under Kennedy's three predecessors.

I am using the phrase "modern presidency" to distinguish the Roosevelt through Carter presidencies from the previous "traditional presidencies."[1] Up to the Hoover administration, there were variations from President to President in how the chief executive conducted his duties. Periodically there were stable shifts in the functioning of the institution itself—for example, the shift to popular election with Jackson and the increased tendency of Presidents to interest themselves in legislation beginning around the turn of the century. With Franklin Roosevelt's administration, however, as part of the general increase in the size and impact of American government, the presidency began to undergo not a shift but rather a metamorphosis. The eight post-Hoover presidencies, those I have called modern, have been different from their thirty traditional predecessors in the following respects:

(1) From a state of affairs in which there was at best a somewhat grudging acceptance that the President would be "interested"

---

[1] For further discussion of the differences between the traditional and modern presidencies, see the preface to Fred I. Greenstein, Larry Berman, and Alvin Felzenberg, *Evolution of the Modern Presidency: A Bibliographical Survey* (Washington, D.C.: American Enterprise Institute, 1977).

in the doings of Congress, it has come to be taken for granted that he *should* regularly initiate and seek to win support for legislative action as part of his continuing responsibilities. The President also has come to be far more active in evaluating legislative enactments with a view to deciding whether to exercise the veto than traditionally was the case.

(2) From a presidency that normally exercised few unilateral powers, there has been a shift to one that is provided—via statutes, court decisions, and informal precedents—with many more occasions for direct policy making through executive orders and other actions not formally ratified by Congress.

(3) From a presidency with extremely modest staff support, there has evolved one in which the President has at his disposal in the Executive Office and "on loan" from elsewhere in the executive branch an extensive bureaucracy to implement his initiatives. It is only because of the rise of a presidential bureaucracy that it has been possible for Presidents to follow through on (1) and (2).

(4) Finally, there appear to have been major changes in the quantity and quality of public attention to incumbent Presidents. For many Americans the complex, uncertain political world of our times seems to be dealt with by personification, in the form of perceptions of the quality of performance and personal virtue of the incumbent President. Presidents are expected to be symbols of reassurance, possessing extraordinary "nonpolitical" personal qualities that traditionally were associated only with long deceased "hero presidents" of the past, such as George Washington. At the same time they are expected to be politically effective, bringing about favorable national and international social conditions. They have become potential beneficiaries of anything positive that can be attributed to the government, but also scapegoats for social and political discontent.[2]

The Formative Period of the Modern Presidency

The emergence of the physical and symbolic defining characteristics of the modern presidency is evident in the several city blocks surrounding 1600 Pennsylvania Avenue. William Hopkins, who began working

[2] Fred I. Greenstein, "What the Presidency Means to Americans: Presidential 'Choice' Between Elections," in James D. Barber, ed., *Choosing the President* (Englewood Cliffs, N.J.: Prentice-Hall, 1974), pp. 121-47.

as White House stenographer under Hoover in 1931, went on to become executive clerk, and held his White House position until his retirement in the Nixon years, remembers that he had shaken hands with President Hoover the year before going to work in the White House. Hoover still found it possible to carry on the leisurely nineteenth-century New Year's Day tradition of personally greeting any person who cared to join the reception line leading into the White House.[3]

In Hoover's time, the presidency had not become so central a symbol for public emotions and perceptions about the state of the nation that elaborate procedures for protecting the White House from potentially dangerous intruders were deemed necessary. The White House of our time is surrounded by a high, electronically sensitized fence; its gates are locked and carefully guarded; and the fence extends across West Executive Avenue to the ornate Old Executive Office Building, creating a two-block "presidential compound." In Hoover's time, the lower, unelectrified fence surrounded only the White House grounds and had open gates. Anyone walking east of the White House from what then was not a presidential office building, but rather the site of the State, Navy, and War Departments, customarily did so by strolling across the White House grounds.

Moreover, when Hoover was President, the West Wing of the White House had sufficient space to accommodate the modest presidential staff. The bureaucracy of the modern presidency now occupies not only the building across the street from the West Wing, but also the red-brick, high-rise New Executive Office Building on 17th Street. Extensions of the presidency are to be found in many other nearby buildings, including the Georgian-façade edifices facing Lafayette Square. There is even a house on the square to accommodate and provide office space for ex-Presidents.

Roosevelt: The Breakthrough to the Modern Presidency. The first stage in the transformation that accounted for these physical changes was an almost overnight rise in expectations about the appropriate duties of the chief executive. This resulted from the convergence of a deep national (and later international) crisis with the accession and long incumbency of perhaps the most giftedly entrepreneurial President in American history, Franklin D. Roosevelt. Nothing was "inevitable" about the appearance in 1933 of entrepreneurial, innovative

---

[3] William Hopkins, Oral History Interview, June 3, 1964, John F. Kennedy Library, Waltham, Mass. I am indebted to Mr. Hopkins for expanding on his oral history in a personal interview.

presidential leadership. FDR's nomination in 1932 had not been a sure thing. As President-elect he barely escaped assassination. It is impossible to believe that the impact of the leader next in succession, Vice President-elect John Nance Garner, would have been very different from Hoover's. One can argue that, whether under Hoover, Garner, or the various other "available" presidential contenders of the time, "social conditions" would have fostered demands for strong leadership.[4] But the outcome, if any, of these demands might well have been some form of indigenous dictatorship, such as that described in Sinclair Lewis's novel *It Can't Happen Here*. Crisis was a necessary but far from sufficient condition for the modern presidency that began to evolve under Roosevelt.

The premodern historical record—especially the record of the nineteenth century—contains countless examples of congressional antipathy to mere suggestions by the President that particular legislation be enacted.[5] There were even congressmen who held that presidential vetoes could not legitimately be used as an expression of policy preference by the chief executive, but rather must be reserved for occasions when he deemed legislation to be unconstitutional.[6] FDR promptly established the practice of advocating, backing, and engaging in the politics of winning support for legislation. By the end of Roosevelt's long tenure in office, presidential legislative activism had come to be taken for granted, if not universally approved.

This activism began within four days of Roosevelt's taking office. The relentless succession of "Hundred Days" legislative enactments passed by the special session of Congress that met from noon, March

---

[4] For a discussion that treats the exigencies of international power politics and other aspects of the international and national environment of the modern presidency as centrally (but not exclusively) responsible for the rise of what I am here calling the modern presidency, see Franz Schurmann, *The Logic of World Power: An Inquiry into the Origins, Currents, and Contributions of World Politics* (New York: Random House, 1974).

[5] Note, for example, Senator George Hoar's comments that in the mid-nineteenth century congressmen "would have considered as a personal affront a private message from the White House expressing a desire that they should adopt any course in the discharge of their legislative duties that they did not approve" and similar congressional assertions quoted in John T. Patterson, "The Rise of Presidential Power before World War II," *Law and Contemporary Problems*, vol. 40 (Spring 1976), pp. 39-57. The Presidents from McKinley to Hoover were in general more disposed to take an interest in legislative outcomes than their nineteenth-century predecessors and in this respect anticipated the great increase in sustained presidential involvement in the legislative process that began with Franklin Roosevelt. Stephen Wayne, *The Legislative Presidency* (New York: Harper and Row, 1978), pp. 13-16.

[6] Charles L. Black, Jr., "Some Thoughts on the Veto," *Law and Contemporary Problems*, vol. 40 (Spring 1976), pp. 87-101.

9, to 1:00 a.m., June 15, 1933—including such major policy departures as the banking act, the securities act, the Civilian Conservation Corps, and the National Industrial Recovery Administration—was appropriately viewed as the result of Roosevelt's leadership. In some cases his leadership involved bringing about the enactment of programs that had long been on the public political agenda, such as the Tennessee Valley Authority, but which needed the impetus of the Hundred Days legislative campaign to achieve approval. In one case—the Federal Deposit Insurance Corporation—Roosevelt received praise for passage of a program that he personally opposed but acceded to after realizing it had too much congressional support to be defeated.[7]

That FDR was given credit for the initiatives of others points to the fact that during his administration people tended more and more to think of the President as a symbol for government. The public dealt with the increasing complexity of government by personifying it. Even before Congress could convene, as the nationally broadcast inaugural ceremony proceeded, the chief executive was almost instantly transformed from a remote, seemingly inert entity to a vivid focal point of national attention. FDR's confident comportment; the high oratory of the inaugural speech, with its grave warning that he would request war powers over the economy if Congress failed to act; his ebullience; the decisiveness of the following day's "bank holiday" executive order—all of this elicited an overwhelmingly favorable public response to the new President. William Hopkins, who was then in the White House correspondence section, remembers that "President Roosevelt was getting about as much mail a day as President Hoover received in a week. The mail started coming in by the truckload. They couldn't even get the envelopes open."[8]

Significantly, the volume of presidential mail has never tapered off. Recent estimates are that over a million letters come to the President annually.[9] Roosevelt evidently was able to wed his own great powers of personal communication to the general sense of national urgency, channeling what hitherto had been a static patriotic sentiment—American veneration of the great Presidents of the past—into a dynamic component of the incumbent President's role. In

---

[7] For general background on the initial months of Roosevelt's first term see Frank Freidel, *Franklin D. Roosevelt: Launching the New Deal* (Boston: Little, Brown, 1973), and E. P. Herring, *Presidential Leadership: The Political Relations of Congress and the Chief Executive* (New York: Rinehart, 1940).

[8] Hopkins, Oral History Interview. Also see L. A. Sussman, *Dear FDR: A Study in Political Letter Writing* (Totawa, N.J.: Bedminister Press, 1963).

[9] Merlin Gustafson, "The President's Mail," *Presidential Studies Quarterly*, vol. 8 (Winter 1978), p. 36.

initiating this characteristic of the modern presidency, he undoubtedly enhanced his ability and that of his successors to muster public support in times of perceived national crisis. But he also undoubtedly established unrealistic and even contradictory standards by which citizens tend to judge both the personal virtue of Presidents and their ability to solve the typically controversial social and political problems that arise during their administrations.

FDR also innovated in accustoming the nation to expect that the President would be aided by a battery of policy advisers and implementers. At first these aides were officially on the payrolls of diverse non-White House agencies but were unofficially "the President's men."[10] Best remembered now is the sequence of academic braintrusters who advised FDR as governor of New York and early in his first term; the lawyers who drafted and politicked for the next stage of New Deal legislation; and Harry Hopkins, who served as war-time presidential surrogate in international diplomacy.

Politically attentive Americans tend to regard unofficial presidential advising—for example, Jackson's use of his Kitchen Cabinet and Wilson's of Colonel Edward House—with suspicious fascination. The fascination draws on the titillation of identifying the "real" powers behind the throne. The suspicion arises from the fear of illegitimate, legally irresponsible power—an especially strong concern in a polity in which so many of the political actors are lawyers inclined to invoke constitutional principles, even in debates over matter-of-fact interest-group conflicts.

In any case, in the fishbowl context of American mass communications, grey eminences do not remain grey for long. The two leading young lawyers who were Roosevelt's principal agents during the so-called Second New Deal, Thomas Corcoran and Benjamin Cohen, were pictured on the cover of *Time* magazine. This visibility of the unofficial aides who were essential to maintaining FDR's momentum as policy initiator threatened the legitimacy of his leadership. To the degree that such aides upstaged him, they also detracted from his centrality as a symbol of national leadership. These costs of using visible unofficial advisers must have contributed to Roosevelt's interest in procedures that would provide the presidency with aides who *were* official and who were *not* conspicuous.

---

10 Patrick Anderson, *The President's Men: White House Assistants of Franklin D. Roosevelt, Harry S. Truman, Dwight D. Eisenhower, John F. Kennedy, Lyndon B. Johnson* (Garden City: Doubleday, 1968), and Stephen Hess, *Organizing the Presidency* (Washington, D.C.: Brookings Institution, 1976).

Just such a corps of aides was proposed in the 1937 recommendations of the Brownlow Committee, the Committee on Administration of the Federal Government that Roosevelt appointed. Arguing that because of the mushrooming responsibilities of the executive branch, "the President needs help," the Brownlow Committee proposed that an Executive Office of the President be established, including a White House Office staffed by skilled, energetic aides who were to have "a passion for anonymity." After extensive political bargaining, the Reorganization Act of 1939 was passed and implemented by executive order.[11]

The shift from exclusive use by Roosevelt of behind-the-scenes advisors to use of a staff authorized by statute is recorded in the *United States Government Manual* released in October 1939. Listed immediately following the page identifying the President of the United States is what continues to be the umbrella heading under which presidential agencies are grouped—the Executive Office of the President (EOP). The White House Office (WHO) is listed next. (In October 1939 only three WHO aides had been selected. In the 1970–1971 *Manual*, about the peak year for size of WHO staff, over fifty were listed.) [12]

Each *Manual* since 1939 has listed next in sequence, following the WHO, the Bureau of the Budget (after 1970, the Office of Management and Budget). BOB/OMB has consistently been by far the most influential Executive Office appendage, except for the White House Office itself. The BOB originally had been established in 1921, after a decade of efficiency-minded lobbying by "good government" reformers who sought to substitute a consolidated and centrally screened Executive Budget as the communication submitted for congressional action, rather than the disaggregated requests from individual agencies that had been submitted until then. Until the passage of the 1939 Reorganization Act, however, the bureau was not a policy-framing agency, but rather a kind of bookkeeping department which sought to achieve mechanical economies in budgetary requests based, in some cases, on exercises of parsimony as picayune as saving paperclips and pencil stubs. Although officially an agency of the President,

---

[11] President's Committee on Administrative Management, *Report with Studies of Administrative Management in the Federal Government* (Washington, D.C., 1937). B. D. Karl, *Executive Reorganization and Reform in the New Deal: The Genesis of Administrative Management, 1900-1939* (Cambridge, Mass.: Harvard University Press, 1963), and R. Polenberg, *Reorganizing Roosevelt's Government* (Cambridge, Mass.: Boston University Press, 1966).

[12] Hugh Heclo, *Studying the Presidency* (New York: A Report to the Ford Foundation, August 1977), p. 37, and Wayne, *The Legislative Presidency*, pp. 220-21.

the old "green eyeshade" BOB was lodged in the Treasury Department and did not attend to presidential policy goals, apart from the general 1920s policy of holding down budgetary requests and expenditures.

The post-Reorganization Act bureau received a new director, Harold D. Smith, who was both passionately anonymous and assiduously devoted to building an organization of highly able public administrators who would have a continuing responsibility to the presidency, no matter who the incumbent was, as well as serving the man who was in office at the time. Smith's unpublished diaries and the memoirs of the Washington insiders of that period make it clear that he privately assumed an active, if invariably diffident, advisory relationship with President Roosevelt.[13] FDR and Smith conferred regularly. The bureau itself was moved in 1939 from the Treasury Department building to office space in the frequently renamed building directly across the street from the West Wing of the White House. Smith continued to have similar regular conferences with the new President during the first year of the Truman presidency. Instructively from the standpoint of anonymity, the bureau was rarely discussed in the press, and during his tenure as director, Smith's name appeared only twice—both times in neutral contexts—in the New York Times Index.

Because the great changes between 1933 and 1945 in expectations about the magnitude, impact, and nature of the presidency were the outcome not only of the political climate during Roosevelt's time in office, but also of FDR's highly personal style, it was not inevitable that what I now confidently describe as "the modern presidency" had to continue into subsequent administrations. Roosevelt's personality-centered presidency might simply have been one of many transitory highs in the recurring cycle of presidential passivity and activism, such as the intense but rather brief legislative activism of the early Wilson administration. Roosevelt's monopoly of political attention and his capacity to arouse public feeling were reminiscent of the visibility and appeal of his cousin, Theodore Roosevelt. His use of emergency powers in response to crisis had strong precedents in the Lincoln administration. Therefore, when Roosevelt died, World War II ended, and a virtually unknown "little man" succeeded him,

---

13 Diary of Harold Smith, Franklin D. Roosevelt Library, Hyde Park, N.Y. Much of the discussion of the Bureau of the Budget and its successor agency, the Office of Management and Budget, in this chapter relies on the comprehensive, archivally based discussion by Larry S. Berman in his "The Evolution of a Presidential Staff Agency: Variations in How the Bureau of the Budget–Office of Management and Budget Has Responded on Presidential Needs," Ph.D. diss., Princeton University, 1977.

there was reason to expect, fear, or hope that, much as in the Wilson-to-Harding transition, the presidency would again move from center stage in national government to a position closer to the wings.

Truman: Institutionalization of the Modern Presidency. Truman's impact on substantive public policies was at best uneven; his impact on the modern presidency as an institution was profound. Under Truman, the presidency did in fact continue to be central in national politics. There was, however, a shift from the ad hoc, personally stimulated policy initiatives of Roosevelt to the methodical development of policy by Truman in consort with WHO and BOB staff members, as well as other public officials. This shift is aptly described by Max Weber's phrase "the routinization of charisma."

As tattered and imprecise as the term "charisma" has come to be, it could not be stretched to describe Truman's leadership, especially the flat, uninspiring impression he communicated during his first eighteen months in office. Truman's initial extremely high Gallup poll rating (87 percent) expressed national mourning for FDR and sympathy for Truman in what obviously was going to be the monumental task of attempting to succeed Roosevelt. After that first Gallup poll, Truman's performance as President frequently garnered more disapproving than approving poll responses. This was an effect of the unsettled political times over which Truman presided. (Roosevelt, like Lincoln, died in time not to face postwar problems virtually guaranteed to erode presidential popularity.) Truman's seeming substantive and rhetorical shortcomings as a national leader also contributed to his endemically low popularity. But he had the added burden that would have been faced by any successor of Roosevelt (and perhaps Roosevelt himself had he survived his fourth term)—that of living up to the standard FDR had set in the depression and during the war as an inspirer of public confidence.

Whatever his inspirational inadequacies, Truman was no back-to-normalcy Harding. This was evident as early as September 1945, when in a twenty-one-point reconversion message he anticipated the major themes of what soon evolved into the Fair Deal program.[14] Truman also was not the inexperienced "failed haberdasher" his critics alleged him to be. In leading a major wartime investigating committee that scrutinized the performance of "home front" activities and in his earlier service on the Senate Appropriations Committee he had over a decade become closely familiar with the operations and

---

[14] Alonzo Hamby, *Beyond the New Deal: Harry S. Truman and American Liberalism* (New York: Columbia University Press, 1973).

policies of the federal government. Moreover, before his entry into the Senate, his extensive experience as a county administrator and his omnivorous reading had left him well furnished with political skills and ideals.

We can see harbingers of the future President in the handful of documents that the Truman Library has been able to salvage from Truman's years in local government. Some of them, in which he methodically accounts for county revenues and expenditures and proposes reforms, anticipate Truman's exceptionally close work with his Budget Bureau staff in examining the many policy issues that quickly fell into the bailiwick of that institution. Other early Truman documents include speeches to patriotic and other civic groups which presage many aspects of his presidential leadership—speeches extolling the centrality of the President in the constitutional system; praising good (that is, decisive, manly, and moral) leaders, including great Presidents; and conceiving of social process as the outcome of the triumph of good over bad leaders.[15]

Much of Truman's impact on the presidency is illustrated by comparing his and Roosevelt's ways of dealing with the Bureau of the Budget. In Harold Smith's diaries, a repeated theme during the Roosevelt years is Smith's concern that he would fail to build a continuing staff agency that could serve successive presidencies. So incorrigibly informal was Roosevelt's way of operating that he often treated Smith simply as if he were another of Roosevelt's many unofficial advisers, rather than the head of a statutory presidential staff agency. Smith expressed in his diaries a concern that the agency he was in the process of carefully filling with the most promising administrators he could find would be compromised institutionally

---

[15] Harry S. Truman, President's Secretary File, Historical, County Judge Address, 1929-33, Box 239, Harry S. Truman Library, Independence, Mo. Here is Truman on the importance of constitutionalism and leadership in the development of the American Constitution: "From the Magna Charta to the Declaration of Independence and the American Constitution is a space of some 560 years, and every step forward was the result of the ideals and self-sacrifice of some great leader. . . . We have an idealist in the White House now, the first we've had since Woodrow Wilson, and he's going to show us how to pull ourselves out of our present woes." Camp Pike, Arkansas, August 1933 (on this occasion Truman was "commandant" of a patriotic gathering of youths, probably a regular program of a veteran's organization). Also see the following undated Washington's Birthday remarks (c. 1932) to a Masonic group. George Washington "was a human, powerful, straightforward man. He liked horse races, liked to take a chance in friendly games, liked a good drink of liquor once in a while and when necessity called for it could swear as well and as effectively as Alexander, Caesar, Napoleon, or any other great commander of men. Men handled in the mass expect the boss to cuss them out when they need it and they like it."

by FDR's continuing impulse to make use of the director as a mediator among feuding departments and wartime agencies. He was distressed, as he put it, at being Roosevelt's "Mr. Fixit."

Under Truman, the bureau itself as well as its director became an integral part of the presidency. During Smith's holdover period and the tenure of his exceptionally able successor, James Webb, the bureau rapidly assumed the role of central coordinating institution for framing and formalizing annual presentations of what came to be called "the program of the President." Truman was a direct party to the soon taken-for-granted expanded role of the Bureau of the Budget, the enlargement of the White House Office staff, and the conversion of that staff into a team meeting daily with "the boss," dividing a workload beyond the capacity of the traditional presidency. By 1947 the efforts of the White House staff and of the Bureau of the Budget had become closely coordinated as a result of Truman's, Smith's, and Webb's efforts.

From time to time BOB aides, especially if they developed strong Fair Deal political convictions, "crossed the street" and became White House aides. Meanwhile, the bureau itself continued to develop its joint roles of helping the President to frame his policy program and examining policy proposals in terms of their consistency with the overall outlines of that program as well as their technical feasibility. It was during Truman's first two years in office that the bureau began, as a standard operating procedure, to examine all departmental appropriations requests in terms of their consistency with the President's program. Even more important (and less probable, given the title of the agency), the bureau became centrally involved in the legislative process. It became a regular BOB duty to clear and coordinate all legislative requests originating within federal departments, to help draft legislation emanating from the White House, to clear and draft executive orders, and to do all of this in terms of program of the President. These actions were in addition to the continuation of a bureau function acquired in the late 1930s—review and clearance with other relevant agencies of all congressional enactments with a view to recommending whether they be signed or vetoed.

The annual BOB compilation of proposed legislation and the final budget document provide the basis for what has become the set-piece initiation of each political year—a state of the union message, backed up by draft legislation. Delivered by the President with dignified republican ceremony to a joint session of Congress and other assembled dignitaries, the contemporary state of the union message enunciates the general outlines of the President's program, as well as containing traditional rhetoric about present national conditions and future prospects.

The state of the union message is one of three major presidential communications that go to Congress in January. The second is the budget document itself, accompanied by the budget message and the *Budget in Brief*, complete with graphic illustrations. The third is the Report of the President's Council of Economic Advisers (CEA). The CEA, which was provided for in the Employment Act of 1946, is one of two continuing accretions to the Executive Office added during the Truman years. Truman's first council had a chairman who wanted the annual report to be an independent assessment of the economy not coordinated with the political emphasis of the overall presidential program. This view of the role of the CEA did not prevail, however. The council became part of the President's team, and its report and the other two January messages quickly became complementary assertions of the same program. A second statutory body, the National Security Council (NSC), grew out of the legislation that brought about the unification of the armed forces. Initially the NSC was conceived of by many congressmen who had supported unification as a potential check on Presidents' autonomy in their commander-in-chief role. Truman, however, "domesticated" the NSC as well as the CEA. Ever since the Truman years both of these, plus numerous more transient EOP agencies, have been further institutional underpinnings of the modern presidency.

Just as the professional staff of the BOB acquired some of the qualities of those British civil servants who perennially aid the executive, whatever party is in power, so the President's January communications have become roughly akin to the messages to new British parliamentary sessions, ghostwritten by the Government in power for delivery by the monarch. But American Presidents face one of the most vigorously autonomous legislatures in any parliamentary democracy. Hence their messages only help set the *terms* of the next legislative session's political debate, whereas the proposals voiced by the British monarch almost invariably are enacted into law. The many legislative defeats Truman received from the 79th through 82nd Congresses illustrate how a presidential program may be consistently blocked by an opposition coalition. In Truman's case the amount of Fair Deal domestic legislation that he succeeded in passing was miniscule, although there were major triumphs in assembling a sufficiently large bipartisan foreign policy coalition to authorize the Truman Doctrine, the Marshall Plan, and other postwar reconstruction and cold war initiatives.

Truman was also responsible not merely for initiating but also for carrying through policy making in areas included in the expanded domain of independent presidential action. Among the most consequential exercises of executive initiative by this believer in a presidency with substantial autonomous powers were the decision to use atomic weapons at the end of World War II, the decision to commit American troops to Korea, and the executive order integrating the military. Many of Truman's autonomous decisions were politically costly, including a number that reflected his commitment to maintaining the independent powers of the presidency—for example, the steel seizure and the relief of General MacArthur.

Despite domestic policy stasis, his low general popularity, and the political costliness of some of his decisions, Truman's practice of executive assertiveness entrenched the tendency of all but the most conservative policy makers to look at the President as the main framer of the agenda for public debate—even when much of the debate consisted of castigation of his proposals. Truman, like Roosevelt, was not alone responsible for the changes in the presidency that occurred during his years in office. Key advisers like Smith and Webb were also influential. Moreover, Truman was operating in an environment of big government, the welfare state, and American international involvement that inevitably tended to place major responsibilities on the executive branch. Nevertheless, like Roosevelt, Truman himself does emphatically seem to have been a major independent influence on the shape of the modern presidency. Not everyone in the postwar period was convinced that the welfare state should continue or that the United States should maintain its international commitments. Conservatives of both parties felt that the New Deal welfare innovations should be repealed or cut back. Conservative isolationists and left-leaning supporters of Henry Wallace's 1948 Progressive party, out of wholly different motivations, opposed American involvement in the international arena. And during the post-World War II years not all democracies acquired assertive, stable executive leadership, the French Fourth Republic being an obvious example of a nation in which the top political executives (although not the permanent bureaucrats) were highly limited in influence and unstable in tenure in office. What then was to be expected of the evolving "center stage" presidency when another President replaced Truman—one who had frequently echoed his newly adopted party's claim that the "balance" of political leadership should be redirected toward Congress?

Eisenhower: Ratification of the Modern Presidency. When the Republicans returned to power in 1953 and the institutional changes and role expectations of the modern presidency were not fundamentally altered, the Great Divide had been crossed. As is well known, drawing on his long military exposure to staff work, Eisenhower arranged for the establishment of a White House office that was more formally organized and, incidentally, larger than Truman's WHO. At least in the official scheme of things, the Eisenhower White House was an organizational hierarchy. Directly under the presidential apex was a chief of staff—for the first six years, the zealous Sherman Adams. As The Assistant to the President, Adams was listed first in the *Organization Manual*; other White House aides were enumerated in an indented list that visually conveyed their subordination to Adams. Adams's counterpart in foreign affairs—again for the first six years—was Secretary of State John Foster Dulles.

We know from a variety of sources, including the newly opened private and confidential files of the President's personal secretary, that Eisenhower was far from being a mere puppet of Adams and Dulles. He was intimately involved in national security policy making and had multiple sources of information about domestic as well as foreign affairs. As a domestic political conservative without a strong desire to innovate, except in modest incremental ways, Eisenhower does, however, seem to have left to Adams and his associates a variety of substantive decisions that would have been made by the President himself in the previous administration, as well as making use of Adams as a framer of alternatives under circumstances where Truman would have canvassed alternatives on his own.

Other steps toward formalization in the Eisenhower White House were the regular and systematic practice of holding cabinet meetings (although, as in other presidencies, the cabinet was not a decision-making body); the establishment of a Cabinet Secretariat; and the creation of an elaborate National Security Council structure, in which special attention was payed not only to formal presentations in weekly meetings of the NSC, but also to the use of a coordinating mechanism (later scrapped by Kennedy) to attend to the implementation of policy.

Many of Eisenhower's formal mechanics of White House organization were supplemented by informal, unpublicized proceedings. The NSC meetings, for example, which by the end of the 1950s had come to be thought of as mechanical rituals, were in fact coordinating and teamwork-generating occasions. Preceding the official meetings, however, there were off-the-record meetings by the President with a subgroup of the NSC, and these appear to have been occasions for a genuine process of hammering out policy in which the President arrived at decisions after hearing contending points of view.[16] And members of the cabinet had individual access to the President to discuss matters that cabinet members invariably find impolitic to discuss openly in the Cabinet Room. Moreover, for the first time the White House Office staff acquired an official legislative liaison office (staffed by a skilled lobbying team that Eisenhower "appropriated" from the Pentagon). As Eisenhower came to be more and more aware that even a conservative who wished to put curbs on policy innovation needed effective representation of his views to Congress, this staff became increasingly systematic in its efforts to advance the President's program.

Above all, under Eisenhower there continued to *be* a President's program. Having talked of "restoring the balance," Eisenhower quickly found himself to be a presidentialist—that is, a defender of the accrued responsibilities of the modern presidency. This ratification of the overall properties of the modern presidency during Eisenhower's two terms is manifested at both the formal and the symbolic levels. On the formal level, his position favoring presidential prerogative is instructive. Eisenhower immediately became intensely active, for example, in the campaign that successfully defeated the Bricker Amendment, which would have made presidential executive agreements with other nations subject to Senate ratification. In terms of maintaining the symbolic function of the office, Eisenhower was able to draw on his longstanding public credit as the most popular figure to emerge from World War II in order to maintain a remarkably consistent high level of prestige and popularity with the electorate, even at times when Washington insiders derided him for his seeming lack of political skill and knowledge. In this sense he was able—with what seems to have been minimum effort—to live up to the high expectations established under FDR that Presidents be endowed with virtuous personal qualities but nevertheless be sufficiently politically competent to carry out their tasks in a way that leaves citizens broadly satisfied with the state of the nation.

A third, and from the standpoint of this essay especially consequential, aspect of the Eisenhower presidency was his continued use of the institutional resource that made it possible for there to be a "program of the President"—the Bureau of the Budget. Eisenhower's first bureau director, Joseph Dodge, became attuned to the bureau's procedures before assuming office, taking advantage of Truman's offer

---

[16] Douglas Kinnard, *President Eisenhower and Strategy Management: A Study in Defense Politics* (Lexington, Ky.: The University Press of Kentucky, 1977).

of interelection "internships" for Eisenhower appointees. Dodge quickly recognized the high quality of the bureau's senior personnel and their readiness to shift from shaping a Truman program to shaping an Eisenhower program. Although there was no first-year Eisenhower legislative program, there was one to accompany his January 1954 state of the union message. The requests for proposed legislation from federal agencies were routinely sent out by the bureau's professional staff in 1953. Before the year was over it became evident that an Eisenhower program would be submitted to Congress.

In August 1956 Eisenhower's secretary, Ann Whitman, replied to an inquiry from Milton Eisenhower as to how the President's workload might be reduced. Her letter, from which I quote selectively, suggests how a basically conservative President, working in a tightly staffed White House, allocated his energies. During much of the previous year the President had been recovering from two major health setbacks, so her remarks apply primarily to Eisenhower's practices up to his September 1955 heart attack. We see his very great attention to national security policy and his greater willingness to delegate policy initiation in domestic than in international affairs.

Regular Weekly Meetings:

1. The National Security Council seems to be the most time-consuming, from the standpoint of number of hours *in* the actual meeting, the briefing before the meeting that has seemed to become a routine, and the time that the President must give, occasionally, to be sure that the meetings reflect exactly the decisions reached. . . . [Mrs. Whitman thought that frequently the President was already well informed on the substance of the prior briefings and of the meetings themselves. She noted "he himself complains that he knows every word of the presentations as they are to be made. However, he feels that to maintain the interest and attention of every member of the NSC, he must sit through each meeting. . . ."]

2. The Cabinet meetings are not usually so long as NSC, but the President feels in some instances that to fill out an agenda, items are included that are not necessarily of the caliber that should come before the Cabinet. . . .

3. The Press Conferences. These meetings are preceded by a half to three-quarter hour briefing by staff members. [Mrs. Whitman felt that in most cases Eisenhower was already sufficiently informed to meet the press without briefings, but added "the meetings do serve the purpose of letting him know how various members of the staff are thinking. . . ."]

4. Legislative Leaders Meetings. When the Congress is in session, these are held weekly but do not last, on the average, more than an hour and a half and only about five minutes' preparation is required.

5. The President has a weekly meeting with the Secretary of Defense.

6. The President usually has a half-hour meeting with [Economic Advisers] Dr. [Gabriel] Hauge and Dr. [Arthur] Burns. I think he finds these meetings valuable and do not believe the sessions are unduly prolonged.

Mrs. Whitman also noted that the President had a half-hour daily intelligence briefing from Colonel Andrew Goodpaster, and she listed roughly a dozen categories of "other items that occupy his time," some of them taking up very little time (for example, independent agencies), some of them involving him in time-consuming ceremonial duties (receiving ambassadors, meeting dignitaries and civic groups, state dinners, and signatures), and others involving policy and intermittently consuming much time. The latter included the State Department ("meetings with the Secretary are irregular, based upon the urgency of the particular crisis of the moment"); additional defense matters ("here is a great time-consuming area. . . . I can't always see why some of the inter-Service problems cannot be resolved before they come to the President"); "other Cabinet matters" ("The President is available at all times to any Cabinet member for consultation"); "personnel, appointments, domestic matters" ("My general impression is that all such items have been pretty well digested [by Sherman Adams] before they reach the President, and that only his final judgment is required"); and speeches ("The President spends a great deal of time personally on his speeches, but I don't think that routine can ever be changed. I think only by the process of editing and reworking does the speech become truly his own—and I think the hours—and I guess he spends twenty to thirty on each major speech—are inevitable.") [17]

The Presidency since 1960: Structural Changes, Oscillations, and Continuity

In any institution it is difficult in the short run to distinguish between permanent changes and changes that will turn out to have been only ephemeral. Many changes in the post-Eisenhower presidency were

---

[17] Ann Whitman to Milton Eisenhower, August 28, 1956, Names Series, Box 13, Dwight D. Eisenhower Library, Abilene, Kansas.

thought to have been permanent at the time but from the persepctive of the late 1970s appear to have been rather drastic zigs and zags in patterns that had been established during the formative first three modern presidencies. Taking as a combined basis of classification the actual functioning of the presidency and the way in which the more widely read commentators on American politics have evaluated its functioning, the Kennedy-to-Carter years can be divided into three phases.

Phase one is the period beginning with Kennedy's efforts—"vigorous" efforts—to initiate a wide range of policies, some of them long-term inheritances from the Democratic party's New Deal–Fair Deal agenda, others projects with a distinctive Kennedy stamp. This period continues through the enactment of the extraordinary volume of Johnson Great Society legislation by the heavily Democratic 89th Congress. The bulk of commentators on the presidency viewed this as a period during which a previously "stalemated" presidency was steadily increasing both in its impact on public policy and also in the merit of its contribution to the political system. Merit, of course, is in the eye of the beholder. The beholders I have in mind are the politically liberal academics and publicists who provide most of the "serious" commentary on public affairs. During the formative presidencies, as we shall see, most such political commentators had become convinced of the institutional desirability of a "strong" presidency. Experiencing the Kennedy qualities of personal leadership, the posthumous idealization of Kennedy, and the passage of Johnson's sweeping domestic policy program during the period from Kennedy's death to roughly the end of the 89th Congress, these commentators typically felt that the presidency was beginning, in practice, to perform precisely the functions in the political system they had long felt that it ought in principle to be performing.

The period of Great Society legislative enactment overlaps with the second phase, from the advent of serious protest at Vietnam escalation through Watergate and President Nixon's resignation. Even before the end of the 89th Congress, increasing American military involvement in Vietnam began to induce commentary on the presidency, which, as in the first post-1960 phase, stressed the growing capacity of Presidents to shape public policy, but which now emphasized "excessive" presidential power. By late in the Watergate sequence, the view that the presidency was a dangerously unchecked institution was no longer monopolized by liberal political commentators. For convenience, I adopt for this period the label that came to be virtually automatic for many writers: "imperial presidency."

The first two phases, that of celebration of presidential strength and that of lamentation about the "imperial" practices of Presidents Johnson and Nixon, have been followed by a phase that, using the most recent catchword, I shall call "postimperial." During the time since President Nixon left office, one President, Gerald Ford, has joined the select ranks of William Howard Taft and Herbert Hoover as the only twentieth-century incumbents to run unsuccessfully for reelection. Ford's successor, Jimmy Carter, limped through an initial year in office, during which he encountered what could charitably be called limited response to his ambitious legislative and foreign policy goals and a substantial erosion in his Gallup poll ratings.[18]

Presidential politics in phase three, at the advent of the final quarter of the century, seems remarkably like the pattern of politics of the formative pre-Kennedy modern presidencies as described in Richard Neustadt's influential essay, "The Presidency at Mid-Century."[19] As a former Truman aide who had worked on the unsuccessful Fair Deal domestic program and who was also aware of the inability of FDR to win support for similar policies after 1938 and of Eisenhower's difficulty in achieving even limited policy goals, Neustadt saw the presidency as a highly restrained institution. Granting that modern Presidents had acquired far enhanced formal powers and role expectations, Neustadt argued that Presidents nevertheless were exceptionally limited in their capacities to turn formal power into effective policy making. Further, the tension between the demands on them and the limitations on their ability to make policy and hence to live up to expectations put them in a position Neustadt likened to that of "a cat on a hot tin roof."

The rather drastic and rapid alternations since 1960 in the way in which the presidency has functioned and, possibly as important, in the way in which it has been perceived to function are to a considerable extent a consequence of one continuing property of the presidency. Among all American national political institutions, none is so profoundly affected by the personal characteristics and performance in office of the incumbent and of the other personalities he chooses or permits to act as his chief associates. One reason why the Roosevelt, Truman, and Eisenhower presidencies could be formative was that their long duration accustomed political actors, including Presi-

[18] "Only Half of Americans Praise Carter's First Year," *Gallup Opinion Index,* Report No. 152, March 1978. Also see the April 14, 1978 *New York Times* report "Approval of Carter Drops to 46% in Poll: Rating is Lowest after 14 Months for any President Except Ford in Wake of Nixon Pardon," p. A.10.

[19] Richard E. Neustadt, "The Presidency at Mid-Century," *Law and Contemporary Problems,* vol. 21 (Autumn 1956), pp. 609-45.

dents themselves and the public at large, as well as other members of the policy-making community, to broadly consistent practices in the conduct of the presidency. Between 1933 and 1961 the *three* formative modern Presidents held office for the equivalent of *seven* four-year terms. Since then *five* presidents have been in office for the equivalent of just over *four* four-year terms.

Just as it was by no means predetermined that the three formative Presidents would have the cumulative impact that they did have in shaping the basic qualities of the modern presidency, there was nothing inexorable about the way the institution has developed since. On the contrary, it has been plausibly maintained that each of the post-Eisenhower Presidents had a major personal impact on the phases through which the presidency has moved since 1960. Would the three phases described above have occurred if the individual named Richard Nixon had defeated Kennedy in 1960? What would have happened if Kennedy had served two full terms? Or if Nixon had never become President?

Although there is no definitive way to answer such questions, it is possible to apply systematic evidence and inference to them. "What if?" questions are the grist of historical explanation. It is only possible to say that *x* caused *y* in a historical sequence by inferring that some plausible non-*x* would have led to a result different from *y*. Putting this concretely, and in terms of the effects of presidential psychology on the evolution of the presidency, we may note that, quite appropriately, there continue to be debates about whether Kennedy would have escalated the Vietnam conflict in the fashion that Johnson did, whether FDR would have presided over the same Truman-led sequence of cold war events that occurred after his death, and so forth. The entire enterprise of psychological interpretation of Presidents and their behavior is dependent on such speculation.[20]

 By the late 1970s the rapid turnover in Presidents had become an important quality of the presidency itself, as well as helping to explain the sequence of cyclical rather than secular changes in certain overall properties of the office. Modern Presidents, at least since the Twenty-second Amendment, have generally been recognized by political ob-

---

[20] Many of the characterizations of twentieth-century Presidents by James D. Barber in his *The Presidential Character: Predicting Performance in the White House* (Englewood Cliffs, N.J.: Prentice-Hall, 1977), 2nd ed., suggest that the personal qualities of an incumbent President were highly consequential for the course of historical events during their administrations. For an abstract discussion of the circumstances under which political leaders' personal qualities are likely to have an impact on events, see Fred I. Greenstein, *Personality and Politics; Problems of Evidence, Inference and Conceptualization* (New York: Norton Library, 1975), chap. 3.

servers as short-run participants in Washington policy making, who therefore tend to have a hurried approach to the making of policy. The more enduring fixtures of the Washington political community—senior members of Congress, justices, lobbyists, and Washington attorneys, for example—can better afford to play a waiting game. If the impact a President seeks is policy innovation rather than the maintenance of the status quo, the President's relatively brief tenure of office encourages him to engage in activities that are politically risky: simply to win office he needs to raise aspirations about what he will be able to contribute to the nation; once in office, the difficulty of meeting those aspirations opens up temptations to cut corners—for example, to rush legislation through Congress and leave considerations of practical implementation for later on, or to circumvent slow-moving or otherwise recalcitrant departments and bureaus by moving policy making into the White House, say, by augmenting the role of the assistant for national security affairs over that of the secretary of state or by establishing a White House "plumbers" group. The temptation to cut corners therefore seems bound to increase.

Shifting Evaluations of the Presidency. In describing the circuitous course of what seemed to be the beginning of enduring changes in the post-1960 presidency, I have deliberately merged institutional functioning and prevailing value judgments about institutional functioning. This is because one of the most significant changes that occurred lay precisely in the evaluation of the institution by writers who, to a considerable extent, were actually responding to their own negative assessments of the policies and performance of individual Presidents, especially Johnson and Nixon. The change in evaluations of the presidency by the most widely read and listened to commentators on that institution has had two consequences. First, it has helped fuel the political debate that has led, for example, to the presidency-curbing legislation of the 1970s. Second, value judgments affect empirical assessments. Since the "imperial" presidency, actions that might previously have seemed to show normal presidential autonomy have been construed as showing a tendency toward augmented unilateral power. As difficult as it is to separate value and empirical judgments in a context where the first type of judgment has contributed to the state of affairs that one seeks empirically to evaluate, it is useful to try to do precisely that.

William Andrews has carefully documented the shifts during the years of the modern presidency in normative appraisals of the institution by academic and, to a lesser extent, nonacademic commentators.[21] His summary pins down and expands on the point made earlier about the politically liberal perspective that has informed most serious writing on the presidency. By the later Truman years, most of the more widely read writers on the presidency had established an academic, and to a lesser extent a journalistic, orthodoxy about the greater intrinsic merit of the presidency as a political institution as compared with other national political institutions. Conservatives still fulminated about excesses in presidential power, but with the exception of the writings of the Princeton University constitutional law theorist Edward Corwin, academic commentary had come to stress the importance of an unfettered, activist President.

The standard themes in both the scholarship and the textbooks of the time [22] are that the President is the nation's single elected official and hence his mandate is broader than the "broken" mirror reflection of public opinion provided by Congress; that the President's institutional vantage point, overlooking other national institutions and facing outward internationally, makes him the most appropriate custodian of the "public interest"; and that the exigencies of an intricately interdependent economy, society, and international environment make it important to have a leader with leeway to act promptly and decisively with a minimum of hindrance and political pulling and hauling. From this standpoint, the major flaw in the presidency is not its susceptibility to the usurpation of power, but its subjection to the political restraints described in Neustadt's "The Presidency at Mid-Century." As we have seen, writers during the first half of the 1960s tended to be delighted that the presidential Gulliver had begun to be freed from the many "parochial" restraints on presidential leadership.

The very same writers who up to the mid-1960s looked to an unfettered presidency as a major positive feature of the political system, during the imperial presidency phase began to sound like the 1940s and 1950s conservatives who had favored the Twenty-second Amendment and the narrowly defeated Bricker Amendment. The bellwether of revisionism on the merits of a strong presidency is Arthur Schlesinger, Jr., whose book (which introduced the term *The Imperial Presidency*) includes an explicit mea culpa for Schlesinger's

---

21 William G. Andrews, "The Presidency, Congress and Constitutional Theory," in Aaron Wildavsky, ed., *Perspectives on the Presidency* (Boston: Little, Brown, 1975), pp. 24-44.
22 Thomas Cronin, "The Text Book Presidency," in Stanley Bach and George T. Sulzner, eds., *Perspectives on the Presidency: A Collection* (Lexington, Mass.: D. C. Heath, 1974), pp. 54-74.

uncritical celebration of presidential activism in his writings on Jackson, Roosevelt, and Kennedy.[23]

Interestingly, Schlesinger goes out of his way to rediscover and to pay his respects to the main scholar of the presidency whose works focus on the chief executive's "aggrandizement of power," Edward Corwin.[24] Since Schlesinger and the many other liberal writers on the presidency only became preoccupied with the dangers inherent in the institution when they became distressed about particular policies pursued by Johnson and Nixon, it is instructive to note the development of Corwin's own thinking. As Andrews shows, Corwin was sufficiently enthusiastic about strong presidential leadership to be the chief academic supporter of Franklin Roosevelt's proposal to expand the size of the Supreme Court in order to reverse its proclivity to strike down New Deal legislation. The press of the day widely viewed Corwin as a major candidate for membership on the proposed "packed" Court.

In the event, "Court packing" never took place; Roosevelt soon had numerous openings to fill, and he never nominated Corwin. By 1940 the first of the four editions of Corwin's textbook criticizing the rise in presidential power had appeared. Without assuming a crass quid-pro-quo motivation on Corwin's part, one can reasonably surmise that his substantive evaluation of FDR had sharply altered after 1937 and that this change—like the changes in the 1960s liberals' views in response to presidential performance in office—was critical in reshaping his overall evaluation of the degree to which the institution itself was appropriately performing its constitutional responsibilities. In short, people often think they are evaluating the presidency when in fact they are evaluating Presidents.

The Use of Persuasion and Command. Command and persuasion are two pivotal terms in Neustadt's book *Presidential Power*.[25] Published in 1960, this work was quickly acknowledged as the most realistic

---

[23] Compare the view of discretionary presidential policy making in Arthur M. Schlesinger, Jr., *The Imperial Presidency* (Boston: Houghton Mifflin, 1973), with that implicit in Schlesinger's *The Age of Jackson* (Boston: Little, Brown, 1946); *The Age of Roosevelt*, 3 vols. (Boston, Houghton Mifflin, 1957, 1959, 1960); and *A Thousand Days: John F. Kennedy in the White House* (Boston: Houghton Mifflin, 1965).

[24] Edward S. Corwin, *The President, Office and Powers, 1787-1957: History and Analysis of Practice and Opinion* (New York: New York University Press, 1957), 4th ed., originally published in 1940.

[25] Richard E. Neustadt, *Presidential Power: The Politics of Leadership with Reflections on Johnson and Nixon* (New York: Wiley, 1976), originally published in 1960.

scholarly account of how the presidency actually functions and what Presidents can do to enhance their leadership. We have seen that Neustadt was not impressed with the shift toward greater capacity for policy initiation and unilateral action by modern Presidents (these developments he described as the President's "clerkship"). Rather, he was concerned with the likelihood that Presidents would fail to be politically effective because of the restraints on them by other elements in the political system and because of their own failure to exercise skilled leadership.

The central leadership skill, in Neustadt's view, was the power of persuasion—a power Presidents can exercise by effective bargaining, maintaining their reputations with other policy makers as skilled and popular leaders, and seeking to arrange that other policy makers find it in their own interest to do voluntarily what the President wants them to do. Truman's wooing of Republican Senator Arthur Vandenberg to win bipartisan support for the Truman Doctrine and the Marshall Plan was Neustadt's illustration of effective persuasion. By command Neustadt meant unilateral presidential orders that are intended to be obeyed without defiance because they lie (or at least the President thinks they lie) in the sphere of decision making within which the President is authoritative, whether on a constitutional, statutory, or some other basis. Neustadt's examples of command were three major decisions: Truman's discharge of MacArthur and his seizure of the steel industry and Eisenhower's dispatch of troops to Arkansas to enforce school integration. All three decisions were unpopular; the steel seizure, in fact, was ruled unconstitutional.

Neustadt's inferences were that commands are evidence of presidential weakness rather than strength; that they do not contribute to the President's later effectiveness; and (presumably) that they are likely to be rare. Numerous presidential decisions during the 1960s and 1970s were construed as exercises of command and seemed to belie these inferences about the utility and frequency of presidential command decision making. First, much attention was paid to types of decisions that seemed not to have concerned Neustadt—namely *routine* command decisions. In later years these began to be recognized as politically significant. Second, many observers felt that *major* command decisions—decisions of the sort that did concern Neustadt— were becoming substantially more common.

Examples of routine command are presidential orders affecting White House administrative staffing and staff organization and presidential orders setting in motion the sophisticated travel and communication facilities at the President's disposal. A much more mundane example is the President's instruction to his secretary to carry out a clerical chore. Routine command is an inevitable component of leadership. If *all* presidential decision making were by persuasion and bargaining, as a literalist might conclude upon reading Neustadt, the President undoubtedly would be hopelessly overloaded.[26] Nevertheless, routine commands can be politically consequential—for example, the command to install a voice-activated tape recording system in the President's office or the command to ready the way for foreign travel, as in the 1972 Nixon trips to China and the Soviet Union, which greatly enhanced the President's popularity and made him a sure election winner.

Moreover, major presidential command decisions clearly *seemed* to be becoming more common during the years after Neustadt's book was published—especially during the imperial phase of the post-1960 presidency. Obvious examples are various of Johnson's and Nixon's decisions in connection with the Indochinese conflict; the instances of political espionage and sabotage by Nixon associates that were brought out in the Watergate episode; and numerous Nixon decisions in domestic politics, such as his aggressive use of presidential spending powers. At least part of the increase in command during the Johnson and Nixon administrations, however, was simply an increase in perceived command. A liberal internationalist who favored Roosevelt's destroyers-for-bases exchange with Britain in 1940 was not likely to classify this as an act of command. The same liberal, as a Vietnam dove, might well have placed many similarly unilateral Johnson and Nixon decisions in the command category.

It follows that the command decisions that are politically costly are decisions that draw unfavorable attention to the President. For most of the public, such decisions need merely to be unpopular to affect the President unfavorably. For fellow leaders, command decisions by the President may be viewed unkindly not only because such leaders and their constituents disagree with their content, but also because they disagree with their wisdom, or even their legitimacy in constitutional terms. This class of major command decision is emphatically open to the kind of backlash that Neustadt had in mind —especially because decisions of this sort are not shared with other leaders, with the result that the blame for them is not shared. The debacles of each of the imperial presidencies document this somewhat modified version of Neustadt's argument.

---

[26] Peter Sperlich, "Bargaining and Overload: An Essay on Presidential Power," in Aaron Wildavsky, ed., *The Presidency* (Boston: Little, Brown, 1969), pp. 168-92 and in Aaron Wildavsky, ed., *Perspectives on the Presidency*.

The Intractable Political Environment of the Postimperial Presidency.
At what Neustadt called "mid-century," Presidents were severely
restrained in their ability to affect policy, especially in spheres other
than those that permitted unilateral action. They were surrounded
by an intractable political environment. As the last quarter of the
century begins, after a period during which Presidents seemed to be
riding high, intractability is back. Many of the restraints on Presidents that seemed unnecessarily oppressive to liberals in the 1950s
and early 1960s are precisely those that so often restrained Ford and
that make Carter's efforts at policy achievement so difficult. The *way*
in which these restraints manifest themselves does seem to have
changed, largely as the result of factors that make it even harder in
the late 1970s than it was during the three formative modern presidencies for Presidents to live up to the continuing belief of many
citizens that the President is singly responsible for the state of the
entire nation.

The most conspicuous obstacle to presidential policy influence is
Congress. From the rise of the congressional conservative coalition
following the 1938 presidential election through Johnson's landslide
election in 1964, the major source of congressional resistance to presidential initiatives was—especially in the Roosevelt, Truman, and
Kennedy years—the resistance by conservative Republicans and
southern Democrats to liberal presidential policy proposals. Eisenhower's domestic policy conservatism was sufficiently disguised by
his advocacy of "modern Republicanism" to make this seem to be
the case even during the single Republican presidency of that period.

The 95th Congress, which in Carter's first year in office passed
none of his major substantive legislative proposals, had approximately
the same one-sided Democratic majority as the 89th Congress, which
in a comparable period of time enacted a sizable proportion of Johnson's Great Society program. One major difference between them
was that Carter's was operating in an "end of liberalism" climate—a
time when the failures of many Great Society programs had produced
widespread skepticism about the efficacy of legislative attacks on
major social problems. In fact, the phrase "the end of ideology"
seems more applicable to the political discourse of the 1970s than it
was to the period in which it was coined, the 1950s. In the 1950s
there were still many political activists and practitioners who took it
for granted that *broadly* liberal or *broadly* conservative political programs, if only enacted, would rectify what they felt to be the nation's
social and political shortcomings. In the present era of economic
"stagflation" and of such cross-cutting conflicts as those between

liberal policy reformers favoring environmental protection and liberal labor union activists favoring economic growth, clear-cut lines of cleavage and hence the bases for organizing coalitions are harder to identify than they were even in the ostensibly unideological 1950s.

Closely related to the decline of predictable ideological groupings in Congress (as elsewhere in society) is a decline since the 1950s in the ability of congressional leaders to serve as effective intermediaries between their colleagues and the President, knowing that on achieving agreement with the President they can deliver significant blocs of votes and bring about the passage of the desired legislation. Consider the negotiations that shaped the final outcome of the Civil Rights Act of 1957. The point at issue was a provision of the legislation that enabled federal judges to exact fines and prison sentences in cases when state officials deprived citizens of their voting rights. If such cases were not decided by judges, but rather by the lily-white southern juries of the time, there would have been no effective sanction against southern officials who ignored the act's provisions. Through the efforts of the two Texas power brokers who led the majority Democratic party, Speaker Sam Rayburn and Senate Majority Leader Lyndon Johnson, a group of swing congressmen had been won over to the provision, which finally became law: fines as great as $300 and jail sentences up to forty-five days would be acceptable without the requirement of a trial. Johnson, who considered this a more favorable compromise than he had hoped for, telephoned President Eisenhower and

> asked the President to see quietly if his boys would agree to that. The President asked for ten minutes. He called [the Republican leaders, William Knowland and Joseph Martin] off the floor; both agreed. . . . [Eisenhower] called Lyndon Johnson back and said everything was okay. He asked for a little time so the proceedings would be in order, which Lyndon agreed to. . . . The President called [his chief of legislative liaison] who was delighted at the compromise.[27]

Even if Carter had managed to establish such solidly grounded bargaining relations with the congressional party leaders of the 95th Congress, there was little likelihood that the leaders themselves would have been able to deliver the goods. Some of the reasons for this change are detailed in Patterson's chapter in this volume: no subsequent congressional party leaders have been as skilled at molding

---

[27] Telephone calls, Conversations between Dwight D. Eisenhower and Lyndon B. Johnson re Civil Rights Bill, August 22, 1957, DDE Diaries, Box 15, Dwight D. Eisenhower Library, Abilene, Kansas.

coalitions as Johnson and Rayburn were; there has been an increasing tendency for incumbent congressmen automatically to be returned to office if they run for reelection, and this undoubtedly increases congressmen's independence in dealing with both their party leaders and the President; and a massive growth in congressional staffs has further decentralized congressional power by giving congressmen their own decision-making resources. Above and beyond these changes, there appears to be a general post-Watergate congressional resistance to cooperation with the White House.[28]

In the 1950s it was widely taken for granted that Congress was a major check on executive autonomy and that the "weakness" of congressional parties limited the chances that partisanship would serve to "bridge the separation of powers" even when the same party was in control of both branches of government. Who would have thought that a quarter-century later one explanation of a President's difficulties in influencing his party would be a still greater decline in the capacity of congressional leaders to mediate between members of Congress and the President? This decline does seem to have occurred, however, and it parallels still another institutional decline— that of the power of party leaders in the states and localities to mediate between their constituencies and the President, especially in presidential-selection politics.

During the formative period of the modern presidency, the "decentralized" national party system was widely viewed as a restraint on the mobilization around the President of national policy-making coalitions. By the 1970s state and local party organizations were so fragmented that, by contrast, the 1930s through the 1950s seem to have been high points of party government. At least in the earlier period there *were* party organizations and leaders with whom Presidents could bargain and who viewed a successful President as a political asset. Accompanying the general decline in the strength of state and local party organizations throughout the 1960s there was a striking decline in candidacies and campaigns using traditional grass-roots party channels. The older decentralized party fiefdoms were at least entities with which Presidents could bargain—for example, when the time came for renomination or for influencing the

---

[28] On recent congressional independence of both executive leadership and leadership by congressional leaders see, in addition to Patterson's chapter in this volume, "Congress: Bold and Balky," *Time*, January 23, 1978; Barry M. Hager, "Carter's First Year: Setbacks and Successes," *Congressional Quarterly Weekly Report*, vol. 35 (December 24, 1977), pp. 2637-42; and Dom Bonafede, "Carter's First Year: An Assessment," *National Journal*, vol. 10 (January 14, 1978), pp. 44-49.

choice of one's successor. Today there is much less to bargain with "out there." Moreover, the change in presidential-selection rules toward multiple primaries, caucus states that are penetrable by disciplined candidate organizations, the disappearance of unit-rule voting at national conventions, and other "democratizing" party reforms further invalidate the textbook description of the President as chief of his party. In 1968, if Johnson had not withdrawn his candidacy, it was by no means certain that he would have been renominated. Ford fought an extremely demanding battle for the 1978 nomination. And while Nixon's renomination was superficially in the traditional pattern of partisan renomination of incumbent Presidents, his main resource was the Committee to Re-elect the President, not the Republican party.[29]

Clearly much of what is intractable about the political environment of the late 1970s results from the inability of Presidents to work effectively with institutions that also restrained the early modern Presidents. The difference is in the nature of this inability. In the past, the resistance came from institutions that possessed sufficient structure and leadership so that bargaining and negotiation were possible. In the present, institutions are more amorphous, less responsive to their own leadership or any other, and are therefore less well suited for presidential coalition-building.

This amorphousness also appears increasingly to apply to cabinet departments, as Heclo suggests in his chapter in this volume and in his larger study of the executive branch.[30] The President's appointees—the cabinet secretaries and assistant secretaries—seem less and less likely to be professional politicians or public figures who have independent bases of political influence. Rather, they are professional participants in the policy domains that concern their departments. In this respect they tend to have views that converge with those of the career officials in the departments—the latter having increasingly become advocates of the substantive policy directions of the programs that they administer. Cabinet secretaries have always "gone native" and civil servants have always had views about their programs, but if

[29] On how local party potentates in the past were both a greater restraint on Presidents than at present and a greater bargaining asset for making policy, see Richard E. Neustadt, "The Constraining of the President: The Presidency after Watergate," *British Journal of Political Science*, vol. 4 (October 1974), pp. 383-97; Lyle W. Dorsett, *Franklin D. Roosevelt and the City Bosses* (Port Washington, N.Y.: Kennikat Press, 1977); David S. Broder, "Of Presidents and Parties," *The Wilson Quarterly*, vol. 2 (Winter 1978), pp. 105-14.
[30] Hugh Heclo, *A Government of Strangers: Executive Politics in Washington* (Washington: Brookings Institution, 1977).

Heclo is correct, there is now less difference between the political appointees and the career bureaucrats than there once was. Above all, the departments are decreasingly available to the President as firm entities with which he can work out alliances in the course of policy making and implementation.

Under the heading of intractability (if not amorphousness) it also is appropriate to mention the mass media, which nowadays expose the President to a kind of scrutiny that probably accounts both for the evanescent high popularity of many Presidents during their early months in office and for their subsequent sharp declines in support. Roosevelt was rarely photographed from the waist down; many Americans do not appear to have been aware of the extent of his physical disability. George Wallace's physical disability was publicized in minute clinical detail; his physical limitations and his emotional state were described in ways that could scarcely have encouraged support for his presidential aspirations. In part, microscopic focus on real or attributed presidential acts and traits (Carter's folksiness, Ford's physical ineptness, Nixon's outbursts of temper during the late stages of Watergate) is a result of the shift from print journalism to television newscasting as the principal source relied upon by most Americans for political news.[31] Without accepting the indictment by Nixon loyalists of the "liberal establishment" mass media, I think that Nixon speech-writer Raymond Price is undoubtedly right in his comment that

> Television has vastly changed the nature of the news business. . . . People turn to the news, whether print or broadcast, for both information and entertainment. Whereas print journalism has tended more toward the presentation of information that entertains, the structure of television news is such that it is designed to be an entertainment that informs.[32]

Media coverage of the President-elect and the first few months of an administration tends to emphasize the endearing personal touches—Ford's preparation of his own English muffins, Carter's fireside chat in informal garb. No wonder both of these Presidents enjoyed high poll ratings during their initial months in office. But the trend can only go downward. Even if the media coverage simply shifts to rather straightforward reporting of initial administration

---

[31] Burns Roper, *Changing Public Attitudes toward Television* (New York: Television Information Service, 1977).

[32] Raymond Price, *With Nixon* (New York: Viking, 1977), pp. 185-86.

efforts to get organized and develop a program, the impact is bound to be unfavorable in contrast to the idyllic initial presentations of the President. Further, after idealizing Presidents, the media quickly search out their warts. More and more it is the shortcomings in presidential performance that are newsworthy. Moreover, tough investigative journalism now is a prime means of making a professional mark. Such journalism may have been an invaluable counterweight to Johnson credibility gaps and Nixon stonewalling. For present purposes, however, what needs to be noted is that aspiring Woodwards and Bernsteins constitute still one more environmental obstacle to presidential leadership.[33]

The Presidents' Reactions to Their Political Environment. During the years when Presidents were widely viewed by liberal political commentators as having an edge over other members of the policy community in their ability to identify and successfully to promote the public interest, some of these commentators were sensitive to the "Caesarist" potential of a politics in which sustained efforts were made to enhance a single leader's influence over other policy makers without providing him with legitimate instruments of leadership.[34] The now barely remembered "responsible party" proposals that were endorsed by many political scientists in the 1950s were designed to domesticate strong presidential leadership by harnessing it to party organizations that would be ideologically cohesive and that would also have a base in widespread participation by idealistic local party members. Needless to say, there has been no move toward strong, responsible political parties along the lines that the party reformers advocated, or along any other lines.

The reformers' concern with Caesarism does, however, seem to have been prophetic. It anticipated the perceived increases in the arbitrary use of presidential command powers during the Johnson, Nixon, and, some would claim, Kennedy years. Some of the excesses of imperial presidential leadership seem to have been attempts to flail out at the very aspects of the political environment that make the

---

[33] Daniel P. Moynihan, "The Presidency and the Press," *Commentary*, vol. 51 (March 1971), pp. 41–52.

[34] As the authors of the famous "Schattschneider report" calling for reform of the American party system put it, presidential power not grounded in issue-oriented parties that have a solid base in the electorate "favors a President who exploits skillfully the arts of demagoguery, who uses the whole country as his political backyard, and who does not mind turning into the embodiment of personal government." *Toward a More Responsible Two-Party System: A Report of the Committee on Political Parties, American Political Science Association* (New York: Rinehart, 1950), p. 94.

presidency a potentially stalemated institution: if bureaucrats seem disloyal, wiretap them; if the media and Congress will surely object to a desired military action, carry it out in secret. Obviously individual Presidents differ in the degree to which they perceive their political environment in adversary terms and are prepared to act ruthlessly. Nevertheless, as the authors of an article reporting the sharp policy differences between Nixon supporters and supergrade civil servants comment, "even paranoids have enemies."[35]

Growth and Evolution of the Presidential Bureaucracy. From early in the 1960s through the end of the Ford administration, the number of people working in the White House Office increased substantially. There have been various published itemizations of the changes, but since practices such as borrowing personnel from other agencies in the executive branch have periodically changed and are difficult to monitor, I simply refer the reader to the several complementary attempts at year-by-year tabulation.[36] There has also been growth in the remainder of the Executive Office of the President, but here the statistics are even less susceptible to summary discussion because the EOP has frequently been used to house agencies that are not engaged in staffing the presidency but have line responsibilities. The most obvious example has been the Office of Economic Opportunity, which for many years was located in the EOP out of a fear that its program would be "absorbed" and that it would lose its innovative aspects and public visibility if it disappeared into the sprawling Department of Health, Education, and Welfare.

Something more than Parkinson's Law has been at work in the growth of the White House staff. In 1961, an administration took office committed to introducing new programs and energizing continuing programs. The Johnson administration was even more activist than Kennedy's, especially if "activism" is used to describe both the monumental outpouring of Great Society programs and also the expansion of hostilities in Vietnam. In these two administrations, the desire to innovate, combined with an impulse to circumvent resistance of the sort discussed in connection with the intractable political environment, led to an increasing tendency "to run the government from the White House." The need to coordinate interdepartmental programs had also expanded greatly. With Nixon, the desire to curb many of the innovations of the previous two administrations in the

---

35 Joel D. Aberbach and Bert A. Rockman, "Clashing Beliefs within the Executive Branch," *American Political Science Review*, vol. 70 (June 1976), pp. 456-68.
36 See, for example, the sources cited in note 12.

context of what seemed to Nixon and his associates to be a uniquely hostile environment (a Democratic Congress, administrators committed to carrying out New Frontier–Great Society programs, and mass media that in their view were not disposed to portray the President favorably) led to an even further expansion of the White House Office staff. Nixon's intense concern with foreign affairs and his close cooperation with Henry Kissinger and the much enlarged National Security Council staff, which served as Kissinger's EOP replica of the State Department, further contributed to the size of the bureaucracy attached to the presidency, as did Nixon's concern with domestic political enemies, which came to a head with the Watergate break-in and its aftermath.

Other important changes in the Executive Office of the President, especially changes in the Bureau of the Budget, which eventually led to a renamed agency with a somewhat changed mission, were underway throughout the post-Eisenhower period. We have seen that much of the Truman domestic program was drafted by Bureau of the Budget staff, working closely with Truman's (by present standards) small White House Office team, especially the aides of the successive special counsels, Clark Clifford and Charles S. Murphy. The bureau proved to be remarkably capable of shifting gears and of responding to Eisenhower's deep commitment to budgetary restraint. After the eight Eisenhower years, however, the bureau did not seem to Kennedy and Johnson to be an administrative entity well suited for framing a large volume of new policy, some of it without much precedent. Even before taking office, Kennedy appointed task forces to help shape his legislative agenda. Johnson made regular use of task forces, linking them to a much expanded White House domestic policy staff. Task forces typically were composed of people from the private sector, presidential aides, and federal officials. Use was made of individual Budget Bureau officials, but frequently they acted not in their institutional status as bureau officials, but rather as individuals who were chosen because they were viewed as personally knowledgeable and imaginative.

The Bureau of the Budget and its successor agency, the Office of Management and Budget (OMB), continued to clear legislation and executive orders, but more and more, routine rather than innovative policies bore the agency's imprint. Perhaps the most stable aspect of the bureau's role since 1960 has been its review of congressional enactments with a view to examining their consistency with the president's program and their practical efficacy.[37] There has been no systematic change in presidential responses to OMB's recommendations about whether or not to exercise the veto.

The 1970 reorganization in which the BOB became the OMB was a direct response to the Nixon administration's desire to have a political impact through the assertive use of the executive branch in policy making—for example, by the impoundment of funds appropriated to maintain Great Society programs. Yet the change was anticipated in Kennedy's and Johnson's view of BOB as too slow-moving and cautious to keep up with their policy-making efforts. Under Kennedy and Johnson and under Nixon, the bureau seemed ill-equipped to meet presidential desires, whether desires to initiate policy or to retrench.

The most distinctive feature of the OMB (which in many ways did continue to carry out the BOB's basic functions) was the introduction of a "layer" of presidential appointees directly under the OMB director. These officials were, in effect, line officers. Their counterparts were the White House Office domestic policy aides. The new layer of politically appointed assistant directors and the bolstered White House staff were intended to make the bureau more systematically responsive to White House directives. During this period, OMB directors also tended to become detached from the professional staffs of their agency. More and more, they were used as personal staff advisers to the President, sometimes physically located in the West Wing and at any rate rarely in touch with the detailed work of the agency in such matters as the legislative clearance of less visible components of the presidential program and the examination of agency budget requests.

At the time of the 1970 transition, a number of long-time senior members of the agency, including some who had held positions of responsibility from as far back as the Smith era, found other employment or went into retirement. At least some of the exodus reflected unhappiness with the agency's changed mission. As Berman's research and other studies show,[38] the OMB is populated with aides who have spent far less time in the agency than was traditionally the case with the BOB and who tend to be reconciled to the notion that

---

[37] Larry Berman, "OMB and the Hazards of Presidential Staff Work: Some Call it TOMB," *Public Administration Review*, forthcoming. Heclo, *A Government of Strangers*, p. 81.

[38] James F. C. Hyde, Jr. and Stephen J. Wayne, "Partners in Presidential Policy-Making: White House–OMB Legislative Relationships," paper prepared for delivery at the 1975 Annual Meeting of the Southern Political Science Association.

their responsibility is directly to the incumbent President. Undoubtedly there is much idealization in the BOB veterans' view that they served both President and presidency and in their feeling of commitment to "neutral competence." Nevertheless, there is reason to believe that the shift from BOB to OMB weakened a valuable restraint on grandiose presidential aspirations. One reason why many of the implementation failures of Great Society programs were not anticipated or more promptly detected was that the BOB staff (which has *not* increased in proportion to the growth of the White House staff) did not have the time and resources to evaluate the cascade of new programs and policy proposals.

Under present circumstances, however, it is far from certain that, even with sufficient resources, the OMB will be as disposed to warn Presidents that proposed policies have hidden costs and impracticalities as the BOB traditionally would have been. Further, an agency with few officials who have long records of service and with a rather high rate of personnel turnover is bound to lack what is commonly called "institutional memory"—the ability to evaluate current proposals in terms of its experience with previous endeavors to accomplish the same ends.[39]

Both the change from BOB to OMB and the great expansion of White House staffs in the 1960s and early 1970s clearly arose out of presidential efforts to respond to a sense that, in spite of the center-stage status of the modern President, he is surrounded by a cast of actors more committed to stealing the show from him than to allowing him to live up to the nation's expectations that his performance be the extraordinary one. There is, however, no evidence that a larger White House staff and a more deferential BOB/OMB have in fact made recent Presidents more successful. On the matter of White House size, Nixon's experience provides the strongest evidence of a contrary effect, as the innumerable memoirs and other Watergate-induced revelations so extensively document. A White House Office that envelops the entire Old Executive Office building and harbors an armed member of a political espionage unit and a special counsel whose safe contains unaccounted-for cash campaign contributions— in short, an office that leaves room for "White House horrors"— symbolizes the broader problem of a presidential bureaucracy that has expanded to the point where the President is victimized rather

---

[39] Hugh Heclo, "OMB and the Presidency: The Problem of Neutral Competence," *The Public Interest*, no. 38 (Winter 1975), pp. 80-98.

than helped by members of a staff whom he himself cannot begin to supervise.[40]

Under Ford, the size of the White House staff did not decline markedly, though one of Nixon's innovations for imposing the presidential will on public policy, John Ehrlichman's Domestic Council, fell into disuse. Carter has sharply cut the size of the White House staff and substituted a domestic policy staff for a council, but the consequences of Carter's reorganization cannot yet be assessed. Much of the reduction is cosmetic—for example, certain personal services are no longer tabulated under the heading White House Office and much White House business will now be conducted by personnel detailed from other agencies. The political layer of OMB has in fact been expanded rather than reduced.

Presidency-Curbing Legislation. In the days when the Bricker Amendment was narrowly defeated by a coalition led by a Republican President, the notion that an already politically restrained presidency needed added legal restraints was abhorrent to liberal commentators on American politics. They saw the presidency as the political institution most likely to have a benign impact on public policy. Opponents of the Bricker Amendment in most cases felt that there had already been a recent and unfortunate presidency-weakening constitutional change—the 22nd Amendment, restraining the President from running for a third term. Many of these same commentators sympathized with such exercises of presidential prerogative as Truman's deliberate refusal to seek a congressional resolution authorizing American military intervention in Korea—a refusal Truman made with some awareness that he was increasing his potential political vulnerability, but on the principled ground that he wanted to avoid setting a precedent that, he felt, would weaken future Presidents. Yet, as Averell Harriman, who at the time recommended that Truman seek such a resolution, has since noted congressional authorization would have "tied the hands" of many later opponents of "Truman's War."[41]

---

[40] The specific illustrations are taken from John Dean, *Blind Ambition* (New York: Simon and Schuster, 1976). For a review of the basic literature on the congeries of events summarized by the term "Watergate," see the bibliographical note to Fred I. Greenstein, "A President is Forced to Resign: Watergate, White House Organization, and Nixon's Personality," in Allan P. Sindler, ed., *America in the Seventies: Problems, Policies and Politics* (Boston: Little, Brown, 1977), pp. 99-101.

[41] Francis H. Heller, ed., *The Korean War: A 25-Year Perspective* (Lawrence: The Regents Press of Kansas, 1977), p. 105.

In connection with the general alterations in views about the presidency that occurred during the Vietnam conflict and Watergate, presidency-curbing legislation came to receive increasing support— much of it from former defenders of a broad construction of the President's power. Largely during the Watergate period, Congress enacted an unprecedented array of presidency-curbing legislation. Most of these laws have not been tested or, when they have been, have not had much effect on existing practices. All told, however, it is hard to believe that their total impact on Presidents will be nil. Certainly if the laws had then been in force many past acts of presidential initiative would have had to be carried out with more systematic attention to congressional support than they were. Here are some of the major legislative changes, beginning with one that is a logical consequence of BOB's transformation into OMB, a more explicitly political agency:

- After fifty-three years during which BOB/OMB had existed as an agency wholly in the President's preserve, in 1973 the OMB director and deputy directors for the first time became subject to congressional confirmation. (P.L. 93-250, 88 Stat 11, 1974.)

- In 1973 Congress allowed the lapse of a presidential power to propose executive branch reorganization plans, which would go into effect unless rejected by Congress within sixty days. In 1977 President Carter succeeded in winning restoration of this power (the Reorganization Act of 1977), but with restraints on the elimination of statutory programs and the provision that no more than three reorganization plans can be pending at any time.

- The Impoundment Control Act of 1974 (Title X of P.L. 93-344) requires that if a President does not want to expend appropriated funds he must report "recission" to Congress. If he wants to *defer* spending funds, he is able to do so unless one house of Congress votes disapproval. Recissions must be approved by both houses within forty-five days.

- The Case Act, passed in 1972 (P.L. 92-403), requires that all executive agreements with foreign powers be reported to the Congress. In fact, however, the Nixon administration failed to report a number of international agreements, notably several made with the government of South Vietnam.

- The War Powers Resolution of 1973 (P.L. 93-148) requires the President to consult with Congress "in every possible instance" before committing troops to combat and to submit a report on his action to Congress, and makes it necessary for the Congress, unless physically unable to meet, to authorize the military action. In the one case to which this has applied, President Ford's rescue of the ship *Mayaguez* and its crew, there was congressional briefing but not consultation, and the episode did not last the sixty days allowed until congressional action was required; most important were the political realities: numerous members of Congress promptly praised Ford's action.[42]

In describing these changes I have used the term commonly applied to them—"President-curbing" legislation. Yet we have also noted the potentially high costs of presidential command actions, especially when these are based on broad interpretations of the extent to which the vague language of Article II entitles the President to engage in autonomous action. At least in the case of Truman and Korea, the War Powers Resolution probably would have yielded the equivalent of the congressional resolution that Harriman urged Truman to seek. And this in turn could have provided Truman with protection from some of the criticism he received as the war lingered on. (Indeed one objection to the resolution by those who felt it did not sufficiently curb presidential war powers was that just such a possibility might occur.) In the legalistic context of American politics it is possible that more explicitly bounded Presidents will be more, rather than less, able to maintain sustained support for their political goals.

Summary and Conclusions

Patterson in his analysis of the contemporary Congress in this volume notes that if Henry Clay had been resurrected and placed in the 95th Congress he would begin to see that, in spite of many detailed changes in the structure of the institution, it continues to function in ways reminiscent of the period before the Civil War. By contrast, we have seen that even a 1920s President would have difficulty making sense of the modern presidency. The changes that have transformed the traditional presidency were evident by the end of the Eisenhower administration. The turbulent experience of the institution since 1960 has also left a few apparently enduring residues—for

---

[42] For a thorough discussion of current legislation and precedents bearing on the separation of powers, see Louis Fisher, *The Constitution between Friends: Congress, the President, and the Law* (New York: St. Martin's, 1977) and Fisher's *Presidential Powers* (Washington, D.C.: Congressional Research Service, Library of Congress, October 25, 1977). Also see Graham T. Allison, "Making War: The President and Congress," in *Law and Contemporary Problems*, vol. 40 (Summer 1976), pp. 86-105.

example, the legislation just summarized and the changes in the White House Office and Executive Office of the President more generally. During the Kennedy, Johnson, and Nixon administrations, more fundamental changes in the presidency seemed to be underway; but to an extraordinary degree the politics of the post-Nixon presidency have been reminiscent of the severely restrained "mid-century" presidencies.

In commenting on the changes in evaluations of the merits of the presidency as an institution that occurred during the post-Eisenhower years, I have not sought to summarize the views of the institution that have been prevalent in the years since Nixon resigned. There are many views of how Ford and (to date) Carter have comported themselves in office, but the "data base" for evaluating the postimperial presidency as an institution is too thin. Even more important, the intellectual resources for such an evaluation are not yet available. The older presidency-celebrating imagery of "lonely grandeur" and "awesome power," and of the need for more power, cannot be resurrected. A common prescription during the Johnson and Nixon years—that the presidency be "demystified"—may slowly be coming to pass, particularly if the nation continues to undergo a series of one-term presidencies. Yet Presidents still do seem to be expected to perform wonders.

My own discussion of the President-curbing legislation stressed the possible contributions that a firmer statutory basis of power might make to effective presidential leadership. I cannot imagine, however, that legislative changes will fundamentally alter dilemmas that arise from high expectations of presidential performance and the low capacity of Presidents to live up to those expectations.

Today's presidency is an institution in search of new role definitions. This is evident in the actions of the President himself, as we see Carter floundering through episodes of self-conscious image-building, self-imposed demands for policy enactments which do not come to pass, a state of the union message stressing the need for lowered expectations from government, and attempts at tough old-fashioned political arm-twisting in connection with Panama Canal Treaty roll calls. Perhaps a President who had not come up as a political outsider, belaboring standard Washington political practices, would have been off to a more effective start. But even as Washington-wise a President as Johnson, whose administration started with widely acclaimed successes, came to grief.

Taking it for granted that FDR's political skills and the widespread sense of crisis that enabled him to put them to work were sui generis, it may be instructive to consider the view of the presidency held by the last two-term incumbent—Eisenhower. As I noted, archives now available at the Eisenhower Library emphatically refute the image that President-watchers of the time had of Ike as a "captive hero," cherubically soothing the American people with his infectious grin and golfing while others ran—or failed to run—the government. We discover a "modern Republican" whose modernity consisted of being an internationalist and of favoring moderate departures from conservative political principles in the interest of providing the Republican party—or at least its President—with sufficient electoral strength to win the support of an electorate unprepared to see basic New Deal programs, like Social Security, repealed. More interestingly, we see a man for whom leadership had been a life-long preoccupation and who in extensive correspondence with his associates enunciated in detail how he conceived of leadership in general and of the presidency in particular.

In my own reflections on what a contemporary presidential role definition might be, I have found instructive such assertions of Eisenhower's as the following comment in a letter to Henry Luce, written in August 1960, ruminating on his tenure in office:

> The government of the United States has become too big, too complex, and too pervasive in its influence on all our lives for one individual to pretend to direct the details of its important and critical programming. Competent assistants are mandatory; without them the Executive Branch would bog down. To command the loyalties and dedication and best efforts of capable and outstanding individuals requires patience, understanding, a readiness to delegate, and an acceptance of responsibility for any honest errors—real or apparent—those subordinates might make.[43]

Eisenhower, with his popularity and his limited domestic policy aspirations, could make such a statement with more assurance than a normal survivor of domestic political wars, especially one committed to substantial political changes. And one doubts whether Sherman Adams would fully have endorsed the last sentence in Eisenhower's statement. Nevertheless, the gist of his message—that the President is not the political system—might usefully inform political thought today. It may be easier to convince Presidents of this than the general public. Presidents have an interest in their own "demystification"

---

[43] Dwight D. Eisenhower to Henry Luce, August 8, 1960, DDE Diaries, Box 33, Dwight D. Eisenhower Library, Abilene, Kansas.

if they are to keep from falling into the perennial trap of seeking overachievement and accomplishing dismal underachievement.[44]

Elsewhere in his letter to Luce, Eisenhower commented that, having had for two years a slim Republican majority and for six years a Democratic majority in Congress, "the hope of doing something constructive for the nation . . . has required methods calculated to attract cooperation, although the natural impulse would have been to lash out." This may be no more than a self-serving way of saying that one has practiced the art of the possible. Again, however, I think Eisenhower's comments suggest a point that may contribute to a redefining of the role of the modern President in more workable terms. The most appropriate redefinition would seem to be one that educates both citizens and political leaders (and, in particular, the President himself) to view the office in terms of a realistic assessment of what Presidents can in fact accomplish in American politics.

This role definition would make it perfectly clear that the buck—a term that presumably refers to all major policy making—neither stops nor starts only in the Oval Office. It circulates among many political actors. Depending upon the President's skill, his interest, the nature of the issues being considered, and the state of the national and international political environment, the President can have a major impact on how the buck circulates and with what results. But he neither is, nor can be, nor should be an unmoved mover.

---

[44] For the argument that another of the major constitutionally mandated institutions, the Supreme Court, would be more politically secure if leaders and other citizens had a less idealized, more politically realistic, conception of how the institution functions in the polity, see Martin Shapiro, "Stability and Change in Judicial Decision-Making: Incrementalism or *Stare Decisis?*," *Law in Transition Quarterly*, vol. 2. (Summer 1965), pp. 134-57.

3

Issue Networks and the Executive Establishment

Hugh Heclo

The connection between politics and administration arouses remarkably little interest in the United States. The presidency is considered more glamorous, Congress more intriguing, elections more exciting, and interest groups more troublesome. General levels of public interest can be gauged by the burst of indifference that usually greets the announcement of a new President's cabinet or rumors of a political appointee's resignation. Unless there is some White House "tie-in" or scandal (preferably both), news stories about presidential appointments are usually treated by the media as routine filler material.

This lack of interest in political administration is rarely found in other democratic countries, and it has not always prevailed in the United States. In most nations the ups and downs of political executives are taken as vital signs of the health of a government, indeed of its survival. In the United States, the nineteenth-century turmoil over one type of connection between politics and administration—party spoils—frequently overwhelmed any notion of presidential leadership. Anyone reading the history of those troubled decades is likely to be struck by the way in which political administration in Washington registered many of the deeper strains in American society at large. It is a curious switch that appointments to the bureaucracy should loom so large in the history of the nineteenth century, when the federal government did little, and be so completely discounted in the twentieth century, when government tries to do so much.

Political administration in Washington continues to register strains in American politics and society, although in ways more subtle than the nineteenth-century spoils scramble between Federalists and Democrats, Pro- and Anti-tariff forces, Nationalists and States-

Righters, and so on. Unlike many other countries, the United States has never created a high level, government-wide civil service. Neither has it been favored with a political structure that automatically produces a stock of experienced political manpower for top executive positions in government.[1] How then does political administration in Washington work? More to the point, how might the expanding role of government be changing the connection between administration and politics?

Received opinion on this subject suggests that we already know the answers. Control is said to be vested in an informal but enduring series of "iron triangles" linking executive bureaus, congressional committees, and interest group clienteles with a stake in particular programs. A President or presidential appointee may occasionally try to muscle in, but few people doubt the capacity of these subgovernments to thwart outsiders in the long run.

Based largely on early studies of agricultural, water, and public works policies, the iron triangle concept is not so much wrong as it is disastrously incomplete.[2] And the conventional view is especially inappropriate for understanding changes in politics and administration during recent years. Preoccupied with trying to find the few truly powerful actors, observers tend to overlook the power and influence that arise out of the configurations through which leading policy makers move and do business with each other. Looking for the closed triangles of control, we tend to miss the fairly open networks of people that increasingly impinge upon government.

To do justice to the subject would require a major study of the Washington community and the combined inspiration of a Leonard White and a James Young. Tolerating a fair bit of injustice, one can sketch a few of the factors that seem to be at work. The first is growth in the sheer mass of government activity and associated expectations. The second is the peculiar loose-jointed play of influence that is accompanying this growth. Related to these two is the third: the layering and specialization that have overtaken the government work force, not least the political leadership of the bureaucracy.

All of this vastly complicates the job of presidential appointees both in controlling their own actions and in managing the bureaucracy. But there is much more at stake than the troubles faced by

---

[1] Hugh Heclo, *A Government of Strangers: Executive Politics in Washington* (Washington, D.C.: Brookings Institution, 1977).

[2] Perhaps the most widely cited interpretations are J. Leiper Freeman, *The Political Process* (New York: Random House, 1965); and Douglass Cater, *Power in Washington* (New York: Vintage, 1964).

people in government. There is the deeper problem of connecting what politicians, officials, and their fellow travelers are doing in Washington with what the public at large can understand and accept. It is on this point that political administration registers some of the larger strains of American politics and society, much as it did in the nineteenth century. For what it shows is a dissolving of organized / politics and a politicizing of organizational life throughout the nation. / ✗

Government Growth in an Age of Improvement

Few people doubt that we live in a time of big government. During his few years in office, President Kennedy struggled to avoid becoming the first President with a $100 billion budget. Just seventeen years later, President Carter easily slipped into history as the first $500 billion President. Even in constant prices, the 1979 federal budget was about double that of 1960.[3] The late 1950s and the entire 1960s witnessed a wave of federal initiatives in health, civil rights, education, housing, manpower, income maintenance, transportation, and urban affairs. To these, later years have added newer types of welfare concerns: consumer protection, the environment, cancer prevention, and energy, to name only a few. Whatever today's conventional skepticism about the success of these programs, posterity will probably regard the last twenty-odd years as an extraordinarily ambitious, reform-minded period. The dominant feeling behind our age of improvement was best expressed by Adlai Stevenson in 1955 when he sensed a new willingness "to feel strongly, to be impatient, to want mightily to see that things are done better." [4]

However, we need to be clear concerning what it is that has gotten big in government. Our modern age of improvement has occurred with astonishingly little increase in the overall size of the federal executive establishment. Figure 3-1 traces changes in the raw materials of government: money, rules, and people from 1949 to 1977. The year 1955 represented a return to more normal times after the Korean conflict and may be taken as a reasonable baseline. Since that year national spending has risen sixfold in current dollars and has more than doubled in constant terms. Federal regulations (as indicated by pages in the *Federal Register*) have also sextupled. In the cases of both money and regulations, it was during the second Eisen-

---

[3] Office of Management and Budget, *The United States Budget in Brief, 1979* (Washington, D.C., 1978), p. 21.

[4] Adlai E. Stevenson, quoted in James L. Sundquist, *Politics and Policy* (Washington, D.C.: Brookings Institution, 1968), p. 385.

Figure 3-1

FEDERAL GOVERNMENT GROWTH:
MONEY, RULES, AND PEOPLE

(1949 = 100)

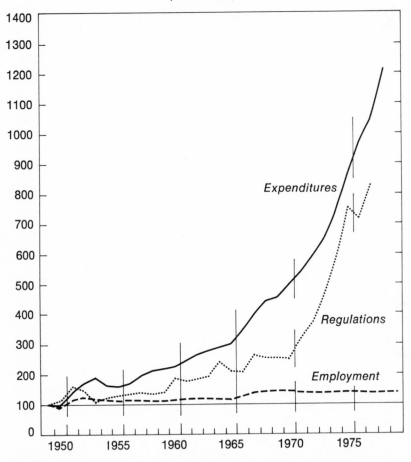

Note: Federal spending on income and product account. Figures are on an accrual basis and include trust account transactions with the public as well as grants-in-aid to state and local governments. Employment covers total end-of-year civilian employees in full-time, permanent, temporary, part-time, and intermittent employment in the executive branch, including the Postal Service. Regulations are indicated by numbers of pages in *The Federal Register*.

Source: The Tax Foundation, *Facts and Figures on Government Finance, 1977*, table 20, p. 33; U.S. Office of Management and Budget, *Special Analyses, Budget of the U.S. Government, 1979*, p. 210. Figures are taken from an unpublished table compiled by the Executive Agencies Division, Office of the Federal Register, Washington, D.C. I wish to express my gratitude to this division for their cooperation in supplying information.

hower administration that a new and expensive activism in public policy began to sweep through the national government. The landslide congressional victory by liberal Democrats in 1958, the challenge of Sputnik, the new stirrings of the civil rights movement—these and other factors created a wave of government spending and regulation that has continued to roll ever since. The force of this growth was felt at least as much in the Nixon-Ford years as in the earlier decade of New Frontier/Great Society programs under Democratic Presidents.

Yet federal employment grew hardly at all in comparison with spending and regulations (up by less than one-fifth since 1955). Despite widespread complaints about the size of government, the federal bureaucracy is entitled to join foreign aid as one of that small band of cases where close to zero-growth has been the norm for the last twenty-five years.

The paradox of expanding government and stable bureaucracy has two explanations. In purely budgetary terms, much of the increase in federal outlays has been due to higher costs of existing policies. It does not necessarily require more bureaucrats to write larger checks. Such cost increases have been especially important in the area of income maintenance programs. Federal payments to individuals (social security, medical care, veterans' pensions, unemployment insurance, and public assistance) increased from $22 billion in 1960 to $167 billion in 1977, accounting for well over half of the total increase in federal domestic spending during these years.[5] Much of this increase came not from adding new programs but from higher bills for existing programs, particularly social security. Thus at the end of 1977, when federal outlays were at $402 billion, President Carter proposed a $500 billion budget for fiscal year 1979. Of the $98 billion increase, about 90 percent was due to the higher cost of existing policies and only 10 percent to new spending recommended by the President.[6] About one-quarter of the total cost increase was due simply to income security programs.

This sort of momentum in government obviously presents serious challenges to politicians in general and to politically appointed executives in particular. These are the people who tend to feel they have a mandate to "change things, shake up the bureaucracy" and who even in the best of circumstances have only a few years in which to do so. But there is a second and at least equally important explana-

---

[5] Office of Management and Budget, *The Budget in Brief, 1979*, p. 21.

[6] Office of Management and Budget, *Special Analyses, Budget of the United States Government, 1979* (Washington, D.C., 1978), table A-4, p. 12.

tion for the stability of the national bureaucracy in an era of increased policy interventionism. This factor creates even more profound problems for government leadership.

In the main, Washington has not attempted to apply its policies by administering programs directly to the general population. It has therefore been able to avoid bureaucratic giantism. This is true in many programs classified as payments to individuals (for example, Medicare and Medicaid funds pass through large numbers of administrative middlemen), and it is especially true in several of the policy areas that have grown the fastest since the mid-fifties. One such area is investment and subsidies for the physical environment. Grants for mass transit, waste treatment plants, highways, and the like have tripled in real terms since 1960. Another area rich in indirect administration falls under the heading of social investment and services; spending for education, health care, employment training, urban development, and social services has risen more than tenfold since 1960.[7] Rather than building and staffiing its own administrative facilities for these programs, the federal government has preferred to act through intermediary organizations—state governments, city halls, third party payers, consultants, contractors, and many others. Administratively, the result is that what was true during the Eisenhower administration remains true today: despite huge increases in government programs, about the only time an ordinary citizen sees a federal bureaucrat is when his mail is delivered, his taxes are audited, or a trip to the local social security office becomes necessary (unless of course an FBI agent knocks on his door).

New policies associated with our modern age of improvement have tended to promote the idea of government by remote control. Political administration in Washington is heavily conditioned by an accumulation of methods for paying the bills and regulating the conduct of intermediary organizations. This pattern is consistent with a long tradition of fragmented and decentralized administration. Moreover, it offers important political and bureaucratic advantages. Spreading cash grants among various third party payers is an important way of building support for policies, translating otherwise indivisible collective goods into terms suitable for distributive politics. Rather than having to convince everyone of the value of a clean environment, government administrators can preside over a scramble for federal funds to subsidize construction of local sewage treatment

---

[7] Charles L. Schultze, "Federal Spending: Past, Present, and Future," in Henry Owen and Charles L. Schultze, *Setting National Priorities: The Next Ten Years* (Washington, D.C.: Brookings Institution, 1976), p. 335.

plants. Likewise, in spending for health, manpower, transportation, and so on, the federal government has sidestepped the tremendously difficult task of creating a broad national consensus for its own administered activities. It has done so by counting on third parties to crave the funds which the national government makes available to serve its purposes. Recently Charles Schultze has argued that Washington should make greater use of market incentives to meet public ends.[8] Yet as far as fiscal relations in the political marketplace are concerned, a strong case could be made that in fact the federal government has done little else.

In terms of using intermediaries to administer the new melioristic policies, the mushrooming of federal regulations has much in common with federal spending. Rather than having to work at building and policing its own delivery mechanisms, the Washington bureaucracy can use regulations and then rest content with telling other public and private bureaucracies what should be done. This has the added advantage of allowing federal policy makers to distribute not only funds but also much of the blame when things go wrong.

One might suppose that the executive establishment in Washington has put itself in an extremely comfortable position, retailing the promise of improved policies and wholesaling the administrative headaches connected with delivery. Unfortunately, life has not been so kind. People increasingly expect Washington to solve problems but not to get in anyone's way in the process. The result is that policy goals are piled on top of each other without generating any commitment to the administrative wherewithal to achieve them. Even in the depths of anti-Washington sentiment, the overwhelming majority of Americans agreed that the federal government should control inflation, prevent depressions, assure international peace, regulate private business, and also ensure that the poor are taken care of, the hungry fed, and every person assured a minimum standard of living. A comparably large majority also felt that the federal government was too "big and bureaucratic."[9] As it turns out, therefore, the executive establishment in Washington tends to get the worst of both worlds—blamed for poor delivery by its public customers and besieged with bills from its middlemen.

---

[8] Charles L. Schultze, *The Public Use of Private Interest* (Washington, D.C.: Brookings Institution, 1977).

[9] U.S. Congress, Senate, Subcommittee on Intergovernmental Relations of the Committee on Government Operations, *Confidence and Concern: Citizens View American Government*, committee print, 93d Cong., 1st sess., 1973, part 2, pp. 111, 117, 118-19, 238.

Fraying at the Center

The strategy of responding to aspirations for improvement while maintaining a no-growth national administrative machine and relying on middlemen has succeeded in doing one thing. It has saved Washington policy makers from having to cope with what would otherwise have been an immense, nationwide bureaucracy. Yet far from simplifying operations, this "success" has vastly complicated the connection between administration and politics in Washington. Lacking their own electoral mandates, political administrators have always been in an ambivalent position in American government. Every ambitious new program, every clever innovation in indirect administration has merely deepened this ambivalence.

What is occurring at the national level is a peculiar "push-pull effect" on the relation between democratic politics and the executive establishment. On the one hand, government growth has pushed more and more policy concerns out of the federal government's own structure and into masses of intermediary, issue-conscious groups. On the other hand, the requirements for managing such a complex system are pulling government leadership further and further away from the nontechnical, nonspecialist understanding of the ordinary citizen and politician. It is worth looking more closely at how it is possible to be both politicizing organizational life and depoliticizing democratic leadership.

All Join In. During 1977–1978, Harvard University hired a Washington lobbyist and joined a loose group called Friends of DNA in an effort to influence federal regulation of research into the creation of new forms of life. The same year, the former militant chairman of the Black Panther party, Bobby Seale, founded a new Washington organization to lobby for community-controlled poverty programs. And the president of the national machinists' union convened a National Energy Coalition composed of environmentalists, neighborhood organizers, and consumer advocates. Perhaps not coincidentally, forty-seven congressmen announced their retirement, citing as the major reason a lack of enjoyment in the job.

Trivial in their own right, these incidents suggest something deeper than the feeling (probably true) that exercising power is not as much fun as it used to be in the clubby days of Washington politics. As more and more puzzling, unfamiliar policy issues have been thrust on government, more and more fluid groups have been unexpectedly mobilized. As proliferating groups have claimed a stake and clamored for a place in the policy process, they have helped to diffuse the focus of political and administrative leadership.

What has happened at the subnational level of government is a striking illustration of this process. Much of the bureaucratic expansion that might otherwise have occurred nationally has taken place in state and local governments. Between 1955 and 1977 state and local public employment grew by more than two and one-half times, to 12 million people, while federal employment hovered at around 2.5 million.[10] The increased interdependence of subnational and national bureaucracies has led to the growth of what Samuel H. Beer has termed the intergovernmental lobby.[11] Those in Washington whose memories go back a generation or more can recall a time when it was something of an occasion for a governor to undertake a mission to Washington. As Senator Moynihan (who was a junior aide to Governor Averell Harriman in the 1940s) put it, "You'd spend time planning how many shirts to take. Going to Washington was a very big deal." [12] Today, not only do governors or mayors as groups have their own specialized staffs permanently stationed in Washington, but large state governments, major units within state governments, and individual cities frequently have their own Washington offices or hired representatives. In addition to umbrella organizations such as the National Governors' Conference, the Conference of State Governments, the U.S. Conference of Mayors, the National League of Cities, the National Conference of State Legislatures, and the National Association of Counties, one finds the intergovernmental lobby peopled with representatives from groups such as the New York State Association of Counties, cities such as Detroit and Boston, major counties, various state water districts, boards of regents, and so on and on and on.

Similarly, an even larger number of private and semi-private organizations have grown up as important extensions of the new federal policies. One of the enduring legacies of every reform movement in the United States—whether it was the Progressives' good government movement, Hoover's attempts at engineering voluntarism, or FDR's New Deal—has been to create new groups with a stake in the reformed processes and programs.[13] So too our own age of improve-

---

[10] Office of Management and Budget, *Special Analyses, 1979 Budget*, p. 33.

[11] Samuel H. Beer, "Political Overload and Federalism," *Polity*, vol. 10 (March 1977).

[12] Unpublished talk at the Brookings Institution, June 8, 1977.

[13] See for example Ellis Hawley, "Herbert Hoover and the Associative State," *Journal of American History*, June 1974; and Grant McConnell, *Private Power and American Democracy* (New York: Alfred Knopf, 1966), pp. 50, 69.

ment has encouraged a blossoming of policy participants and kibitzers. In this instance (and this differentiates it somewhat from earlier periods) virtually everyone has accepted the idea that the national government in Washington is the decisive arena and will continue to be so indefinitely.

Some groups are nurtured by the government's own need for administrative help. For example, new neighborhood associations have been asked to take a major part in Washington's urban and housing programs. Or when the Consumer Product Safety Commission sets new standards for extension cords, the National Electrical Manufacturers' Association plays a major part in drawing up the new designs. Some groups are almost spontaneously called into being by what they can gain or lose from new federal policies or—perhaps just as often—the unforeseen consequences of these policies. For example, in the early 1970s Washington launched vigorous new efforts to promote grain exports. This generated not only new borrowing by farmers to expand production but also a new, militant farmers' organization (American Agriculture) when prices later fell from their export-led highs.

A key factor in the proliferation of groups is the almost inevitable tendency of successfully enacted policies unwittingly to propagate hybrid interests. The area of health care is rich in examples. Far from solidifying the established medical interests, federal funding and regulation of health care since the mid-1960s have had diverse impacts and therefore have tended to fragment what was once a fairly monolithic system of medical representation. Public policy has not only uncovered but also helped to create diverging interests among hospital associations, insurance companies, medical schools, hospital equipment manufacturers, local health planning groups, preventive medicine advocates, nonteaching research centers, and many others.[14] This does not necessarily mean that every group is in conflict with all of the others all of the time. The point is that even when government is not pursuing a deliberate strategy of divide and conquer, its activist policies greatly increase the incentives for groups to form around the differential effects of these policies, each refusing to allow any other group to speak in its name.

While nothing should necessarily be assumed about their political power, trade and professional associations offer a revealing pattern

---

[14] A similar tendency for public involvement to divide private interests occurred with earlier health initiatives in other countries. See Arnold Heidenheimer, Hugh Heclo, and Carolyn Adams, *Comparative Public Policy* (New York: St. Martin's Press, 1976).

of growth. The number of such groups has grown sharply during three periods: during the First World War, the first half of the 1930s, and the Second World War. Since 1945 the total number has been continuously increasing, and in recent years more and more of these groups have found it useful to make their headquarters in Washington. During the 1970s the number of trade and professional associations headquartered in Washington surpassed that in New York for the first time, climbing to 1,800 organizations with 40,000 employees in 1977. Well over half of the nation's largest associations (those with annual budgets of over $1 million) are now located in the Washington metropolitan area.[15] This takes no account of the large number of consumer and other public interest groups that have sprouted all over the nation's capital since the early 1960s.[16]

Of course Americans' love affair with interest groups is hardly a new phenomenon. From abolitionists to abortionists there has never been a lack of issue-conscious organizations; in the 1830s, Tocqueville described how the tariff question generated an early version of local consumer groups and a national lobbying association.[17] Yet if the current situation is a mere outgrowth of old tendencies, it is so in the same sense that a 16-lane spaghetti interchange is the mere elaboration of a country crossroads. With more public policies, more groups are being mobilized and there are more complex relationships among them. Since very few policies ever seem to drop off the public agenda as more are added, congestion among those interested in various issues grows, the chances for accidental collisions increase, and the interaction tends to take on a distinctive group-life of its own in the Washington community. One scene in a recent Jacques Tati film pictures a Paris traffic circle so dense with traffic that no one can get in or out; instead, drivers spend their time socializing with each other as they drive in endless circles. Group politics in Washington may be becoming such a merry-go-round.

How these changes influence the substance of public policy processes depends on what it is that the burgeoning numbers of par-

---

[15] Craig Colgate, Jr., ed., *National Trade and Professional Associations* (Washington, D.C.: Columbia Books, 1978).

[16] For example, a statement issued by Ralph Nader on April 24, 1978, criticizing the Carter energy program included endorsements by the National Resources Defense Council Inc., Friends of the Earth Inc., the Environmental Policy Center, the Environmental Action Foundation, Environmentalists for Full Employment, the Wilderness Society, Consumer Action Now, the Sierra Club, the Environmental Defense Fund Inc., the National Parks and Conservation Association, and the National Consumers League.

[17] Alexis de Tocqueville, *Democracy in America* (New York: Harper and Row, 1966), p. 176.

ticipants want. Obviously their wants vary greatly, but to a large extent they are probably accurately reflected in the areas of greatest policy growth since the late 1950s—programs seeking social betterment in terms of civil rights, income, housing, environment, consumer protection, and so on—what I will simply refer to as "welfare policies." The hallmark of these policies seems to reflect attitudes in the general public.[18] What is wanted is not more equal outcomes or unfair preferences. No, if there is a theme in the clamor of group politics and public policy, it is the idea of compensation. Compensation for what? For past racial wrongs, for current overcharging of consumers, for future environmental damage. The idea of compensatory policy—that the federal government should put things right—fits equally well for the groups representing the disadvantaged (special treatment is required for truly equal opportunity to prevail) and for those representing the advantaged (any market-imposed loss can be defined as a special hardship). The same holds for newer public interest groups (government action is required to redress the impact of selfish private interests). If middle-class parents have not saved enough for college costs they should be compensated with tuition tax credits. If public buildings are inaccessible to the physically handicapped, government regulations should change that. If farmers overinvest during good times, they should be granted redress from the consequences of their actions. The old American saying "there oughtta be a law" had a negative connotation of preventing someone from getting away with something. Today the more prevalent feeling is "there oughtta be a policy," and the connotation of getting in on society's compensations is decidedly positive.

In sum, new initiatives in federal funding and regulation have infused old and new organizations with a public policy dimension, especially when such groups are used as administrative middlemen and facilitators. Moreover, the growing body of compensatory interventions by government has helped create a climate of acceptance for ever more groups to insist that things be set right on their behalf. What matters is not so much that organizations are moving to Washington as that Washington's policy problems are coming to occupy so many different facets of organizational life in the United States.

Policy as an Intramural Activity. A second tendency cuts in a direction opposite to the widening group participation in public policy. Expanding welfare policies and Washington's reliance on indirect administra-

18 Seymour Martin Lipset and William Schneider, "The Bakke Case: How Would It Be Decided at the Bar of Public Opinion?" *Public Opinion* (March/April 1978), pp. 41-42.

tion have encouraged the development of specialized subcultures composed of highly knowledgeable policy-watchers. Some of these people have advanced professional degrees, some do not. What they all have in common is the detailed understanding of specialized issues that comes from sustained attention to a given policy debate.

Certain of these changes are evident in the government's own work force. Employees in the field and in Washington who perform the routine chores associated with direct administration have become less prominent. More important have become those officials with the necessary technical and supervisory skills to oversee what other people are doing. Thus the surge in federal domestic activities in the 1960s and 1970s may not have increased the overall size of the bureaucracy very much, but it did markedly expand the upper and upper-middle levels of officialdom. Compared with an 18 percent rise in total civilian employment, mid-level executive positions in the federal government (that is, supergrade and public law 313 equivalents) have increased approximately 90 percent since 1960. Some of these changes are due to a slow inflation of job titles and paper credentials that can be found in private as well as public organizations. But case studies in the 1960s suggested that most of this escalation occurring in the Washington bureaucracy could be traced to the new and expanded public programs of that decade.[19] The general effect of these policy changes has been to require more technical skills and higher supervisory levels, overlaying routine technicians with specialist engineers, insurance claims examiners with claims administrators, and so on. Approximately two-fifths of mid-level executives in the bureaucracy (grades 16–18 or the equivalent) are what might loosely be termed scientists, though frequently they are in fact science managers who oversee the work of other people inside and outside of the government.

Increasing complexity and specialization are affecting leaders in all modern organizations, even profit-oriented enterprises with stable sets of clear goals. For decision makers in government—where the policy goals have been neither stable nor clear in the last twenty years—the pressures for more expert staff assistance have become immense. This is as true for legislators as it is for public executives. President Nixon estimated that he personally saw no more than 200,000 of the 42 million pieces of paper in his own presidential materials. Recent studies of Congress estimate that the average member of the House of Representatives has, out of an eleven-hour

---

[19] McKinsey and Company, Inc., "Strengthening Control of Grade Escalation" (Office of Management and Budget Archives: processed, June 1966).

workday, only eleven minutes to devote personally to reading and only twelve minutes in his or her own office to spend personally on writing legislation and speeches.[20] Congress, like the executive branch, has responded to the pressures by creating more specialists and top-side staff. Since 1957 the total number of personal and committee staff on the Hill has climbed from 4,300 to 11,000 and over 20,000 more persons service the legislature from institutional staff positions (the General Accounting Office, Congressional Budget Office, and so on).[21] At the core of this blossoming congressional bureaucracy are bright, often remarkably young, technocrats who are almost indistinguishable from the analysts and subject matter specialists in the executive branch.

There are many straws in the wind to indicate the growing skill base of policy professionals in Washington. Executive search firms (so-called headhunters) have found a booming market in recent years, with many new firms being founded and prestigious New York organizations opening up Washington offices. One indicator of this movement, the amount of "professional opportunity" advertising in the press, now puts Washington on a par with Los Angeles and New York as an executive hunting ground for the private sector. The reason is clear. As government activities and regulations have grown, the value of policy specialists who understand the complex Washington environment has appreciated in the eyes of all of the private organizations with a stake in government activity. Another indicator is the mushrooming of new Washington law firms. Typically these firms are headed by former government officials and practice in substantive areas of law and policy that did not exist twenty years ago. Table 3-1 gives some idea of this trend.

Again it is tempting to borrow a term from Professor Beer and to refer to these groups of policy specialists as constituting a "professional-bureaucratic complex." Certainly there are many core groups with scientific or professional training which have carved out spheres of bureaucratic influence over health, highways, education, and so on. Likewise the familiar nexus of less professional, economic interests can still be found linking various parts of the Washington community. But the general arrangement that is emerging is somewhat different from the conventional image of iron triangles tying together executive bureaus, interest groups, and congressional committees in all-powerful alliances.

20 *Washington Post*, August 28, 1977, p. 1.
21 Harrison W. Fox, Jr. and Susan Webb Hammond, *Congressional Staffs* (New York: Free Press, 1977).

Table 3-1

THE NEW WASHINGTON LAW FIRMS

Firm	Year Founded	Area of Activity	Background of Leading Partners
Beveridge, Fairbanks and Diamond	1974	environmental law	former head of Environmental Protection Agency; official in tax division of Justice Department; assistant in EPA and White House adviser on energy and environmental policy
Epstein and Becker	1972	health care	official in Health Maintenance Organization Service of Department of Health, Education, and Welfare
Blum, Parker and Nash	1977	energy, international business	associate counsel of Senate subcommittee on multinational corporations; appellate attorney in tax division of Justice Department; assistant counsel, Senate anti-trust subcommittee
Brownstein, Zeidman, Schomer and Chase	1970	housing and urban development	assistant secretary of Department of Housing and Urban Development; commissioner of Federal Housing Administration; general counsel of Small Business Administration
Lobel, Novins and Lamont	1972	consumer litigation	legislative assistant to senator; official in Justice Department; assistant counsel to Senate subcommittee on small business
Garner, Carton and Douglas	1977	defense	general counsel of Defense Department; secretary of the army
Bracewell and Patterson	1975	energy	former assistant administrator of Federal Energy Administration
Breed, Abbott and Morgan	1976	general	former solicitor of Labor Department; head of Office of Federal Contract Compliance Programs
Lane and Edson	1970	housing	general counsel of U.S. National Corporation for Housing Partnerships; former Justice Department official; former official in Department of Housing and Urban Development

Source: "The Boom in Small Law Firms," *National Journal*, February 4, 1978, p. 172.

.tunately, our standard political conceptions of power and
are not very well suited to the loose-jointed play of influence
s emerging in political administration. We tend to look for one
up exerting dominance over another, for subgovernments that are
strongly insulated from other outside forces in the environment, for
policies that get "produced" by a few "makers." Seeing former government officials opening law firms or joining a new trade association,
we naturally think of ways in which they are trying to conquer and
control particular pieces of government machinery.

Obviously questions of power are still important. But for a host
of policy initiatives undertaken in the last twenty years it is all but
impossible to identify clearly who the dominant actors are. Who is
controlling those actions that go to make up our national policy on
abortions, or on income redistribution, or consumer protection, or
energy? Looking for the few who are powerful, we tend to overlook
the many whose webs of influence provoke and guide the exercise of
power. These webs, or what I will call "issue networks," are particularly relevant to the highly intricate and confusing welfare policies
that have been undertaken in recent years.

The notion of iron triangles and subgovernments presumes small
circles of participants who have succeeded in becoming largely autonomous. Issue networks, on the other hand, comprise a large number
of participants with quite variable degrees of mutual commitment or
of dependence on others in their environment; in fact it is almost
impossible to say where a network leaves off and its environment
begins. Iron triangles and subgovernments suggest a stable set of
participants coalesced to control fairly narrow public programs which
are in the direct economic interest of each party to the alliance. Issue
networks are almost the reverse image in each respect. Participants
move in and out of the networks constantly. Rather than groups
united in dominance over a program, no one, as far as one can tell,
is in control of the policies and issues. Any direct material interest is
often secondary to intellectual or emotional commitment. Network
members reinforce each other's sense of issues as their interests,
rather than (as standard political or economic models would have it)
interests defining positions on issues.

Issue networks operate at many levels, from the vocal minority
who turn up at local planning commission hearings to the renowned
professor who is quietly telephoned by the White House to give a
quick "reading" on some participant or policy. The price of buying
into one or another issue network is watching, reading, talking about,
and trying to act on particular policy problems. Powerful interest

102

groups can be found represented in networks but so too can individuals in or out of government who have a reputation for being knowledgeable. Particular professions may be prominent, but the true experts in the networks are those who are issue-skilled (that is, well informed about the ins and outs of a particular policy debate) regardless of formal professional training. More than mere technical experts, network people are policy activists who know each other through the issues. Those who emerge to positions of wider leadership are policy politicians—experts in using experts, victuallers of knowledge in a world hungry for right decisions.

In the old days—when the primary problem of government was assumed to be doing what was right, rather than knowing what was right—policy knowledge could be contained in the slim adages of public administration. Public executives, it was thought, needed to know how to execute. They needed power commensurate with their responsibility. Nowadays, of course, political administrators do not execute but are involved in making highly important decisions on society's behalf, and they must mobilize policy intermediaries to deliver the goods. Knowing what is right becomes crucial, and since no one knows that for sure, going through the process of dealing with those who are judged knowledgeable (or at least continuously concerned) becomes even more crucial. Instead of power commensurate with responsibility, issue networks seek influence commensurate with their understanding of the various, complex social choices being made. Of course some participants would like nothing better than complete power over the issues in question. Others seem to want little more than the security that comes with being well informed. As the executive of one new group moving to Washington put it, "We didn't come here to change the world; we came to minimize our surprises." [22]

Whatever the participants' motivation, it is the issue network that ties together what would otherwise be the contradictory tendencies of, on the one hand, more widespread organizational participation in public policy and, on the other, more narrow technocratic specialization in complex modern policies. Such networks need to be distinguished from three other more familiar terms used in connection with political administration. An issue network is a shared-knowledge group having to do with some aspect (or, as defined by the network, some problem) of public policy. It is therefore more well-defined than, first, a shared-attention group or "public"; those

---

[22] Steven V. Roberts, "Trade Associations Flocking to Capital as U.S. Role Rises," *New York Times*, March 4, 1978, p. 44.

in the networks are likely to have a common base of information and understanding of how one knows about policy and identifies its problems. But knowledge does not necessarily produce agreement. Issue networks may or may not, therefore, be mobilized into, second, a shared-action group (creating a coalition) or, third, a shared-belief group (becoming a conventional interest organization). Increasingly, it is through networks of people who regard each other as knowledgeable, or at least as needing to be answered, that public policy issues tend to be refined, evidence debated, and alternative options worked out—though rarely in any controlled, well-organized way.

What does an issue network look like? It is difficult to say precisely, for at any given time only one part of a network may be active and through time the various connections may intensify or fade among the policy intermediaries and the executive and congressional bureaucracies. For example, there is no single health policy network but various sets of people knowledgeable and concerned about cost-control mechanisms, insurance techniques, nutritional programs, prepaid plans, and so on. At one time, those expert in designing a nationwide insurance system may seem to be operating in relative isolation, until it becomes clear that previous efforts to control costs have already created precedents that have to be accommodated in any new system, or that the issue of federal funding for abortions has laid land mines in the path of any workable plan.

The debate on energy policy is rich in examples of the kaleidoscopic interaction of changing issue networks. The Carter administration's initial proposal was worked out among experts who were closely tied in to conservation-minded networks. Soon it became clear that those concerned with macroeconomic policies had been largely bypassed in the planning, and last-minute amendments were made in the proposal presented to Congress, a fact that was not lost on the networks of leading economists and economic correspondents. Once congressional consideration began, it quickly became evident that attempts to define the energy debate in terms of a classic confrontation between big oil companies and consumer interests were doomed. More and more policy watchers joined in the debate, bringing to it their own concerns and analyses: tax reformers, nuclear power specialists, civil rights groups interested in more jobs; the list soon grew beyond the wildest dreams of the original energy policy planners. The problem, it became clear, was that no one could quickly turn the many networks of knowledgeable people into a shared-action coalition, much less into a single, shared-attitude group believing it faced the moral equivalent of war. Or, if it was a war, it was a Vietnam-type quagmire.

It would be foolish to suggest that the clouds of issue networks that have accompanied expanding national policies are set to replace the more familiar politics of subgovernments in Washington. What they are doing is to overlay the once stable political reference points with new forces that complicate calculations, decrease predictability, and impose considerable strains on those charged with government leadership. The overlay of networks and issue politics not only confronts but also seeps down into the formerly well-established politics of particular policies and programs. Social security, which for a generation had been quietly managed by a small circle of insiders, becomes controversial and politicized. The Army Corps of Engineers, once the picturebook example of control by subgovernments, is dragged into the brawl on environmental politics. The once quiet "traffic safety establishment" finds its own safety permanently endangered by the consumer movement. Confrontation between networks and iron triangles in the Social and Rehabilitation Service, the disintegration of the mighty politics of the Public Health Service and its corps—the list could be extended into a chronicle of American national government during the last generation.[23] The point is that a somewhat new and difficult dynamic is being played out in the world of politics and administration. It is not what has been feared for so long: that technocrats and other people in white coats will expropriate the policy process. If there is to be any expropriation, it is likely to be by the policy activists, those who care deeply about a set of issues and are determined to shape the fabric of public policy accordingly.

The Technopols

The many new policy commitments of the last twenty years have brought about a play of influence that is many-stranded and loose. Iron triangles or other clear shapes may embrace some of the participants, but the larger picture in any policy area is likely to be one involving many other policy specialists. More than ever, policy making is becoming an intramural activity among expert issue-watchers,

[23] For a full account of particular cases, see for example Martha Derthick, *Policy-Making for Social Security* (Washington, D.C.: Brookings Institution, forthcoming); Daniel Mazmanian and Jeanne Nienaber, *Environmentalism, Participation and the Corps of Engineers: A Study of Organizational Change* (Washington, D.C.: Brookings Institution, 1978). For the case of traffic safety, see Jack L. Walker, "Setting the Agenda in the U.S. Senate," *British Journal of Political Science*, vol. 7 (1977), pp. 432-45.

their networks, and their networks of networks. In this situation any neat distinction between the governmental structure and its environment tends to break down.

Political administrators, like the bureaucracies they superintend, are caught up in the trend toward issue specialization at the same time that responsibility is increasingly being dispersed among large numbers of policy intermediaries. The specialization in question may have little to do with purely professional training. Neither is it a matter of finding interest group spokesmen placed in appointive positions. Instead of party politicians, today's political executives tend to be policy politicians, able to move among the various networks, recognized as knowledgeable about the substance of issues concerning these networks, but not irretrievably identified with highly controversial positions. Their reputations among those "in the know" make them available for presidential appointments. Their mushiness on the most sensitive issues makes them acceptable. Neither a craft professional nor a gifted amateur, the modern recruit for political leadership in the bureaucracy is a journeyman of issues.

Approximately 200 top presidential appointees are charged with supervising the bureaucracy. These political executives include thirteen departmental secretaries, some half a dozen nondepartmental officials who are also in the cabinet, several dozen deputy secretaries or undersecretaries, and many more commission chairmen, agency administrators, and office directors. Below these men and women are another 500 politically appointed assistant secretaries, commissioners, deputies, and a host of other officials. If all of these positions and those who hold them are unkown to the public at large, there is nevertheless no mistaking the importance of the work that they do. It is here, in the layers of public managers, that political promise confronts administrative reality, or what passes for reality in Washington.

At first glance, generalization seems impossible. The political executive system in Washington has everything. Highly trained experts in medicine, economics, and the natural sciences can be found in positions where there is something like guild control over the criteria for a political appointment. But one can also find the most obvious patronage payoffs; obscure commissions, along with cultural and inter-American affairs, are some of the favorite dumping grounds. There are highly issue-oriented appointments, such as the sixty or so "consumer advocates" that the Ralph Nader groups claimed were in the early Carter administration. And there are also particular skill groups represented in appointments devoid of policy content (for example, about two-thirds of the top government public relations positions were filled during 1977 with people from private media organizations). In recent years, the claims of women and minorities for executive positions have added a further kind of positional patronage, where it is the number of positions rather than any agreed policy agenda that is important. After one year, about 11 percent of President Carter's appointees were women, mainly from established law firms, or what is sometimes referred to as the Ladies' Auxiliary of the Old Boys' Network.

How to make sense of this welter of political executives? Certainly there is a subtlety in the arrangements by which top people become top people and deal with each other. For the fact is that the issue networks share information not only about policy problems but also about people. Rarely are high political executives people who have an overriding identification with a particular interest group or credentials as leading figures in a profession. Rather they are people with recognized reputations in particular areas of public policy. The fluid networks through which they move can best be thought of as proto-bureaucracies. There are subordinate and superordinate positions through which they climb from lesser to greater renown and recognition, but these are not usually within the same organization. It is indeed a world of large-scale bureaucracies but one interlaced with loose, personal associations in which reputations are established by word of mouth. The reputations in question depend little on what, in Weberian terms, would be bureaucratically rational evaluations of objective performance or on what the political scientist would see as the individual's power rating. Even less do reputations depend on opinions in the electorate at large. What matters are the assessments of people like themselves concerning how well, in the short term, the budding technopol is managing each of his assignments in and at the fringes of government.

Consider, for example, the thirteen department secretaries in Jimmy Carter's original cabinet. In theory at least, one could spin out reasons for thinking that these top political appointments would be filled by longstanding Carter loyalists, or representatives of major Democratic party factions, or recognized interest group leaders. In fact, none of these labels is an accurate characterization. One thing that stands out clearly is the continuation of a long-term trend away from relying on party politicians, others active in electoral politics, or clientele spokesmen, to fill executive positions. Nelson Polsby has concluded that at most, three members of the original Carter cabinet fell into the clientele or party political category.[24] Polsby goes on to divide the remainder into specialists and generalists, but a closer look at individual careers suggests how almost all of them—the Vances and the Califanos, the Browns and the Schlesingers—came out of or had a lasting affinity to particular issue networks.

The background of Carter's cabinet can be described in terms of movement among four great estates: academia, corporate business and the law, the government bureaucracy, and (to a lesser extent) elective politics. To represent these movements on a motionless page is difficult, but even a rough, schematic presentation of top public executives' careers reveals several outstanding features (see Table 3-2). Obviously no one estate is able to dominate all of the top positions. Moreover, every cabinet secretary has seen service in more than one of the major sectors. While there is movement from lower to higher positions, few people move up through the ranks of a single organiza-tion or sector in order to reach the top slots. Rather they move in hierarchies that stretch across the estates. Lower academic or business positions are parlayed into higher political appointments; lower political appointments into higher business positions; and so on.

Finally, and most importantly, all of President Carter's new cabinet secretaries had established reputations for handling leading problems that were regarded by issue-watchers as having a place on the public agenda. The secretary of interior had an outstanding record in dealing with conservation and environmental issues. The secretary of labor was a recognized expert in labor economics, particularly the problems of minorities. The secretary of health, education, and wel-fare had presided over the creation of the Johnson Great Society pro-grams a decade earlier. The secretary of defense was one of the insiders in the arcane world of defense technology. The secretary of commerce had a well established reputation as an advocate for con-sumer, minority, and women's issues. And so it went. For the one new field where issues and networks were poorly formed, the Energy Department, Carter chose a respected technocrat's technocrat with a strong track record in strategic theory, defense management, and bureaucratic politics.

The emergence of the policy politicians in our national politics goes back many years, at least to the new policy commitments of the New Deal era. Policy initiatives undertaken in the last generation have only intensified the process. For example, since 1960 the selec-

[24] Nelson W. Polsby, "Presidential Cabinet Making," *Political Science Quarterly*, vol. 93 (Spring 1978). Brief biographies of the original Carter cabinet are given in Congressional Quarterly, *President Carter* (Washington, D.C.: Congressional Quarterly, 1977), pp. 17-22.

Table 3-2

CAREER PATTERNS OF SELECTED MEMBERS OF CARTER'S FIRST CABINET

Cabinet Member	Academia	Government	Corporate Business/Law	Elective Politics
Michael Blumenthal (Treasury)	Ph.D. economics teacher 1953-57		manager 1957-59 vice president 1959-61	
		deputy assist. secretary 1961-63 U.S. trade representative 1964-67		
			executive 1967-72 president and chairman 1973-76	
		cabinet secretary		
Harold Brown (Defense)	Ph.D. physics teacher 1947-49 research scientist 1949-52 laboratory manager 1952-60	consultant 1956-61 director of research office 1961-65 air force secretary 1965-69		
	university president 1969-77	cabinet secretary		

Table 3-2 continued

Cabinet Member	Academia	Government	Corporate Business/Law	Elective Politics
Joseph Califano (Health, Education, and Welfare)	LL.B.	Judge Advocate General's Office 1955-58	law practice 1958-61	
		special assistant 1961-63 general counsel 1963-64 deputy secretary 1964-65 presidential assistant 1965-68		
		cabinet secretary	law practice 1969-71 law firm partner 1971-76	
Bob Bergland (Agriculture)		regional official 1961-62 regional director 1963-68	(independent farmer)	
			(independent farmer) 1968-70	
		cabinet secretary		congressman 1971-76

Juanita
Kreps
(Commerce)

instructor 1942-43

economist 1943-44

instructor 1945-46
Ph.D. 1948
lecturer 1952-55
associate professor 1963-68
dean 1969-72
vice president 1973-76

various advisory positions 1963-76

cabinet secretary

Patricia
Harris
(Housing and
Urban Development)

LL.B.

attorney 1960-61

associate dean 1962-65

dean 1967

ambassador 1965-67

law firm partner 1967-76

various part-time party positions 1960-76

cabinet secretary

Note: Part-time membership on corporate boards is not included.
Source: Compiled by the author from biographies supplied by the respective cabinet secretaries' offices.

tion process for presidential appointees has seen important changes.[25] Using somewhat different techniques, each White House staff has struggled to find new ways of becoming less dependent on the crop of job applicants produced by normal party channels and of reaching out to new pools of highly skilled executive manpower. The rationale behind these efforts is always that executive leadership in the bureaucracy requires people who are knowledgeable about complex policies and acceptable to the important groups that claim an interest in the ever growing number of issue areas. Not surprisingly, the policy experts within the various networks who are consulted typically end by recommending each other. Thus over half of the people President-elect Carter identified as his outside advisers on political appointments ended up in executive jobs themselves. Similarly, while candidate Carter's political manager promised to resign if establishment figures such as Cyrus Vance and Zbigniew Brzezinski were given appointments after the election, at least half of the candidate's expert foreign policy advisers (including Vance and Brzezinski) wound up in major political positions with the administration.

Historical studies tend to confirm the impression of change in the political executive system. In the past, there have generally been short-term fluctuations in a few social attributes (religion, types of school attended) that can be associated with changes in party control of the presidency. But, especially since the early 1960s, changes in party control of the White House have produced few distinctive differences in the characteristics of political appointees. Instead, the longer-term trend toward specialized policy expertise tends to wash over the short-term political fluctuations. Law, the traditional career base for generalists, has become progressively less important in filling the ranks of political executives. Academia, think tanks, and people with specialized credentials have been gaining in importance. If law itself were broken down into general versus specialized practice, the trend would probably appear even more sharply. In any event, the historical findings tentatively support the view that "there is a growing distance between electoral coalitions and governing coalitions. . . . The bases a presidential candidate needs to touch in order to win election are progressively unrelated to the bases a president needs to govern."[26]

---

[25] Changes in the presidential personnel process are discussed in Hugh Heclo, *A Government of Strangers* (Washington, D.C.: Brookings Institution, 1977), pp. 89-95.

[26] Kenneth Prewitt and William McAllister, "Changes in the American Executive Elite, 1930-1970," in Heinz Eulau and Moshe Czudnowski, *Elite Recruitment in Democratic Politics* (New York: Wiley, 1976), p. 127.

Below the level of cabinet secretaries, the same changes in political administrators stand out even more sharply. Fifty years ago there were few political subordinates to the top executives in the departments, and scholars dismissed the career background of those who were there as a "miscellany of party assignments and political posts." [27] Today the people filling the much larger number of subordinate political executive positions are rarely partisan figures with any significant ties to party or electorate. Instead they are part of a political bureaucracy of policy specialists that sits atop and beside the permanent career bureaucracy in Washington. The key indicators for these changes are not just the obviously larger numbers of appointees. More revealing of the political bureaucracy is the growing compartmentalization by functional specialty and the increased layering of appointed executives. Figure 3-2 offers three snapshots of the top political manpower in one department: before the arrival of the New Deal, before the Kennedy-Johnson Great Society, and at the present time. Despite the picture that Figure 3-2 presents of bureaucratic expansion in political manpower, the Labor Department is actually among the smallest agencies, with a reputation for one of the leanest staff structures, in Washington.

The Agriculture Department offers another good example of change in one of the oldest and most traditional domestic departments. At one time, agricultural policies could be accounted for fairly economically in terms of general purpose farmers' organizations, particular bureaus in the Department of Agriculture, and a congressional farm bloc in legislative committees and subcommittees. Today one would have to feed into the equation not only more specialized expressions of agricultural interests (different associations for particular commodities, corporate "farmers," grass-roots family farm groups, and so on) but also environmentalists, international economic and foreign policy advocates, and civil rights, nutritional, and consumer groups. Whereas a previous agriculture secretary might have surrounded himself with a few political cronies and a clutch of Farm Bureau (or National Farmers' Union) insiders, the current secretary's inner circle is described as including "three women (one of them black), a Mexican-American, an environmentalist, two economists, and a politician." [28] Within a year of his appointment the

---

[27] Arthur W. Macmahon and John D. Millett, *Federal Administrators* (New York: Columbia University Press, 1939), pp. 295, 302.

[28] Daniel J. Balz, "Agriculture under Bergland—Many Views, Many Directions," *National Journal*, December 10, 1977, p. 1918. For an interesting case study of the multifaceted play of influence in recent agricultural policy see I. M. Destler, *United States Foreign Economic Policy-Making* (Washington, D.C.: Brookings Institution, 1978).

Figure 3-2
POLITICAL APPOINTEES ABOVE THE LEVEL OF BUREAU HEADS, DEPARTMENT OF LABOR, 1933, 1960, AND 1976

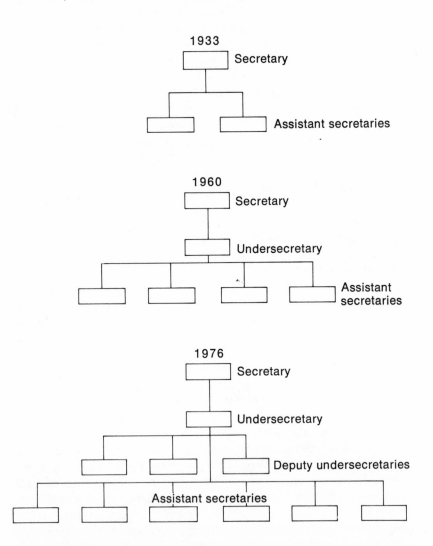

Source: U.S. Congress, Senate, Committee on Civil Service, *Positions Not Under the Civil Service,* document no. 173, 72d Cong., 2d sess., January 1933, pp. 4 and 19; U.S. Congress, Senate, Committee on Post Office and Civil Service, *United States Government Policy and Supporting Positions,* committee print, 86th Cong., 2d sess., 1960, p. 92; U.S. Congress, House, Committee on Post Office and Civil Service, *United States Government Policy and Supporting Positions,* 94th Cong., 2d sess., 1976, pp. 64-65.

politician was gone after reported fights with one of the "women," who was also the former executive director of the Consumer Federation of America.

Of course, if appointed executives were part of a coherent political team, the larger numbers and deeper issue specialization might suggest a stronger capacity for democratic leadership in the bureaucracy. But as participants themselves often come to realize, this is not the case. Political executives' tenure in a given position is short. Their political bases of support in the electorate at large are ambiguous at best. Any mutual commitment to each other is problematic. Thus coherent political leadership in the bureaucracy—especially leadership with any ties to ordinary democratic politics—is normally at a premium. What one can count on finding in and at the fringes of every specialized part of the political bureaucracy are policy networks. It is likely to be in these that judgments about performance are made, reputations established or lost, and replacements for appointees—whoever may be the President—supplied.

The Executive Leadership Problem

Washington has always relied on informal means of producing political leaders in government. This is no less true now than in the days when party spoils ruled presidential appointments. It is the informal mechanisms that have changed. No doubt some of the increasing emphasis on educational credentials, professional specialization, and technical facility merely reflects changes in society at large. But it is also important to recognize that government activity has itself been changing the informal mechanisms that produce political administrators. Accumulating policy commitments have become crucial forces affecting the kind of executive leadership that emerges. E. E. Schattschneider put it better when he observed that "new policies create new politics." [29]

For many years now the list of issues on the public agenda has grown more dense as new policy concerns have been added and few dropped. Administratively, this has proliferated the number of policy intermediaries. Politically, it has mobilized more and more groups of people who feel they have a stake, a determined stake, in this or that issue of public policy. These changes are in turn encouraging further specialization of the government's work force and bureaucratic layering in its political leadership. However, the term "political" needs

---

[29] E. E. Schattschneider, *Politics, Pressures and the Tariff* (Hamden: Archon, 1963), p. 288 (originally published 1935).

to be used carefully. Modern officials responsible for making the connection between politics and administration bear little resemblance
to the party politicians who once filled patronage jobs. Rather, today's
political executive is likely to be a person knowledgeable about the
substance of particular issues and adept at moving among the networks of people who are intensely concerned about them.

What are the implications for American government and politics?
The verdict cannot be one-sided, if only because political management
of the bureaucracy serves a number of diverse purposes. At least
three important advantages can be found in the emerging system.

First, the reliance on issue networks and policy politicians is
obviously consistent with some of the larger changes in society.
Ordinary voters are apparently less constrained by party identification and more attracted to an issue-based style of politics. Party
organizations are said to have fallen into a state of decay and to
have become less capable of supplying enough highly qualified executive manpower. If government is committed to intervening in more
complex, specialized areas, it is useful to draw upon the experts and
policy specialists for the public management of these programs.
Moreover, the congruence between an executive leadership and an
electorate that are both uninterested in party politics may help
stabilize a rapidly changing society. Since no one really knows how
to solve the policy puzzles, policy politicians have the important
quality of being disposable without any serious political ramifications
(unless of course there are major symbolic implications, as in President Nixon's firing of Attorney General Elliot Richardson).

Within government, the operation of issue networks may have
a second advantage in that they link Congress and the executive
branch in ways that political parties no longer can. For many years,
reformers have sought to revive the idea of party discipline as a
means of spanning the distance between the two branches and turning their natural competition to useful purposes. But as the troubled
dealings of recent Democratic Presidents with their majorities in
Congress have indicated, political parties tend to be a weak bridge.

Meanwhile, the linkages of technocracy between the branches
are indeliberately growing. The congressional bureaucracy that has
blossomed in Washington during the last generation is in many ways
like the political bureaucracy in the executive branch. In general,
the new breed of congressional staffer is not a legislative crony or
beneficiary of patronage favors. Personal loyalty to the congressman
is still paramount, but the new-style legislative bureaucrat is likely to
be someone skilled in dealing with certain complex policy issues,

possibly with credentials as a policy analyst, but certainly in using other experts and their networks.

None of this means an absence of conflict between President and Congress. Policy technicians in the two branches are still working for different sets of clients with different interests. The point is that the growth of specialized policy networks tends to perform the same useful services that it was once hoped a disciplined national party system would perform. Sharing policy knowledge, the networks provide a minimum common framework for political debate and decision in the two branches. For example, on energy policy, regardless of one's position on gas deregulation or incentives to producers, the policy technocracy has established a common language for discussing the issues, a shared grammar for identifying the major points of contention, a mutually familiar rhetoric of argumentation. Whether in Congress or the executive branch or somewhere outside, the "movers and shakers" in energy policy (as in health insurance, welfare reform, strategic arms limitation, occupational safety, and a host of other policy areas) tend to share an analytic repertoire for coping with the issues. Like experienced party politicians of earlier times, policy politicians in the knowledge networks may not agree; but they understand each other's way of looking at the world and arguing about policy choices.

A third advantage is the increased maneuvering room offered to political executives by the loose-jointed play of influence. If appointees were ambassadors from clearly defined interest groups and professions, or if policy were monopolized in iron triangles, then the chances for executive leadership in the bureaucracy would be small. In fact, however, the proliferation of administrative middlemen and networks of policy watchers offers new strategic resources for public managers. These are mainly opportunities to split and recombine the many sources of support and opposition that exist on policy issues. Of course, there are limits on how far a political executive can go in shopping for a constituency, but the general tendency over time has been to extend those limits. A secretary of labor will obviously pay close attention to what the AFL-CIO has to say, but there are many other voices to hear, not only in the union movement but also minority groups interested in jobs, state and local officials administering the department's programs, consumer groups worried about wage-push inflation, employees faced with unsafe working conditions, and so on. By the same token, former Secretary of Transportation William Coleman found new room for maneuver on the problem of landings by supersonic planes when he opened up the setpiece debate between pro- and anti-Concorde groups to a wider play of influence through public hearings. Clearly the richness of issue politics demands a high degree of skill to contain expectations and manage the natural dissatisfaction that comes from courting some groups rather than others. But at least it is a game that can be affected by skill, rather than one that is predetermined by immutable forces.

These three advantages are substantial. But before we embrace the rule of policy politicians and their networks, it is worth considering the threats they pose for American government. Issue networks may be good at influencing policy, but can they govern? Should they?

The first and foremost problem is the old one of democratic legitimacy. Weaknesses in executive leadership below the level of the President have never really been due to interest groups, party politics, or Congress. The primary problem has always been the lack of any democratically based power. Political executives get their popular mandate to do anything in the bureaucracy secondhand, from either an elected chief executive or Congress. The emerging system of political technocrats makes this democratic weakness much more severe. The more closely political administrators become identified with the various specialized policy networks, the farther they become separated from the ordinary citizen. Political executives can maneuver among the already mobilized issue networks and may occasionally do a little mobilizing of their own. But this is not the same thing as creating a broad base of public understanding and support for national policies. The typical presidential appointee will travel to any number of conferences, make speeches to the membership of one association after another, but almost never will he or she have to see or listen to an ordinary member of the public. The trouble is that only a small minority of citizens, even of those who are seriously attentive to public affairs, are likely to be mobilized in the various networks.[30] Those who are not policy activists depend on the ability of government institutions to act on their behalf.

If the problem were merely an information gap between policy experts and the bulk of the population, then more communication might help. Yet instead of garnering support for policy choices, more communication from the issue networks tends to produce an "everything causes cancer" syndrome among ordinary citizens. Policy forensics among the networks yield more experts making more

---

[30] An interesting recent case study showing the complexity of trying to generalize about who is "mobilizable" is James N. Rosenau, *Citizenship Between Elections* (New York: The Free Press, 1974).

sophisticated claims and counterclaims to the point that the non-specialist becomes inclined to concede everything and believe nothing that he hears. The ongoing debates on energy policy, health crises, or arms limitation are rich in examples of public skepticism about what "they," the abstruse policy experts, are doing and saying. While the highly knowledgeable have been playing a larger role in government, the proportion of the general public concluding that those running the government don't seem to know what they are doing has risen rather steadily.[31] Likewise, the more government has tried to help, the more feelings of public helplessness have grown.

No doubt many factors and events are linked to these changing public attitudes. The point is that the increasing prominence of issue networks is bound to aggravate problems of legitimacy and public disenchantment. Policy activists have little desire to recognize an unpleasant fact: that their influential systems for knowledgeable policy making tend to make democratic politics more difficult. There are at least four reasons.

Complexity. Democratic political competition is based on the idea of trying to simplify complexity into a few, broadly intelligible choices. The various issue networks, on the other hand, have a stake in searching out complexity in what might seem simple. Those who deal with particular policy issues over the years recognize that policy objectives are usually vague and results difficult to measure. Actions relevant to one policy goal can frequently be shown to be inconsistent with others. To gain a reputation as a knowledgeable participant, one must juggle all of these complexities and demand that other technocrats in the issue networks do the same.

Consensus. A major aim in democratic politics is, after open argument, to arrive at some workable consensus of views. Whether by trading off one issue against another or by combining related issues, the goal is agreement. Policy activists may commend this democratic

---

[31] Since 1964 the Institute for Social Research at the University of Michigan has asked the question, "Do you feel that almost all of the people running the government are smart people, or do you think that quite a few of them don't seem to know what they are doing?" The proportions choosing the latter view have been 28 percent (1964), 38 percent (1968), 45 percent (1970), 42 percent (1972), 47 percent (1974), and 52 percent (1976). For similar findings on public feelings of lack of control over the policy process, see U.S. Congress, Senate, Subcommittee on Intergovernmental Relations of the Committee on Government Operations, *Confidence and Concern: Citizens View American Government*, committee print, 93d Cong., 1st sess., 1973, pt. 1, p. 30. For a more complete discussion of recent trends see the two articles by Arthur H. Miller and Jack Citrin in the *American Political Science Review* (September 1974).

purpose in theory, but what their issue networks actually provide is a way of processing dissension. The aim is good policy—the right outcome on the issue. Since what that means is disputable among knowledgeable people, the desire for agreement must often take second place to one's understanding of the issue. Trade-offs or combinations —say, right-to-life groups with nuclear-arms-control people; environmentalists and consumerists; civil liberties groups and anti-gun controllers—represent a kind of impurity for many of the newly proliferating groups. In general there are few imperatives pushing for political consensus among the issue networks and many rewards for those who become practiced in the techniques of informed skepticism about different positions.

Confidence. Democratic politics presumes a kind of psychological asymmetry between leaders and followers. Those competing for leadership positions are expected to be sure of themselves and of what is to be done, while those led are expected to have a certain amount of detachment and dubiety in choosing how to give their consent to be governed. Politicians are supposed to take credit for successes, to avoid any appearance of failure, and to fix blame clearly on their opponents; voters weigh these claims and come to tentative judgments, pending the next competition among the leaders.

The emerging policy networks tend to reverse the situation. Activists mobilized around the policy issues are the true believers. To survive, the newer breed of leaders, or policy politicians, must become well versed in the complex, highly disputed substance of the issues. A certain tentativeness comes naturally as ostensible leaders try to spread themselves across the issues. Taking credit shows a lack of understanding of how intricate policies work and may antagonize those who really have been zealously pushing the issue. Spreading blame threatens others in the established networks and may raise expectations that new leadership can guarantee a better policy result. Vagueness about what is to be done allows policy problems to be dealt with as they develop and in accord with the intensity of opinion among policy specialists at that time. None of this is likely to warm the average citizen's confidence in his leaders. The new breed of policy politicians are cool precisely because the issue networks are hot.

Closure. Part of the genius of democratic politics is its ability to find a nonviolent decision-rule (by voting) for ending debate in favor of action. All the incentives in the policy technocracy work against such decisive closure. New studies and findings can always be brought to bear. The biggest rewards in these highly intellectual

HUGH HECLO

groups go to those who successfully challenge accepted wisdom. The networks thrive by continuously weighing alternative courses of action on particular policies, not by suspending disbelief and accepting that something must be done.

For all of these reasons, what is good for policy making (in the sense of involving well-informed people and rigorous analysts) may be bad for democratic politics. The emerging policy technocracy tends, as Henry Aaron has said of social science research, to "corrode any simple faiths around which political coalitions ordinarily are built."[32] Should we be content with simple faiths? Perhaps not; but the great danger is that the emerging world of issue politics and policy experts will turn John Stuart Mill's argument about the connection between liberty and popular government on its head. More informed argument about policy choices may produce more incomprehensibility. More policy intermediaries may widen participation among activists but deepen suspicions among unorganized nonspecialists. There may be more group involvement and less democratic legitimacy, more knowledge and more Know-Nothingism. Activists are likely to remain unsatisfied with, and nonactivists uncommitted to, what government is doing. Superficially this cancelling of forces might seem to assure a conservative tilt away from new, expansionary government policies. However, in terms of undermining a democratic identification of ordinary citizens with their government, the tendencies are profoundly radical.

A second difficulty with the issue networks is the problem that they create for the President as ostensible chief of the executive establishment. The emerging policy technocracy puts presidential appointees outside of the chief executive's reach in a way that narrowly focused iron triangles rarely can. At the end of the day, constituents of these triangles can at least be bought off by giving them some of the material advantages that they crave. But for issue activists it is likely to be a question of policy choices that are right or wrong. In this situation, more analysis and staff expertise—far from helping—may only hinder the President in playing an independent political leadership role. The influence of the policy technicians and their networks permeates everything the White House may want to do. Without their expertise there are no option papers, no detailed data and elaborate assessments to stand up against the onslaught of the issue experts in Congress and outside. Of course a President can replace a political executive, but that is probably

---

[32] Henry J. Aaron, *Politics and the Professors* (Washington, D.C.: Brookings Institution, 1978), p. 159.

merely to substitute one incumbent of the relevant policy network for another.

It is, therefore, no accident that President Carter found himself with a cabinet almost none of whom were either his longstanding political backers or leaders of his party. Few if any of his personal retinue could have passed through the reputational screens of the networks to be named, for example, a secretary of labor or defense. Moreover, anyone known to be close to the President and placed in an operating position in the bureaucracy puts himself, and through him the President, in an extremely vulnerable position. Of the three cabinet members who were President Carter's own men, one, Andrew Young, was under extreme pressure to resign in the first several months. Another Carter associate, Bert Lance, was successfully forced to resign after six months, and the third, Griffin Bell, was given particularly tough treatment during his confirmation hearings and was being pressured to resign after only a year in office. The emerging system of political administration tends to produce executive arrangements in which the President's power stakes are on the line almost everywhere in terms of policy, whereas almost nowhere is anyone on the line for him personally.

Where does all this leave the President as a politician and as an executive of executives? In an impossible position. The problem of connecting politics and administration currently places any President in a classic no-win predicament. If he attempts to use personal loyalists as agency and department heads, he will be accused of politicizing the bureaucracy and will most likely put his executives in an untenable position for dealing with their organizations and the related networks. If he tries to create a countervailing source of policy expertise at the center, he will be accused of aggrandizing the Imperial Presidency and may hopelessly bureaucratize the White House's operations. If he relies on some benighted idea of collective cabinet government and on departmental executives for leadership in the bureaucracy (as Carter did in his first term), then the President does more than risk abdicating his own leadership responsibilities as the only elected executive in the national government; he is bound to become a creature of the issue networks and the policy specialists. It would be pleasant to think that there is a neat way out of this trilemma, but there is not.

Finally, there are disturbing questions surrounding the accountability of a political technocracy. The real problem is not that policy specialists specialize but that, by the nature of public office, they must generalize. Whatever an influential political executive does is done with all the collective authority of government and in the name of the public at large. It is not difficult to imagine situations in which policies make excellent sense within the cloisters of the expert issue watchers and yet are nonsense or worse seen from the viewpoint of ordinary people, the kinds of people political executives rarely meet. Since political executives themselves never need to pass muster with the electorate, the main source of democratic accountability must lie with the President and Congress. Given the President's problems and Congress's own burgeoning bureaucracy of policy specialists, the prospects for a democratically responsible executive establishment are poor at best.

Perhaps we need not worry. A case could be made that all we are seeing is a temporary commotion stirred up by a generation of reformist policies. In time the policy process may reenter a period of detumescence as the new groups and networks subside into the familiar triangulations of power.

However, a stronger case can be made that the changes will endure. In the first place, sufficient policy-making forces have now converged in Washington that it is unlikely that we will see a return to the familiar cycle of federal quiescence and policy experimentation by state governments. The central government, surrounded by networks of policy specialists, probably now has the capacity for taking continual policy initiatives. In the second place, there seems to be no way of braking, much less reversing, policy expectations generated by the compensatory mentality. To cut back on commitments undertaken in the last generation would itself be a major act of redistribution and could be expected to yield even more turmoil in the policy process. Once it becomes accepted that relative rather than absolute deprivation is what matters, the crusaders can always be counted upon to be in business.

A third reason why our politics and administration may never be the same lies in the very fact that so many policies have already been accumulated. Having to make policy in an environment already crowded with public commitments and programs increases the odds of multiple, indirect impacts of one policy on another, of one perspective set in tension with another, of one group and then another being mobilized. This sort of complexity and unpredictability creates a hostile setting for any return to traditional interest group politics.

Imagine trying to govern in a situation where the short-term political resources you need are stacked around a changing series of discrete issues, and where people overseeing these issues have nothing to prevent their pressing claims beyond any resources that they can offer in return. Imagine too that the more they do so, the more you lose understanding and support from public backers who have the long-term resources that you need. Whipsawed between cynics and true believers, policy would always tend to evolve to levels of insolubility. It is not easy for a society to politicize itself and at the same time depoliticize government leadership. But we in the United States may be managing to do just this.

4

The Semi-Sovereign Congress

Samuel C. Patterson

Congress is not unique. It belongs to a class of political institutions which, generically, are called representative assemblies.[1] There are more than 100 major institutions of this sort in the world today. They exhibit many structural differences and variously perform their representative functions. The comparative study of these representative institutions is one of the important challenges of modern political inquiry.[2] At the same time, Congress is probably the most impressive specimen of its genre. Among other things, it is a very powerful *legislative* body. In an era in which law making has in most countries fallen heavily into the hands of executives, the American Congress continues to be a significant, independent lawmaking institution, capable of legislative innovation and able to undertake the creative act of law making without executive leadership if necessary.[3]

This chapter is an exercise in taking stock of the Congress of the 1970s. The assessment focuses upon three central questions: (1) What changes have been taking place in the relationship between Congress and its constituency? (2) How has Congress changed as a legislative organization? and (3) What changes have occurred in congressional decision making? These are questions for which very extensive

[1] One compendium which provides information about fifty-six national representative assemblies is Valentine Herman and Françoise Mendel, eds., *Parliaments of the World* (London: Macmillan, 1976).

[2] See Gerhard Loewenberg and Samuel C. Patterson, *Comparing Legislatures* (Boston: Little, Brown, 1978).

[3] See Gary Orfield, *Congressional Power: Congress and Social Change* (New York: Harcourt Brace Jovanovich, 1975); Ronald C. Moe and Steven C. Teel, "Congress as Policy-Maker: A Necessary Reappraisal," *Political Science Quarterly*, vol. 85 (September 1970), pp. 443-70; John R. Johannes, "Congress and the Initiation of Legislation," *Public Policy*, vol. 20 (Spring 1972), pp. 281-309.

answers are possible. In contrast to most national representative assemblies, the American Congress has been singularly observed, investigated, and analyzed. The study of Congress has proliferated since the mid-1960s, so that today there is quite a rich literature dealing with the institution.[4] This chapter can only provide selective attention to a highly complex, intricate, and hoary national legislature.

Many changes, large and small, have taken place in the organization and procedure of the Congress of the 1970s. Of the previous decade and before, Ralph Huitt said, "Congress changes, as all living things must change; it changes slowly, adaptively, as institutions change."[5] The pace of congressional change has quickened. There are, accordingly, more changes for the observer of Congress to study than in most of the years before the 1970s. But, perhaps paradoxically, the meaning of congressional change is in many respects still difficult to weigh. We cannot promise to unravel the profound effects of recent changes in the institution, but we can bring some order to the complexity of these changes. Doing so can help us to take a step in the direction of understanding what congressional changes mean.

The 95th Congress

A new Congress of the United States convened on Capitol Hill for the ninety-fifth time in January 1977. A large Democratic majority had been elected in the preceding November, along with a Democratic President, Jimmy Carter. For the first time in eight years, the

---

[4] Little, Brown and Company of Boston has published an excellent group of books about Congress in The Study of Congress Series; see Lewis A. Froman, Jr., *The Congressional Process: Strategies, Rules, and Procedures* (1967), Randall B. Ripley, *Majority Party Leadership in Congress* (1969), John S. Saloma III, *Congress and the New Politics* (1969), Charles O. Jones, *The Minority Party* (1970), John F. Manley, *The Politics of Finance* (1970), Richard F. Fenno, Jr., *Congressmen in Committees* (1973), and Robert L. Peabody, *Leadership in Congress* (1976). Important additional studies include Randall B. Ripley, *Congress: Process and Policy* (New York: W. W. Norton, 1975); Norman J. Ornstein, ed., *Congress in Change* (New York: Praeger, 1975); David R. Mayhew, *Congress: the Electoral Connection* (New Haven: Yale University Press, 1974); Harvey C. Mansfield, Sr., ed., *Congress Against the President* (New York: Praeger, 1975); Lawrence C. Dodd and Bruce I. Oppenheimer, eds., *Congress Reconsidered* (New York: Praeger, 1977); Roger H. Davidson and Walter J. Oleszek, *Congress Against Itself* (Bloomington: Indiana University Press, 1977); Morris P. Fiorina, *Congress: Keystone of the Washington Establishment* (New Haven: Yale University Press, 1977); and Susan Welch and John G. Peters, eds., *Legislative Reform and Public Policy* (New York: Praeger, 1977).

[5] Ralph K. Huitt and Robert L. Peabody, *Congress: Two Decades of Analysis* (New York: Harper & Row, 1969), p. 229.

Democrats controlled both the White House and Capitol Hill. Of the 435 members of the House of Representatives, 292 were Democrats; of the 100 senators, 61 were Democrats. A large number of the House members were new to the 95th Congress, although not as many as had been elected in the Democratic landslide of 1974, and an unusually large proportion of the 1974 Democratic newcomers had been reelected. Of the 67 House freshmen, 47 were Democrats and 20 Republicans—30 lawyers, 14 businessmen, 3 farmers, 4 journalists, 4 former congressional aides, 5 educators, 2 manual workers, a social worker, a probation officer, and 3 who accounted themselves "politicians."

Thirty-three Senate seats were filled in the November 1976 elections, of which twenty-one were won by Democrats, eleven by Republicans, and one by an Independent. The Independent was Senator Harry F. Byrd, Jr. of Virginia. He was elected as an Independent but when the Senate convened he joined with the Democratic majority for purposes of seniority and committee assignments and thus made the putative partisan margin sixty-two to thirty-eight. Eighteen new senators were elected to the 95th Congress, the largest number of freshmen to enter the Senate since 1958. Of the ten new Democratic and eight new Republican senators, half were lawyers. The other half included a farmer, a veterinarian, two educators, three businessmen, an astronaut, and a "politician."

Although the partisan coloration of the 95th Congress was about the same as that of its predecessor, and the other characteristics of its members were about the same as before, some things about the new Congress were different. Most notably, both houses chose new leaders, a moderately rare event. Senator Mike Mansfield (D.-Mont.), majority floor leader since 1961, and Congressman Carl Albert (D.-Okla.), speaker since 1971, did not run for reelection to the 95th Congress, nor did the previous Senate minority leader, Senator Hugh Scott (R.-Penn.).

When House Democrats caucused in December, they unanimously selected former floor leader Thomas P. "Tip" O'Neill, Jr. of Massachusetts to be the new speaker. After a vigorous four-way contest, the Democratic caucus chose Representative Jim Wright of Texas as majority leader. House Republicans reelected John J. Rhodes of Arizona as minority leader. In the Senate, Robert C. Byrd of West Virginia was elected Democratic leader without opposition after the strategic withdrawal of Senator Hubert H. Humphrey of Minnesota, and Alan Cranston of California was elected deputy floor leader. By a one-vote margin, Senate Republicans selected Howard H.

Baker, Jr. of Tennessee as floor leader over Robert P. Griffin of Michigan. Thus, along with a new Democrat in the White House, the large Democratic majorities in both House and Senate opened the 95th Congress with new and rather different kinds of leaders.

In addition to new leadership, both House and Senate were in the midst of some procedural and organizational remodeling. In the House, subcommittees were in the process of acquiring increased autonomy, the seniority system had been relaxed, efforts were afoot to make the administrative affairs of the House more efficient and to streamline House committees, the Democratic caucus had become more assertive, procedural changes had been designed to make the conduct of House business more open and public, and the powers of the speaker had been enhanced. Speaker O'Neill, repeatedly vowing to be "a strong speaker," was in a position to capitalize upon changes in Democratic party caucus rules made in 1974 which gave the speaker considerable control over committee assignments and influence upon the Rules Committee—the House committee that regulates the flow of legislation to the House floor. The House Democratic caucus meetings in December 1976 further embellished the speaker's powers by giving him special discretion over bills referred to more than one committee.

Changes made in the rules of the House Democratic caucus in 1971 and 1973 provided for caucus votes on individual nominees for committee chairmanships. The Democrats of the 94th Congress amended their rules so as to permit nominations of candidates for committee chairmen to be made from the floor of the caucus meeting and to require caucus approval of the subcommittee chairmen of the Appropriations Committee, whose subcommittees are among the most important in the House. In 1975, the House Democrats used their new control of the seniority system to replace three incumbent chairmen. The 1974 congressional election had brought seventy-five freshman Democrats to the House, many of them eager to test the new caucus rules. Especially vulnerable to attack were those chairmen who had gotten a substantial number of "no" votes in the 1973 caucus voting on chairmanships. Their number included all three of the chairmen deposed in 1975: William R. Poage (D.-Tex.) of the Agriculture Committee, F. Edward Hébert (D.-La.) of the Armed Services Committee, and Wright Patman (D.-Tex.) of the Committee on Banking, Currency, and Housing. Two of these three elderly Southerners were replaced by the committee members next to them in seniority—Poage by Thomas S. Foley (D.-Wash.), Hébert by Melvin Price (D.-Ill.)—and Patman was replaced by Henry S. Reuss

(D.-Wis.), the fourth-ranking Democrat on Banking, Currency and Housing.[6]

Two years later, in mid-January 1977, the Democratic caucus again voted on each of the nominees proposed by the Steering and Policy Committee—the party committee chaired by the speaker that handles committee assignments and chairmanships—for the twenty-two full committee chairmanships. Except for the committees on Merchant Marine and Fisheries and Small Business, the senior Democrat in every case was recommended and approved as chairman. Because of a change in rules made by the House Democratic caucus in 1976 prohibiting the chairman of a full committee from serving as a subcommittee chairman on another committee, three senior Democrats on Merchant Marine and Fisheries and two on Small Business turned down the chairmanships of these two committees in order to retain their subcommittee chairmanships. As a result, John J. Murphy (D.-N.Y.) became chairman of Merchant Marine and Fisheries although he was fourth ranked, and third-ranking Neil Smith (D.-Iowa) became chairman of Small Business. Later in January, the caucus approved twelve of the thirteen nominees of the Appropriations Committee for subcommittee chairmanships; Congressman Robert L. F. Sikes (D.-Fla.) was replaced as chairman of the Subcommittee on Military Construction because of his censure by the House the year before for unethical conduct. The new rules for selecting House committee chairmen and their application in 1975 and 1977 showed that seniority, while still the main criterion of selection for committee leadership, was no longer inviolate.

The Senate convened in an unusually heady atmosphere. In addition to selecting new leadership, the Senate faced proposals to make substantial changes in its committee system—the most sweeping changes since the passage of the Legislative Reorganization Act of 1946. A temporary Select Committee to Study the Senate Committee System had been established during 1976, chaired by Senator Adlai E. Stevenson III (D.-Ill.). The proposals of the Select Committee, after some alterations had been made by the Committee on Rules and Administration to which the reform proposals had been referred, were adopted in large measure by the Senate in early February. The number of Senate committees was reduced from thirty-one to twenty-five, with a further reduction to twenty-one anticipated. Accordingly, committee jurisdictions were reshuffled.

---

[6] For a more detailed description of these events, see Malcolm E. Jewell and Samuel C. Patterson, *The Legislative Process in the United States*, 3rd ed. (New York: Random House, 1977), pp. 196-99.

For example, virtually all energy legislation, previously divided among a number of committees, now was under the aegis of the new Committee on Energy and Natural Resources, chaired by Senator Henry M. Jackson (D.-Wash.). In addition, limitations were placed upon the number of committee and subcommittee chairmanships that a senator could hold. And for the first time committee chairmen were elected by secret ballot by the caucus of Senate Democrats; all of the incumbent chairmen were reelected by large margins.

Changes in leadership and organizational reforms made in the first few weeks of the 95th Congress reinforced and extended congressional changes that had been undertaken since the early 1970s. Although the complexion of Congress was not greatly different, the changes in the House and Senate were more than cosmetic. What do these changes mean?

The Meaning of Congressional Change

The new developments in the 95th Congress, some harkening back to signals of reform emitted as long ago as 1958, have generally been received as beneficial. The leadership is more activist and aggressive than before, and organizational changes appear to contribute to greater congressional efficiency and accountability. But the deeper meaning of congressional change is not so clear.

Incremental Change. The deeper meaning of congressional change is difficult to assess. Part of the difficulty lies in the state of the analytical art. Congress is not easy to analyze holistically. It is a subtle and complex collective decision-making body with intricate linkages to its constituencies and to other governmental agencies. While much is known about Congress as an institution, analysis of the congressional manifold is not so finely tuned as to detect easily the systematic effects of relatively small changes in the short term. Reform is ubiquitous in the congressional arena, and changes tend to be both small in scope and large in number. Probably it is not too much of an exaggeration to say that Congress changes persistently. The constancy of change and the incremental character of change make it difficult to acquire a firm grasp of the meaning of change.[7]

Leadership change in Congress has seldom had a dramatic impact upon the institution itself. That is not to say that the leader-

---

[7] See Samuel C. Patterson, "On the Study of Legislative Reform," in Welch and Peters, eds., *Legislative Reform and Public Policy*, pp. 214-22.

ship is unimportant; significant political outcomes may be influenced by the congressional leadership. Leadership may make a contribution to the enactment of particular legislation, but within the institutional constraints that characterize the Congress. The foremost student of congressional leadership change says that "the party leadership's contribution to most . . . legislative endeavors is marginal at best; they schedule legislation, work out appropriate floor strategy, and corral a few votes here and there." The marginal, incremental character of the leadership's contribution is significant. Indeed, "although leadership contributions may be marginal, most important political choices are made at the margins." [8]

In making organizational adjustments, such as modifying the rules of procedure or reshuffling committee jurisdictions, Congress is adapting itself to changes in the political, economic, or social environment. Such reforms are often hailed at the time of their adoption as "revolutionary"—or, if they are not inoffensive, denounced as "crippling" by their opponents. But it is a rare congressional reform that produces a clear fundamental consequence.

In 1975, one of the shrewdest students of Congress asked, "Will Reform Change Congress?" [9] The answer then was, in effect, nobody knows for sure. Short-term changes are notable—some may lose committee chairmanships, some may get more staff help, some may acquire new policy hegemony. But Congress quickly adjusts to the new, and usually small-scale, distribution rules. Long-run consequences are more problematical, depending upon how a complexity of other factors impinge upon the unfolding of change. An equally cogent question might be, "Will Congress change reform?" Is Congress likely to adopt, or be subject to, fundamental change in one direction or another? Not likely. Congress has as one of its purposes in the American political system the task of adapting, through incremental change, to alterations in its environment. In this sense, Congress is always in "crisis," in a perpetual state of reform.

The Reincarnation of Henry Clay. Henry Clay was America's most remarkable congressional politician. Just after the turn of the nineteenth century he served in the Kentucky legislature, which twice sent him to the United States Senate. Then he was elected to the 12th Congress as a member of the House of Representatives. As a freshman congressman, he was elected speaker, and he served as speaker

---

[8] Peabody, *Leadership in Congress*, p. 9.
[9] Charles O. Jones, "Will Reform Change Congress?" in Dodd and Oppenheimer, eds., *Congress Reconsidered*, pp. 247-60.

off and on between 1811 and 1825. His leadership contributed importantly to the development of the House as an autonomous and politically unified policy-making body. After his House service, he was a presidential candidate in 1824, 1832, and 1844, and a U.S. senator from Kentucky from 1831 to 1842 and from 1849 to 1852.

Clay was a congressman and senator during the years when Congress was becoming an imposing and powerful national legislative body. Although what we might call the "modern" Congress was not fully developed until after the 1880s, the institution came to be, in many fundamental ways, much as it is today during the period of Clay's service.[10]

If Henry Clay were alive today, and he were to serve again in the House and Senate to which he was chosen so many times in the nineteenth century, he would find much that was very familiar. He would certainly recognize where he was, and perhaps after some initial shock he surely would be reasonably comfortable in the modern congressional envelope. Of course, things have changed. Congress has a much larger membership. There were only 186 members of the House that Clay first entered as member and speaker; there were only 52 senators in the 1830s. Members and committees have vastly more staff help. A far greater array of policy decisions is required of Congress nowadays than before the Civil War. There is a fancy electronic gadget for voting in the House. The party memberships are less coherent, and the committee system is much more complex. Many more congressmen are professionals now, in contrast to the relative amateurism of the pre-Civil War Congresses. The scale of things has grown; but the fundamental character of the institution has not changed so very much.

Congress is an extraordinarily stable institution. Many changes have occurred in the party leaderships, the committee systems, and the norms of the Congress, but the intrinsic internal order of the institution has shown enormous continuity. Although relationships between Congress and the executive were altered as the country came to be an urban, industrial society with a pivotal role in international affairs, Congress, unlike the legislative bodies of many other industrial nations, continues to be a highly autonomous institution. Certainly since the mid-nineteenth century Congress has been embedded in its environment; this feature and its responsiveness as it performs

---

[10] For a concise analysis of the emergence of Congress as an institution, see Randall B. Ripley, *Congress: Process and Policy* (New York: W. W. Norton, 1975), pp. 27-57; and Malcolm E. Jewell and Samuel C. Patterson, *The Legislative Process in the United States*, 3rd ed. (New York: Random House, 1977), pp. 30-59.

its constituent function have become profoundly institutionalized. It has been said that the United States is a modern country with an antique political system, and in a sense that is true.[11] American governing institutions emerged in a particular way in the nineteenth century, and many of their present-day core features are readily traceable to earlier times. That is why Henry Clay, if he were a congressman today, would surely find that Congress had not become unrecognizable. Institutions simply do not change very much, which is why they are called institutions.

Keeping that in mind is helpful to understanding the Congress of the 1970s. Congress has never experienced a "revolutionary" change. Congress is very stable. Stable institutions change as they adapt themselves to changes in the world around them. Thus, congressional changes are most appropriately viewed as the adaptations through which a very stable system maintains itself. Accordingly, reforms of Congress, relatively small in magnitude, are consequential largely in the ways in which they maintain the existing congressional structure. A marked transformation of a political institution like the Congress is not impossible, but it simply has not occurred in the whiggish context of American political history. As a result, it is the stability of Congress, and not changes in it, that is the most remarkable in the long term. Perhaps, therefore, we should distinguish between adaptive and transformative institutional change; changes in Congress are all adaptive.

Strains Toward Change. Congress does change, and its adaptive changes are important to us. If such changes do not alter the intrinsic character of the institution, they often have important consequences for the politics of the day. Such changes, often cyclical in nature, seem to be called forth in three distinct circumstances. First, adaptation of the congressional organization occurs when the magnitude, complexity, and diversity of *demands* made upon it increase sharply. The first dramatic demand overload occurred after the Civil War, when the United States emerged as an industrial nation. As a result, important changes in leadership and committee structure took place in Congress. Increased demands after World War II for public policies to cope with domestic economic crisis, and the new international role of the United States, help account for the congressional reforms of the mid-1940s.

---

[11] Samuel P. Huntington, *Political Order in Changing Societies* (New Haven: Yale University Press, 1968), pp. 93-139.

Second, pressures for congressional change develop out of tension between the *coordination* and the *dispersion* of congressional power. The party leaderships in Congress tend to be coordinative; they are involved in pulling things together. The committee system is dispersive—prone to increasing decentralization of influence over public policy. It is not easy to say precisely when this tension comes to be over-stretched. But congressional history provides us with one pretty unequivocal example—the case of the revolt against "Cannonism" in 1910–1911. The House reduced the substantial congressional power of Speaker Joseph Cannon by removing him from the Rules Committee and withdrawing his power to appoint members of the standing committees. The upshot of these simple changes in the rules was a significant decentralization of congressional power to committees.

Third, pressures for congressional change arise out of tensions between *congressional* and *executive* power. Although a variety of stimuli generated reform activity in the early 1970s, the presidency of Richard M. Nixon seems to have been the most important one. President Nixon entered the White House, and was subsequently reelected, in the very rare circumstance of an opposition party with a substantial majority in control of the Congress. His extraordinary interpretation of the powers of the President, especially in regard to executive privilege and the impoundment of funds appropriated by Congress, certainly helped to precipitate congressional reforms intended to recapture political control.

The 95th Congress was no oddity, no political parvenu. It was, nevertheless, elected in an era when interesting adaptive change was taking place. The danger for political analysis in every new Congress is that it alone will become the major basis upon which trends are identified or the future predicted. The opportunity that the 95th Congress presents is that it, like those that went before, stimulates us to assess the character of the congressional institution. The new Congress, like the old, is linked to its constituency through the dynamics of election and representation. It is an institution with organizational needs to cope with demands on its members, to provide leadership, to consume information, and to divide and process work. And it is a decision-making body, expressing its will, so to speak, by voting on policy questions and protecting its independence as a decision maker. Constituent, organizational, and decision-making changes can be observed and assayed, with profit to an understanding of Congress in the 1970s, and to these changes we now turn.

Constituent Changes in Congress

The nexus between congressmen and their constituents can be assessed in three important ways. First, we can evaluate the outcome of the way in which members are distributed over the number of constituencies. The United States Senate is, of course, based upon the principle of the equal representation of states, with two senators elected from each state. House members are apportioned among the states in accord with the state populations, with the constitutional stipulation that every state will have at least one member. House district boundary lines are drawn within each state, normally by the state legislatures, within the constraints of decisions by the United States Supreme Court that the congressional districts must be equal in population as ascertained in the decennial census.

Second, we can evaluate the consequences of the way in which the electoral system rewards the political parties in congressional seats for the votes they accrue in congressional elections. All members of Congress are elected in single-member districts, and the candidate with at least a plurality of the popular vote is elected. This kind of electoral system contains a well-known bias—the so-called Matthew Effect—in which the party winning the most votes wins a disproportionately large share of the legislative seats, and the minority party gets fewer seats than its share of the vote would dictate.[12]

Third, we can investigate the activities of congressmen in their constituencies, as they work for reelection, provide services to their constituents, and otherwise "nurse" their districts.

Representation of Population. Because the Constitution gives each state two senators regardless of population, senators represent widely disparate numbers of people. Senators Jacob Javits (Rep.) and Daniel Patrick Moynihan (Dem.) of New York represent more than 18 million people; Senators Alan Cranston (Dem.) and S. I. Hayakawa (Rep.) of California represent more than 21 million people. But Republican Senators Clifford Hansen and Malcolm Wallop of Wyoming have only 374,000 constituents, and Alaska Senators Ted Stevens (Rep.) and Mike Gravel (Dem.) represent only 352,000. About 60 percent of Americans live in the twelve largest states, represented by less than a

---

[12] This electoral system bias is called the Matthew Effect after the proverb in Matthew 13:12: "For whosoever hath, to him shall be given, and he shall have more abundance; but whosoever hath not, from him shall be taken away even that he hath." Electoral laws are analyzed in Douglas W. Rae, *The Political Consequences of Electoral Laws*, rev. ed. (New Haven: Yale University Press, 1971).

fourth of the members of the Senate; another fourth of the senators represent the twelve smallest states, which contain less than 4 percent of the national population. These egregious population disparities do not bother Americans very much, and no efforts to reapportion the Senate have ever been seriously proposed.

In contrast, the House of Representatives has always been representative on the basis of the states' populations. In *Wesberry v. Sanders* (1964) and subsequent decisions, the Supreme Court held that congressional districts must be equal in population according to the most recent national census.[13] Prior to the redistricting done by the state legislatures, House seats are apportioned among the states so as to minimize the differences in the average number of persons represented by a congressman from one state to another. Although the redistricting of the 1960s was hailed as a "reapportionment revolution" and did rectify a few districts that were either too large or too small, in general the House has not been systematically malapportioned or maldistricted. Figure 4–1 shows Lorenz curves for the populations of congressional districts in 1964, 1969, and 1970; while these curves do not hug the equality line, they indicate a very trivial amount of population inequality in congressional districts.

Without a change in the Constitution, it is impossible to make congressional districts perfectly equal in population across the country, even though they may be made equal within a particular state. On the basis of the 1970 census, every congressional district should ideally have had a population of about 465,000. But two considerations suggest why actual districting produces inevitable variances from this ideal size. First, every state gets one member of Congress irrespective of its population, so that Alaska, Wyoming, and Vermont get one congressman each even though their populations are well below the ideal national average, and Nevada, Delaware, and North Dakota are entitled to only one House member in spite of the fact that their populations are above the national average for district populations. Second, congressional district boundary lines may not cross state lines.

In spite of these constraints, the House has been reasonably representative in an equal-population sense since at least the turn of the century. Table 4–1 presents an assessment of congressional apportionment and districting for nine Congresses since 1900. In every case, the Gini index, which measures the area between a line standing for perfect population equality of districts and a curve

---

[13] See Nelson W. Polsby, ed., *Reapportionment in the 1970s* (Berkeley: University of California Press, 1971).

Figure 4-1

POPULATION INEQUALITY IN CONGRESSIONAL
APPORTIONMENT, 1964, 1969, AND 1970

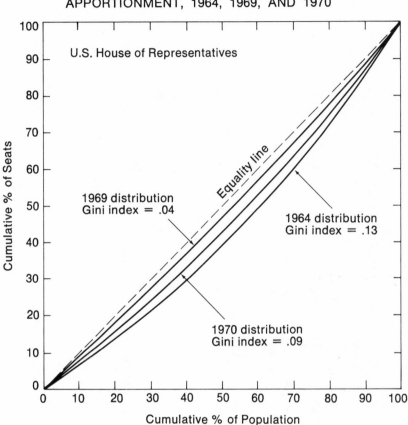

Source: Author.

representing the actual cumulative payoff of population in seats, is very small. No one would want to defend a congressional districting in which districts were overly large or small in population or assert that redistricting has had no political consequences. Nevertheless, it is true that in the twentieth century the periodic adjustments in the number of congressmen to which the states are entitled and the adjustments in the boundaries of congressional districts after the national censuses have been effected in such a way as to retain quite a reasonable measure of population equality in representation in the House of Representatives.

Table 4-1
DEVIATIONS FROM POPULATION MEANS FOR CONGRESSIONAL DISTRICTS, 1905–1970
(in percentages of districts)

Deviation Range (in percentage points)	1970	1969	1964	1955	1945	1935	1925	1915	1905
0 – 5	24	60	24	21	29	25	18	37	33
5 – 10	28	29	21	22	20	18	18	21	27
10 – 15	17	5	14	19	9	12	17	13	17
15 – 20	12	3	8	12	12	13	16	11	11
20 – 25	8	1	10	8	10	7	7	7	4
Over 25	11	2	23	18	20	25	24	11	8
Total	100	100	100	100	100	100	100	100	100
Mean population per district	465,025	411,936	415,170	347,499	304,222	286,853	243,195	216,016	196,357
Gini index	.09	.04	.13	.11	.12	.15	.13	.09	.07

Source: Author.

The Congressional Electoral System. The Republicans have only succeeded in winning a majority of seats in the Congress twice since World War II (in 1946 and in 1952). In the 95th Congress, Democrats occupied 67 percent of the House seats and 62 percent of the Senate seats. As Figure 4–2 shows, the party margins in the House of Representatives have fluctuated since the 1940s, although Democratic hegemony has generally increased. Figure 4–2 also shows the Democratic and Republican votes in House elections, indicating since the mid-1950s a greater yield in seats for Democratic than for Republican votes.

Figure 4–3 displays the general relationship between votes and seats for the House of Representatives. In the post-World War II years, neither party's candidates have garnered fewer than 40 percent of the total vote or more than 60 percent. As Figure 4–3 shows, the Matthew Effect is quite pronounced and is generally advantageous to the Democrats inasmuch as they have been the dominant party (a one percentage-point increase in their general election vote yields approximately 2 percent of the seats in the House). The Democrats have always dominated southern congressional elections. Until the mid-1960s, the electoral system systematically advantaged the Republicans in the northern states, but since then the system has favored the Democrats in both North and South. These changes in the payoff of the electoral system stem from changes in the distribution of Democratic and Republican voters. Today there are more Democratic safe seats than there were in the 1960s and before, there are fewer marginal Republican seats, and Democratic voters are somewhat "overrepresented" because their low turnout rate means that the number of voters is lower in Democratic districts than in Republican districts.[14]

The performance of the American electoral system is highly characteristic of single-member district, plurality voting systems. It confers a large congressional majority on the party that captures a majority (or a very large plurality) of the popular votes. The system is about equally responsive to Democratic and Republican votes, but because of its post-World War II dominance at the polls in congressional elections, the bias of the system favors the Democratic party. On average, about 48 percent of the popular vote could yield a majority of House seats to the Democrats, while the Republicans

---

[14] See Edward R. Tufte, "The Relationship Between Seats and Votes in Two-Party Systems," *American Political Science Review*, vol. 67 (June 1973), pp. 540-54; and Robert S. Erikson, "Malapportionment, Gerrymandering, and Party Fortunes in Congressional Elections," *American Political Science Review*, vol. 66 (December 1972), pp. 1234-45.

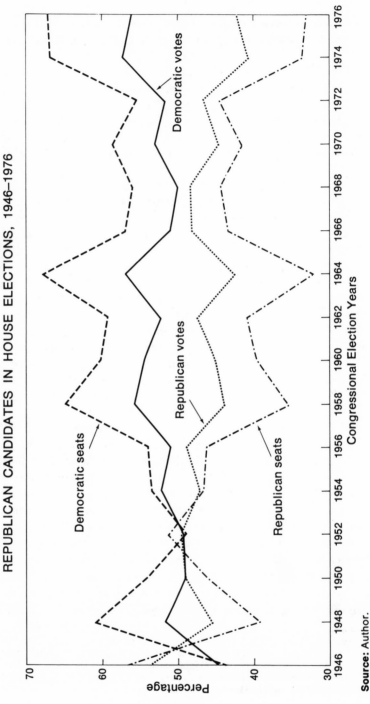

Figure 4-2

VOTES AND SEATS WON BY DEMOCRATIC AND
REPUBLICAN CANDIDATES IN HOUSE ELECTIONS, 1946–1976

Source: Author.

Figure 4-3

SEATS AND VOTES IN HOUSE ELECTIONS, 1946–1976

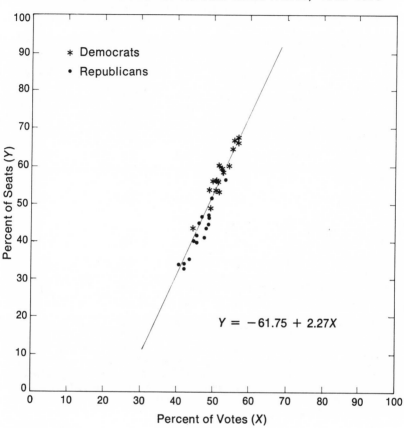

$$Y = -61.75 + 2.27X$$

Source: Author.

require slightly over half of the popular vote to win a majority of House seats. In actuality, of course, Democratic candidates have won considerably more than a majority of popular votes in most postwar elections.

Within this electoral framework, incumbent candidates for both House and Senate seats have a marked tendency to be reelected. While a very large proportion of seats is contested in every election, incumbents have always been advantaged in the outcome. The "incumbency effect" in congressional elections has, moreover, become more striking, especially in House elections since the mid-1960s. The magnitude of this effect is portrayed in Tables 4–2 and 4–3. Of the

141

Table 4-2

THE REELECTION OF INCUMBENTS TO
THE U.S. HOUSE OF REPRESENTATIVES, 1956–1976

	Incumbents Seeking Reelection			Incumbents Reelected	
Year	Total	Defeated in the primary	Defeated in the general election	Total	As a percentage of those seeking reelection	As a percentage of the total House
1956	411	6	16	389	95	89
1958	394	3	37	354	90	81
1960	403	5	26	372	92	86
1962	393	11	14	368	94	85
1964	397	8	44	345	87	79
1966	407	5	40	362	89	83
1968	404	3	5	396	98	91
1970	398	8	12	378	95	87
1972	381	7	13	361	95	83
1974	391	8	40	343	88	79
1976	384	3	13	368	96	85

Source: Charles O. Jones, "Will Reform Change Congress," in Lawrence C. Dodd and Bruce I. Oppenheimer, eds., *Congress Reconsidered* (New York: Praeger, 1977), p. 254; *Congressional Quarterly Weekly Report*, vol. 34 (November 6, 1976), pp. 3121-22.

incumbent House members running for reelection in 1976, three were defeated in primary elections and thirteen lost the general election, producing an incumbent return rate of nearly 96 percent. The 1974 election had been a Democratic landslide; more than a fifth of the Republican incumbents seeking reelection were defeated by Democrats.[15] Of the seventy-nine new Democrats elected to the House in 1974 or afterward, seventy-eight sought reelection in 1976 and seventy-five were successful.

On the whole, the rate at which Senate incumbents have been returned in elections is considerably lower than for House incumbents.

[15] For a thorough analysis of the 1974 congressional election, see Walter Dean Burnham, "Insulation and Responsiveness in Congressional Elections," *Political Science Quarterly*, vol. 90 (Fall 1975), pp. 411-35.

Table 4-3
THE REELECTION OF INCUMBENTS
TO THE U.S. SENATE, 1956–1976

Year	Incumbents Seeking Reelection			Incumbents Reelected	
	Total	Defeated in the primary	Defeated in the general election	Total	As a percentage of those seeking reelection
1956	28	0	3	25	89
1958	31	0	11	20	65
1960	29	0	1	28	97
1962	35	1	5	29	83
1964	36	4	4	28	78
1966	32	3	1	28	88
1968	28	4	4	20	71
1970	30	1	6	23	77
1972	27	2	5	20	71
1974	27	2	2	23	85
1976	25	0	9	16	64

Source: *Congressional Quarterly Weekly Report*, various issues.

Only 64 percent of Senate incumbents seeking reelection 1976 were returned, the lowest return rate since the war. Nine incumbents were defeated in the general election, eight incumbents did not seek to be reelected, and Governor Wendell Anderson of Minnesota was appointed to replace Senator Walter Mondale, who became vice president.

There is no reason to believe that the high rate of return of incumbents to Congress sharply distinguishes it from parliaments in most other countries where there are no constitutional or other restrictions on the number of terms that a representative may serve. The presence of a substantial proportion of incumbents in the legislature provides it with an important measure of continuity and allows for the development of expertise on the part of members. A legislative body like the House of Representatives, all of whose members are up for election every two years, could not function effectively if a large number of its members could not be reelected over a number of elections, thus acquiring experience in both representing their constituencies and performing as legislators.

143

Congress is increasingly criticized on the ground that the high rate of return of incumbents indicates rigidity, locking the institution into a changeless and stultifying pattern of complacency and unresponsiveness. This criticism would carry greater weight if there were some evidence to support the claim that undemocratic and otherwise undesirable consequences flow from the present congressional incumbency rate. No one knows what an optimal incumbency rate would be for Congress; admittedly, it probably would not be desirable for a representative institution to experience no change in its membership over extended periods of time. But, as we shall see, this is far from the case. Both House and Senate receive what seem to be quite ample injections of "new blood"; the turnover of membership over longer periods is far greater than the high rate of incumbency return in a period as short as two years would suggest. Moreover, what evidence there is about the responsiveness of winners of congressional elections (mostly incumbents) to the views of their constituents strongly suggests that they are more likely to be in harness with the constituency than their challengers and that policy agreement between congressmen and constituents is more robust for members elected in safe districts than for those representing competitive districts.[16]

In House races, the advantages of incumbency have increased. Systematic estimates of the incumbency advantage vary in magnitude. One set of estimates suggests that "the gain to a candidate from running as an incumbent for the first time and the loss to a party when its incumbent retires increased from roughly two percent to about five percent of the vote" between the 1950s and the 1960s.[17] Other estimates corroborate the increased advantage of incumbency since the mid-1960s and indicate an average incumbency advantage in elections between 1966 and 1974 of around 6 to 7 percent of the vote.[18] There is evidence that the importance of incumbency increased

---

[16] For suggestive studies, see: Warren E. Miller, "Majority Rule and the Representative System of Government," in *Mass Politics: Studies in Political Sociology*, Erik Allardt and Stein Rokkan, eds. (New York: Free Press, 1970), pp. 284-311; John L. Sullivan and Robert E. O'Connor, "Electoral Choice and Popular Control of Public Policy: The Case of the 1966 House Elections," *American Political Science Review*, vol. 66 (December 1972), pp. 1256-68; and Charles H. Backstrom, "Congress and the Public: How Representative Is the One of the Other?" *American Politics Quarterly*, vol. 5 (October 1977), pp. 411-35.

[17] Erikson, "Malapportionment, Gerrymandering and Party Fortunes in Congressional Elections," p. 1240; and Robert S. Erikson, "The Advantage of Incumbency in Congressional Elections," *Polity*, vol. 3 (Spring 1971), pp. 395-405.

[18] Albert D. Cover and David R. Mayhew, "Congressional Dynamics and the Decline of Competitive Congressional Elections," in *Congress Reconsidered*, p. 60.

in Senate elections between 1946 and 1970.[19] But the advantage of incumbency has not increased as much for Senate as for House incumbents, and Senate incumbency is not as great an advantage as House incumbency. States are more socially and economically diverse than congressional districts and thus are less politically homogeneous and more competitive. The relatively poor showing of Senate incumbents in 1976, plus a more normal responsiveness of the 1972–1976 House elections to shifts in voter preferences, suggests the possibility that the incumbency effect has "bottomed out."[20] Or perhaps more precisely, it may be that the electoral process has begun to stabilize around a generally lower level of intra-district competitiveness than characterized it before the mid-1960s.

No conclusive explanation has been discovered for the increase in the incumbency effect after the mid-1960s. It does not appear that the redrawing of congressional district boundary lines in the late 1960s and early 1970s could be the culprit, since (1) the incumbency reelection rate is no different in redistricted and unredistricted constituencies, (2) the difference between the electoral prospects of incumbents and nonincumbents was no greater in districts that had been redrawn than in those that had not, and (3) the advantage of incumbency increased some for senators, and clearly the states were not gerrymandered in any redistricting process.[21] Gerrymandering does not appear to have had a lasting effect on any significant number of congressional races for either Democrats or Republicans.

Nevertheless, in the 1970s there has been a marked increase in the "safeness" of congressional elections (for House seats, and for Senate seats in the northern states). Table 4–4 shows the proportion

[19] Warren L. Kostroski, "Party and Incumbency in Postwar Senate Elections: Trends, Patterns, and Models," *American Political Science Review*, vol. 67 (December 1973), pp. 1213-34.

[20] The 1972-1976 "swing ratio" increased to 2.3 after a marked decline in the 1960s (1960-64=1.7; 1966-70=.7). The swing ratio, which is the estimated slope of the regression of votes and seats, indicates the responsiveness of the partisan division of legislative seats to changes in the partisan division of the general election vote. Of course, calculating the swing ratio from election triplets implies confidence in statistical comparisons based upon very small frequencies. As the graphic presentation in Figure 4-3 shows, the votes-seats relationship in the United States has produced a very tight linear fit over all postwar congressional elections. See Tufte, "Relationship Between Seats and Votes," p. 550.

[21] Charles S. Bullock, III, "Redistricting and Congressional Stability, 1962-72," *Journal of Politics*, vol. 37 (May 1975), pp. 569-75; Albert D. Cover, "One Good Term Deserves Another: The Advantage of Incumbency in Congressional Elections," *American Journal of Political Science*, vol. 21 (August 1977), pp. 528-31; John A. Ferejohn, "On the Decline of Competition in Congressional Elections," *American Political Science Review*, vol. 71 (March 1977), pp. 167-68.

Table 4-4
DECLINE IN THE COMPETITIVENESS ✓
OF HOUSE ELECTIONS, 1956–1976
(in percentages)

Year	Incumbents Winning 60% of the Vote or More	Districts with Margin of Victory of Less than Five Percentage Points
1956	59	20
1958	63	22
1960	59	*
1962	64	*
1964	59	*
1966	68	16
1968	72	14
1970	77	13
1972	78	*
1974	66	*
1976	70	8

* Not calculated.

Source: Albert D. Cover and David R. Mayhew, "Congressional Dynamics and the Decline of Competitive Congressional Elections," in Lawrence C. Dodd and Bruce I. Oppenheimer, eds., *Congress Reconsidered* (New York: Praeger, 1977), p. 55; Edward R. Tufte, "The Relationship between Seats and Votes in Two-Party Systems," *American Political Science Review*, vol. 67 (June 1973), p. 550; *Congressional Quarterly Weekly Report*, vol. 35 (March 19, 1977), pp. 491-98.

of safe seats since 1956, defining as safe those districts in which the incumbent won 60 percent or more of the vote. The table also shows, for selected congressional election years, the proportion of close contests—those in which the margin of victory was less than five percentage points. In 1976, 70 percent of the House incumbents running for reelection got at least 60 percent of the vote, and in only 8 percent of the districts was the victory margin less than five percentage points. In 1976, Senate races were more closely contested— only 42 percent of the Senate incumbents won 60 percent or more of the vote—but only 9 percent were "horse races" where the winner's margin was less than five percentage points. Most congressional races are contested (only 7 percent of House and 6 percent of Senate seats were uncontested in 1976), but in the 1970s contests with incumbents have been very one-sided and a declining percentage of races have been close.

The increase in the incumbency effect in congressional elections—the propensity of voters to reelect incumbents—and the concomitant decline in the competition of congressional contests appear to stem largely from changes in patterns of voting behavior. There is evidence that political party identification accounts for a declining proportion of the congressional election vote. [22] Since the mid-1960s there has been some increase in the proportion of Independents in the electorate. But more important, partisan cues for voting behavior appear to have become less important than they were for those who have a political party attachment of some kind. Defections from party in congressional voting have increased, even among "strong" party identifiers. As Figure 4–4 shows, these defections have significantly advantaged incumbents since 1966, and there has been an especially sharp increase in partisan defections among those voters who are identified with the political party of the congressional challenger. The spurt in defections to the congressional incumbent among voters identified with the challenger's party in 1972–1974 may have occurred as many dismayed Republicans voted for Democratic incumbents in reaction against the Nixon presidency and the Watergate affair.

But the evidence indicates a profounder weakening of partisan cues to congressional election voting, and a tendency for congressional elections to be more responsive to national forces (such as the state of the economy and the perceived performance of the President), although local forces continue to have a great impact on voting. [23] When partisan cues for voting are weakened, and when incumbent congressmen can effectively appeal to voters in terms of highly salient national political concerns, which they can capitalize on without being expected to resolve, the electoral advantage of incumbency can be enhanced.

---

[22] See Robert B. Arseneau and Raymond E. Wolfinger, "Voting Behavior in Congressional Elections," paper presented at the 1973 Annual Meeting of the American Political Science Association, New Orleans.

[23] Edward R. Tufte, "Determinants of the Outcomes of Midterm Congressional Elections," *American Political Science Review*, vol. 69 (September 1975), pp. 812-26; Francisco Arcelus and Allan H. Meltzer, "The Effect of Aggregate Economic Variables on Congressional Elections," *American Political Science Review*, vol. 69 (December 1975), pp. 1232-39; Howard S. Bloom and H. Douglas Price, "Voter Response to Short-Run Economic Conditions: The Asymmetric Effect of Prosperity and Recession," *American Political Science Review*, vol. 69 (December 1975), pp. 1240-54; Samuel Kernell, "Presidential Popularity and Negative Voting: An Alternative Explanation of the Midterm Congressional Decline of the President's Party," *American Political Science Review*, vol. 71 (March 1977), pp. 44-66.

Figure 4-4

PARTISAN DEFECTIONS IN CONGRESSIONAL VOTING,
1958–1974

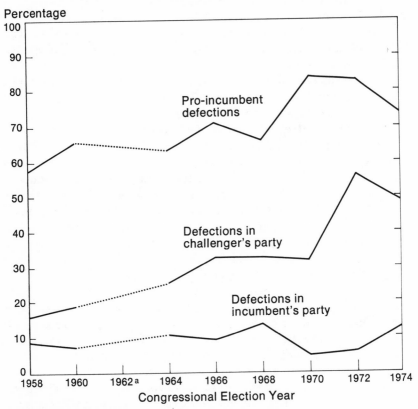

ᵃ Data not available.

Source: Albert D. Cover, "One Good Term Deserves Another: The Advantage of Incumbency in Congressional Elections," *American Journal of Political Science,* vol. 21 (August 1977), pp. 534–35.

Weakened partisanship in the electorate presumably increases the difficulty of mounting an effective challenge to incumbents in their districts. Congressmen can "run for Congress by running against Congress," or against the President, or in behalf of solutions to a host of national problems—solutions for which they cannot be held accountable as merely individual members of a collective body. Incumbents have acquired very handsome resources for use in their districts, and with these they present themselves as helping the district, as responsible for the distributive largesse of the national welfare state, and as struggling faithfully, if helplessly, against great national crises, evils, and policy problems. Accordingly, incumbency cues for voting may have become more important in voters' choices.

Servicing the Districts. There is no doubt that congressmen are in a far better position today to nurse their constituencies than they were twenty years ago. First, members are authorized a far larger number of trips to their districts or states, and they spend more time at home. In the early 1960s, House and Senate members were authorized to take three government-paid trips home annually. That number was doubled in 1966, and doubled again in 1968; in 1973, eighteen round trips were authorized; in 1976, House members were given twenty-six trips home, and senators more than forty; in 1977, the House authorization was increased to thirty-three round trips a year. Interviews with 219 House members indicated that in 1973 members went home an average of thirty-five times and, altogether, spent 38 percent of their time in their districts (nearly a third went home every weekend).[24]

Second, the traffic in mail between congressmen and their constituents has markedly increased. The House Commission on Administrative Review reported in 1977 that incoming mail to the House had grown threefold between 1971 and 1977 and that members were getting an average of 31,600 letters annually. The outgoing mail has increased dramatically as well. About 40 million pieces of franked mail were sent out by House and Senate members in 1954; by 1970 the amount had grown to about 200 million.[25] This change far exceeds the population growth: in 1954 about one in every four Americans could have gotten a letter from a member of Congress; in 1970, the mail averaged one letter for every American. As Figure 4–5 shows, the amount of franked congressional mail has climbed in the 1970s, stimulated by a new "constituent communication allowance" in the House permitting members to send two newsletters to constituents a year at congressional expense. The volume of franked mail is, as Figure 4–5 indicates, notably larger in election years than in nonelection years.

Third, members' staffs have increased substantially. In the early 1960s, a House member could have a staff of nine persons; now a staff of eighteen is authorized, with a total "clerk hire" allowance of $255,144. Senators' staffs have doubled since 1960; depending upon

---

[24] Richard F. Fenno, Jr., "U.S. House Members in Their Constituencies: An Exploration," *American Political Science Review*, vol. 71 (September 1977), p. 890.

[25] David R. Mayhew, "Congressional Elections: The Case of the Vanishing Marginals," *Polity*, vol. 6 (Fall 1974), pp. 295-317, reprinted in Robert L. Peabody and Nelson W. Polsby, eds., *New Perspectives on the House of Representatives*, 3rd ed. (Chicago: Rand McNally, 1977), p. 38.

Figure 4-5

HOUSE MEMBERS' USE OF THE FRANKING PRIVILEGE FOR
MAILINGS TO THEIR CONSTITUENTS, 1971–1974

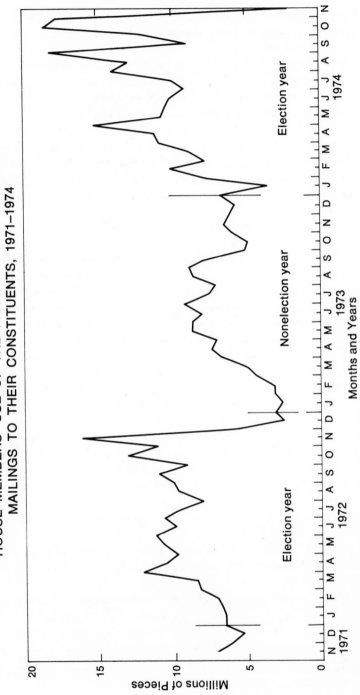

Source: Congressional Quarterly, *Inside Congress* (Washington, D.C., 1976), p. 29.

the populations of the states, senators are now authorized staff allowances ranging from $413,082 to $844,608. But probably more important than the growth in the size of congressional staffs is the burgeoning of district and state offices. Constituent service activities have increasingly been moved out of members' Washington offices and into offices in their districts. In 1960, 14 percent of House members' staffs were assigned to their district offices; this had grown to 26 percent in 1967, 34 percent in 1974, and 36 percent in 1977.[26] For the 95th Congress, House members averaged nearly two district offices each, and senators more than two state offices. In 1977, 16 percent of House members had assigned half or more of their staff to their district offices. Senators have established more than 300 branch offices in the states, staffed by more than 400 aides who dispense constituent services.[27]

Fourth, the volume of "casework" for constituents and constituency projects has expanded a great deal in the 1970s as the coverage of welfare laws and veterans' benefits has been enlarged and as federally funded projects in states and communities have proliferated. Although there is no systematic monitoring of this growth, the senators from the largest states, New York and California, now have casework loads ranging between 30,000 and 50,000 cases a year, and for about two-thirds of Senate offices this work has been transferred to the state offices. A study of Senate staff activity conducted in 1972 showed that two-thirds of the staff dealt with constituency projects once a day or more, and more than 40 percent of the Senate aides estimated that they handled casework more than once a day.[28]

Finally, candidates for Congress are spending more money in their election efforts. In 1976, the average sum spent by Democratic House candidates was $80,965, by Republican candidates $77,440. Senate Democratic candidates averaged $569,902 in campaign spending, Republicans $616,501. Although these are large average amounts, the average cost per vote for House candidacies was only $1.22; for Senate candidacies the cost per vote was $1.52. Moreover, campaign expenditures vary sizably from place to place. Senator William Proxmire (D.-Wis.) got 72 percent of the vote with a total expenditure of only $697. In contrast, Senator H. John Heinz III (R.-Pa.) spent

[26] Percentages for 1960, 1967, and 1974 are from Fiorina, *Congress: Keystone of the Washington Establishment*, p. 58. Figures for 1977 were calculated from the 1977 *Congressional Staff Directory*.
[27] U.S. Congress, Senate, Commission on the Operation of the Senate, "Constituent Service," by Janet Breslin in *Senators: Offices, Ethics, and Pressures*, Committee Print (Washington, D.C., 1977), p. 19.
[28] Harrison W. Fox, Jr. and Susan Webb Hammond, *Congressional Staffs* (New York: Free Press, 1977), p. 186.

$3 million. In the House races, half of all of the campaign money spent was expended by 10 percent of the candidates, and 43 percent of the candidates spent less than $15,000 each. At the other extreme, in California's 27th congressional district the Republican candidate who won spent $403,675 and the Democratic loser spent $637,080.[29]

In 1974 and 1976 Congress enacted new legislation regulating campaign spending. The main provisions of the new law limited spending in primary and general elections, limited contributions that could be made to campaigns, and required detailed reporting and disclosure of campaign financing. A Federal Election Commission was created to implement the new campaign regulations. There has been persistent controversy over the limitations and reporting requirements of the campaign law, and concern has been expressed about the presumed advantages conferred on incumbents by the law. In 1976, although House incumbents spent more than challengers and were overwhelmingly reelected, money and incumbency failed to tip the balance for the third of the Senate incumbents who were defeated. On the whole, campaign spending appears to add little to the already very substantial advantages of incumbency.[30]

The impact of the growth in constituency service activities is not easy to assess precisely. It has been demonstrated that the frequency with which House members travel to their districts and their allocation of staff resources to their districts are not correlated with the members' election margins; safe-seat congressmen do not differ significantly in these matters from those elected in marginal districts.[31] Increased constituency nursing has not brought about a change in the proportion of Americans who can recall the name of their congressman, and incumbents have no greater advantage in name visibility over challengers than was the case twenty years ago.[32] Nevertheless, it is

[29] Congressional Quarterly Weekly Report, vol. 35 (June 25, 1977), pp. 1291-94, and (October 29, 1977), pp. 2299-2311.

[30] On the effects of campaign spending and regulation, see Lawrence Shepard, "Does Campaign Spending Really Matter?" Public Opinion Quarterly, vol. 41 (Summer 1977), pp. 196-205; Gary W. Copeland and Samuel C. Patterson, "Reform of Congressional Campaign Spending," Policy Studies Journal, vol. 5 (Summer 1977), pp. 424-31; Gary C. Jacobson, "The Electoral Consequences of Public Subsidies for Congressional Campaigns," paper presented at the 1977 Annual Meeting of the American Political Science Association, Washington, D.C.; and Timothy A. Hodson and Roland D. McDevitt, "Congressional Campaign Finance: The Impact of Recent Federal Reforms," paper presented at the 1977 Annual Meeting of the American Political Science Association, Washington, D.C.

[31] Fenno, "U.S. House Members in Their Constituencies," pp. 890-97.

[32] Ferejohn, "On the Decline of Competition in Congressional Elections," p. 170; Corer and Mayhew, "Congressional Dynamics and the Decline of Competitive Congressional Elections," p. 67.

possible that an increased proportion of constituents are responding to incumbent congressmen *qua* incumbents, based more on voters' evaluation of members' constituency service performance than on their party or their policy-making activities in Washington.[33]

A Harris Survey conducted for the House Commission on Administrative Review in January 1977 provides some shreds of evidence about the impact of congressmen's contacts with constituents and their constituency service activities. Some of the results of this survey are given in Table 4–5. Half of the respondents could recall the name of their House member; 54 percent made favorable and only 13 percent made negative comments when they were asked to mention things their congressman "has done in office or what he (she) stands for." Although only 15 percent reported that they or a member of their family had directly requested help from their congressman, nearly 70 percent of those who had asked for help said they were satisfied with the help they received. Sixty-six percent reported having received mail from their congressman, and 68 percent said they had read about their congressman's activities in the press or heard about their member on television.

In addition, the survey showed that constituents evaluated their congressman quite positively, more so than Congress as a whole. Forty percent rated their own congressman as "excellent" or "pretty good" (38 percent said they were not sure about their member's performance), but only 22 percent rated Congress equally highly (and only 14 percent were not sure). There are no survey data that conclusively establish that increased constituency nursing has brought about wider salience for incumbents among their constituents, but some of the evidence is consistent with the claim that this has been the case.

Changes in Congressional Organization

The most acclaimed changes in Congress in recent years have been in the congressional organization itself. The organization's membership has changed, and its workload has greatly altered. These changes have not necessarily been inexorable, but they have not been so susceptible as organizational features have been to deliberate manipulation by Congress itself. Changes in the organizational mechanics of Congress—in the committee structure, the party leadership, and the staff—have aroused spirited congressional debate and precipitated

---

[33] This is Fiorina's argument in *Congress: Keystone of the Washington Establishment*.

Table 4-5

AMERICANS' ATTITUDES TOWARD CONGRESSMEN, 1977

Survey Item	Percentage
"Very" or "fairly" interested in the activities of Congress	58
Can recall congressman's name	50
Comments positively about congressman's activities or stands	54
Read newspaper story or heard television story about congressman	68
Received mail from congressman	66
Sent letter or telegram, or signed petition, to congressman	29
Met congressman or heard congressman speak at a public meeting	26
Respondent or family members requested assistance from member of Congress or staff	15
Contributed financially to candidate	11
Personally visited congressman	8
Campaigned for congressional candidate	7
Own congressman "excellent" or "pretty good"	40
Same as or better than other congressmen	63
Congress "excellent" or "pretty good"	22

Source: Based upon interviews in January 1977 with 1,510 respondents conducted by the Harris Survey for the U.S. House of Representatives' Commission on Administrative Review.

deliberate legislative reorganization. Moreover, Congress has made new attempts to cope with the burgeoning information technology of the 1970s.

Membership. In spite of the growing incumbency effect in congressional elections, the turnover of the membership has been substantial. The 1974 House election produced ninety-two new members, the second largest influx of freshmen congressmen since the early 1950s (second only to the slightly larger turnover resulting from the Democratic landslide of 1964). The 1976 senatorial elections resulted in the largest number of new senators in eighteen years. More than 55 percent of the House members of the 95th Congress had been elected in 1970 or thereafter; 36 percent were first- or second-term members. Since only a third of the senators are elected at each congressional election, straight comparisons with the House are not appropriate; but over the three elections in which most senators in the 95th Congress were chosen (1972, 1974, 1976), 41 percent have been freshmen. By any appropriate standard of comparison, congressional turnover is as high as or higher than the membership turnover of the parliaments of western Europe, Canada, and the United Kingdom.[34]

On the whole, the recent turnover of the House and Senate memberships has been at the expense of the Republicans; even senior, incumbent Republicans have often not fared successfully at the polls in recent years.[35] Although a high proportion of incumbents win any given election, a substantial percentage of incumbents lose over a period of time. For instance, of the House members elected in 1972 who had first won a House seat in or after 1954, 36 percent entered by defeating an incumbent.[36] The fact that a few incumbents do lose is sufficient to remind congressmen that electoral defeat is a real possibility, and members running in what objectively appear to be safe districts often run scared. In addition to turnover produced by the defeat of incumbents or their death, there has been a steady growth since the mid-1960s in the proportion of members of Congress, especially House members, who have retired or left their seats to run for other offices (see Figure 4–6). Eight senators retired in 1976. By May 1978, ten senators and forty-two representatives had announced they would not seek reelection in the November congressional election.

On the whole, the composition of Congress has not changed in the social or personal characteristics of members. However, there has been some "younging" of both House and Senate. The average age of members of the 95th Congress was 49.3 for the House members and 54.7 for senators, making it the youngest Congress in a long time.

A more notable change has been the fairly long-term decline in the proportion of southerners among congressional Democrats, a

---

[34] Loewenberg and Patterson, *Comparing Legislatures;* Jean Blondel, *Comparative Legislatures* (Englewood Cliffs, N.J.: Prentice-Hall, 1973), pp. 87, 160.

[35] Charles S. Bullock III, "House Careerists: Changing Patterns of Longevity and Attrition," *American Political Science Review,* vol. 66 (December 1972), pp. 1295-1300.

[36] Robert S. Erikson, "Is There Such a Thing as a Safe Seat?" *Polity,* vol. 8 (Summer 1976), p. 66. A safe seat in one election may, in fact, be an electorally insecure seat. Fifty-eight percent of the House members of the 93rd Congress had at least once won a general election with less than 55 percent of the vote, and this was true for 70 percent of the senators in the 93rd Congress. See David R. Mayhew, *Congress: The Electoral Connection,* p. 33.

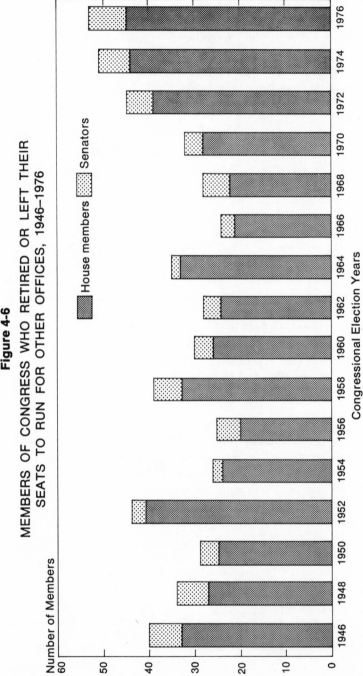

Figure 4-6

MEMBERS OF CONGRESS WHO RETIRED OR LEFT THEIR
SEATS TO RUN FOR OTHER OFFICES, 1946–1976

Source: *Congressional Quarterly Weekly Report*, vol. 34 (April 24, 1976), p. 1003.

trend shown in Figure 4–7. Less than a third of the Democrats are southerners now, compared to more than half in the 1950s. The number of southern congressional seats has declined, and the proportion of southerners among Republicans has increased some. Accordingly, southern representation in the positions of seniority leadership in Congress has declined very sharply. From the 1920s to the 1940s, about three-fourths of the Democratic seniority leaders in the House were southerners; in the 1950s and 1960s this proportion had declined to about two-thirds; by the early 1970s, somewhat more than two-fifths were southerners. By the 95th Congress, only slightly over one-fifth (23 percent) of the seniority leadership was southern. Moreover, of the five southern standing committee chairmen in the 95th Congress (out of a total of twenty-two committees), three were from Texas and one from Kentucky; only one chairman was from a Deep

Figure 4-7

PROPORTION OF SOUTHERNERS AMONG CONGRESSIONAL DEMOCRATS, 1947–1977

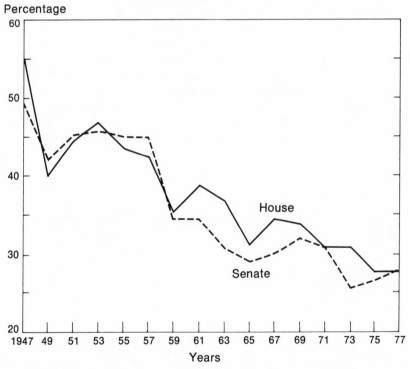

Source: Norman J. Ornstein, ed., *Congress in Change* (New York: Praeger, 1975), p. 74; *Statistical Abstract of the United States*, 1977, p. 462.

South state (the Georgian John R. Flynt, Jr., chairman of the Committee on Standards of Official Conduct).[37] In the Senate, southerners have fared better than in the House in terms of sheer numbers (holding a third of the standing committee chairmanships in the 95th Congress), largely because the Senate's composition has not been much affected by the demographic changes that have shaped the membership of the House. Moreover, these powerful Senate committees are chaired by southerners: Agriculture, Armed Services, Finance, Foreign Relations, and Judiciary. But the average age of these five Senate chairmen is seventy-one, and the workings of seniority will almost certainly elevate northern Democrats to every one of these chairmanships when their incumbents are no longer serving in the Senate.

As a consequence of membership changes, recent Congresses, especially the 94th and 95th, have contained a large number of Democrats, particularly from the North, the Midwest, and the West, and a high proportion under forty years old. Along with these changes in the membership has gone a marked ideological shift, so that both the House and Senate are substantially more liberal than they were in the late 1950s and early 1960s, and in the House, at least, there are many more liberal southern Democrats.[38] Finally, an important membership change has been the increasing number of women and black members. Eighteen women served in the 95th Congress, all in the House, a decline of one woman member from the record high of nineteen in the 94th Congress. Seventeen blacks were members of the 94th and 95th Congresses, sixteen in the House and one in the Senate (Senator Edward Brooke, R.-Mass.).

The Pressures of Work. The workload of Congress has steadily increased, and there has been especially dramatic growth in congressional work since the 1960s. As Figure 4–8 shows, the extent of floor sessions and committee or subcommittee meetings has escalated. This growth is particularly telling in the House, where the number of committee and subcommittee meetings doubled between the 84th and 94th Congresses. Since Congress has not grown in membership, this means that members are much more heavily burdened in their performance of legislative work. In addition, members serve on more

---

[37] Davidson and Oleszek, *Congress Against Itself*, p. 41.
[38] See Norman J. Ornstein, Robert L. Peabody, and David W. Rohde, "The Changing Senate: From the 1950s to the 1970s" and Lawrence C. Dodd and Bruce I. Oppenheimer, "The House in Transition," in Dodd and Oppenheimer, eds., *Congress Reconsidered*, pp. 3-53.

Figure 4-8

INCREASES IN CONGRESSIONAL ACTIVITY, 1955–1976

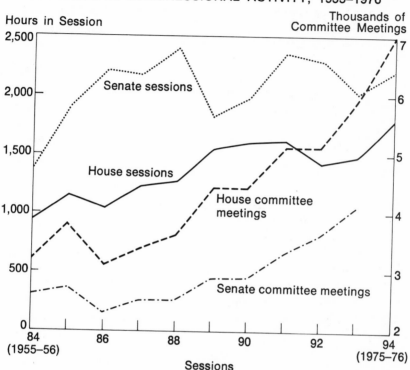

Source: U.S. Congress, House, Commission on Administrative Review, *Administrative Reorganization and Legislative Management,* vol. 1, H. Doc. 95–232, 95th Cong., 1st sess., 1977, p. 4; U.S. Congress, Senate, Commission on the Operation of the Senate, *Policy Analysis on Major Issues* (Washington, D.C., 1977), p. 6.

committees and subcommittees. In the 95th Congress, 347 House members had two or more committee assignments, and 257 members had four or more subcommittee assignments. In the 94th Congress, the average senator served on four committees and fourteen subcommittees. Consequently, overburdened work schedules and a morass of conflicting meeting times have been a mounting congressional problem.

Both houses have attempted to alleviate the work pressures on members by establishing special commissions to recommend improvements in work scheduling. The House Commission on Administrative Review (the Obey Commission, so called after its chairman, David R. Obey, D.-Wis.), established during the 94th Congress, and the Com-

159

mission on the Operation of the Senate, created in 1975, conducted thorough studies of House and Senate operations. Both commissions found that members worked an eleven-hour day on the average, that they were required to engage in too many legislative activities because of their multiple committee assignments, and that work schedules had become overly demanding and filled with conflicting obligations. Both commissions agreed that members' days had become "long, fragmented, and unpredictable." Both made recommendations for changes in the scheduling of legislative work and in administrative practices, and quite a few of these recommendations were adopted. But fundamentally the congressional problem of coping with accelerating demands for policies and services lay in the hands of its committees and staffs.

Congressional Committees. The most striking feature of congressional organization is decentralization, and congressional government by subcommittee has grown in the 1970s. Table 4–6 shows the growth in the number of subcommittees in selected years since 1945. In the 95th Congress, the House had 29 committees (22 standing and 7 select) with 149 subcommittees. Persistent efforts have been made to streamline the House committee structure since the passage of the Legislative Reorganization Act of 1946. A Select Committee on Com-

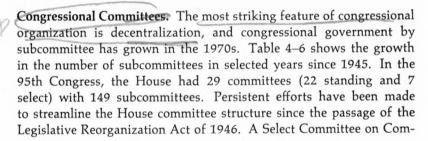

Table 4-6
CONGRESSIONAL SUBCOMMITTEES, 1945–1977

| Year | Number of Subcommittees of | | | |
	House committees	Senate committees	Joint committees	Total Number of Subcommittees
1945	106	68	6	180
1959	121	100	8	229
1961	131	109	13	253
1968	139	104	15	258
1970	138	104	15	257
1975	146	139	14	299
1977	149	113	5	267

Source: Malcolm E. Jewell and Samuel C. Patterson, *The Legislative Process in the United States,* 3rd ed. (New York: Random House, 1977), p. 39; *Congressional Staff Directory,* 1977.

mittees (called the Bolling Committee after its chairman, Richard Bolling, D.-Mo.) was created in 1973, and it proposed a thorough modernization of House committees. However, its proposals were not supported in the Democratic party caucus when they were considered in 1974.[39] Instead, the Democratic House majority adopted committee proposals formulated by its own caucus Committee on Organization, Study, and Review, chaired by Julia Butler Hansen (D.-Wash.). The result was the Committee Reform Amendments of 1974, which further dispersed committee power to the House subcommittees.[40]

The Senate of the 94th Congress had 24 committees with 139 subcommittees. Former Senate Majority Leader Mike Mansfield (D.-Mont.) once observed, "This body is getting subcommittee-happy." In 1976, the Senate established a temporary Select Committee to Study the Senate Committee System, chaired by Adlai E. Stevenson III (D.-Ill.). Late in that year, the reform committee issued recommendations for a sweeping overhaul of the Senate committee system. These proposals were greatly modified by the Senate Committee on Rules and Administration and on the Senate floor, but in February 1977 the Senate adopted a resolution providing for extensive committee changes. The major changes involved reducing the number of committees and revising committee jurisdictions so that work on major new legislative responsibilities could be more effectively concentrated. Most committees were left intact, and some were renamed, but major jurisdictional changes were made in order to recreate the old Interior and Insular Affairs Committee as the new Committee on Energy and Natural Resources with control over most energy matters. The reform resolution also prohibited full committees from creating subcommittees without the approval of the full Senate.

The new Senate committee arrangements have reduced policy fragmentation in that body some, but the problem remains in the House. In the first five months of the 95th Congress, 1,956 measures were referred to more than one committee. The policy fragmentation of the House committee system is poignantly illustrated by the committee referrals of energy and health bills, shown in Table 4–7. Energy bills are especially widely dispersed across the committee structure. Nineteen committees handled energy bills, and although a

---

[39] For a very perceptive insiders' analysis of the Bolling Committee's work and its fate, see Davidson and Oleszek, *Congress Against Itself.*

[40] An analysis of the work of the Hansen Committee from 1970 to 1973 is in Norman J. Ornstein, "Causes and Consequences of Congressional Change: Subcommittee Reforms in the House of Representatives, 1970-73," in Ornstein, ed., *Congress in Change,* pp. 88-114.

161

Table 4-7

ENERGY AND HEALTH BILLS REFERRED TO HOUSE
COMMITTEES IN THE FIRST FIVE
MONTHS OF THE 95TH CONGRESS
(in percentages)

Committee Referred to	Energy Bills	Health Bills
Agriculture	4	2
Appropriations	1	1
Armed Services	1	1
Banking, Finance, and Urban Affairs	9	1
Education and Labor	3	—
Government Operations	3	10
House Administration	1	1
Interior and Insular Affairs	10	1
International Relations	8	1
Interstate and Foreign Commerce	27	45
Judiciary	4	3
Merchant Marine and Fisheries	5	1
Post Office and Civil Service	1	2
Public Works and Transportation	9	1
Rules	1	1
Science and Technology	9	—
Small Business	3	—
Veterans' Affairs	—	2
Ways and Means	2	28
Total	100	100

Source: U.S. Congress, House, Commission on Administrative Review, *Administrative Reorganization and Legislative Management*, vol. 2, H. Doc. 95-232, 95th Cong., 1st sess., 1977, p. 33.

plurality were referred to the Committee on Interstate and Foreign Commerce, five other committees each considered 8–10 percent of the energy bills. Health legislation was more concentrated, with Interstate and Foreign Commerce and the Committee on Ways and Means dealing with most of the bills, but fourteen other committees handled some health legislation.

When the House got President Carter's energy legislation in early 1977 something had to be done to coordinate the handling of this complex package. Speaker O'Neill got House approval to establish an ad hoc subcommittee on energy which could provide comprehensive consideration of this major policy area in addition to its separate consideration by the standing committees. More recently, consideration was begun in November 1977 of the President's omnibus welfare reform bill by a twenty-nine-member ad hoc subcommittee drawn from the memberships of the committees on Agriculture, Education and Labor, and Ways and Means. These temporary arrangements are symptomatic of House committee fragmentation and indicate the difficulties the House has in attempting to come to grips with major policy questions that cut across the dispersive power structure of subcommittee governments.

Committee work has not only proliferated; it has also become more public. In 1973, the House adopted a resolution requiring most committee meetings to be open to the public and the press. Two years later the Senate adopted a similar rule, and both houses approved open meetings of joint House-Senate conference committees. As Figure 4–9 shows, the proportion of closed meetings had already declined before these "sunshine" resolutions were adopted, particularly after House Appropriations subcommittee sessions were opened to the public in 1971.

Congressional Staffs. Twenty years ago, only a few hundred staff people worked on the Hill. Today, they are counted in the thousands. The Capitol and the House and Senate offices are literally overflowing with staff. So abundant have staff resources become that a study for the House Commission on Administrative Review reported in 1977 that "approximately three more office buildings similar to the existing buildings would be required before the facilities of the House would approach those of the executive branch."[41]

The growth of congressional staffing for the last thirty years is depicted in Figure 4–10. The rate of growth of House members' personal staffs has been particularly sharp. As was noted earlier, a considerable proportion of these staff people are in the members' districts, mainly performing constituent service tasks. The most important single source of growth for the personal office staffs of senators has been the addition of legislative assistants. Major increases

---

[41] U.S. Congress, House, Commission on Administrative Review, *Administrative Reorganization and Legislative Management*, vol. 2, H. Doc. 95-232, 95th Cong., 1st sess., 1977, p. 127.

Figure 4-9

DECLINE IN CLOSED CONGRESSIONAL COMMITTEE MEETINGS, 1965–1975

Percent of Committee Meetings Closed

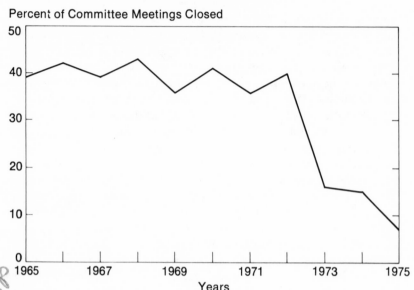

Years

Source: *Congressional Quarterly Weekly Report*, vol. 34 (January 24, 1976), p. 152

have occurred in both professional and specifically investigative staffs of committees. The relatively large influx of new staff people since the mid-1960s has brought a substantial number of young people to work on the Hill, many serving in very influential policy positions.[42] Members' staffs are denoted by their loyalty to the congressman or senator; committee staffs operate in a more closeted environment, constrained by norms of specialization, anonymity, and limited partisanship.[43]

Increased congressional staffing has had at least three important consequences. (1) it has heightened the need for managerial skills on the part of representatives and senators, a growing proportion of whom are now required to be managers in a bureaucratic sense; (2) it has greatly enlarged the presence of members in their districts or states; and (3) it has contributed to the fragmentation of the

[42] For a good recent analysis, see Fox and Hammond, *Congressional Staffs*.
[43] See Samuel C. Patterson, "The Professional Staffs of Congressional Committees," *Administrative Science Quarterly*, vol. 15 (March 1970), pp. 22-37.

Figure 4-10
GROWTH OF CONGRESSIONAL STAFFS, 1947–1977

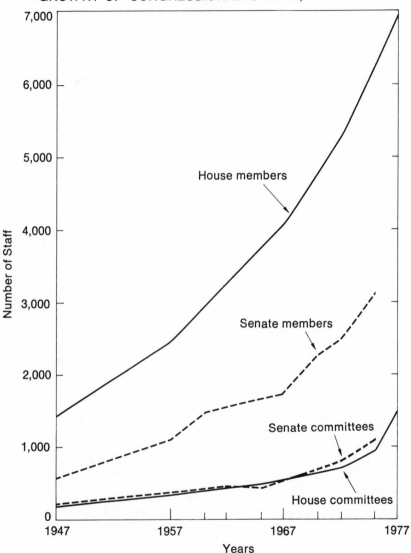

Source: U.S. Congress, House, Commission on Administrative Review, *Administrative Reorganization and Legislative Management,* vol. 2, H. Doc. 92–232, 95th Cong., 1st sess., 1977, p. 3; U.S. Congress, Senate, Commission on the Operation of the Senate, *Senators: Offices, Ethics, and Pressures* (Washington, D.C., 1977), p. 6; Harrison W. Fox, Jr. and Susan W. Hammond, "The Growth of Congressional Staffs," in Harvey C. Mansfield, Sr., ed., *Congress Against the President* (New York: Praeger, 1975), p. 115.

congressional policy process by strengthening committees, and especially subcommittees. Twenty years ago there was a crying need for increases in staff assistance to congressmen. Today, concern about the consequences of burgeoning staffs is more often expressed. The House Commission on Administrative Review concluded that "Committee staffs have grown and tended to become entrenched. As a consequence, committee staffs often appear, at least to some Members, to be more concerned about the power interests of their committees than about what is good for the House." Moreover, the Obey Commission concluded that "there has been increasing concern that Members are becoming too dependent on a permanent bureaucracy of staff aides, particularly committee staff aides, who by virtue of their tenure and expertise 'control' policy decisions." [44]

In addition to the staffs of members and committees, four support agencies assist in the work of the Congress. The Congressional Research Service, an arm of the Library of Congress, provides wide-ranging research services for congressmen and committees. In 1977 it had more than 800 employees. The General Accounting Office, in addition to performing a range of auditing assignments, supplies reviews of the economy, efficiency, and effectiveness of government programs to Congress; more than a third of the work of the GAO staff now responds to direct requests from congressmen and committees. In 1977 its staff exceeded 5,000 people. The Office of Technology Assessment provides policy analysis for Congress on subjects having to do with science and technology; OTA is authorized to have 130 employees in 1978. Finally, the Congressional Budget Office, with a staff of about 200, furnishes fiscal and economic research for Congress and is intended to work in tandem with the new House and Senate Budget Committees. Since 1970, the CRS and GAO have been given a larger role in providing research and policy analysis for Congress. The OTA opened for business in 1973, and the CBO was created by the Congressional Budget and Impoundment Control Act of 1974.[45] These support agencies provide a very impressive "policy analysis" capability for the Congress; whether congressional

---

[44] U.S. Congress, House, Commission on Administrative Review, *Administrative Reorganization and Legislative Management*, vol. 2, H. Doc. 95-232, 95th Cong., 1st sess., 1977, p. 59. Also, see Michael J. Malbin, "Congressional Committee Staffs: Who's in Charge Here?" *Public Interest*, no. 47 (Spring 1977), pp. 16-40.

[45] A thorough evaluation of these support agencies was prepared for the Commission on the Operation of the Senate. See U.S. Congress, Senate, Commission on the Operation of the Senate, *Congressional Support Agencies*, Committee Print, 94th Cong., 2d sess., 1976.

leaders and committees can use policy analysis effectively is another question.[46]

Allied to the growth of congressional staffing has been the development of computerized information systems for Congress. In the "technetronic era" Congress has, however reluctantly, coped with the massive inflation of information by establishing computer facilities for the use of members and committees.[47] The most substantial is the House Information System staff of more than 200 members created by the House Administration Committee.[48] In 1977 about 250 House offices were equipped with remote computer terminals through HIS, and 97 of the 100 Senate offices had terminals linking them either to the Library of Congress computer or to various private data banks.[49]

Leadership. Leadership changes in Congress surely are observable, although their effects are not always easy to assess. Two elemental facts about congressional leadership are clear. First, committee leadership has been diffused. The adulteration of the seniority rule for the selection of committee and subcommittee chairmen and the increased autonomy of subcommittees have diluted the position of full committee chairmen and enlarged the sheer number of committee leaders. In the 95th Congress, very nearly half the House Democrats chair a committee or subcommittee, and three-quarters of the House Republicans are ranking members of a committee or subcommittee. Committee leadership is widely dispersed in the Senate as well, and junior senators frequently get leadership assignments. Of the ten new Senate Democrats in the 95th Congress, seven were made subcommittee chairmen forthwith; and all eight of the new Republicans were ranking minority members of at least one subcommittee.

Second, the party leadership of Congress has been at least somewhat strengthened, most notably in the House. Speaker O'Neill is a much more vigorous leader than his predecessor, Speaker Albert.[50]

---

[46] See Allen Schick, "The Supply and Demand for Analysis on Capitol Hill," and Roger H. Davidson, "Congressional Committees: The Toughest Customers," *Policy Analysis*, vol. 2 (Spring 1976), pp. 215-34, 299-323.

[47] The term "technetronic era" refers to the age of technology and electronics. See Zbigniew Brzezinski, *Between Two Ages: America's Role in the Technetronic Era* (New York: Viking Press, 1970).

[48] U.S. Congress, House, House Administration Committee, *Computer-Based Information Resources for the United States House of Representatives*, Committee Print, 94th Cong., 1st sess., 1975.

[49] *Congressional Quarterly Weekly Report*, vol. 35 (May 28, 1977), pp. 1045-51.

[50] For an excellent analysis of leadership changes in the House and Senate from 1955 to 1974, see Peabody, *Leadership in Congress*.

The House Rules Committee, a vital gatekeeper in the legislative process, has shifted from an obstacle to the party leaders to an arm of the leadership, largely because of the changed composition of the committee and a change in its chairman.[51] In 1975 the House Democratic caucus transferred the authority to appoint members of committees from the Democratic members of the Committee on Ways and Means to the Democratic Steering and Policy Committee, a caucus committee chaired by the speaker; and changes in the House rules have given the speaker more control over legislation, especially in strengthening his control over the referral of bills to committees. Observation of the first year's performance of the new House leadership "supports the impression that the new House Democratic leadership team—Speaker O'Neill, Majority Leader Wright, Majority Whip Brademas, Chief Deputy Whip Rostenkowski and Caucus Chairman Foley—is the strongest the House has experienced since the heyday of Speaker Sam Rayburn." [52]

With the selection of Senator Byrd as Democratic leader, party leadership in the Senate has undergone some change. In particular, Byrd is a more vigorous leader than his low-keyed predecessor, Mike Mansfield (although the change from Mansfield to Byrd is modest compared to the very great contrast in leadership between Majority Leader Lyndon B. Johnson and Mansfield, his successor).[53] The Senate of the 1970s is less amenable to forceful policy leadership than was the Senate of the 1950s. It seems a correct assessment of contemporary Senate leadership to say that

> Today's leaders are housekeepers, tending more to the scheduling than to the substance of legislation. They work to maintain a steady flow of Senate business and to protect the procedural rights of Members—important tasks for a collegial body. As the leadership has concentrated on caretaker activities, it has lost much of its partisan stripe.[54]

There can be little doubt that the more aggressive leadership in the houses of the 95th Congress enhanced the legislative fortunes of the new Democratic President. But the tensions in congressional leader-

---

[51] See Spark M. Matsunaga and Ping Chen, *Rulemakers of the House* (Urbana: University of Illinois Press, 1976), esp. pp. 95-118.

[52] Bruce I. Oppenheimer and Robert L. Peabody, "The House Majority Leadership Contest, 1976," paper presented at the 1977 Annual Meeting of the American Political Science Association, Washington, D.C., p. 78.

[53] See Peabody, *Leadership in Congress*, pp. 321-57.

[54] Allen Schick, "Complex Policymaking in the United States Senate," in U.S. Congress, Senate, Commission on the Operation of the Senate, *Policy Analysis on Major Issues*, Committee Print, 94th Cong., 2d sess., 1977, p. 19.

ship which arise from the fragmenting forces of dispersed committee leadership and the coordinating forces of strengthened party leadership make it difficult to get congressional work done expeditiously or to achieve smooth legislative-executive relations even wnen a Democrat is in the White House.

Decision-Making Change

Decision-making changes have manifested themselves in Congress in changes in voting patterns and in modifications of processes related to the decisional autonomy of the two houses of Congress. Structurally, the proliferation of subcommittees has meant an enlargement in the number of decisional units in the House and Senate, and this structural fragmentation probably is, in general terms, the most important change in congressional decision making. As it has been said, "it is not easy for a feudal system to make national policy."[55] At the same time, the strengthening of subcommittee government, and particularly the enhancement of committee staffing, have contributed to the independence and autonomy of Congress, especially in its relations with the executive branch.

Voting Patterns. Congressional voting behavior has been abundantly studied, largely because roll-call votes have supplied grist for the analytical mills of many students of Congress.[56] Analyses of congressional voting over a period of time indicate great continuity in voting patterns, which persist irrespective of changes in the composition of the membership.[57] Nevertheless, some aggregate patterns exhibit interesting fluctuations. One is in the pattern of party voting, which is displayed in Figure 4–11. In both houses, party voting levels increased in the 1950s, declined in the 1960s, and have been increasing slowly but regularly since 1970. In some part, the recent increases in party voting are attributable to the growing partisan activity of the party caucuses, notably in the House. But more of the increase in party voting can be attributed to the increasing, ideologically liberal

[55] Ralph K. Huitt, "Congress, the Durable Partner," in Ralph K. Huitt and Robert L. Peabody, *Congress: Two Decades of Analysis* (New York: Harper & Row, 1969), p. 229.

[56] A useful recent contribution which contains a thorough bibliography is Joseph Cooper, David W. Brady, and Patricia A. Hurley, "The Electoral Basis of Party Voting: Patterns and Trends in the U.S. House of Representatives, 1887-1969," in Louis Maisel and Joseph Cooper, eds., *The Impact of the Electoral Process* (Beverly Hills, Calif.: Sage Publications, 1977), pp. 133-65.

[57] Aage R. Clausen, *How Congressmen Decide: A Policy Focus* (New York: St. Martin's, 1973).

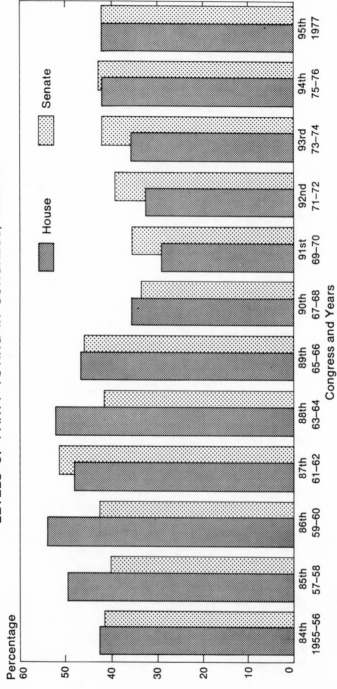

Figure 4-11

LEVELS OF PARTY VOTING IN CONGRESS, 1955–1977

Source: Malcolm E. Jewell and Samuel C. Patterson, *The Legislative Process in the United States* (New York: Random House, 1977), p. 390; *Congressional Quarterly Weekly Report*, vol. 34 (November 13, 1976), pp. 3173–74 and vol. 36 (January 14, 1978), p. 79.

homogeneity of congressional Democrats and to the growing galvani-
zation of Democratic opposition to Republican Presidents Nixon and
Ford in the early 1970s.

That congressional voting persistently reflects cross-party coalition building is indicated by the continued appearance of the so-called
conservative coalition in voting on a significant proportion of issues,
especially those having to do with civil rights and social welfare. The
conservative coalition is said to exist when a majority of the southern
Democrats vote together with a majority of Republicans *against* a
majority of northern Democrats. Figure 4–12 shows the extent to
which the coalition appeared in the 1960s and 1970s. Although this
cross-party coalition continues to appear in congressional voting
roughly a quarter of the time, it can be seen that its success rate has
declined noticeably since the Nixon-Ford years.

Although all Presidents have a way of losing congressional
support as time goes on, congressional support for the issue positions
taken by the President has been especially low in the 1970s. Figure
4–13 shows these changes in presidential support in Congress since
the 1950s. Although all Presidents since the 1950s have gotten congressional approval of at least half of the measures on which they
took a position, specific presidential requests have not fared so well.
Of the last five presidents (Eisenhower through Ford), only Lyndon
Johnson had a "batting average" with Congress above 50 percent for
his specific legislative proposals, and his success was most prominent
during the 89th Congress when two-thirds of his Great Society
proposals were adopted. Presidents Nixon and Ford, facing a large
Democratic opposition in Congress, succeeded in getting Congress to
enact only about a third of their legislative proposals. American
Presidents generally do not get a very good reception in Congress for
their legislative programs. In most other countries, a legislative record
as poor as that of the American President would precipitate a government crisis and general elections; in the United States, with its legislative body very much independent of the executive, this state of affairs
is normal.

Decisional Autonomy. Since the mid-1960s, Congress has strengthened its autonomy as a legislative institution in a variety of ways.
The pace of congressional oversight of executive agencies has quickened markedly, especially in the House. House committees have
increased the time they spend in oversight activities from 39 percent
in the 91st Congress (1969–1970) to 54 percent in the 94th Congress

171

Figure 4-12

THE CONSERVATIVE COALITION IN
HOUSE AND SENATE ROLL CALLS, 1959–1977

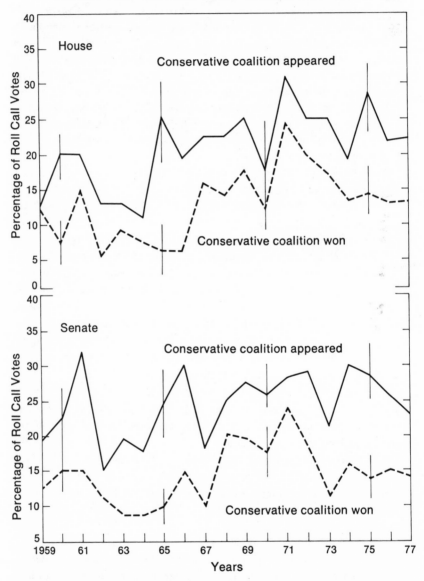

Source: Malcolm E. Jewell and Samuel C. Patterson, *The Legislative Process in the United States* (New York: Random House, 1977), p. 393; Congressional Quarterly, *Congressional Quarterly Almanac,* vols. 31 and 32; *Congressional Quarterly Weekly Report,* vol. 36 (January 7, 1978), pp. 4–5.

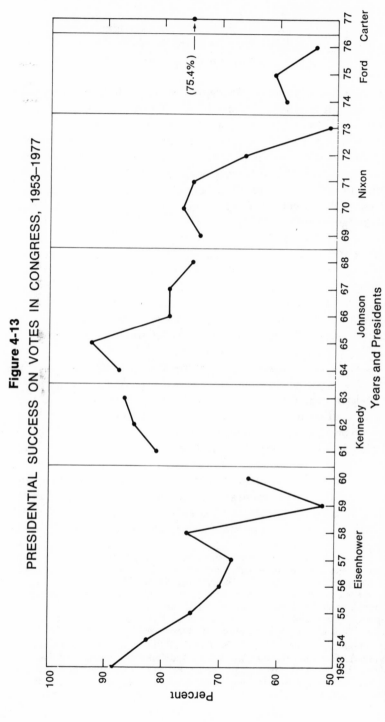

Figure 4-13

PRESIDENTIAL SUCCESS ON VOTES IN CONGRESS, 1953–1977

Source: Randall B. Ripley, *Congress: Process and Policy*, 2d ed. (New York: W.W. Norton, forthcoming); *Congressional Quarterly Weekly Report*, vol. 36 (January 21, 1978), p. 116.

(1975–1976).[58] The growth in the number of oversight subcommittees and investigative staffs, partly stimulated by mounting congressional hostility to the Nixon administration, accounts for this expanding oversight activity.

Congress sought a larger degree of control over the federal budget when it enacted the Congressional Budget and Impoundment Control Act of 1974. The act placed limitations on the ability of the President to interdict the expenditure of appropriated funds and expanded the scope of participation in the congressional budget process. New Budget Committees were established in the House and Senate, and the Congressional Budget Office was created to provide Congress with budget information and analysis. The new congressional budget process permits greater control over appropriations, budgetary priorities, and fiscal policy.[59]

Under the new budget procedures, Congress can impose a ceiling on budget authority and outlays and set a floor under receipts through the adoption of "budget resolutions." The House and Senate Budget Committees, supported by their own staffs and the Congressional Budget Office, are required to report two concurrent budget resolutions each year. The first resolution is a tentative budget setting targets for expenditures and receipts and the size of the public debt. These targets serve as guidelines for the appropriations and revenue committees in each house but are not binding. After the appropriations and tax committees have finished their detailed work and their bills are reported to their respective houses, Congress is required to take a second look at the overall budget totals. A second budget resolution is adopted which confirms or revises the targets initially set and reconciles changes required by the actions taken in the appropriations process. This second resolution provides binding spending ceilings for major program categories and minimums for tax receipts, although it is subject to later amendment.

This reformed congressional budget process is too new to permit

---

[58] Joel D. Aberbach, "The Development of Oversight in the United States Congress: Concepts and Analysis," paper presented at the 1977 Annual Meeting of the American Political Science Association, Washington, D.C., p. 26. For the development of oversight activities prior to the 91st Congress, see Lawrence C. Dodd and George C. Shipley, "Patterns of Committee Surveillance in the House of Representatives, 1947-70," paper presented at the 1975 Annual Meeting of the American Political Science Association, San Francisco.

[59] For details, see Allen Schick, "The Battle of the Budget," in Mansfield, ed., *Congress Against the President*, pp. 51-70; and John W. Ellwood and James A. Thurber, "The New Congressional Budget Process: The Hows and Whys of House-Senate Differences," in Dodd and Oppenheimer, eds., *Congress Reconsidered*, pp. 163-92.

firm evaluation of its success. It ran its full course for the first time for the 1977 budget. President Ford had recommended a budget for fiscal year 1977 totaling $394.2 billion; the second budget resolution passed by Congress provided $413.1 billion. When President Carter assumed office, he recommended an "economic stimulus package" to Congress which required additional federal spending. Congress quickly accommodated the President's wishes by passing a third budget resolution raising the ceiling from $413.1 to $417.5 billion. When President Carter later decided to withdraw his tax rebate proposal, yet another adjustment in congressional budgetary authorization was required; a Democratic Congress somewhat less cooperatively approved what amounted to a fourth budget resolution lowering the spending ceiling to $409.2 billion. The fact that the budget resolutions can be so easily amended in order to accommodate vacillations in economic conditions, erroneous guesses of budgetary needs, or changes in presidential preferences makes the new procedures rather blunt instruments of congressional control of the budget. Nevertheless, they do permit Congress to consider taxing and spending as a whole, rather than in bits and pieces as under the previous procedures.

 Finally, Congress has become much more active in the realm of foreign policy. The War Powers Act of 1973, enacted despite the President's veto, established congressional review powers regarding the commitment by the President of U.S. armed forces abroad. The Executive Agreements Act of 1972 requires the President to transmit international agreements other than treaties to Congress so that it is informed about such commitments. Congressional oversight of intelligence activities, once sacred cows, has expanded, and congressional activism in foreign policy has generally accelerated. The executive-legislative consensus on foreign policy that was exemplified in such post-World War II policies as the Truman Doctrine, American participation in the United Nations, the Marshall Plan, and the more recent Gulf of Tonkin Resolution has largely evaporated, and Congress has become more an adversary than an ally of the President in the fields of national security and foreign affairs. The device of the "legislative veto"—which permits Congress to override actions of the President—has been included in foreign policy legislation in the 1970s much more frequently than before as a way to assure congressional involvement in foreign policy implementation.[60]

---

[60] See U.S. Congress, House, Committee on International Relations, *Congress and Foreign Policy—1976*, Committee Print (Washington, D.C., 1977). Also see Fred Kaiser, "Oversight of Foreign Policy: The U.S. House Committee on International Relations," *Legislative Studies Quarterly*, vol. 2 (August 1977), pp. 255-79.

Conclusion

It is an open question whether Henry Clay would find the Congress of the 1970s an improvement over the Congress in which he served. But there is reason to believe that he would be impressed. While retaining its basic shape and form, Congress has adapted itself in many important ways to the demands of a changing society. Thirty years ago, the architect of the Legislative Reorganization Act of 1946 wrote:

> Congress lacks adequate information and inspection facilities. Its internal structure is dispersive and duplicating. It is a body without a head. Leadership is scattered among the chairmen of 81 little legislatures who compete with each other for jurisdiction and power. Its supervision of executive performance is superficial. Much of its time is consumed by petty local and private matters which divert its attention from national policy-making. Elected by the people to protect the public interest, it yields too often to the importunities of lobbyists for special-interest groups. It lacks machinery for developing coherent legislative programs and for promoting party responsibility and accountability. Its posts of power are held on the basis of political age, regardless of ability or agreement with party policies. And its members are overworked and underpaid—the forgotten men of social security.[61]

Congress has acquired impressive staffs and information processing facilities; improvements have been made in its system of committees; oversight of the executive has expanded measurably; because of the growth in the scope and immediacy of national policy issues and the professionalization of its membership, far less of its time is spent on merely parochial issues; mainly on account of its extensive and expert staffs, it is substantially more impervious to special-interest pressure; seniority is no longer an automatic guarantee of committee power; and certainly its members are not underpaid (a 1977 increase raised members' pay to $57,500 a year).

Congress has great political power and an enormous capacity to frustrate the legislative ambitions of the President, as President Jimmy Carter discovered in the course of his first year in the White House. It tasted sovereignty during the exhilarating days of 1973 when it nearly removed a President, Richard Nixon, from office, and surely

---

[61] George B. Galloway, *Congress at the Crossroads* (New York: Thomas Y. Crowell, 1946), p. 334.

would have had he not resigned. We do not have congressional government in the United States in the sense that an omnipotent Congress makes all the laws, which the President and the executive branch merely enforce. Such a simplistic system never existed. But Congress is far more formidable as a political body today than it was in the more quiescent days of the 1950s and early 1960s. Congress is semi-sovereign.

It remains, nevertheless, a peculiar institution. The electoral connections of its members are highly individual and localized. Although its membership has become more ideologically homogeneous, and accordingly somewhat more partisan, its party leadership remains relatively weak. Its internal power structure continues to be highly dispersed, with legislative influence over policy decisions scattered over a large number of members manning its many subcommittees and conducting business in a remarkably open and public manner. It jealously guards its independence, enlarges the scope of its legislative activities, strengthens its capacity to scrutinize the executive, and demands a greater role in realms of policy previously left largely to the President. Its aggregate decision making is "individualistic" in the sense that party or committee influence on members' voting is not compelling. In short, Congress is an unusually democratic legislative institution. This makes it a very frustrating policy-making body for those politicians and intellectuals who have the "received truth." And its democratic character makes it often seem painfully slow and incompetent to its attentive constituents. Its own internal dynamic, along with these external frustrations and annoyances, brings about cyclical pressures for reform. So it surely will be true that the Congress of the 1980s will not be very different from the Congress of the 1970s—but, equally, it will not be the same.

5

The Supreme Court:
From Warren to Burger

Martin Shapiro

The Supreme Court as Independent Policy Maker

In the past twenty-five years the Supreme Court has been a major domestic policy maker in the United States. It has initiated at least five major policies. The first is school desegregation. The second is reapportionment. Before the Court's decisions in *Baker* v. *Carr*,[1] *Wesberry* v. *Sanders*,[2] and *Reynolds* v. *Sims*,[3] some congressional and state legislative districts had as many as eighteen times the number of voters as others. Today no district varies by more than about 20 percent from comparable districts in the same state. The third is a major reform of the criminal justice system. The Court has guaranteed every accused person a lawyer and made substantial inroads into police misconduct in searches and interrogations by excluding illegally obtained confessions and evidence from trials. The fourth is an emasculation of federal and state obscenity laws that has made pornographic book stores and movie houses an almost commonplace sight all across America. The fifth is the opening up of birth control and abortion services to millions of working-class women and girls.

In addition to these major policy breakthroughs, there have been dozens of other smaller policy changes that have had a substantial impact on American life. For instance, the Court's bans on long residency requirements for voting, the poll tax, and high filing fees for candidates collectively have had a substantial effect on electoral politics. The Court has cut into the use of the death penalty. It has

---

[1] 369 U.S. 186 (1962).

[2] 376 U.S. 1 (1964).

[3] 377 U.S. 533 (1964).

substantially affected welfare administration by abolishing residency requirements and requiring hearings before benefits are cut off. It has massively reduced the effectiveness of state libel laws, leaving the media far freer to comment on public figures. It has inhibited several attempts by the American presidency to use the foreign affairs powers to extend the administration's coercive and surveillance powers over Americans at home. It has expanded the legal concepts of standing and class action to facilitate a much broader use of litigation as a form of interest group politics. It has given government employees, students, convicts, and illegitimates whole sets of new legal rights. It has struck at various forms of sexual discrimination.[4]

Aside from their sheer magnitude, a number of other aspects of the Court's policy interventions ought to be noted. Most important, all of the major and many of the minor interventions occurred quite independently, without the cooperation or encouragement of other parts of government or of either of the political parties.[5] Many portions of this chapter will stress the interaction of the courts with other political institutions, but it must be made clear at the outset that the Supreme Court has shown a capacity for independent action that has been surprising in the light of the total subservience—indeed, the near demise—of judicial authority that New Deal commentators and justices often announced.

It should also be noted that aside from school desegregation, which was spurred by long-term, well-planned, and well-financed lobbying by the NAACP, the major policies and many of the minor ones were judicially initiated without the support of substantial organized constituencies, interest groups, or identifiable blocs of voters. To be sure, in a number of instances, particularly that of birth control and abortion, there were organized, highly articulate, and politically sophisticated groups anxious to trigger the Court's policy. But in none of these areas, again excepting desegregation, was the Court acting on behalf of one of the major, politically focused American interests, like labor or agriculture. Nor was it acting in response to, or anticipation of, major political pressure or support. In-

---

[4] The course of these policy initiatives can be easily traced in any standard constitutional law casebook. See, for example, Martin Shapiro and Rocco J. Tresolini, *American Constitutional Law*, 5th ed. (New York: Macmillan, forthcoming).

[5] Compare Jonathan Casper, "The Supreme Court and National Policy Making," *American Political Science Review*, vol. 60 (1976), pp. 50-61, with Robert Dahl, "Decision-Making in a Democracy: The Supreme Court as a National Policy-Maker," *Journal of Public Law*, vol. 6 (1957), pp. 279-95.

deed, in all five areas, the Court could readily anticipate more political opposition than support—and opposition from sources with a lot of political clout such as state political elites and the Catholic church. In school desegregation the Court could expect strong support from a large constituency, namely blacks. That constituency was not, however, one that most politicians at the time thought it was politically wise to court. Few American politicians even today would care to run on a platform of desegregation, pornography, abortion, and the "coddling" of criminals. If, as we are so often told, the Supreme Court follows the election returns, it nevertheless does not act in a directly election-oriented way.

The Court as Enunciator of Diffuse Values. The distinguishing feature of the Court's interventions has not been their utility in building a support coalition of politically powerful, focused constituencies. Rather, it has been their consonance with some widely held but inchoate values of the American people and with ideas whose "time has come." Few politicians could have won an election on the slogan "one man one vote" in 1962. Those who sought to overturn the Court's reapportionment decisions nevertheless found that one man one vote was too close to the democratic bone to be attacked successfully. Neither the clichés of states rights nor the sophistications of political science voting analysis could stand up against a Court armored in democratic truism. Nor could rural and urban constituencies be mobilized to fight for more than their fair share of the vote. Similarly, law and order could and did become a campaign issue. And the rules that excluded from trial truthful evidence that would have sent guilty men to prison were, and remain, a political liability to the Court. But the root holding, that everyone accused of a crime is entitled to a lawyer, could hardly be attacked successfully. And the political viability of that holding is not a result of the fact that American lawyers are a powerful interest group looking after its economic well being. Rather, it results from the fact that most Americans cannot help believing that everyone accused of a crime is entitled to a fair trial, which obviously means having a lawyer among other things.

As to desegregation, obscenity, and abortion, they were all ideas whose time had come. We can debate about how fundamentally racist American society was in the 1950s and later. It is clear, however, that after World War II Jim Crow had become an anomaly of American life. Few white Americans outside the South could openly defend official government discrimination against Negroes. The question in 1954 was not how the Court could announce desegregation. It was how at that late date the Court could possibly have held racism to be constitutional. By the 1960s and 70s American sexual mores had so changed that the Court's recognition in its obscenity, birth control, and abortion decisions of both the prevalence and problems of sexual expression was little more than a legal confirmation of the felt necessities of the times.

It is precisely this phenomenon of Supreme Court expression of diffuse but basic beliefs and values that makes the Court such a political mystery. For, as a number of other chapters in this book make clear, political science is extremely uncomfortable about the relation between generalized public opinion or basic political values on the one hand and political action on the other. In the light of the striking parallelism between what the Court has done and the general drift of American life and thought, it is difficult to depict the Court as a pure example of a political elite doing whatever it pleases. In the light of its massive policy initiatives, it is also impossible to depict it as a mere ritualistic legitimizer of what those political actors more closely linked to particular political forces choose to do.[6]

The Court as a Member of the National Governing Coalition. One major clue to explaining the Court's policy-making role may be that nearly all of its most successful interventions have been primarily against state governments and in areas like education, police, and morals that had traditionally been left primarily to state law. Since John Marshall's time we have been accustomed to thinking of the Court as a nationalizing force. In the twentieth century we have come to concentrate more upon the presidency as a centralizing political authority and on the enormous growth of federal statutes, the federal bureaucracy, and federal spending as the major vehicle of nationalization. There remains a lively debate about the continued vitality of American federalism.[7] There is no serious challenge, however, to the proposition that the central government has extended both the scope and the intensity of its regulation of state and local government activity. In this sense, while the Court has often acted independently or in advance of its central government partners, it has acted as part of the partnership.

Sometimes it has acted in close cooperation with its partners. In the civil rights area, Court decisions and the major civil rights

---

[6] See Charles Black, *The People and the Court*, chap. 3 (New York: Macmillan, 1960).

[7] See Chapter 9.

statutes have followed closely upon one another. In one of the clearest examples, at a time when Congress was actively concerned with proposed antidiscrimination provisions in housing legislation, the Court discovered that long neglected provisions of the 1866 Civil Rights Act already banned discrimination in the sale and rental of housing.[8]

There are also instances in which the Court seemed to be breaking the way for anticipated congressional-presidential action, although there is always the chance that the Court action was purely coincidental. For instance, in the late sixties the Nixon administration was pushing plans for a negative income tax, one of whose principal virtues would have been to reduce the grave disparities between support levels for the poor in different states. Among the major causes of these disparities were federal formula grants for welfare such as Aid for Dependent Children. At this point the Court handed down *Shapiro* v. *Thompson*[9] which banned state residency requirements for welfare recipients. The result of *Shapiro* was that the states with high welfare benefits no longer had any effective means of fending off invasions of welfare eligibles seeking to move from low-support to high-support states. *Shapiro* underlined and aggravated the problem of the disparities that resulted from state-by-state welfare programs at the very time the President was advocating the nationalization of welfare. If the President had persisted and finally won, no doubt *Shapiro* would have been widely marked as a major act of cooperation between Court and presidency. As it was, the President dropped his plans and *Shapiro* became a minor skirmish in a lost campaign.

Instead, the Court-presidency cases that are best remembered are *New York Times* v. *U.S.*[10] and *U.S.* v. *Nixon*[11] in which the Court acted "against" the presidency. As we have noted, both are atypical of the Court's big decisions, most of which have been directed against the states. And neither goes very far. *New York Times* v. *U.S.* arose out of the publication by the *New York Times* and other newspapers of excerpts from the Pentagon Papers. The government sought to enjoin publication on the grounds that publication of this classified material would do it irreparable injury. The Court's decision did not challenge the constitutionality of the security classification system. Instead it refused the government's claim on

---

[8] Jones v. Alfred H. Mayer Co., 392 U.S. 409 (1968).
[9] 394 U.S. 618 (1969).
[10] 403 U.S. 713 (1971).
[11] 418 U.S. 683 (1974).

the narrowest possible grounds. Prior restraint, that is censorship in advance of illegal publication rather than punishment by criminal or civil prosecution after publication, has always been considered particularly abhorrent to our freedom of speech traditions. In *New York Times* the Court ruled only that, while the ban on prior restraint was not absolute, the government had not met the heavy burden of proof of irreparable injury that would justify such restraint.

In *U.S.* v. *Nixon*, arising out of the Watergate trials, the President claimed that "executive privilege" defended him against demands that he surrender presidential papers and tapes. Executive privilege was a novel constitutional doctrine that had never previously been pled before or acknowledged by the Supreme Court. In *Nixon* the Court *upheld* the executive privilege doctrine. It also held, however, that the privilege must give way in the particular circumstances of the case, that is, to a carefully circumscribed demand by a court for evidence necessary to a criminal prosecution. *Nixon* was a terrible defeat for President Nixon. Indeed, it drove him from the White House. It also quashed the extreme constitutional theory he had propounded, that the President was above the law. But in the long run the case will be remembered as pro-presidency, the first that acknowledged the constitutional validity of the executive privilege doctrine.

Both *New York Times* and *Nixon* came at a time when public opposition to the Vietnam War was peaking. They were hardly brave constitutional naysaying by the Court to war-inflamed majorities. Rather, they came after majority support for presidential Vietnam policies had disappeared. They reflected and abetted the major political currents of the moment rather than standing in opposition to them.

The Court as Effective Policy Maker

Thus, while the Court turns out to have been a major policy maker in recent times, its movement seems to have been largely in the same direction as the nationalizing tendency of American politics, the liberalizing trend in American thought and mores, and the general constellation of Washington forces. Yet many of its decisions, such as those on obscenity, the rights of the accused, abortion, school prayer, and desegregation, have been highly controversial. How has a Court, which is not elected and has neither a large budget with which to buy support nor an enforcement arm to compel it, gotten away with these decisions? Four complementary answers may be offered.

Partial Success and Outside Assistance. First, it has not gotten away with them completely or unaided.[12] The school prayer decisions are those that have been most fully studied. These studies indicate that, in those sections of the country where opposition to the Court's holdings was the strongest, the prayers have simply continued. Similarly, the exclusionary rule of *Mapp* and *Miranda* was designed to deter police misconduct by barring the fruits of such conduct from trial. While the evidence is mixed, it seems probable that in many police departments, basic conduct has been changed very little by the decisions. Police may work a little harder or lie a little more in court to show that their searches were done with the consent of the suspect, or involved seizure of material in "plain sight," or were part of "stop and frisk" or vehicular-stop situations, all of which are exempted from the warrant requirement.[13] Or they may get warrants to conduct the same searches that they used to conduct without them. In many jurisdictions, "dropsie" evidence is routinely offered by the police and accepted by judges. While the Court rules seem to have been evolved basically to protect the privacy of dwellings, their greatest potential inhibiting effect on the police seems to be in street searches. So many police validate illegal street searches by claiming that what they actually found in the defendant's pockets was dropped or thrown away by the defendant as the police approached.

In the obscenity area, the great relaxation of legal constraints was, to be sure, triggered by the Court's decisions;[14] but it has been implemented by juries that, in many jurisdictions, simply refuse to find even the most blantantly pornographic material obscene. While triggering some opposition, the Court's decisions basically ran with a vogue for pornography and other sexual deviance that was sweeping the Western world.

The long-term opposition to the Court's desegregation decisions also illustrates this first answer. Clearly in the initial twenty years after *Brown* v. *Board*[15] in 1954, the Court did not wholly get away with its decision. Implementation was very slow. The Court deliberately kept out of the battle and allowed the district and circuit courts

---

[12] The literature on compliance and impact more generally is surveyed in Stephen Wasby, *The Impact of the United States Supreme Court: Some Perspectives* (Homewood, Ill.: Dorsey Press, 1970).

[13] See David W. Neubauer, *Criminal Justice in Middle America* (Morristown, N.J.: General Learning Press, 1974), pp. 166-68.

[14] See Roth v. United States, 354 U.S. 476 (1957); A Book v. Attorney General, 383 U.S. 413 (1966).

[15] 347 U.S. 483 (1954).

to take the brunt.[16] "White flight" has been an effective response for many white families who evade the Court's mandate by moving out of racially mixed cities into all-white suburbs. So far the Court has not ordered the interdistrict remedies that would force these families' children into racially mixed schools.

Not only has the Court's mandate been incompletely met, but where it has been met it is often because the Court has received a great deal of aid. For instance, a study of the Georgia schools shows that more or less complete integration came when the flow of federal grant money to the Georgia schools was threatened.[17] Congressional civil rights statutes, HEW and Justice Department action, and the voluntary cooperation of many other state and federal agencies have helped in getting desegregation as far as it has gotten.

So the first answer to the question of how the Court obtains compliance is that in fact many of those who don't want to obey it don't. On the other hand, those who do want to obey it do—and sometimes help the Court to overcome opposition.

Interest Group Allies. The second answer is a variant of the first. Court decisions may call into being, encourage, or greatly strengthen interest groups that will then aid the Court in achieving its policies. The Court's school desegregation decision followed a long and carefully orchestrated litigational campaign by the NAACP. The decision in turn greatly strengthened the NAACP and acted as a catalyst for the civil rights movement which brought to the fore such leaders as Martin Luther King. The movement in turn pressed for enforcement of the decision both by direct action and by further litigation. Actually a certain division of labor seemed to arise. The newer groups specialized in marches, boycotts, and other direct action aimed both at coercing local authorities and at recruiting general public support for further desegregation. The NAACP concentrated on the enormous campaign of follow-up litigation necessitated by the Court's "all deliberate speed" remedy. One way of looking at the Court's tactic of declaring school desegregation unconstitutional but ordering that it be eliminated not immediately but only over time is that the Court was giving southern governments time to obey. In the actual event, the additional time was most significant not as a resource for government

---

16 Stephen L. Wasby, Anthony D'Amato, and Rosemary Metrailer, *Desegregation from Brown to Alexander: An Exploration of Supreme Court Strategies* (Carbondale, Ill.: Southern Illinois Press, 1977).

17 Charles Bullock and Harrell Rodgers, *Law & Social Change: Civil Right Laws and Their Consequences* (New York: McGraw-Hill, 1972).

obedience but as a resource through which constituencies favorable to the decision could greatly expand and perfect their political organization in order to help bring about compliance.

The school prayer [18] and abortion decisions [19] illustrate a different pattern of interest group response. If the religious groups had stood united against the prayer decisions, the Court might have faced a serious crisis. In fact, some religious denominations favored prayer in the schools and others were opposed. Thus the decisions themselves triggered their own defense. They elicited public responses from organized religion that clearly illustrated the Court's main point—that school prayer was religiously divisive—and at the same time showed that attacks on the Court as irreligious were bound to meet only very limited success. Similarly, the abortion decisions, while controversial, have elicited strongly organized support, and also strongly organized attack. This balance of forces has led to a prolonged debate on the issues but has prevented a wholesale attack on the Court.

Summating Preferences. A third and closely related approach to the Court's political viability is in terms of its ability to summate constituencies. Along one dimension this summating capacity involves intensities. A relatively weak, very widespread, diffusely held value may receive little representation from the legislative or executive organs of either state or national government, most of which are better designed to respond to intensely held values concentrated in specific, easily identified constituencies. Supreme Court decisions may tap highly diffuse support, for instance pro freedom of speech sentiment, that rarely becomes sufficiently focused or organized to generate direct pressure on legislative or administrative bodies. It is not being argued here that such diffuse sentiment somehow prompts the Court to act, but only that, where it exists, anti-Court reactions from more organized groups tend to be dampened, diffused, and ultimately ignored.

There is another dimension to the Court's ability to summate interests. The Little Rock story that evolved around *Cooper* v. *Aaron*[20] is a good example. After *Brown* a number of southern authorities promised massive resistance. The governor of Arkansas

---

[18] Engel v. Vitale, 370 U.S. 421 (1962), Abington School District v. Schempp, 374 U.S. 203 (1963).

[19] Roe v. Wade, 410 U.S. 113 (1973); Doe v. Bolton, 410 U.S. 179 (1973); Maher v. Roe, 97 S. Ct. 2394 (1977).

[20] 358 U.S. 1 (1958).

called out his state's National Guard to prevent integration in Little Rock. President Eisenhower found himself in the middle. He was not a strong public proponent of desegregation and his private views were the opposite of crusading. Having won his party's nomination and the presidency against a background of fears about military men in the White House, he certainly did not want to be known as the President who had "used the troops" against his fellow citizens—no matter what their political persuasion. Yet in the end he sent federal paratroops to Little Rock. Why?

The explanation seems to lie in the additive capacities of the Court. There was broad but diffuse American sentiment in favor of desegregation. There was much broader and much more intensely held American sentiment in favor of obedience to law by public officials. The spectacle of a state governor defying "the law" with armed force while the President of the United States stood idly by was one that a great many Americans found intolerable no matter what their views on desegregation. It was a spectacle that President Eisenhower could not tolerate either. And having been maneuvered into it by the Supreme Court and the governor of Arkansas, he found that his only way out was to send the troops to enforce the Court's policy. He was forced to do so because a racial justice value *plus* a law and order value proved a winning combination in the political forum.

Working Out the New Deal Program. A fourth answer to the question of the Court's success in the last twenty-five years is to be found by reviewing the events of the past forty. Such a review is not easy to do in an objective way because of a curious phenomenon of American intellectual history. It is worth describing this phenomenon very briefly because scholarly commentary about the Court is such an important feature of the Court's political life. The Court's opinions are legal documents directed in part at lawyers. The justices are not only important politicians but also leaders of the bar. In their opinions, they themselves construct endless commentaries on the law and the Court. In the briefs and oral arguments, they are constantly bombarded by the commentaries of others. The bar is one of the Court's attentive publics, and about its only constant attentive public, because other such publics are essentially "issue publics" that come and go as the issues change. And the general public finds it appropriate that lawyers tell it about the Court. Thus the justices are far more deeply concerned with legal commentary about the Court than, for example, the President is with political science commentary about the presidency.

Perhaps the most important thing a beginning student of the Supreme Court can know is that most of what he reads about the Court, including what the Court itself says, is the product of men whose political perspectives were profoundly shaped by the New Deal experience and who have spent most of their lives propagating a New Deal myth about the Court. The word "myth" here is not meant to suggest a falsehood as such, but rather a selective version of reality made larger than life and employed as a guide to the interpretation of all subsequent reality.

The myth is simply stated. President Roosevelt took office in 1932 with overwhelming public support and immediately initiated a set of ingeniously pragmatic government programs to save the nation from the Depression. In the grip of a sterile and outmoded laissez-faire economic philosophy, the Court declared these programs unconstitutional. In his righteous wrath, the President then rose up to threaten the Court with his "court packing" bill, and in 1937 the Court surrendered. The surrender consisted of the Court's abandoning the protection of so-called economic rights, which really consisted of nothing more than reading its own economic policy preferences into the Constitution, and instead taking up the cause of civil rights and liberties, which really are protected by the specific wording of the Bill of Rights.

The perpetrators of the myth fall into two schools. The first is that of judicial self-restraint. New Deal commentators on the Supreme Court agreed that constitutional judgments were necessarily public policy judgments in disguise and essentially involved the balancing of various social interests. In a democracy, Congress was the place best suited to do this interest balancing. Therefore, the Court should defer to the congressional policy judgment embodied in each statute and never, or hardly ever, declare congressional statutes unconstitutional.[21]

The teachings of New Deal Court commentators combined with the teachings of New Deal commentators on the presidency to produce a curious and generally unnoticed result, for during the period in which the theory of judicial self-restraint was most dominant, the theory of the "strong presidency" was also being propounded.[22]

[21] See Wallace Mendelson, *Justices Black and Frankfurter: Conflict in the Court* (Chicago: University of Chicago Press, 1961).

[22] The most extended statement summarizing much of the earlier commentary is James MacGregor Burns, *The Deadlock of Democracy* (Englewood Cliffs, N.J.: Prentice-Hall, 1963).

Congress consisted of many individuals and committees elected by and representing small and special constituencies. The President was one man elected by the nation as a whole. The President must therefore provide strong leadership in the national interest. More particularly he must become "chief legislator." The Congress's job was to enact the President's legislative program. The President's job was to employ all of the various powers and influences at his command to persuade Congress to do so.

When we add these two strains of thought together, the result is clear. The Supreme Court is to defer to Congress. The Congress is to defer to the President. Therefore the Supreme Court is to defer to the President. In the scholarly writing and popular commentary on the institutions of American government from the 1940s onward, the myth of 1937 is magnified and generalized and played over and over again as the very model of the correct functioning of the American political system.

The second school of New Deal commentators on the Supreme Court are "judicial activists" but under the guidance of the "preferred position" doctrine. That doctrine was intiated by Justice Stone,[23] a Republican appointee, but Roosevelt's choice as chief justice. The crux of the doctrine was that in economic rights cases the Court should be absolutely deferent to the legislature, but that it should undertake a special, active role in defending Bill of Rights freedoms like freedom of speech and in protecting racial minorities. The constitutional rationale for providing this preferred position for political and civil rights over economic rights is less important than its ideological functon.[24]

The New Deal had built its organizational and electoral success on the basis of a coalition of union members, the poor, Negroes, and liberal intellectuals. To that coalition were soon added the masses of government workers that the New Deal and World War II created. The principal opposition to the New Deal came from business and the propertied class. To some New Dealers, the only response to the Supreme Court's terrible sin against Roosevelt was to destroy its power utterly through the doctrine of self-restraint. But after 1937 the Court was controlled by Roosevelt appointees. To other New Dealers, it seemed a shame to destroy a major political agency over which they had just gained control. For them the problem was not to destroy the Court but to transfer its patronage from a Republican

---

[23] In United States v. Carolene Products Co., 304 U.S. 144 (1938), footnote 4.
[24] For the constitutional rationale, see Thomas I. Emerson, *The System of Freedom of Expression* (New York: Random House, 1970).

to a Democratic clientele. That is the function of the preferred position doctrine.

In the realm of labor relations, the federal district courts necessarily carried the main load. Their performance had been so anti-union that the Democrats abandoned hope of reforming them. The New Deal simply created a new court and a new law for labor cases, the National Labor Relations Act and the National Labor Relations Board, and then packed the new court with pro-union judges.[25] For the other members of the coalition, however, the old Supreme Court would serve, through the preferred position doctrine.

There is not space here to trace the slow development of the service that the Court performed.[26] We must confine ourselves here to a brief summary. The poor and government employees were served by an extension of the preferred position doctrine that, by magic, turned *their* economic rights, as opposed to those of business and the wealthy, into civil or individual rights worthy of protection.

The traditional view of both government employment and government assistance like welfare was that they were not rights but privileges which the government could cut off for any reason or indeed for no reason at all. Gradually the Court evolved a set of doctrines, sometimes referred to as the "new property," which held that government workers and the recipients of government aid had a constitutionally protected interest in the continuance of their employment or benefits free of arbitrary government action.

Now these interests were indubitably economic. There is no more economic right than the right to a paycheck or a welfare check. The problem was to create a rationale for serving these economic interests that would commit the Court to these particular economic interests *only* and not those of the rich. The Court adopted a number of piecemeal solutions. A few examples must suffice here. Perhaps the most bizzare is the best. *Shapiro* v. *Thompson*[27] involved a state statute that required a person to have been resident in the state for a certain length of time before he or she became eligible for state welfare payments. The Supreme Court held the residency requirement unconstitutional as an invasion not of an economic right to welfare but of a civil right to travel. The Court argued that

---

[25] The Supreme Court did its share by announcing that the NLRB rather than the courts had "primary jurisdiction" in most labor cases. Martin Shapiro, *Law and Politics in the Supreme Court*, chap. 3 (New York: Macmillan, 1964).

[26] See Martin Shapiro, "The Supreme Court and Economic Rights," in M. Judd Harmon, ed., *Essays on the Constitution of the United States* (New York: Kennikat Press, 1978).

[27] 394 U.S. 618 (1969).

people would be deterred from traveling to Connecticut if they knew they could not get on welfare immediately upon their arrival.

In government employment, the McCarthy period eased the way. In the 1950s, the jobs of many government employees were put at risk because they were alleged to be Communists or Communist sympathizers. Often they were fired without proper investigation or a fair hearing on the charges. Thus government employment cases came to the Court in the context of First Amendment and procedural due process arguments as government employees alleged they were being fired without proper procedures for what they had said or what politics they had engaged in off the job rather than for their job performance. In this context the Court developed the doctrine that government employment was a right and not a privilege, and in this context it was easy to call such a right a free speech or procedural right rather than an economic one.[28]

Subsequently the Court has managed to bring many other rights to government services under the due process umbrella. For instance, in *Goldberg* v. *Kelly*,[29] it in fact created a right to welfare by holding that a welfare recipient could not have his benefits terminated without a fair hearing. Ironically enough, this protection of economic interests under the due process clause is precisely the tactic for which the New Dealers had denounced the old Supreme Court, giving it that dreaded and opprobrious label, "economic substantive due process."[30] But somehow these economic interests of the poor had become civil liberties. Under the preferred position doctrine, they were entitled to special judicial concern, unlike the merely economic rights of the rich, which were entitled to no constitutional protection at all.

Much less trouble was needed to use the preferred position doctrine on behalf of Negroes and liberal intellectuals. The doctrine as enunciated by Stone had specifically mentioned minorities subject to prejudice. The Court eventually spelled this out in a "two-tiered"[31] test for the equal protection clause of the Fourteenth Amendment. Race was a suspect classification. The use of a racial classification in a statute, therefore, triggered "strict scrutiny" by the Supreme

---

[28] See Keyishian v. Board of Regents of the University of the State of New York, 385 U.S. 589 (1967).

[29] 397 U.S. 254 (1970).

[30] See Robert G. McCloskey, "Economic Due Process and the Supreme Court: An Exhumation and Reburial," *Supreme Court Review* (Chicago: University of Chicago Press, 1962), pp. 34-68.

[31] See below, p. 207.

Court. In other words, the Court would actually engage in judicial review. On the other hand, where no suspect classification was involved, the Court would defer to the legislature. Since the only suspect classification was race, presto quicko the Court could be absolutely active in all race matters and absolutely passive toward equal protection claims made by everyone else.

As for the liberal intellectuals, intellectuals it must be remembered are people who earn their living with words. The first real use of the preferred position doctrine was in the early 1940s in freedom of speech cases.[32] There it was used to argue that while the Court should be self-restrained in all other areas, it should be activist in protecting the most important of all civil rights, and the one most specifically acknowledged in the Constitution itself, freedom of speech.

Thus the preferred position doctrine with suitable additions and appurtenances served as a gigantic umbrella and blueprint for transferring Supreme Court political services from Republican to Democratic clienteles. Once the doctrine is understood in this light, it can be seen that what appeared to be a bitter battle between two schools of commentators and two wings of the Court—the judicial activists and the judicial self-restrainers—was in reality a New Deal consensus on the validity of the New Deal myth and the virtue of the New Deal clientele. At worst there was only a difference of opinion on whether the Supreme Court should leave the President alone or actively assist him in the care and feeding of the New Deal coalition.

Once the commentary is understood, the history can be more easily understood, and so can one basic reason for the Court's successful activism. The history of the Court at its activist peak in the 1950s and 1960s, and even into the 1970s, is actually the history of a political institution working out the implications of the victory of the New Deal coalition and the dominance of the New Deal consensus. This reality has been obscured by the fact that it was a "Republican" Court, the Warren Court, that broke out of the period of judicial self-restraint. Thus it appeared that a new Republican Court had broken from the old Democratic consensus on judicial self-restraint. Why was it then that it had broken in a liberal not a conservative direction and that Republicans like Nixon now urged restraint? Put this way the whole thing seemed to make no sense. In reality, however, the Warren Court simply moved from the negative to the posi-

---

[32] See Martin Shapiro, *Freedom of Speech, the Supreme Court and Judicial Review* (Englewood Cliffs, N.J.: Prentice-Hall, 1966), p. 58 ff.

tive side of the New Deal approach. It received broad support because, a decade or two after the New Deal, it finally moved to incorporate service to the New Deal victors into constitutional law, just as Congress and the presidency earlier had incorporated such service into statutory law. The Supreme Court got away with its activism because it was activism on behalf of the winners not the losers of American politics. The losers were the propertied interests. The preferred position stance left them firmly in the status of unpersons with unrights, even in the new age of judicial activism.

The Court and the Law. The fifth and final factor to be examined in accounting for the success of the Court in policy making is that it retains its status as a court and as guardian of the Constitution. The "courtness" of the Supreme Court remains its most potent political asset.

In recent years, we have benefited from a major study of public opinion about the Supreme Court.[33] It indicates that the public reacts to the Court in just about the same way it does to other government institutions. The general public has little specific information about the Court and therefore few specific agreements or disagreements with what the Court does. Certain segments of the public know much more about a particular issue that concerns them, such as abortion, and approve or disapprove of the Court's actions in the specific area of their concern. These specific agreements or disagreements do not seem greatly to affect the overall evaluation of the Court even by these special "issue publics." At the level of thought and feeling that can be tapped by survey research, the popular sense of the legitimacy of the Court tends to fluctuate over time along just about the same curves as the felt legitimacy of other American institutions. The Court fairly consistently scores somewhat higher than Congress and the presidency, but in recent years its level of popular support has run at only about 50 percent. None of these data yield any very clear picture of why the Supreme Court is considered a court or why what it says is considered to be the law.

---

[33] See Walter Murphy, Joseph Tanenhaus, and Daniel Kastner, "Public Evaluations of Constitutional Courts," Sage Professional Papers, 01-045 (Beverly Hills, Calif.: Sage Publications, 1973); Murphy and Tanenhaus, "Explaining Diffuse Support for the U.S. Supreme Court," *Notre Dame Lawyer*, vol. 49 (1974), pp. 1037-60. See also John Kessel, "Public Perceptions of the Supreme Court," *Midwest Journal of Political Science*, vol. 10 (1966), pp. 175-84; Kenneth M. Dolbeare, "The Public Views the Supreme Court," in Herbert Jacob, ed., *Law, Politics and the Federal Courts* (Boston: Little, Brown, 1967).

Political scientists are naturally loath to attach great political significance to phenomena they cannot understand. Nevertheless, of key importance to explaining the success of the Court is the fact that it retains its public image as a court whose declarations are "the law." While its mandates are sometimes disobeyed by those most immediately hurt by them, those very mandates are viewed by everyone else as law. And Americans still believe that laws ought to be obeyed. The teachings of those scholars who hold that the Court's constitutional pronouncements are mere policy fiats has not, or at least not yet, become an operative part of American political culture. All else being equal, and particularly when someone else's ox is being gored, a Supreme Court pronouncement is the law. It follows that so long as the Court does not gore too many oxen at any given moment, it continues to tap American respect for the rule of law. We do not know why Americans still identify the Court with the law of the Constitution rather than with simple policy making. We suspect, however, that part of the reason is that the Supreme Court is called a court, its members are called justices, and its law making continues to be dressed in the language of discovering, not making, the meaning of the Constitution.

When all is said and done, the Supreme Court's power stems not only from its service to particular constituencies or its collaboration with other segments of government but also from the fact that its pronouncements are perceived as "the law" in a nation that believes in obeying the law—and not only "the law," but "the constitutional law" in a nation that believes that the Constitution is a higher and better law.

The Policy-Making Process

The Supreme Court has been a relatively important, relatively independent, and relatively successful public policy maker over the last twenty-five years or so. How does it make policy? What determines the policy choices of the justices? These questions may be approached along a number of different routes. The judicial behavior school tells us that the justices have certain basic ideological patterns along two dimensions, one involving civil rights and the other economic liberties.[34] (By the way, the discovery of these two dimensions indicates just how deeply the New Deal ideology of preferred position has penetrated the Court.) In each individual case, a justice's vote

---

[34] This work is summarized in Glendon Schubert, *The Judicial Mind* (Evanston, Ill.: Northwestern University Press, 1965).

for one or the other party is triggered by the correspondence of the issues or parties to his attitudinal set. Thus a justice who has conservative attitudes in the economic realm will vote for business and against government in regulation cases. A justice who is a liberal in the civil rights and liberties realm will vote for the speaker and against the government in freedom of speech cases.

There has been considerable debate about whether the research techniques of the behaviorists can "prove" that "attitudes" determine votes or even whether what the behaviorists identify as attitudes are truly independent variables that can properly be used to explain anything. What is shown indisputably by their work, however, is that many of the justices vote with very considerable consistency for certain classes of parties over other classes: government over business, unions over management, the accused over the state, and so on. Whatever theory of judicial psychology we wish to construct from these facts, the brute facts of judicial preferences remain.

For some years political science has been concerned with the internal dynamics of small decision-making groups such as congressional committees. Some work on the Court has also stressed its small-group processes, suggesting that both votes and the wording of the controlling opinion in a case may be influenced by coalition building and bargaining among the justices.[35] For instance, it has been suggested that Chief Justice Burger has sometimes used his privilege of assigning opinion writing when he is in the majority to keep opinions away from Justices Douglas and Brennan. The justices circulate draft opinions among themselves for comment. Scholars working in the justices' papers have discovered that a great deal of such comment occurs at times and that at least some tacit bargaining takes place.[36] In spite of this work there seems to be some embarrassment about describing what actually goes on in the Court. The justices themselves say a bit.[37] The former clerks are discreet. The news media are polite although a bit of gossip sometimes emerges.

---

[35] Much of this work is summarized in Joel B. Grossman and Richard S. Wells, *Constitutional Law and Judicial Policy Making* (New York: John Wiley, 1972), pp. 168-79.

[36] See, for example, Michael Parrish, "The Supreme Court and the Rosenbergs," *AHR*, vol. 82 (1977), pp. 805-42.

[37] See, for example, Justice Brennan's address to the Florida Bar Convention published in Alan Westin, ed., *An Autobiography of the Supreme Court* (New York: Macmillan, 1963); L. F. Powell, "Myths and Misconceptions about the Supreme Court," *American Bar Association Journal*, vol. 61 (1975), pp. 1344-47; and most notably, W. J. Brennan, "A National Court of Appeals: Another Dissent," *University of Chicago Law Review*, vol. 40 (1973), pp. 473-85.

Nevertheless, it is possible to describe in plain English roughly what goes on. Each year the Court receives several thousand petitions for certiorari and appeal. In theory, appeals are treated differently than certiorari. In fact, they are processed in about the same way. Each justice's clerks work their way through the papers guessing which ones will be of interest to their justice. The clerks are recent law school graduates, typically first in their class and with law review experience. They usually come from the most prestigious law schools, although a kind of geographic distribution modifies this somewhat. Some have clerked for other judges before coming to the Court. Most stay two years. Some justices do part of the petition-culling work themselves. Some indicate what kinds of things they want to see. Others barely supervise the work of the clerks. Each justice eventually prepares a list of pending cases he wishes the Court to consider. Any case listed by any one justice is likely to receive some personal attention from the others. Eventually any case that four justices wish to take will be accepted by the Court. Although this work is done rapidly and largely by the clerks, there is little need for a more elaborate process. Certain clues like conflict on the circuits or appeal by the government easily tag many cases as ready for the Court.[38] Everyone around the Court has a general sense of what the big issues of the moment are, and of what are the current trends in litigation. Each term dozens of cases will raise approximately the same issue. It is highly unlikely that any major issue that the justices would want to consider if they knew about it slips by them in the clerk-dominated petition stage. Even if it did so in one term, it would undoubtedly be back the next.

Once a case is accepted, both parties file written briefs and a date is set for oral argument. Today's Supreme Court brief in any major case really consists of two parts although they may be interwoven. One is a legal argument citing, distinguishing, and otherwise disposing of the cases in point and the legal arguments made by opposing counsel and in treatises and law review articles. It may sometimes influence the outcome of cases. But its principal role, like that of most lobbying, is not to persuade "the guys on the other side" but to provide good arguments for "our guys." In addition to the law, the brief will contain a substantial public policy analysis of the issue

---

[38] See Joseph Tanenhaus et al., "The Supreme Court's Certiorari Jurisdiction: Cue Theory," in Glendon Schubert, ed., *Judicial Decision-Making* (New York: The Free Press, 1963), pp. 111-27. See also Sidney Ulmer et al., "The Decision to Grant or Deny Certiorari: Further Consideration of Cue Theory," *Law and Society Review*, vol. 6 (1972), pp. 640-55.

raised and a good deal of supporting data to show that the resolution recommended by counsel will constitute the best outcome for society at large and the fairest treatment of the equities of the two parties. The root of the modern brief is not the legal analysis but the attempt to persuade the Court what the best thing to do would be.

Some of the justices read some of the briefs before some of the oral arguments. No one seems to suggest that all of the justices read all of the briefs before all of the oral arguments. The oral argument itself usually lasts an hour split between the two opposing counsel who address the whole Court in the Supreme Court chamber. The justices complain about the poor quality of oral argument. In pre-flying days, a small ring of Washington lawyers conducted most of the oral argument. Today many more lawyers appear before the Court, most of them with little or no previous experience in presenting arguments to it. The justices interrupt with questions. At weekly or bi-weekly intervals the justices meet to vote on the cases they have heard argued. Some justices apparently vote in many cases on the basis of what they have heard in oral argument plus memoranda written by the clerks. Clearly all the justices have not thoroughly read the briefs in all the cases and evaluated them on the basis of their own independent research before they cast their initial votes. The chief justice speaks first and then the others in order of seniority on the Court, so some justices may be influenced by what they hear the others say.

The justice to whom the opinion in a particular case is assigned prepares a draft and circulates it to his colleagues and those justices who choose to prepare concurrences and dissents also write drafts. It is clear from reading the opinions that there is some reading of each others' drafts. It is also clear that dissenters often do not bother specifically to meet the arguments of the majority and vice versa although a real debate occurs in some instances. Real collaboration or even bargaining takes place rather infrequently among the majority. In many instances a majority justice simply votes silently with the majority in spite of language in the majority opinion he does not like. Since the 1950s there has been a rapidly growing tendency to file brief concurrences to indicate differences over language or rationale. A large number of "opinions of the Court" are signed by only four justices. In a number of important cases in recent years, the Court has resorted to a brief per curiam opinion signed "by the Court" and then individual opinions by each of the justices. It is now fairly routine for five or six justices to file written opinions in a single case.

It is a long-time open secret, although rarely discussed in print, that most of the words in most of the opinions are written by clerks. At one extreme, a justice may tell his clerks which party he wants to win in a given case and then let them do the whole job, merely reading the clerk's finished product and signing it. At the other, a justice may write the entire opinion asking his clerks only for research assistance on particular points. Some of the justices fall near the first extreme in the handling of nearly every case. Others choose to do a good deal of original writing in certain select cases. There may be a few justices who actually write a majority of the words they sign as their own each year.

The justices are clearly hard working.[39] Nevertheless, the Supreme Court is not a place where nine scholarly men think, study, discuss, and carefully ponder their decisions and then write reasoned elaborations of the careful path of legal analysis that they have pursued before coming to a conclusion. Most cases seem to be decided by most justices after a little reading and talking and some more or less structured thinking, and on the basis of their best guess about what resolution of the issues will be fair to the parties and promote the best public policy. Most of the justices are not practicing legal scholars of the first order. Few are policy specialists with a vast fund of expertise in any area of government operations or social or economic affairs. They do the best they can under the circumstances— and the circumstances are that, like most other politicians, they confront too many problems, for most of which neither the state of our social knowledge nor the capacity of our social technology provides clear solutions.

All of this is not to say that the justices act "by guess or by God" or by delegating decision making to the parties or to their clerks. Few of the issues that reach the Court are brand new. Most cases involve only a slight variation on facts and issues that have been before the Court dozens of times before. A justice may have made up his mind after a half a dozen vehicular search cases that the cops ought to be allowed to search cars whenever they have any half-way decent reason for doing so. Then he does not have to spend more than a few minutes on the latest case, which may be novel only in the sense that this car was in a parking lot while the cars in the previous eight cases had been in the street. He need only look at the facts

---

[39] Henry M. Hart, Jr., "The Time Chart of the Justices," *Harvard Law Review*, vol. 73 (1959), pp. 95–112, describes the workload of the late 1950s. It has gotten worse since. Justice Whittaker noted the work pressures as a major factor in his retirement.

briefly to make sure the police were not acting in a totally arbitrary way. If they weren't, his vote is routine. Moreover, he may be quite sure of where all his fellow justices stand and be pretty sure that none could be convinced to change their views by any facts or arguments that he has at his disposal. Under such circumstances there is little purpose in his rethinking the basic questions, seeking to convince or bargain with his fellow justices, or spending time carefully honing an elaborate opinion. Even if he is assigned the opinion-writing chores for the majority or feels compelled to file a separate opinion, there is no reason that one of his clerks should not compose it. In short, like most other government policy makers, the justices are usually confronted with choices that they can treat as incremental variations on choices that they have made in the past.

The Warren Court

To what extent, however, do the justices treat the really big cases that raise major new issues differently? To answer this question, a brief review of the Warren and Burger Courts is necessary. After its first few terms of incremental adjustments,[40] the Warren Court had a fairly clear direction. Its concern was to serve the value of equality and to incorporate that value more deeply in the Constitution.[41] While the structure was never completed, the blueprint was clear. The Court was moving toward the creation of constitutional guarantees of national basic minimums in education, housing, subsistence, legal services, political influence, birth control services, and other facets of the modern welfare state for all persons regardless of race. This equality thrust turned up not only in the Court's equal protection clause decisions, but in all sorts of other cases that purported to be about rights to due process, privacy, travel, counsel, voting, or what have you. For instance, while the Court's rights of accused decisions rested on half a dozen different constitutional provisions, they were all directed at ensuring that the poor and ignorant received treatment from the criminal justice system equal to that meted out to the educated and well-to-do. Its ground-breaking *Griswold* decision,[42] which struck down state bans on birth control and led the way to the later abortion decisions, supposedly rested on a whole range of con-

---

[40] See Robert G. McCloskey, *The Modern Supreme Court* (Cambridge, Mass.: Harvard University Press, 1972), chap. 4.

[41] See Robert G. Dixon, *Democratic Representation* (New York: Oxford University Press, 1968).

[42] Griswold v. Connecticut, 381 U.S. 479 (1965).

stitutional grounds—of which the equal pro
one. Yet it was obvious that the Court's jud,
the conclusion that birth control services were
to the middle classes and the basic effect of th
deprive only the poor of such services. It is i
tarian thrust of the Court that its most confusec
was in the area of freedom of speech, which
liberty rather than equality issues.[43]

This drive toward equality was led by Chief Justice Warren and
Justice Brennan, the first of whom provided the public symbol and
the second much of the actual consensus building on the Court. The
chief sometimes wrote the big opinions, but it was Brennan, using
the balance-of-interests doctrines that could be all things to all men,
who seems to have worked hardest at actually bargaining out differences and producing opinions of the Court that a majority could sign.
Warren and Brennan were routinely joined by the old left on the
Court, Douglas and Black, the former because his values too were
egalitarian, the latter because his philosophy of judicial activism in
the service of specific constitutional commandments corresponded
with the equality goals of the others, at least in the short run.

Justices Clark and Stewart were at first swing justices, Justice
Stewart eventually moving over fairly completely into the Warren
and Brennan camp. Justices White, Goldberg, Fortus, and Marshall
essentially shared the egalitarian goals. With a solid bloc of four to
five, and some real concern for consensus building, the Warren-
Brennan leadership had a high batting average. The Warren-Brennan
camp contained no careful legal scholar of the sort beloved by the
law schools. Both Frankfurter and Harlan fulfilled this role with
great excellence, but typically in dissent. Of course it is easier to be
a great legal scholar in dissent, and not only because dissenters do
not have to write compromise decisions to recruit votes. The Warren
Court was attempting to change the Constitution and impose its own
will on that of other governmental bodies, particularly the state legislatures. Under such circumstances, conventional legal scholarship
would necessarily run against it.

Few justices may ever have cared. Earlier courts may have been
no better. The goal of equality may be more important than the
niceties of legal reasoning. Whatever defenses may be offered, it was
pretty clear that by the late 1960s nobody in the Warren-Brennan
majority really cared much about anything but the policy outcomes
of the cases. At least a dozen leading law professors had fun ridiculing

---

[43] See Shapiro, *Freedom of Speech.*

urt's ineptness at legal argumentation [44]—not a hard task when
players obviously did not care enough about the game even to
try to obey the rules.

The Burger Court

By the time of Chief Justice Warren's retirement, the Court had gone
a long way in the equality direction in the areas of race, rights of
accused, voting, and birth control. While the materials were still
scattered and incomplete, it seemed on the verge of moving toward
declaring constitutional rights to subsistence, housing, and education.
The crucial halt to this movement came in *San Antonio Independent
School District* v. *Rodriguez* [45] in 1973, which really announced that the
Burger Court had arrived. The vote in the case was the four Nixon
appointees (Justices Powell, Blackmun, Rehnquist, and Chief Justice
Burger) against the egalitarian bloc of the later Warren Court (Justices
Marshall, Douglas, White, and Brennan). Justice Stewart concurring
provided the victory to the new members.

Rodriguez involved a challenge to a state system of school
financing that allowed rich districts to maintain a lower local tax rate
and yet spend far more per student than poor districts. All fifty
states used such systems. Two state supreme courts had already
declared them unconstitutional. In *Rodriguez* the U.S. Supreme Court
refused to do so. In the age of the service and welfare state, the
ability of persons of differing socioeconomic status to sort themselves
out residentially and then receive public services appropriate to their
class status is crucial to maintaining social stratification. This has
been particularly clear in education where the upper middle class
ensures the superior education of its children not by sending them to
private schools but by forming upper-middle-class, self-governing
suburbs that provide superior "public" education. Public education
has been a model of how to maintain major class differentiations
even in the enjoyment of public sector benefits.

The opposite decision in *Rodriguez* would have invalidated the
school taxing and spending policies of forty-eight states. While
wealthy districts might have still found ways to maintain their
islands of superior education, the overall effect would probably have
been substantially greater equality in American education, although
not of course necessarily any improvement in quality. At the constitutional level, the opposite decision would have been an announce-

---

[44] See, for example, Philip Kurland, "Equal in Origin and Equal in Title to the
Legislative and Executive Branches of the Government," *Harvard Law Review*,
vol. 78 (1964), pp. 143-76.
[45] 411 U.S. 1 (1973).

ment that the Warren Court's quest for equality would be continued and pushed into major new spheres.

In the same year, the same egalitarian bloc of Brennan, Douglas, White, and Marshall sought to make sex, like race, a suspect classification in *Frontiero v. Richardson*.[46] And the same bloc of Nixon appointees voted against them, with Justice Stewart again providing the key vote for the new appointees. Since *Frontiero* the Burger Court has refused to extend the list of suspect classifications or fundamental rights. It has continued the egalitarian crusade of the Warren Court in only a few select areas, notably birth control and abortion.

Those who disliked the policies of the Warren Court often chose to attack its "activism" rather than the policies themselves. President Nixon made an issue of appointing "strict constructionists" to the Court. As a result, there was an initial temptation to characterize the Burger Court's halt to the Warren Court's egalitarianism in terms of a switch from Warren Court activism to Burger Court self-restraint.[47] It would be quite wrong, however, to describe the Burger Court as restrained.

In many ways the transition from the Warren Court is like that from the Marshall to the Taney Court. In both instances the partisan political setting of the transition leads to overstatements of the differences. In both instances the new justices have somewhat different policy preferences from the old and thus often reach somewhat different resolutions of particular cases. In both, however, the new Court receives and accepts the basic increments to judicial power and the basic theory of judicial review established by the old. Like the Taney Court, the Burger Court did not retreat from the basic assertions of judicial power or the basic policies made by its predecessor. Yet its policy preferences are somewhat different. And, as we have noted in the equality sphere, it sometimes dramatically refuses to tread further down paths broken by its predecessor.

---

[46] Frontiero v. Richardson, 411 U.S. 677 (1973). This case involved less favorable treatment of the dependents of female than male military personnel. Subsequently the Nixon and Burger Courts have struck down a number of state and federal statutes on sex discrimination grounds but have refused to hold that sex is a suspect classification. Instead the Court holds that, in order to satisfy its equal protection standard, sex classification "must serve important governmental objectives and must be substantially related to achievement of those objectives." Craig v. Boren, 429 U.S. 190 (1976).

[47] On the transition from the Warren Court to the Burger Court see Richard Y. Funston, *Constitutional Counter-Revolution* (New York: John Wiley, 1977); Stephen L. Wasby, *Continuity and Change: From the Warren Court to the Burger Court* (Pacific Palisades, Calif.: Goodyear Publishing, 1976); Wallace Mendelson, "From Warren to Burger: The Rise and Decline of Substantive Equal Protection," *American Political Science Review*, vol. 66 (1972), pp. 1226-33.

In many areas of the Warren Court's march to equality, the Burger Court has simply dragged its feet. In an assortment of "minor" cases, it signaled that it would not extend Warren Court holdings to new areas or push them to their logical extreme.[48] In some areas, the Court actually engaged in a slight rollback of Warren Court policies. For instance, where the Warren Court had required prosecutors in obscenity cases to prove that the material was "utterly without social importance,"[49] the Burger Court assigned them the lighter burden of showing lack of "serious literary . . . or scientific value."[50] In the "new property" area, it tended to be more grudging in the scope of the property right it granted to government employees.[51] It sometimes allowed slightly larger disparities in the size of electoral districts than the Warren Court probably would have.[52] In general it has emphasized that in neither apportionment nor school desegregation will it require exact numerical equality. In the desegregation area as a whole, it is following the Warren Court's strategy of deciding few cases and making few general commitments. And it has actually approved more extreme desegregation plans than the Warren Court ever got around to. On the other hand, it has dropped broad hints that it is "moderate" on desegregation issues.[53]

---

[48] For example, compare Goldberg v. Kelly with Mathews v. Eldridge, 424 U.S. 319 (1976). *Goldberg* had ruled that welfare benefits could be terminated only after an evidentiary hearing. *Mathews* does not reverse *Goldberg* but refuses to extend its rule to the termination of disability benefits. *Mathews* was then followed in cases involving revocation of a driver's license [Dixon v. Love, 431 U.S. 105 (1977)] and the removal of children from foster homes [Smith v. Organization of Foster Families, 431 U.S. 816 (1977)].

[49] A Book v. Attorney General.

[50] Miller v. California, 413 U.S. 5 (1973).

[51] See Bishop v. Wood, 426 U.S. 341 (1976); Massachusetts Board of Retirement v. Murgia, 427 U.S. 307 (1976).

[52] See Mahan v. Howell, 410 U.S. 315 (1973).

[53] See Swann v. Charlotte-Mecklenburg Board of Education, 402 U.S. 1 (1971); Keyes v. School District, 413 U.S. 18 (1973); Milliken v. Bradley, 418 U.S. 717 (1974). *Swann* suggests that where a previously segregated school district is desegregated by the school board and then resegregates itself through changes in residential patterns, the school board is under no obligation to desegregate it again. *Keyes* indicates that under certain circumstances the finding of de jure segregation in a single school need not trigger a judicial demand for integration of the whole district. *Milliken* rejected a district court demand for interdistrict integration where there was no showing that the suburban districts to be thrown in with the central city had themselves practiced de jure segregation. Compare Pasadena City Board of Education v. Spanger, 427 U.S. 424 (1976), which rejects a district court's desegregation plan requiring annual reassignment of students in order to insure that no school has a majority of minority students, with Milliken v. Bradley, 433 U.S. _____ (1977) (Milliken II), which authorizes a district court to order remedial education as part of a desegregation package.

In the rights-of-accused area, the Burger Court has sometimes moved a step beyond the Warren Court. For instance, it has extended the right to counsel to misdemeanor as well as felony cases. On the key issue of the exclusionary rule, however, it has been chipping away at the Warren Court position [54] and calling for Congress to abolish the rule. Indeed, it seems fairly close to abolishing the rule or seriously modifying it itself.[55]

In one area, however, the Burger Court has marched on down the path blazed by the Warren Court, that of birth control and abortion. The Court's major abortion decisions [56] derive three sets of constitutional rules—one for each trimester of pregnancy—from no particular constitutional provision at all. They manage a form of blatant, unrationalized constitutional law making that surpasses any achievement of the Warren Court. With the aid of a specific constitutional provision, the Burger Court goes almost as far in the death penalty cases,[57] declaring state death penalty statutes unconstitutional although it is quite clear that the founding fathers could not have intended the cruel and unusual punishment clause to invalidate them.

Burger Court Activism. Thus, while the Burger Court may want somewhat different things from the Warren Court, it is hardly less activist. The crucial difference is in the style of its activism. Judges, or indeed any politicians wielding hierarchical, legal authority, may be active in one of two ways. They may announce major new rules that embody large step changes in policy. Such rules have the advantage of determining a large amount of the decision making of subordinates at a stroke, assuming reasonable levels of compliance. They have, however, the disadvantage of binding the top rule makers themselves as well as their subordinates, at least in countries where there is a strong tradition of the rule of law. The second mode of activism is to refuse to announce general rules and retain the power

---

[54] See Harris v. New York, 401 U.S. 22 (1971); United States v. Calandra, 414 U.S. 338 (1974). In these two cases the Court held that certain evidence otherwise inadmissible was admissible for the impeachment of the testimony of a defendant who chose to take the stand in his own behalf and in grand jury proceedings.

[55] See Stone v. Powell, 428 U.S. 465 (1976). The Court holds that, where the state provides a full opportunity to litigate an exclusion claim, a federal court may not intervene to decide it under federal habeas corpus jurisdiction. In this case, Justice Powell becomes the fifth justice of the current Court to indicate skepticism about the rule.

[56] Roe v. Wade and Doe v. Bolton.

[57] Furman v. Georgia, 408 U.S. 238 (1972).

to make case-by-case decisions rather than delegate it to one's subordinates. Indeed, in a sense the refusal to make rules is the refusal to delegate since the subordinate unguided by rules can hardly make authoritative decisions. The disadvantage of the refusal to make general rules is obviously that the work load of the top echelons is increased. Unlegitimized by rules, subordinate decisions will be challenged and appealed to the top more frequently. The advantage is that, unbound even by its own previous rules and in receipt of a large number of appeals, the top decision maker increases the area in which he can exercise his own discretion. Is a Court any less activist that maximizes its discretion than one that maximizes its rule making?

For some curious reasons having to do with the struggles between the self-restraint and activist schools of the New Deal period, it has appeared so. But the appearance is deceiving. One of the favorite tricks of Justice Frankfurter and company was to condemn all judicially made general rules as "mechanical" and unrealistic. Such blunt rules were no substitute, Justice Frankfurter would argue, for the sensitive balancing of interests that was the real heart of legal decision. Then, however, Justice Frankfurter would go on to say that of course it was the legislature not the Court that was the appropriate and most capable institution for balancing interests in a democracy. Therefore the courts should do nothing. Q.E.D.[58] In short, in the 1940s and early 1950s the rejection of rules in favor of case-by-case "balancing of interests" was only an elaborate code for the surrender of the Supreme Court to the presidency that we described earlier.

As a result, even in the 1970s many commentators tend to see a Court that balances as more self-restrained than one that announces new rules. Balancing, however, underwent a profound change in the hands of the Warren Court. We have noted that much of the success of the Warren Court stemmed from its playing out of the final stages of the New Deal consensus. One of its neatest consolidations of New Deal ideology was its synthesis of the activist and self-restraint wings of New Deal jurisprudence in what I have elsewhere called "preferred position balancing."[59] In *Gibson* v. *Florida Legislative Investigating Committee*[60] the Court declared that it would follow the balancing technique taken from the most notorious of all the balancing self-restraint cases, *Barenblatt* v. *United States*.[61] Where, however, a

---

[58] The highpoint of this Frankfurter technique is his concurrence in Dennis v. United States, 341 U.S. 494 (1951).

[59] Shapiro, *Freedom of Speech*, chap. 4.

[60] 372 U.S. 539 (1963).

[61] 360 U.S. 109 (1959).

fundamental constitutional right like freedom of speech and association was involved, the state would have to show a "compelling" interest before it could prevail over the individual's interest in exercising his right. It was the Court that would decide whether the state interest was compelling. Thus, the Warren Court changed balancing from an excuse for judicial surrender to an occasion for judicial choice. Of course, it did so only in the service of New Deal clients whose interests could be characterized as civil rather than economic rights.

The balancing of interests that the Burger Court has done must be seen in the light of this fundamental change already completed by the Warren Court. Fortunately, Professor Gunther has catalogued the Burger Court's activities for us with great precision.[62] He shows that in the equal protection area the Court has actually employed three basic techniques. The first is traditional New Deal deference to the legislative body and is used essentially for "old property" cases. The third is a preferred-position, "two-tiered" formula. If a "fundamental right" is infringed or a "suspect classification" is employed, the Court engages in "strict scrutiny." In other words, it comes very close to presuming unconstitutionality and requires the government to show a compelling state interest to justify its actions. As we noted earlier, the Burger Court has refused to expand the categories of suspect classification and fundamental rights.

The second, or "in between," technique Gunther has labeled reasonableness "with bite" or "the newer equal protection." Here the Court invokes the traditional formula that the classification employed must be "reasonably related" to the purpose of the statute. Then, however, there is a change from the New Deal presumption of the reasonableness of the means and the legitimacy of the purpose. Using the New Deal approach, the Court would hold a statute valid if the justices could themselves dream up any conceivable reason why the classification might serve any imaginable purpose that they could invent for the statute. All this creative imagination was exercised by the justices themselves if the legislature had failed to give reasons or specify purposes. Indeed, it was often exercised in the face of what were clearly the legislature's real reasons and purposes, reasons and purposes that raised serious constitutional doubts. Under the "newer

---

[62] Gerald Gunther, "The Supreme Court: 1971 Term; In Search of Evolving Doctrine on a Changing Court: A Model for a Newer Equal Protection," *Harvard Law Review*, vol. 86 (1972), pp. 1-48. He follows later developments in Gerald Gunther, *Constitutional Law*, 9th ed. (Mineola, N.Y.: The Foundation Press, 1975) and its annual supplements. See also J. Harvie Wilkinson, III, "The Supreme Court, the Equal Protection Clause, and the Three Faces of Constitutional Equality," *Virginia Law Review*, vol. 61 (1975), pp. 945-87.

equal protection" standard, the Court refuses to presume and refuses to imagine. Instead it asks what purpose is actually articulated in the statute and then engages in a realistic analysis of whether the classification employed actually contributes sufficiently to the state's purpose to justify its injury to those who suffer from it. In short, it balances the interests of the government against the interests of those adversely affected by the government's policy.

This technique is highly flexible. It is bounded at one extreme by cases like *Massachusetts Board of Retirement* v. *Murgia*[63] in which, while purporting to do independent analysis, the Court comes very close to the New Deal presumption. At the other extreme, particularly in cases involving sex and illegitimacy classifications,[64] it comes very close to the "two-tiered" formula. Nevertheless, considering the cases as a whole, it is fairly distinct from the two extreme approaches. What it comes down to is the Court doing its own legislative analysis of whether the statute constitutes good public policy that adequately serves all the major interests involved.[65] Except for the fact that these cases involve the new property rather than the old, the language and holdings in these cases cannot readily be distinguished from those in *Lochner* v. *New York*[66] and the other much maligned pillars of "substantive due process." The pre-1937 Court presumed that free enterprise was the rule and regulation the exception. The Burger Court presumes that government action is the rule and freedom from government the exception. Both those presumptions fit the general ideology and the general stance of the government of their day. The Burger Court, like the old Court, is prone to develop two lines of precedent, one on each side of the issue, so that it is always free to go whichever way it pleases. It is far more prone than the old Court to refuse to state general rules at all. Its normal style is to assert that the constitutional question raised by the particular case is one of balancing or degree and then to go on to do its own balancing.

This technique occurs not only in equal protection but across the board. Thus the Court condemns not entanglement between church and state but "excessive" entanglement, with the justices deciding just how much entanglement is too much.[67] The Court has announced a

---

[63] 427 U.S. 307 (1976).
[64] See, for example, Weber v. Aetna Casuality & Surety Co., 406 U.S. 164 (1972); Weinberger v. Wiesenfeld, 95 S. Ct. 1225 (1975).
[65] Justice Powell's opinion for the Court in *Weber* is a very clear example.
[66] 198 U.S. 45 (1905).
[67] See Lemon v. Kurtzman, 403 U.S. 602 (1971); Tilton v. Richardson, 403 U.S. 672 (1971).

pure balancing standard for freedom of speech in *Buckley* v. *Valeo*.[68] That case involved a complex, multi-provision statute regulating campaign financing, almost every one of whose provisions the Court admitted infringed on free speech. The Court marched through the statute, upholding some provisions and invalidating others, on no other basis than its view that some did more good than harm and others did more harm than good.

The most dramatic example of all is in the cruel and unusual punishment area. There the Court's initial condemnation of the death penalty in *Furman* v. *Georgia*[69] could be seen as essentially procedural. The statutes were struck down because decisions under them as to who was and who was not condemned to death appeared arbitrary. In a sense *Furman* was typical of the Burger Court style because in it the Court made itself into a super legislature. In effect the states were instructed to rewrite their death penalty statutes and resubmit them to the Supreme Court. Then the Court would approve those that it liked and send back those that it didn't for yet another redrafting.

In fact, the Court was going even further. In *Coker* v. *Georgia*[70] it holds that, even where appropriate procedures are employed, the death penalty is per se cruel and unusual punishment for rape, at least where the rape is of an adult and is not aggravated by serious physical injury to the victim. The only reason the Court really offers for this conclusion is that it feels deep down that rape just is not serious enough to warrant the death penalty—that the punishment is disproportionate to the crime. The Burger Court has declared itself to be the Mikado. It will decide just which crimes are serious enough to warrant just which penalties.

The Burger Court Style. Whether one agrees or disagrees with the substantive policy outcomes achieved by the Burger Court, it is surely fair to say that the Burger Court's style mirrors the reality of its decision making. No member of the current Court cares much about legal scholarship. None seems to combine a sufficiently centrist position with sufficient desire for, and skill at, consensus building to achieve a solid front. We have come to expect five or six opinions in major cases, none of which does more than state the author's policy preferences dressed up in cursory and pro forma legal argument.

---

[68] 424 U.S. 1 (1976).
[69] See Furman v. Georgia and Gregg v. Georgia, 428 U.S. 153 (1976).
[70] 433 U.S. 584 (1977).

There is no reason not to say openly what the justices care so little to disguise, that they make their decisions on the basis of seat-of-the-pants predictions of the immediate and direct policy benefits of the various alternatives available to them.

This is not to say that the justices are careless, arbitrary, stupid policy makers—or at least it is not to say that they are more careless, arbitrary, and stupid than other Washington policy makers. From the evidence of the questions at oral argument and from the opinions, most observers would probably agree that the justices prepare themselves pretty well on most major issues. Essentially they follow the normal Washington tactic of letting the issue stew for a while so that there is an opportunity for all to be heard and for the decision maker to absorb what is to be heard. They often make tentative or partial experiments in new areas before going the whole way. They seem to be aware of and responsive to public sentiment and the general political climate, although like other politicians they may occasionally miscalculate. When they miscalculate, they sometimes retreat a bit.[71]

Earlier we posed the question, does the Court handle big questions differently from little ones? The answer is no and yes. It does not seem to become a more careful, precise, and refined legal scholar on big issues than on little ones. Indeed, the reverse is probably true. On the other hand, most of the justices seem to have thought long and hard about the big policy issues that confront the Court. They seem to have made their policy choices on the basis of their own estimates of where the factual data point and their own vision of what the good life in the good state would be.

---

[71] For instance, see Maher v. Roe. The Court's initial abortion decisions had inspired an organized, active, and well-financed "pro-life" movement which has been vigorously challenging the Court's policy particularly by putting pressure on health authorities to reduce or cut off funding and facilities for abortion. In *Maher* the Court ruled that state legislatures were under no constitutional obligation to provide state funds for abortion services if they did not want to. Similarly in Washington v. Davis, 426 U.S. 299 (1976) the Court held that a local government personnel policy was not a violation of the equal protection clause "solely because it has a racially disproportionate impact" absent any showing of a "racially discriminatory purpose." Thus the Court eased away from a strict quota approach just when that approach was widely coming under fire. Initially it had held that Title VII of the 1964 Civil Rights Act did sometimes forbid differential racial impact even in the absence of discriminatory purpose. See Griggs v. Duke Power Co., 401 U.S. 424 (1971). Notice that in both these instances the Court has passed the buck to the legislatures, indicating that they may go further than the Court is prepared to go if they want to. The Court indicates that, by statute, the legislature may provide a higher level of abortion services for women and employment opportunities for minorities than the Court is going to provide by its independent reading of the Constitution.

More than most previous Courts, the Burger Court openly acknowledges that this is what it is doing. Its reaction to nearly any problem is to enhance its own policy discretion and then wield that discretion case by case to achieve what it believes to be desirable social results. So long as it does not get markedly out of step with the policy preferences of the rest of the political system, there is no reason why this should be an unfruitful or dangerous role for the Court. So far the Burger Court does not seem to be out of step.

6

The Political Parties:
Reform and Decline

Austin Ranney

Few elements of the American political system have changed as much in recent years as the major political parties. Almost all of these changes have taken place since the 1960s. As I shall detail in this chapter, there have been major alterations in the parties' internal rules, the national and state laws regulating them, the numbers, social characteristics, and attitudes of people participating in their affairs, the distribution of power between their national agencies and state affiliates, and the cultural and technological environment in which they operate. As a result, the parties' traditional roles in choosing presidential candidates and in financing and directing presidential campaigns have diminished so greatly that presidential politics has become, in substance if not in form, something closely approaching a no-party system.

There is some temptation to qualify the foregoing by remarking that these changes have taken place almost entirely in the Democratic party and that the Republicans, as befits the more conservative group, remain much the same as they were in the 1960s and before. However, that is not the case. The Democrats, to be sure, have made many more rules changes than the Republicans, but the Republicans have not stood pat. The Republican National Committee's Delegates and Organization Committee (1968–1972) persuaded the 1972 national convention to adopt new rules that, among other things, banned proxy voting, eased access to caucuses and conventions selecting national convention delegates, prohibited ex officio delegates, and encouraged the state parties to "take positive action to achieve the broadest possible participation by everyone in party affairs, including such participation by women, young people, minority and heritage [ethnic] groups and senior citizens in the delegate selection process."[1] And the RNC's "Rule 29 Committee" (1972–1975) spelled out how these objectives might be reached, though stopping well short of fixed quotas. Even more important, the many changes in state primary laws and federal campaign finance laws have affected the Republicans almost as much as the Democrats.[2] Hence, while the Democrats may have changed somewhat more than the Republicans, both parties were very different in the late 1970s from what they had been a decade before.

Some commentators hail these changes as reforms in the great American tradition of "increasing the individual citizen's power over and responsibility for the collective political destiny."[3] Others deplore the changes as being prime causes of the parties' "decomposition" or "dismantling."[4] Now, "increasing the individual citizen's power" seems highly praiseworthy and "dismantling the parties" seems most reprehensible. But before we can determine whether either is actually taking place, we have to know what is meant by "increasing citizen power" and "dismantling parties" and what evidence shows that

---

[1] Quoted in William J. Crotty, *Political Reform and the American Experiment* (New York: Thomas Y. Crowell Co., 1977), p. 257. For a review of the Republicans' rules changes, see ibid., pp. 255-60, and Charles Longley, "Party Reform and the Republican Party," a paper presented at the annual meeting of the American Political Science Association, New York, N.Y., August 31–September 3, 1978.

[2] There was one notable exception. All thirty states holding presidential primaries altered their laws governing Democratic primaries so as to bring them into compliance with the party's new Rule 11 requiring the allocation of delegates "in a fashion that fairly reflects the expressed presidential preference . . . of the primary voters." Eighteen of the states also imposed substantially the same requirement on the Republicans, despite the fact that the latter had no national party rule requiring such "proportional representation." But twelve states—including California, Florida, Indiana, New Jersey, and Wisconsin—allowed the Republicans to continue using some version of the traditional winner-take-all principle: see the summary of the states' primary laws in *Congressional Quarterly Weekly Report*, January 31, 1976, pp. 229-42.

[3] Crotty, *Political Reform*, p. 293. For similar evaluations, see John S. Saloma III and Frederick H. Sontag, *Parties: The Real Opportunity for Effective Citizen Politics* (New York: Random House Vintage Books, 1973); and the official report of the Democrats' original Commission on Party Structure and Delegate Selection (the "McGovern-Fraser commission"), *Mandate for Reform* (Washington, D.C.: Democratic National Committee, 1970).

[4] See, for example, Walter Dean Burnham, "The End of American Party Politics," *Trans-action* (December 1969); Jeane Jordan Kirkpatrick, *Dismantling the Parties* (Washington, D.C.: American Enterprise Institute, 1978); David S. Broder, *The Party's Over* (New York: Harper & Row, 1972); Everett Carll Ladd, Jr., " 'Reform' is Wrecking the U.S. Party System," *Fortune*, vol. 96 (November 1977), pp. 177-88; and Frank J. Sorauf, *Party Politics in America*, 3d ed. (Boston: Little, Brown & Co., 1976), chap. 17.

either or both have resulted from the many changes made in the parties since the late sixties.

We are not greatly helped in either regard by the fact that the commentators do not seem to be talking about quite the same things. William Crotty, John Saloma, and Frederick Sontag talk mainly of changes in the number of people who participate in grass roots precinct caucuses and state primaries to choose delegates to national party conventions. Walter Dean Burnham speaks mainly of what is going on in the voters' minds—of their weakening party identifications and the declining influence of those identifications on voting choices. Jeane Kirkpatrick is concerned mainly with the party leaders' loss of power to control or even influence significantly who are the parties' members and workers and who wins presidential nominations. And David Broder focuses mainly on the parties' low cohesion and consequent inability to develop or implement meaningful programs.

V. O. Key, the great scholar of the prereform American parties, might well have said of this confusion that it is another instance of a familiar phenomenon: Burnham is talking about the parties-in-the-electorate; Crotty, Saloma, Sontag, and Kirkpatrick are talking mainly about party organizations; and Broder is talking mainly about the parties-in-government.[5] But, as Key said, there is nothing wrong with this if we use one meaning at a time and if we are always clear about which meaning is being used at the moment.

In that spirit, this chapter has two main purposes: first, to review the leading changes that have taken place in the electoral parties[6] and in the organizational parties since the late 1960s; and second, to estimate the impact of the changes on the parties' role in presidential politics and in the larger political system.

The Electoral Parties: More Participation and Less Loyalty

There have been two main changes in the parties-in-the-electorate since the mid-1960s, and they make an odd couple. One change is the major increase in the number of participants in the parties' presidential nominating processes resulting from a number of reforms intended to make the presidential parties more open and participatory. The other change is the decline in the electorate's proportion of party

---

[5] For Key's definitions of these interchangeable meanings of "party," see his *Politics, Parties and Pressure Groups*, 5th ed. (New York: Thomas Y. Crowell Co., 1964), pp. 163-65.

[6] This is also analyzed by Jeane J. Kirkpatrick in Chapter 7.

loyalists and the increase in its proportion of "independents," so that the more "open" and "democratic" parties of the 1970s have substantially fewer supporters than the more "closed" and "boss-ridden" parties of the 1960s. Let us review the particulars of each change.

Increased Participation.[7] In 1968, a total of around 11 million Americans participated in primaries, caucuses, and conventions directly involved in the selection of the Democratic and Republican candidates for President. In 1976, the total rose to around 30 million. This near-trebling of the number of participants resulted from two developments: changes in the parties' rules, and the proliferation of presidential primaries.

From changes in the party rules. The first, and in many respects the most sweeping and consequential, changes in party rules were those made by the Democrats' Commission on Party Structure and Delegate Selection—generally known as the McGovern-Fraser commission after its two chairmen, Senator George McGovern (S.D.) and Representative Donald Fraser (Minn.).[8] The commission was mandated by the 1968 national convention and in 1969 recommended eighteen "guidelines" for the state parties to follow in selecting their delegates to future national conventions. The Democratic National Committee accepted all eighteen, incorporated them in the call for the 1972 convention, and made compliance with them a prerequisite for seating party delegates at the convention. Two subsequent commissions, the Mikulski commission (1972–1974) and the Winograd commission (1975–1978), revised the McGovern-Fraser rules somewhat, and the revised rules controlled the selection of delegates to the party's national conventions of 1972 and 1976 and national conferences (or "mini-conventions") of 1974 and 1978. The Democrats' new delegate selection rules have the following main thrusts:[9]

First, *rules facilitating participation.* For example, Rule 1 requires that state parties adopt and publicize explicit written rules covering all aspects of delegate selection. Rule 3 requires ample public notice of all party meetings involved in choosing delegates. Rule 4

---

[7] The discussion in the text is drawn mainly from my *Participation in American Presidential Nominations, 1976* (Washington, D.C.: American Enterprise Institute, 1977).

[8] For accounts of the commission's origins, politics, and impact, see my *Curing the Mischiefs of Faction: Party Reform in America* (Berkeley: University of California Press, 1975); Theodore H. White, *The Making of the President 1972* (New York: Bantam Books, 1973), chap. 2; and Crotty, *Political Reform*, pp. 238-47.

[9] The most recent compilation available is *Delegate Selection Rules for the 1976 Democratic National Convention* (Washington, D.C.: Democratic National Committee, 1975).

prohibits the exclusion from the selection process of anyone for failure to pay a cost or fee.

Second, *rules encouraging participation by disadvantaged groups.* The McGovern-Fraser Guidelines A-1 and A-2 required the representation on each state delegation of women, young people, and minority groups "in reasonable relationship to their presence in the population of the State." Most people in 1972 interpreted this to mean mandatory numerical quotas for each group.[10] The Mikulski commission's Rule 18 altered the requirement to one of "affirmative action" to encourage participation by these groups (and added Native Americans to the list), but prohibited the use of mandatory quotas.

Third, *rules making the delegates' preferences a "fair reflection" of Democratic voters' preferences.* Rule 11 requires the most extensive use yet made in America of the principle of "proportional representation" so common in European electoral systems:

> At all stages of the delegate selection process, delegations shall be allocated in a fashion that fairly reflects the expressed presidential preference, uncommitted, or no preference status of the primary voters, or if there be no binding primary, the convention and caucus participants, except that preferences securing less than 15 percent (15%) of the votes cast for the delegation need not be awarded any delegates.

From the proliferation of presidential primaries. Between 1968 and 1976, there was a greater increase in the number of states holding presidential primaries than at any time since the original surge of 1908–1916. The details are shown in Table 6-1.

The state governors and legislators who worked for new presidential primaries after 1968 had a variety of motives. Some decided that the easiest way to comply with the Democrats' new delegate selection rules was to adopt a presidential primary and thereby isolate presidential politics and rules from all of the other activities of the state's parties. Others calculated that the "kooks" of the left or the right were less likely to capture the state parties if delegates were chosen by primaries rather than by the "participatory" caucuses and conventions thrust on the states by the new rules. Still others believed that primaries offered the most democratic way to choose delegates.

Consequences. Whatever may have been the causes for the proliferation of presidential primaries, it had, in combination with

---

[10] For an account of the metamorphosis of "reasonable relationship" into numerical quotas in California in 1972, see Bill Cavala, "Changing the Rules Changes the Game," *American Political Science Review,* vol. 68 (March 1974), pp. 27-44.

Table 6-1

PROLIFERATION OF PRESIDENTIAL PRIMARIES, 1968–1976

Party and Coverage	1968	1972	1976
Democratic Party			
Number of states using a primary for selecting or binding national convention delegates	17	23	29[a]
Number of votes cast by delegates chosen or bound by primaries	983	1,862	2,183
Percent of all votes cast by delegates chosen or bound by primaries	37.5	60.5	72.6
Republican Party			
Number of states using a primary for selecting or binding national convention delegates	16	22	28[a]
Number of votes cast by delegates chosen or bound by primaries	458	710	1,533
Percent of all votes cast by delegates chosen or bound by primaries	34.3	52.7	67.9

[a] Does not include Vermont, which held a nonbinding presidential-preference poll but chose all delegates of both parties by caucuses and conventions.
Source: Austin Ranney, *Participation in American Presidential Nominations, 1976* Washington, D.C.: American Enterprise Institute, 1977), table 1, p. 6.

the more accessible caucuses and conventions ordered by the Democrats' new rules, a major impact on the sheer number of participants in presidential nominations. For instance, in the 1968 presidential primaries, a total of 10,478,395 votes were cast, which constituted only 8.7 percent of the national voting-age population. In the 1976 primaries, the total vote was 28,925,253—19.3 percent of the voting-age population. But the turnout *rate* of eligible voters did not increase —in fact, it was four percentage points lower in 1976 than in 1972.[11] But the jump in the number of states holding primaries from seventeen to thirty meant that in 1976 nearly three times more people participated in presidential primaries than in any previous year.

We have no reliable data for earlier years on the number of participants in caucuses and conventions in the nonprimary states, but *Congressional Quarterly* estimated that in 1976 about 717,200 persons participated in Democratic precinct caucuses.[12] If we guess that another 400,000 participated in comparable Republican gatherings,

[11] Ranney, *Participation*, p. 22.
[12] See table 2 in ibid., p. 16.

we can conclude that over a million people participated in delegate selection in the nonprimary states.

All in all, then, far more people participated in making the two parties' presidential nominations in 1976 than ever before. If "open parties" and "participatory politics" are what we want, we came the closest yet to achieving them in the processes that produced the nominations of Jimmy Carter and Gerald Ford.

At present, several bills are pending before Congress to establish some form of a national presidential primary. Most propose a same-day national primary held throughout the nation without regard to state lines, with the provision that if no candidate receives as much as 40 percent of the votes, a runoff will be held a few weeks later between the two top finishers in the first round. Such proposals have been cropping up ever since 1911, and none has yet even gotten out of committee. But public opinion polls show that around 70 percent of the people favor the idea, and its time may be at hand.[13] Certainly when it arrives, our presidential parties will approach the goal of perfect openness and participation. But whether those participants will value and nurture the parties they control is another question.

Fading Party Loyalties.[14] One of the reasons most frequently given for believing that the presidential parties are "decomposing" or being "dismantled" is the sharp decrease since the mid-1960s in the proportions of strong party identifiers, as measured by the studies of the national electorate conducted by the Center for Political Studies of the University of Michigan since 1952. The data are summarized in Table 6-2.

If we group the strong, weak, and independent identifiers in the two parties for each year shown in Table 6-2, we find that between 1960 and 1976 there was a sharp drop (eleven percentage points) in the proportion of adults describing themselves as strong identifiers, a rise (seven percentage points) in the proportion calling themselves independents but leaning to one of the parties, and a near-doubling (8 to 14 percent) of "pure independents," who express no party preference whatever.

Ironically, then, while the number of participants in party affairs has increased greatly since the 1960s, the party loyalties of the general population have weakened noticeably. That is bad news for those

---

[13] The proposals are described and the arguments for and against each are analyzed in Austin Ranney, *The Federalization of Presidential Primaries* (Washington, D.C.: American Enterprise Institute, 1978).

[14] For a more detailed discussion of trends in party identification see the next chapter, especially pp. 258-63 and 268-74.

Table 6-2
PARTY IDENTIFICATIONS, 1960–1976
(in percentages)

Party Identification	Presidential Election Year				
	1960	1964	1968	1972	1976
Strong Democrat	21	27	20	15	15
Weak Democrat	25	25	25	26	25
Independent Democrat	8	8	9	10	12
Independent	8	8	11	13	14
Independent Republican	7	6	9	11	10
Weak Republican	13	13	14	13	14
Strong Republican	14	11	10	10	9
Other	4	2	2	2	1
Total	100	100	100	100	100

Source: Arthur H. Miller and Warren E. Miller, "Partisanship and Performance: 'Rational' Choice in the 1976 Presidential Election," a paper presented at the annual meeting of the American Political Science Association, Washington, D.C., 1977.

who believe in strong as well as open and participatory parties. But how bad? Some commentators believe it is strong evidence that the parties-in-the-electorate are "decomposing."[15] Others are not so sure. Raymond Wolfinger and his associates, for instance, point out that in every important respect the party leaners behave much more like strong party identifiers than like pure independents. Indeed, they are more partisan than weak identifiers in that they are more likely to vote for their parties' presidential candidates regularly and less likely to flip back and forth between the parties from one election to the next.[16]

On the other hand, the near-doubling of the proportion of pure independents since 1964 constitutes a sure sign of weakened electoral

[15] Cf. Norman H. Nie, Sidney Verba, and John R. Petrocik, *The Changing American Voter* (Cambridge, Mass.: Harvard University Press, 1976), chap. 4; and Burnham, "The End of American Party Politics." See also the discussion by Jeane J. Kirkpatrick in Chapter 7 of this volume.

[16] Bruce R. Keith, David B. Magleby, Candice J. Nelson, Elizabeth Orr, Mark Westlye, and Raymond E. Wolfinger, "The Myth of the Independent Voter," a paper presented at the annual meeting of the American Political Science Association, Washington, D.C., September 1977. See also Richard A. Brody, "Stability and Change in Party Identification: Presidential to Off-Years," a paper presented at the annual meeting of the American Political Science Association, Washington, D.C., September 1977.

parties. Or does it? One of the most firmly established generalizations in the voting behavior literature is that the younger people are, the less likely they are to have strong party identifications. This became politically important in 1971 when the Twenty-sixth Amendment to the Constitution lowered the voting age to eighteen (it had been twenty-one in all but three states) and thereby at a stroke added to the electorate about 11.5 million new voters who were not likely to hold strong party preferences. Nie, Verba, and Petrocik ascribe much of the recent decline in professed partisanship to this "youthing" of the electorate:

> Much of the change in the partisan commitment of Americans appears to come from those new voters who entered the electorate in the late 1960s. Their impact is made greater by the fact that young voters have been an increasing proportion of the electorate. In 1952, 8 percent of our sample was between twenty-one and twenty-four; twenty years later 12 percent of the sample falls in that age group (and if one adds the eighteen to twenty year olds, one has an electorate in 1972 in which 17 percent of its members was not eligible to vote in the previous election). The combination of the fact that the new voters are a larger proportion of the electorate and the fact of their greater independence makes clear that these new voters contribute disproportionately to the decay of partisanship.[17]

Nevertheless, while youthing may account for much of the weakening of the parties-in-the-electorate, it cannot account for all of it. The data in Table 6-2 show that while there was a sharp decline in attachment to the parties from 1968 to 1972, there was an even sharper decline from 1964 to 1968, well before the Twenty-sixth Amendment took effect. It is also noteworthy that the decline slowed down considerably between 1972 and 1976. This may mean that the antiparty trend has "bottomed out" and the attachment to parties may make a comeback, but at the present writing it is too early to tell.

Declining Straight-Ticket Voting. The other evidence of the electoral parties' debilitation is the substantial decrease in straight-ticket voting since the 1960s. Nie, Verba, and Petrocik show that this most partisan kind of voting hit a postwar peak in 1960, when 65 percent of the voters reported casting ballots for all the candidates on their

---

[17] Nie, Verba, and Petrocik, *Changing Voter*, pp. 64-65. See also Arthur H. Miller and Warren E. Miller, "Partisanship and Performance: 'Rational' Choice in the 1976 Presidential Elections," a paper presented at the annual meeting of the American Political Science Association, Washington, D.C., September 1977.

parties' tickets. The proportion plummeted to 43 percent in 1964, 34 percent in 1968, and 33 percent in 1972.[18] In 1976, the figure stayed about the same, and it may be that this trend too has "bottomed out." But in any case, there is no clear relationship between the weakening of party identifications and the decrease in straight-ticket voting. By far the sharpest drop in the latter came between 1960 and 1964 when party identifications were at their peak. And the rates of decrease in straight-ticket voting are smaller than those in party identification in the period since 1964.

In summary, the evidence suggests that there has indeed been some weakening of the parties-in-the-electorate since 1964, in terms of both the number of persons professing party identifications and the power of those identifications to impel voters to vote their parties' straight tickets. The weakening does not seem to warrant quite so drastic a label as "decomposition," but it certainly has gone far enough to concern admirers of strong and well-rooted parties.

The Presidential Party Organizations: More Centralization and Less Control

Most party-watchers in America find it useful to maintain a clear organizational distinction between the "presidential parties" and the "congressional parties." The presidential parties include the organizations (national conventions, national committees, national commissions), leaders (Presidents, presidential candidates, national chairs), workers, and voters who participate in some direct way in nominating presidential candidates, writing national platforms, and formulating the rules concerning those activities. The congressional parties include the organizations (caucuses, steering and policy committees, campaign committees), leaders (floor leaders and whips), and other representatives and senators who bear party labels and participate in party-connected activities in one congressional chamber or the other.

Each party's congressional organization has little or no formal connection with its presidential organization, and the political fortunes of each are largely if not entirely independent from the other's. The best proof of this is the striking difference in competition levels between presidential and congressional politics since World War II. Presidential politics has been highly competitive. Four of the eight presidential elections from 1948 to 1976 have been won by Re-

---

[18] Nie, Verba, and Petrocik, *Changing Voter*, figure 4.3, p. 53.

publicans and four by Democrats. Moreover, Republican candidates have won an aggregate of 270 million votes, while Democratic candidates have won 256 million—in short, a two-party system with a slight edge to the Republicans. Congressional politics is a very different matter. In the sixteen congressional elections from 1946 to 1976, the Republicans won control of either chamber only twice (1946 and 1952). Republican House candidates have won an aggregate of 373 million votes to the Democrats' 421 million, and Republicans have captured a total of 2,922 seats to the Democrats' 4,025. Congressional politics, unlike presidential politics, has constituted a modified Democratic one-party system.

As is usual (though not necessarily desirable) with discussions of American national parties, most of this chapter focuses on the presidential parties. But a few parenthetical remarks on what has happened to the congressional parties seem in order here.

A Few Stirrings in the Congressional Caucuses. As Samuel Patterson notes in Chapter 4 of this book, the most noteworthy development in the congressional parties since the 1960s has been the considerable assumption and modest exercise of new powers by the House Democratic Caucus.[19] In the 1960s and for many decades before, all chairmen of the House's standing committees were chosen almost automatically by the operation of the seniority rule. That rule stipulated that the member of the majority party with the longest continuous service on a committee would be its chairman, regardless of how unpopular he was with his fellow partisans on the committee or in the House. And advocates of disciplined, cohesive, and therefore "responsible" parties long deplored this mode of selection as one of the major barriers against developing such parties.[20]

In 1971, the House Democratic Caucus changed its rules to provide that at the beginning of each new session of Congress each chairman of a standing committee would have to be approved by a vote of the caucus. The caucus first used its new power in 1975, when it voted three very senior Democrats out of their longstanding chairmanships of the committees of Agriculture, Armed Services, and Banking and Currency and replaced them with Democrats more in tune with the caucus's wishes.[21] No similar move was made in 1977,

---

[19] For another analysis of these changes, see Norman J. Ornstein, "The Democrats' Reform Power in the House of Representatives, 1969-75," in *America in the Seventies*, ed. Allan P. Sindler (Boston: Little, Brown & Co., 1977), pp. 2-48.

[20] Cf. James MacGregor Burns, *Congress on Trial* (New York: Harper & Row, 1969), and Broder, *The Party's Over*, pp. 217-18.

[21] *Congressional Quarterly Weekly Report*, January 18, 1975, pp. 114-18.

but the events of 1975 made it clear that henceforth, among the House Democrats at least, the party organization would have to be reckoned with a little more and the seniority system a little less.

Otherwise, not much has happened. Patterson's chapter describes the many changes Congress has undergone since the 1960s, but, with the exception just noted, none have had much to do with the organization and role of the parties. Patterson shows that there was no significant increase in the cohesion of either Democrats or Republicans in the House and Senate. Moreover, the increasing difficulty of defeating incumbent members of the House of either party suggests that party labels, in congressional as in presidential elections, are becoming less important than in the 1960s as prime influences on the voters' choices among candidates.

On the other hand, party labels continue to be moderately useful as predictors of how congressmen and senators will vote, although cohesive party voting has been slowly declining in both chambers since the early 1900s. In the 1960s and earlier, some commentators spoke of "Congress's three-party system"—that is, cohesive northern Democrats opposing cohesive Republicans, with cohesive southern Democrats forming coalitions sometimes with one group, sometimes with the other. In the 1970s, the northern Democrats have become more divided, especially on such issues as forced busing for racial integration of schools, federal funding of abortions for indigent women, and the creation of a consumer protection agency; southern Democrats have come to include a somewhat higher proportion of liberals; and the Republicans have remained mostly conservative with a sprinkling of liberals. The net result has been a slight additional weakening of Democratic and Republican cohesion that masks a larger redistribution of positions among the Democrats.[22]

The quiescence of the congressional parties has been more than outweighed by changes in the presidential party organizations, as the following pages detail.

The Nationalization of the Presidential Parties.[23] Up to the mid-1970s almost every political scientist writing on the structure of American

---

[22] For the details, see Julius Turner, *Party and Constituency: Pressures on Congress* (Baltimore: Johns Hopkins Press, 1970 edition revised by Edward V. Schneier, Jr.); David R. Mayhew, *Party Loyalty among Congressmen* (Cambridge, Mass.: Harvard University Press, 1966); and *Congressional Quarterly Weekly Report*, January 14, 1978, pp. 79-83.

[23] This account is taken mainly from *Curing the Mischiefs of Faction*, pp. 171-87; and Charles D. Longley, "Party Reform and Party Nationalization: The Case of the Democrats," a paper presented at the annual meeting of the Midwest Political Science Association, Chicago, Illinois, 1976.

parties stressed *decentralization*—the fragmentation and dispersion of power among the parties' many national, state, and local organs—as their most salient trait. Most commentators took their lead from E. E. Schattschneider's statements that "the American major party is a loose confederation of state and local bosses for limited purposes" and that the national party machinery is in reality "only the transparent filaments of the ghost of a party."[24] The leading textbook of the 1950s and 1960s said: "In a sense, no nationwide party organization exists. . . . Rather, each party consists of a working coalition of state and local organizations."[25] And the leading textbook of the 1970s says: "So extreme are the traditional observations on the decentralization of the American parties that one is tempted to dismiss them as empty rhetoric or pure hyperbole. . . . [But] closer examination of the American parties reveals that what seems to be hyperbole is merely a statement of reality."[26]

Decentralization under the old rules. Descriptions like the foregoing were accurate enough up to the late 1960s. The presidential parties consisted of two main organs, each of which was set up by the state parties for very limited purposes. The national conventions were the national parties' "supreme governing bodies." But they met for only a few days once every four years; they consisted entirely of delegates from the state and territorial parties; and—this was the key fact—each state's delegates were chosen entirely by rules and procedures laid down by its state party organization and legislature. As a result, the delegates were chosen by a wide variety of procedures, ranging from election in an open primary (Wisconsin) to handpicking by the state party chairmen (Georgia).[27] The national committees were established by the conventions to handle housekeeping matters, mainly making the arrangements for future conventions, in the four-year interims between conventions. With a few minor exceptions, every state party, no matter how small, had the same number of members as every other state party, no matter how

---

[24] E. E. Schattschneider, *Party Government* (New York: Farrar & Rinehart, Inc., 1940), footnote 76, p. 158; p. 163.

[25] Key, *Parties*, p. 315.

[26] Frank J. Sorauf, *Party Politics in America*, 3d ed. (Boston: Little, Brown & Co., 1976), p. 114.

[27] For a summary of the prereform rules, see Paul T. David, Ralph M. Goldman, and Richard C. Bain, *The Politics of National Party Conventions* (Washington, D.C.: Brookings Institution, 1960), chaps. 10-11. Brief summaries of states' and territories' rules in 1968 are given in *Mandate for Reform*, pp. 56-63.

large. The leading scholarly book on the national committees was aptly entitled *Politics without Power.*[28]

Truly, then, the national parties up to the late 1960s were "only the transparent filaments of the ghost of a party." But no longer.

Centralization under the new rules. We observed earlier that since the 1960s the Democratic party has adopted a whole new set of rules governing how the state parties' delegates to national party conventions are chosen. We also noted the new rules' part in increasing the number of participants in the parties' presidential nominating processes. And later we shall examine the impact of the rules on the kind of people who participate and the kind of candidates who are advantaged. But for our present purposes, the new rules are significant because they constitute the first increase in the power of a party's *national* organs since the heyday of presidential nominations by congressional caucuses from 1800 to 1824.

Remember that from the 1820s to the 1960s, each state's Democratic party and/or legislature decided for itself how the state's delegates to the national conventions would be chosen and who would do the choosing. So no matter how "national" the conventions were in appearance, the real power over who attended them resided entirely in the states.

In the 1970s, however, the party's new rules provide, among other things, that: only Democratic voters can participate in choosing national convention delegates; no proxy voting is permitted; the unit rule is outlawed; all candidates for delegate must make known their presidential preferences, if any, prior to the selection process; each presidential candidate must approve the delegate candidates running as his or her supporters; delegates must be chosen in a manner which "fairly reflects the division of preferences expressed by those who participate"; no ex officio or "automatic" delegate slots may be reserved for party notables; and every state party must adopt and implement an "affirmative action" program "to encourage full participation by all Democrats, with particular concern for minority groups, Native Americans, women, and youth."

Everywhere the state parties now turn, they are hedged in by these rules. Note, moreover, that the rules were drawn up by a series of commissions mandated by national conventions and appointed by national chairmen. They are incorporated in the national committees' calls for the succeeding national conventions. The states' adherence

---

[28] Cornelius P. Cotter and Bernard C. Hennessy, *Politics without Power: The National Party Committees* (New York: Atherton Press, 1964).

to the affirmative action rules is monitored by a Judicial Council. And the ultimate sanction enforcing these rules is the national conventions' power to deny seats and votes to the delegates of any state whose selection is held to be in noncompliance with the rules.

The new rules have stuck and stuck hard. Moved by the fear of losing their seats at the national convention and/or by their agreement with the spirit and substance of the new rules, most state parties were in full compliance in both 1972 and 1976. If there had been any question about whether the new rules had teeth, it was answered when the 1972 convention refused to seat the delegation from Cook County, Illinois, which had been handpicked by the most powerful local party "boss" of the time, Mayor Richard J. Daley of Chicago.

Consequently, in the late 1970s there is no doubt that the power to determine all rules and procedures for selecting delegates to the national conventions has passed entirely—and in all probability permanently—from the state parties and legislatures to the national conventions, commissions, and committees. Moreover, the national party rules are superior not only to state party rules but even to state laws.

The legal supremacy of national party rules over state laws.[29] A number of the Democrats' new national rules run squarely counter to some state laws. For example, Rule 2-A requires that only Democratic voters be allowed to participate in any Democratic delegate selection process, including primary voting. But the election laws of Wisconsin require an "open primary" in which any voter is allow to vote in either party's primary without any test of party membership or even any public declaration of which party's primary he has chosen. As we saw earlier, in 1976 the Compliance Review Commission gave the Wisconsin Democrats a last-minute "exception" to the rule against open primaries. But they reserved the right to refuse seats to a future Wisconsin delegation if it were elected by Republicans as well as Democrats.

The critical case, however, involved Mayor Daley's Cook County slate of delegates in 1972. The story is worth recounting in some detail.[30] In preparation for the Illinois presidential primary in March 1972, Mayor Daley and his organization, as they had for many previous primaries, held a private confab in which they chose a carefully balanced slate of Daley loyalists for the fifty-nine delegate posts from Cook County. The slate was put before the voters as the

---

[29] This discussion is drawn mainly from Longley, "Party Nationalization," pp. 10-14.

[30] For a fuller account, see Theodore H. White, *The Making of the President 1972* (New York: Bantam Books, 1973), pp. 217-19.

"Mayor's" or "official" slate. It was opposed by an opposition slate led by dissident Alderman William Singer. And in the primary, conducted entirely according to Illinois's election laws, the Daley slate—as usual—swept the field by a wide margin. But at the convention the Singer group challenged the seating of the Daley delegates because the manner in which they had been elected violated two national party rules: (1) Guideline C-5, which required that no slate of candidates be put forth as the official slate; and (2) C-6, which required open access for all interested Democrats to all meetings involved in forming slates of candidates.

In response to the Singer group's challenge, the national convention's Credentials Committee voted, by seventy-one to sixty-one, that the Daley slate was indeed in violation of the rules, that they should therefore be denied their seats, and that the Singer group should be seated in their place.

This flat assertion of the supremacy of national party rules over state laws led to two lines of litigation. The first culminated in the ruling by the Supreme Court three days before the convention met that there was insufficient time to conduct hearings and render an authoritative opinion on the constitutional questions involved, and therefore the issue would have to be decided by the party machinery.[31] It was: the convention backed up the Credentials Committee, the Daley delegation was thrown out, and the Singer delegation was seated.

The other line of litigation resulted in the Supreme Court's clearest statement yet of the principle that national party rules supersede state laws. Shortly after the vote of the Credentials Committee, one Paul Wigoda, acting on behalf of the Daley delegates, got an injunction from the Cook County Circuit Court prohibiting the Singer delegates from taking their seats or otherwise acting as delegates from Illinois at the convention. The Singer group ignored the injunction, took their seats, and participated fully as delegates. Shortly thereafter, criminal proceedings were initiated against them for disobeying the injunction. The validity of the injunction was upheld by the Illinois Appellate Court, which declared that the election laws of Illinois were legally of higher standing than the rules of the national Democratic party. As they put it:

> Because election to the office of convention delegate in Illinois is governed by nondiscriminatory state legislation, the instant case is not merely an intraparty factional dispute

---

[31] O'Brien v. Brown, 409 U.S. 1 (1972).

to be settled by party discipline. In this case, the law of the State is supreme and party rules to the contrary are of no effect. . . . We think the convention, a voluntary association, was without power or authority to deny the elected delegates their seats in the Convention and most certainly could not force them upon the people of Illinois as their representatives contrary to their elective mandate. Such action is an absolute destruction of the democratic process of this nation and cannot be tolerated.[32]

The Illinois court's view was certainly widespread up to 1972, but it was soon overruled by the federal courts. The Singer group appealed the Illinois decision to the United States Supreme Court, and in the leading case of *Cousins* v. *Wigoda* (1975) the Court declared that the national party rules are in most circumstances superior to state laws. Justice Brennan, writing for the Court majority, argued thus: The right to organize and associate with others in a political party is part of the freedom of association protected by the U.S. Constitution's First and Fourteenth Amendments. It can therefore be abridged or limited by the state law only when "a compelling State interest" makes it absolutely necessary. In this case, Illinois's interest in protecting the integrity and authority of its presidential primary was not sufficiently compelling to warrant any such infringement of freedom of association. After all, the states have no constitutionally mandated role in the selection of candidates for President and vice president. That role is performed by the national party conventions, and they therefore have the final word about whether a delegation should be seated. And finally, this clinching argument:

If the qualifications and eligibility of delegates to National Political Party Conventions were left to state law, "each of the fifty states could establish the qualifications of its delegates to the various party conventions without regard to party policy, an obviously intolerable result." Such a regime could seriously undercut or indeed destroy the effectiveness of the National Party Convention as a concerted enterprise engaged in the vital process of choosing Presidential and Vice-Presidential candidates—a process which usually involves coalitions cutting across state lines. The Convention serves the pervasive national interest in the selection of candidates for national office, and this national interest is greater than any interest of an individual State.[33]

---

[32] 14 Ill. App., 3d 460, N.E. 2d at 627, 631, quoted in Longley, "Party Reform," p. 12.

[33] Cousins v. Wigoda, 419 U.S. 477 (1975), at 490.

The concurring opinion of Justices Rehnquist, Burger, and Stewart suggested that *all* national party rules may not be superior to *all* conflicting state laws under *all* circumstances, though they did not specify the conditions under which state laws would supersede. So at the end of the 1970s, it is clear that the national party organs' power to make rules governing presidential nominating processes is, in both political reality and legal principle, at its highest peak by far since the early 1820s. Yet the new rules, as we shall see, have all but destroyed the power of national and state party leaders to control the nominating game played under those rules.

Who Participates? The New Presidential Elite [34]

The old elite. We have noted that the Democrats' new delegate selection rules were intended in part to increase the sheer number of participants in the party's presidential nominating process and that they succeeded admirably. They were also intended to facilitate and encourage participation by people quite different from those who had dominated delegate selection in the past.

By all the evidence we have, the "old presidential elite" was predominantly male (85 percent or more), middle-aged (95 percent or more over the age of thirty), and white (95 percent or more). Most of the old elite were "party regulars"—that is, faithful supporters of and/or contributors to the party year-in, year-out regardless of the nature of the candidate or platform in any particular year. Most were handpicked by state and local party leaders as rewards for past services and/or anticipated future services *to the party.* Quite a few had held some kind of party or public office. And, as one would expect of such people, most placed a high value on such goals as choosing the candidate most likely to win the election, uniting the party behind him, and leaving the party in the best possible condition to fight not only the current election but future elections.[35]

The new rules. Many of the rules adopted from 1969 on were designed to ensure that the participants in presidential politics would be quite different from the old elite. For example, several of the rules strip party leaders and other party regulars of any special advantage

---

[34] The phrase is borrowed from the most thorough exploration of the topic yet: Jeane J. Kirkpatrick, *The New Presidential Elite* (New York: Russell Sage Foundation and Twentieth Century Fund, 1976).

[35] See David, Goldman, and Bain, *Politics of National Party Conventions,* chap. 14; and Nelson W. Polsby and Aaron Wildavsky, *Presidential Elections,* 4th ed. (New York: Scribners, 1976), chaps. 1, 6.

their greater experience might give them over "outsiders" previously inactive in party affairs who wanted to support a particular candidate or policy in a particular presidential year. Thus Rule 3-A requires that all delegate selection processes take place in the calendar year of the national convention. Rules 3-B and 3-C stipulate that all delegate selection meetings must be scheduled at convenient and uniform times and that those times must be well-publicized in advance of the meetings. Rule 13 prohibits anyone from being given a delegate post by virtue of any party or public office he or she holds. And Rule 18-A requires each state party to adopt an "affirmative action plan" designed "to encourage full participation by all Democrats, with particular concern for minority groups, Native Americans, women, and youth, in the delegate selection process and in all Party affairs."

The results: demographics The "quotas" of 1972 and the "affirmative action plans" of 1976 have had a major impact upon the distribution of certain demographic characteristics of Democratic national convention delegates, as is clear from the data in Table 6-3.

Table 6-3 shows, among other things, that the de facto quotas in 1972 produced proportions of women, blacks, and young people among the delegates that were quite close to the groups' proportions in the general population. In 1972-1973, the Mikulski commission moderated the quotas into "affirmative action," and as a result there was some slippage in the proportions of all three demographic groups in the 1976 convention. This fact was not lost on any of the favored groups, but the women were the best organized to do something about it. At the 1976 convention, they were able, with the approval of candidate Jimmy Carter, to persuade the convention to adopt a resolution that, "consistent with the tradition of the Democratic Party, the calls to the 1978 Midterm Convention and future National Conventions shall promote equal division between delegate men and delegate women from each State and Territory." [36]

Subsequent interpretations ruled that this did not quite impose on the party an immediate mandatory requirement that 50 percent or more of the delegates in 1978 and 1980 be women, but the 1976 resolution constituted a long step on that path. Table 6-3 also shows that the delegates were predominantly middle-class in both conventions. There were many more women, youth, and blacks than in 1968, to be sure; but, like the middle-aged WASP males who survived, they were mainly college-educated, upper-income, upper-status people.

---

[36] *Congressional Quarterly Weekly Report*, July 17, 1976, p. 1938.

Table 6-3
DEMOGRAPHIC CHARACTERISTICS OF DEMOCRATIC
NATIONAL CONVENTION DELEGATES AND ALTERNATES,
1968–1976
(in percentages)

Characteristic	Convention Delegates			General Population
	1968	1972	1976	1970
Sex				
Women	13	40	33	51
Men	87	60	67	49
Race				
Nonwhite	5.5	15	11	11
White	94.5	85	89	89
Age				
Under 30	3	22	15	21
30 and over	97	78	85	79
Annual Income				
Under $10,000	—	13	8	44
Over $20,000	—	52	70	12
Education				
No college	—	17	10	78
Some college,				
college graduate	—	54	40	18
Graduate degree	—	29	50	4

Source: The 1968 data are taken from the Commission on Party Structure and Delegate Selection, *Mandate for Reform* (Washington, D.C.: Democratic National Committee, 1970), pp. 26-29. The 1972 data are from Jeane Kirkpatrick, *The New Presidential Elite* (New York: Russell Sage Foundation and the Twentieth Century Fund, 1976), chap. 3. The 1976 data were furnished by the staff of the Democratic National Committee's Commission on Presidential Nomination and Party Structure, 1978. Data for the general population, 1970, were taken from the Bureau of the Census, *Statistical Abstract of the U.S., 1974* (Washington, D.C.: Bureau of the Census, 1974).

Kirkpatrick's study of the 1972 delegates shows, further, that the proportions of professionals—lawyers, teachers, journalists—increased and that the proportions of businessmen, workers, and farmers decreased. She suggests that these changes are bound to affect not only the nature of the delegates but the whole character of presidential politics. In her words:

Self-employed businessmen seek profits; workers are aggressively concerned with wages, hours, and working conditions. Both groups are frankly self-interested. Professionals, by contrast, are more likely to see themselves as participating in politics for reasons unrelated to material rewards. The business and trade union ethos alike stress economic self-interest as a legitimate incentive. The professional ethos stresses service. This does not mean that the professional is necessarily more altruistic than the businessman or worker; it does mean that a politics dominated by professionals will differ in style and probably also in substance from a political process in which businessmen and workers are more numerous. Politics conducted by professionals will probably feature more emphasis on the symbolic aspects of politics and less on the output of goods and services.[37]

The results: participation by officeholders. In the prereform days, it was customary in most states to reserve delegate slots for the parties' main elected officials, particularly governors, U.S. senators, and U.S. representatives. Quite often, such people were most influential in making the conventions' decisions. But the Democrats' new rules, as we have seen, took dead aim at any such special privilege. Rule 13 requires that "no person shall serve as an automatic or ex officio voting delegate at any level of the delegate selection process by virtue of holding a public or Party office." Any party or public officeholder who wanted to participate in 1972 or 1976 had to compete in the state caucuses, conventions, and primaries just like everyone else. Evidently, many were reluctant to do so, and some who did were rejected because they backed the wrong presidential candidate. The results appear in Table 6-4.

Table 6-4
DEMOCRATIC PUBLIC OFFICEHOLDERS SERVING AS NATIONAL CONVENTION DELEGATES, 1956–1976
(in percentages)

Convention Year	U.S. Senators	U.S. Representatives	Governors
1956	90	33	100
1960	68	45	85
1964	72	46	61
1968	68	39	83
1972	36	15	80
1976	18	15	47

Source: Furnished by the staff of the Democratic National Committee's Commission on Presidential Nomination and Party Structure, 1978.

As Table 6-4 shows, the proportion of officeholders serving as delegates took a sharp dip in the 1972 convention and dropped even further in the 1976 convention.

[37] Kirkpatrick, *Presidential Elite*, p. 71.

The results: the delegates' policy preferences and representative-ness. Herbert McClosky's classic study comparing the policy prefer-ences of convention delegates and of rank-and-file party identifiers in 1956 found that Democratic delegates were substantially more liberal than ordinary Democratic identifiers, and Republican delegates were comparably more conservative than the Republican rank and file.[38] Jeane Kirkpatrick's study of delegates to the two 1972 conventions found the same kind of leader/follower differences that McClosky had found, but much greater differences among Democrats than among Republicans. Indeed, she found that the differences between the Democratic delegates and the Democratic identifiers were so great that the policy preferences of ordinary Democratic identifiers were much better represented by *Republican* delegates than by Democratic delegates! The data are shown in Table 6-5.

Table 6-5 shows that on five of seven leading issues in 1972 the preferences of ordinary Democratic identifiers were much nearer to those of delegates to the Republican convention than to those of delegates to the Democratic convention. I have no 1976 data for the Republicans, but studies of the Democrats show that the differences between their identifiers and convention delegates in 1976, while narrower than in 1972, were still quite marked, as Table 6-6 makes clear.

In summary, then, there has been a major change in the nature as well as the number of participants in the presidential parties since the late 1960s. The main differences can be tabulated thus:

Participants in Presidential Nominations

1960s, before the Reforms	*1970s, after the Reforms*
Mainly "party regulars"	Mainly "issue and candidate enthusiasts"
Predominatly male, white, middle-aged	Many more women, minorities, youth
Included most of the party's public officeholders	Included only a few of the party's public officeholders
Higher socioeconomic status than identifiers	Even higher gap with identifiers' socioeconomic status
Policy preferences somewhat more liberal than those of identifiers	Policy preferences much more liberal than those of identifiers

[38] Herbert McClosky, Paul J. Hoffman, and Rosemary O'Hara, "Issue Conflict and Consensus Among Party Leaders and Followers," *American Political Science Review*, vol. 54 (1960), pp. 406-27.

Table 6-5

POLICY PREFERENCES OF PARTY
DELEGATES AND IDENTIFIERS, 1972

(in percentages)

	Policy Preferences			
	Democratic		Republican	
Policy Alternatives	Delegates	Identifiers	Delegates	Identifiers
Main consideration in social welfare				
Abolish poverty	57	22	10	13
Obligation to work	28	69	75	79
Busing for school integration				
Bus to integrate	66	15	8	5
Keep children in neighborhood school	25	82	84	93
Main consideration in dealing with crime				
Protect rights of accused	78	36	21	28
Stop crimes regardless of accuseds' rights	13	50	56	56
Government action toward inflation				
Govt. should do all possible	87	78	74	63
No govt. action necessary	4	9	6	14
Attitude toward political demonstrators				
Favorable	59	14	14	8
Unfavorable	22	67	72	76
Attitude toward the military				
Favorable	42	67	84	71
Unfavorable	43	16	4	12
Attitude toward police				
Favorable	71	81	94	84
Unfavorable	13	7	2	5

Source: Jeane Kirkpatrick, *The New Presidential Elite* (New York: Russell Sage Foundation and Twentieth Century Fund, 1976), chap. 10.

Table 6-6
POLICY PREFERENCES OF DEMOCRATIC
DELEGATES AND IDENTIFIERS, 1976
(in percentages)

Policy Preference	Delegates	Identifiers
Favor busing for school integration	50	24
Feel nation is spending too much for defense	60	30
Favor right to abortion without restriction	83	42
Favor death penalty for serious crimes	54	76
Feel too much attention has been paid to welfare of minorities	14	42
Describe themselves as "conservative"	8	36

Source: Everett Carll Ladd, Jr., " 'Reform' is Wrecking the U.S. Party System," *Fortune*, vol. 96 (November 1977), p. 181.

The rules of the game have changed and the nature of the players has changed as well. What difference, if any, do these changes make for who wins and who loses? That is our final concern.

The Parties' Role in Presidential Politics

Presidential Nominations: Parties as Prizes, Not Judges. Up to the late 1960s, political scientists typically described the role of the parties in presidential politics something like this: Most delegates to the national conventions were party regulars who owed their presence there to the favor of state and local party chiefs, called "bosses" by their opponents and "leaders" by their supporters. Thus, the delegates' prime loyalties belonged to their party chiefs, not to national presidential aspirants, and they voted in the conventions as the chiefs ordered. Consequently, presidential nominations were made after negotiation and bargaining by coalitions of the chiefs, each of whom could deliver the votes he promised to fulfill his part of a deal.

After the nomination, the candidate turned to organizing his campaign to win the November election. He retained the chiefs who had made up his nominating coalition, augmented them with most of the chiefs who had joined losing coalitions, and depended upon them to plan and execute his campaign strategy and tactics, mobilize the state and local parties on his behalf, and raise the money to support the whole effort. He usually put his own man in as national chairman, who then became the campaign director. After the November election, the national party organizations went into hibernation until presidential politics began to heat up three years later when the new crop of aspirants began to seek support for the next nomination or the incumbent President told his national committee it was time to get going on his renomination.

So the party organizations played a central role in presidential politics. No matter that they were merely confederations of state parties dominated by state and local party leaders. No matter that they slept for thirty-seven months out of every forty-eight. When they *were* awake, they ran the show. A colleague and I, writing in 1956, summed it up thus:

> [The parties] make nominations and write platforms, and so "boil down" the number of alternatives to a manageable number; they organize, finance, and conduct campaigns, and so acquaint the voters with what is involved in the choice among them; and they staff the election machinery, oversee its operation, and get out the vote, thereby assisting the voters to use their powers . . . today they are the main suppliers of the fuel and energy that animates and operates the legal election machinery.[39]

The most recent presidential nomination made in the traditional way was that of Hubert Humphrey by the Democrats in 1968. It may well have been the last. In all essentials, it was like the nomination of Adlai Stevenson in 1952. An incumbent President (Harry Truman, Lyndon Johnson) was challenged by a dissident senator (Estes Kefauver, Eugene McCarthy). The dissident did unexpectedly well in the first primary, in New Hampshire, and the incumbent withdrew. The dissident continued to do well in the primaries, but the primaries elected or bound only 40 percent of all delegates. Most of the nonprimary delegates followed their national, state, and local party organization leaders; and most of the leaders rejected the dissident in favor of another aspirant they believed would be a more appealing candidate in the general election and a better President if elected (Adlai Stevenson, Hubert Humphrey). Even though the leaders' choice entered no primaries and the dissident proclaimed himself "the choice

---

[39] Austin Ranney and Willmoore Kendall, *Democracy and the American Party System* (New York: Harcourt, Brace & Co., 1956), p. 505. For a similar description, see Key, *Politics*, chaps. 15, 17.

of the grass roots," the leaders had enough clout among the delegates to get their man chosen.[40]

After the 1968 convention, the anti-Vietnam War Democrats and McCarthy supporters were outraged by the "bosses' steal" of the nomination and the "flouting of the popular will." They pressed for and obtained a commission to reform the rules that had made such injustice possible. The McGovern-Fraser commission was appointed in 1969, and the basic thrust of its many reforms was to end, once and for all, the traditional dominance of regular party leaders and their followers. Commissioner David Mixner's rhetoric may have been more colorful than his fellow commissioners', but he spoke for the views of the majority when he declared:

> Mr. Chairman, every time you let these party people have any role in the process, they'll find some way to cheat you. If it's not Winner-Take-All, it's slating, or it's manipulation of some other rule. And boy can they deal at the convention, if you let them get to the convention, with the power they have over winner-take-all. If there's ever backroom deals, they're going to be made after the second and third ballot, by these party people. It'll be, "I'll deliver you my delegation for this and this and this." It's happened and it will continue to happen. You've got to get these party people out of the process, you've got to, at least you've got to have a system which is so open that they get overwhelmed. I think most reformers now agree that you cannot allow these regular party people to have control over anything, and still hope that you will have democracy in the parties.[41]

In this spirit, the commission majority wrote the new rules designed to transfer power over presidential nominations from party regulars to people committed, not necessarily to the party, but to a particular presidential aspirant or policy in the year of the convention. They succeeded. In the late 1970s, as we have seen, the situation is radically different from that in 1968 or 1952. The national party organs now override the state parties and even state laws in laying down the rules governing the selection of delegates. Most delegates owe their seats not to the favor of any state or local "boss" but to

---

[40] For 1952, see Paul T. David, Malcolm Moos, and Ralph M. Goldman, *Presidential Nominating Politics in 1952* (Baltimore: The Johns Hopkins Press, 1954), Vol. I; for 1968, see Theodore H. White, *The Making of the President 1968* (New York: Pocket Books, 1970).

[41] McGovern-Fraser commission transcripts, November 19-20, 1969, furnished by courtesy of the staff of the Democratic National Committee's Commission on Presidential Nomination and Party Structure.

their identification with a national presidential aspirant ("favorite sons" are outlawed) who did well in their state's caucuses and convention or primary—and perhaps also to their sex, ethnic identity, or age group. Their commitments are mainly to their candidate or their demographic group, certainly not to the party. Most state and local regular organization chiefs are not even at the conventions, and those who are have no power whatever to "control" the delegates' votes. Presidential nominations are contested by candidate-centered organizations. Each organization is assembled by the candidate and his inner circle. Each is financed in part by funds it raises and in part by federal matching funds (see below). Each appeals to the party rank and file in primaries, caucuses, and conventions with little concern for what the state organization leaders do or don't do. The party organizations simply are not actors in presidential politics. Indeed, they are little more than custodians of the party-label prize which goes to the winning candidate organization. The parties have long since ceased to be judges *awarding* the prize.

Political scientist Christopher Arterton puts the present picture in sharp focus:

> Conventions are no longer best conceptualized as gatherings of important party members to select a candidate. With the passing of control over delegate selection processes from party to national candidate organizations, conventions have become meetings of individuals with a primary, though varying, commitment to a particular candidate. The evolution toward candidate-centered conventions suggests the need for a re-examination of much of the established thinking about conventions.
>
> First, consider the relationship between delegates and the constituencies they represent. To the extent that conventions have become arenas for competing candidate organizations, the question of the correspondence of delegate attitudes on public policy issues to the attitudes of party voters becomes a tangential matter. Rather, as delegates come to resemble mere instruments of their campaign, the germane issues involve mechanisms for insuring delegate loyalty and the correspondence in candidate preferences between voters and convention delegates. Second, in a candidate-centered convention, platform writing and party governance issues will naturally and inextricably become linked to the nomination question. Although the platform and rule issues do provide real and symbolic prizes, useful for unifying the party around the nomination outcome, we need to consider the consequences of having all party business deter-

mined by the nomination struggle. Such a system is tantamount to parties being no more than arenas for candidate competition.[42]

The Democrats' two postreform nominations illustrate Arterton's comments. In 1972, the candidacy of George McGovern was opposed by most party organization leaders and supporters because McGovern was thought to be too radical and unelectable. But the new rules put a premium on the kind of dedicated, issue-oriented army of enthusiasts that McGovern, like McCarthy four years earlier, mobilized. They dominated the caucuses and conventions, maximized the translation of primary votes to delegates won, and generally took advantage of the advantages conferred on them by the new rules. McGovern won on the first ballot where McCarthy had lost in 1968.

In 1976, Jimmy Carter started the year as perhaps the most "outside" of all "outsiders" in the history of presidential politics. He had had no experience in national office and little in national party affairs. He was little known to most national and state leaders. He had previously been governor of a southern state that never in history had supplied a major-party presidential candidate, and he had been out of even that office for two years. But none of that mattered. He campaigned all-out for two full years before the first 1976 caucuses and primaries, and he followed the correct strategy of running everywhere and of putting his main efforts on the early delegate selections so that he would soon become the front-runner. His shrewd strategy and maximum effort—aided by the new rules and no doubt also by a considerable anti-Washington mood in the country—worked magically. Against great odds, he not only won the nomination but locked it up earlier than any candidate had in a contested nomination for many years.[43]

Even the Republicans were affected by the new situation. Although they began 1976 with the greatest asset a presidential party can have—an incumbent President eligible and running for a second term—they almost dumped Gerald Ford in favor of Ronald Reagan, another ex-governor who had been campaigning for two years. In the end, they stuck with their incumbent, although only after one of the closest struggles in many years. And after Ford's narrow squeak, no incumbent President of either party can assume that his renomina-

---

[42] F. Christopher Arterton, "Strategies and Tactics of Candidate Organizations," *Political Science Quarterly*, vol. 92 (Winter 1977-78), pp. 663-71.

[43] One of the best accounts is Jules Witcover, *Marathon: The Pursuit of the Presidency, 1972-1976* (New York: Viking Press, 1977).

tion is inevitable or that it can be won against serious opposition without a stiff fight.

Campaign Finance: From Fund-Raisers to Innocent Bystanders. The "Watergate" crimes of 1972–1974 were perpetrated entirely by the nonparty Committee to Reelect the President (CREEP), and the Republican *party* organization had nothing to do with them. Indeed, had the party been as powerful as it was in, say, the 1950s, it might well have prevented them. Certainly it would have had a powerful incentive to do so, for while CREEP's sole objective was to secure the largest possible plurality for Richard Nixon, the Republican party had to look to other offices than the presidency and to other elections than those of 1972. It is therefore particularly ironic that one of the chief responses to Watergate was the enactment of a campaign finance law that weakened the national parties still further. Let us review its main provisions before we consider its consequences.

The Federal Election Campaign Act (FECA) was adopted in 1971, and major amendments were added in 1974 and 1976. As amended, its main provisions are as follows:

(1) Limits on contributions. Each person is limited to contributing $1,000 to a candidate in primary elections and another $1,000 in the general election. He is also limited to a total of $25,000 of all such contrubutions in any calendar year. Organizations are limited to $5,000 contributions to any candidate in any election.

(2) Restrictions on expenditures. Presidential aspirants are limited to $10 million in expenditures for the nomination, and $20 million in those for the general election. Party committtes are allowed to spend up to two cents per voter on the general election campaign, which amounts to about $4 million.

(3) Federal financing of campaigns. If an aspirant for a presidential nomination qualifies, the federal government will finance up to 50 percent of his campaign expenses. To qualify, he must raise at least $5,000 in contributions of no more than $250 each in each of at least twenty states. If he does, the government will match every contribution of $250 or less up to a total of $5 million. But if he accepts federal funds (as every candidate did in 1976), he must limit his total spending to $10 million. For the general election, each candidate may receive up to $20 million for his campaign without bothering with matching funds. But if he accepts federal money, he may not raise funds privately or spend beyond the $20 million limit. And whatever he raises and spends, both as aspirant for the nomination and candidate for the presidency, must be accounted for in

reports regularly submitted to the Federal Election Commission, which rules on whether or not he is complying with the law.

Impact on the parties.[44] Neither Common Cause, which was the principal pressure group pushing FECA, nor Congress, which adopted it, was out to "get" the parties. Their objective was to "clean up" the financing of federal campaigns and to remove the influence of "special interest" money. But, intentionally or not, the machinery they adopted further weakens the parties. The main reasons are these:

(1) Candidates, not parties, get the money. The federal matching funds provided for the prenomination and general election campaigns go to the candidates and their organizations, not to party committees for distribution to candidates. The parties are given $2 million each to finance their national conventions and about $4 million to do a little general-election campaigning. But 90 percent of the matching funds for the general elections and 100 percent for the prenomination campaigns go to the candidates, not the parties.

This has several effects, all bad for the parties. One is to accelerate the parties' decline as campaign managers. Rendering the party leaders insignificant as sources of campaign funds removes one of the few reasons left for giving them important roles in making and executing campaign strategy. And the less prominent they are in general election campaigning, the less important it is to deal with them in the prenomination campaigns.

(2) Permitting only small contributions hurts the parties. Most studies of campaign finance prior to 1976 stressed the fact that political parties characteristically raised most of their funds by relatively large contributions from relatively few contributors. The national committees have made occasional attempts to attract large numbers of small donations, but they have never produced very much.[45] There is no great mystery about why this should be so. Party organizations, after all, are *continuing* bodies. They appear under the same names election after election, regardless of the issues or candidates that are prominent in any particular election. They are not ad hoc committees pulled together for the short-term purpose of pushing a special cause

---

[44] This section borrows freely from my paper "The Impact of Campaign Finance Reforms of American Presidential Parties," presented at the Conference on Political Money and Election Reform: Comparative Perspectives, University of Southern California, Los Angeles, December 10, 1977.

[45] Cf. Delmer D. Dunn, *Financing Presidential Campaigns* (Washington, D.C.: Brookings Institution, 1972), pp. 108-10; and Herbert Alexander's studies of campaign finance in 1960 and 1964 (published by the Citizens Research Foundation in 1962 and 1966) and in 1968 and 1972 (published by the D.C. Heath Company in 1971 and 1976).

or a unique candidate. Hence, it is not surprising that they characteristically rely mainly on their long-term connections with wealthy donors, not on their ability to inspire and capitalize on short-term enthusiasm for issues or candidates of the moment.

The FECA's limits on contributions, especially the $250 limit on contributions that will be matched by federal funds, put a heavy premium on the ability to generate very large numbers of small contributions. And experience has shown that the best technique for this purpose is direct-mail solicitation of many thousands of names on computerized lists of persons who have previously made contributions to causes and candidates (there aren't enough who have made contributions to parties to bother with).

Like most techniques of modern campaigning, direct-mail solicitation is a highly complex, mechanized, and professionalized operation. Its most successful practitioner in the 1970s was Richard Viguerie, who raised over $3 million for conservative candidates and causes from the "priceless computerized mailing lists he has built up in more than a decade of work." It should also be noted that Viguerie was strongly committed to conservatism and weakly committed to the Republican party. Indeed, he said of the GOP, "it will have to become a conservative vehicle or it will die." [46]

The FECA, then, has largely rendered obsolete the money-raising techniques most suitable for party organizations and put a premium on techniques most suitable for nonparty—indeed, antiparty—groups dedicated to ideological causes and candidates. It has thereby minimized the parties' role in a function they used to dominate.

(3) Expenditure limitations make for personalistic, nonparty campaigns. Just about everyone, participants and observers alike, agrees that the FECA's expenditure ceilings were too low in 1976 to permit the campaigns to include all the activities they used to include. A minor effect of this financial austerity was the general disappearance of campaign buttons, bumper stickers, local rallies, and other campaign items that people used to enjoy. A major effect was the decision of most candidate organizations to allocate greater shares of their funds than ever before to TV spot advertisements and programs. FECA did not, of course, create the new emphasis on TV campaigning. The trend started as early as 1952. But FECA's expenditure limits certainly accelerated it in 1976.

As several analysts have pointed out, TV campaigning has a strong tendency to focus on the candidates' personalities and on the issues—that is, the issues as identified and interpreted by network

[46] *Congressional Quarterly Weekly Report*, June 11, 1977, pp. 1141-43.

commentators. TV has a concomitant tendency to blur the candidates' party affiliations and ignore the party organizations behind those affiliations. After all, the basic reason for TV's effectiveness is the sense, however spurious, it conveys of establishing direct, unmediated personal relationships between the candidate in the studio and the viewers at home. In such relationships, there is no place for the parties; for what are they but the same old gang of politicians doing their same old thing of organizing meetings, decorating halls, setting up parades, and in general intruding themselves between the sovereign people and their future President? Democrats and Republicans have been around forever, and who cares about them anyway? But Carter and Ford are new (after all, where were *they* in the public gaze when McGovern and Nixon were battling it out in 1972?), and their contest is new, different, and, if not exactly exciting, at least a lot more interesting than the national committees and the party platforms.[47]

Thus, anything that increases the role of TV in national campaigns diminishes the role of the parties. And while many developments in society and technology have contributed to the tube's growing importance in recent campaigns, the FECA's regulations gave it a big boost in 1976.

(4) Strict accounting made for arms-length candidate-party relations. In June 1977, the Kennedy School at Harvard University assembled a conference of twenty-five people who had played prominent roles in various presidential candidate organizations of 1976. According to the conference report, most participants felt the law had forced the candidate campaign organizations and the parties to operate quite separately from one another. Their lawyers advised the party organizations to be careful not to use the presidential and vice presidential candidates' names in connection with any party fund-raising efforts, voter registration drives, or advertising lest the money spent for such activities be charged by the FEC against the candidates' $20 million limits. Indeed, the candidate organizations lived in fear that some operation might be challenged by the FEC on the ground that it was a clandestine effort by the candidate to get around the law. As a leader of one of the candidate organizations put it, "We could not afford the 'mish-mash' of helping the party. It doesn't take much to look like a crook. And Congress is as remote from the parties as we

---

[47] These points are made in many different studies, including Thomas E. Patterson and Robert D. McClure, *The Unseeing Eye* (New York: G. P. Putnam's Sons, 1976); Steven H. Chaffee, ed., *Political Communication* (Beverly Hills, Calif.: Sage Publications, 1975); and Michael J. Robinson, "Television and American Politics, 1956-1976," *The Public Interest*, vol. 48 (Summer 1977), pp. 3-39.

are." And another asked, "What the hell does the party do for the nominee?"[48]

In the 1970s, not much.

Conclusion: Two Parties or No Parties?

At the outset, I remarked that the national parties have been so weakened since the late 1960s that presidential politics has become, "in substance if not in form, something closely approaching a no-party system." Now that we have reviewed much of the relevant evidence, the question becomes: *how* closely?

Clearly, the parties-in-the-electorate are significantly weaker than they were in the 1960s, whether measured by the waning of party identification, the growing proportion of independents, or the increase of split-ticket voting. But it is equally clear that the electoral parties have not disappeared altogether. Even now, only about 15 percent of the population have no party preferences whatever, 24 percent are still strong identifiers, and at least one-third still cast straight party tickets. The party labels of presidential candidates continue to appear on the November ballots, and they are still the prime voting cues for tens of millions of voters. For such voters, at least, presidential politics is still two-party politics. But for a number of others—a number steadily increasing since the 1960s—the no-party system has arrived.

Some readers may feel that in this chapter far too much has been made of the weakening of the presidential party organizations. After all, it can be argued that they never have been well-knit, European-style hierarchies of leaders enjoying the effective power to choose the candidates and write the platforms. They have never been more than short-lived, ad hoc coalitions of state and local party leaders and followers, labor and business leaders, and issue and candidate enthusiasts. Each has been pulled together to support a particular candidate in a particular year, and each has dispersed after the election. That has been the case in the postreform seventies as much as in the prereform sixties.

Perhaps so—but with one crucial difference. Most of the prereform nominating coalitions were dominated by state and local party organization leaders, whose interests and outlooks inclined them to seek well-known, well-regarded, reliable, and moderate candidates and

[48] Xandra Kayden, "Report of a Conference on Campaign Finance Based on the Experience of the 1976 Presidential Campaigns," mimeo., the Campaign Finance Study Group of the Institute of Politics, John F. Kennedy School of Government, Harvard University, October 1977, pp. 48-50.

to seek ways of strengthening the party to fight not only the current election but future elections as well. The Democrats' reform rules were designed to destroy the power of such leaders over the conventions in order to maximize "open access" for people with weak party commitments or none and produce a "fair reflection" of their presidential preferences. The rules have worked like a charm. The Democrats' two reformed conventions have been dominated by a different kind of delegate, and each has nominated a new kind of candidate. George McGovern had policy views sharply different from those of his party's identifiers, and Jimmy Carter was a complete outsider with policy views and leadership qualities largely unknown prior to (and even after) his nomination.

Thus, where the prereform Democratic party was able to turn back a Kefauver for a Stevenson and a McCarthy for a Humphrey, the postreform party was easily captured by outsiders. Whatever one may think of the relative merits of the winning and losing aspirants, and however weak in some absolute sense the national parties may have been in the 1960s, they are significantly weaker in the 1970s.

They may be weaker still in the 1980s. The Democrats have not yet finished changing their rules, and the Republicans are considering further moves in the same direction. Several bills are pending before Congress to establish a national presidential primary superseding the conventions and ignoring state lines. These proposals have not yet gotten out of committee, but the public opinion polls show that the idea has the support of well over two-thirds of the general population.

Perhaps they are right. After all, if what we want more than anything else is the most open possible nominating process and the fairest possible reflection of grass roots presidential preferences, a national primary beats *any* kind of reformed convention hands down. Openness and participation? Most ordinary people find it a great deal easier to vote in a government-run primary than to participate in a party-run caucus. This is clear from the fact that turnout in presidential primaries is nearly ten times higher than that in "participatory caucuses."[49] Accordingly, a national presidential primary is sure to attract millions more participants than the present combination of caucuses, conventions, and primaries that select national convention delegates.

Fair reflection of presidential preferences? A national party convention, no matter how widely proportional representation is used in allocating its delegates among presidential aspirants, is still an *indirect* device for expressing the presidential preferences and issue

---

[49] Ranney, *Participation*, pp. 15-16.

positions of the party rank and file. Consequently, some slippage between the convention's choice and the grass roots' preference is always possible. The only way to eliminate that possibility entirely is to end indirect nominations by conventions and establish direct nominations by national presidential primaries.

The reader may say that this is all very well as far as it goes, but maximum participation and fair reflection are not the only values at stake. What about the health of the parties? A national presidential primary would certainly weaken the presidential party organizations still further and perhaps wipe them out altogether.

What if it did? The Republic would not collapse, at least not right away. The party labels would persist for a while and serve as cues for the dwindling number of voters for whom they were still meaningful. The candidate organizations, the women's caucuses, the black caucuses, the right-to-life leagues, and the like would become the only real players in the game. The mass communications media would become the sole agencies for sorting out the finalists from the original entrants and for defining the voters' choices. And the societal functions of interest-aggregation, consensus-building, and civil war-prevention would presumably be left to the schools, the churches, and perhaps Common Cause and Nader's Raiders.

Would they perform those functions as well as the parties? At the moment, we can only guess at the answer. But perhaps we shall learn it from firsthand experience in the 1980s.

7

Changing Patterns of
Electoral Competition

Jeane J. Kirkpatrick

Students of American politics have paid much attention to elections and voting in recent years for a variety of reasons. Elections are, after all, *the* process through which popular participation and political accountability are secured, *the* nexus of a system of interlocking institutions through which political leaders are recruited, governments criticized, alternatives presented and examined, and decisions finally made by masses of people about who should rule and to what broad ends. Elections are also one of the relatively few political events that attract the attention and participation of large numbers of citizens— and so constitute a useful point at which to "cut into" the mass level of a political system to study such diverse subjects as the relations between political and social structure, the ways in which ordinary citizens think about leadership, citizenship, and public policy, the patterns of consensus and cleavage, and the dynamics of leadership and change. In addition, elections have the fascination, drama, and human interest of a major sporting event, with the added attraction of producing outcomes that are expressed in numbers. In an age when political scientists have been preoccupied with precision and measurement, this last is a matter of no small importance.

For whatever reasons, widespread interest in elections and voting behavior is a hallmark of contemporary political science, and as a consequence there has been developed a body of research and writing on elections and the electorate that is unusual in its richness, its cumulative character, and its theoretical sophistication.[1] Drawing on

---

[1] A number of such books have appeared in the last decade or so. Among these are Walter Dean Burnham, *Critical Elections and the Mainsprings of American Politics* (New York: W. W. Norton, 1970); Norman H. Nie, Sidney Verba, and John R. Petrocik, *The Changing American Voter* (Cambridge, Mass: Harvard University Press, 1976); Warren E. Miller and Teresa E. Levitin, *Leadership and*

this body of research, I discuss in this chapter some of the characteristics of presidential politics that seem most pertinent to the future of
American politics. Whether these patterns of presidential politics are
changing in fundamental ways is one of the most interesting questions
concerning American politics today.

To many observers of the American scene, Jimmy Carter's
election as President of the United States appeared to be a return to
normal—to the good old days of reliable Democratic victories based
on a coalition of the relatively less privileged against the better off.
This view had a certain prima facie plausibility: because a Democrat
won the presidency for the first time in more than a decade, because
economic issues were more salient in 1976 than in any other recent
presidential race, because the pattern of Carter's victory seemed to
herald a return of those historic Democratic constituencies—the
South, the Catholics, the white working class—to the Democratic
fold. In this view, the "new politics" of polarization, direct action,
"abnormal" landslides, dealignment, and realignment that characterized the political scene from the mid-sixties to the mid-seventies
ought to be considered not as part of a long-range trend but as the
consequence of short-term dislocations resulting from several unique
historical events—urban riots, Vietnam, Watergate—which happened
to occur coincidentally. And though on close examination it does not
turn out to be quite true that Carter's victory marked the reconsti-
tution of the Roosevelt coalition (white Southerners and union
families gave Roosevelt much greater support than Carter, and black
support was much more important to Carter's victory than to Roosevelt's) it can be persuasively argued that expectations and predictions
of the transformation of the party system may indeed turn out to
have been exaggerated.

However, other close observers of American politics remain
impressed by the many ways in which the politics of the sixties and
seventies differ from those of the previous period, and many believe
that the changes currently being observed are not epiphenominal but
are manifestations of long-range political trends rooted in broader
processes of social and cultural change. These latter views are ex-

Change (Cambridge, Mass.: Winthrop Publishers, Inc., 1976); James L. Sundquist, Dynamics of the Party System (Washington, D.C.: The Brookings Institution, 1973); Everett Carll Ladd, Jr. with Charles D. Hadley, Transformations of
the American Party System (New York: W. W. Norton & Co., Inc., 1975);
Walter De Vries and Lance Terrance, Jr., The Ticket Splitters: A New Force in
American Politics (Grand Rapids, Mich.: Eerdmens, 1972); David Broder, The
Party's Over: The Failure of Politics in America (New York: Harper & Row,
1972); Jeane J. Kirkpatrick, The New Presidential Elite (New York: The Russell
Sage Foundation and The Twentieth Century Fund, 1976).

pressed in titles of books such as *The Changing American Voter, Transformations of the American Party System, The Party's Over,* and in several widely discussed hypotheses that were born from projecting into the future the atypical political behavior of the recent past. The "decomposition," "dealignment," and "realignment" hypotheses are examples; so are the theories of "post-industrial" politics, the "sun belt" hypothesis, and various other change-oriented predictions. The behavior of the American electorate in presidential elections is a critical aspect of these projections; it is that behavior that will concern us here.

The Base Lines: "Normal Politics"

A discussion of change implies some norm from which the events or phenomena in question can be said to have deviated. In discussions of American electoral politics among political scientists the norm assumed usually has three dimensions. It embraces: (1) the electoral alignment born out of the New Deal, (2) the "Downsian" model of two-party competition, and (3) the theory of voting behavior derived from *The American Voter.* Because these conceptions have exercised a compelling influence on most of those who think and write about American politics, I delineate their essential elements here.

The New Deal. The "New Deal" coalition that resulted from the last major realignment of American politics divided voters on a new basis, produced new coalitions in the electorate and in Congress, and produced new party images that have served ever since as the basis of the Democratic electoral advantage.

The event that precipitated this restructuring of the American electorate was, of course, the Great Depression; the principal issue was whether government's power should be used to protect individuals against economic catastrophes growing out of social upheavals beyond their control. The new coalition pitted those who supported the broader use of government's power to solve economic problems against a smaller number of voters who opposed a more activist role for government in the economy. Of the resulting Democratic and Republican parties, it may be said that the Democrats were generally less well off and less well educated and that they enjoyed less high status positions than the Republicans. The chief results of the realignment at the political level were four successive Roosevelt victories and a dramatic increase in the number of persons who identified with the Democratic party. The chief result at the governmental level was the construction of the welfare state.

The Roosevelt coalition has often been described as consisting principally of "the cities and the South." That description is roughly accurate if the character of both the urban and southern voters of the epoch is borne in mind. The southern voters were white and had been voting Democratic for a long time. It did not require a depression to attract them into the Democratic party. The Civil War, racial policy, reconstruction, a distinctive agricultural base, and evangelical Protestantism were all related in the region's strong support for Democratic presidential nominees since the Civil War. The onset of the depression not only kept normally Democratic southern voters in the Democratic column, it also produced a regional landslide for Roosevelt, who attracted three-fourths of all votes cast in 1932. Southern blacks, most of whom were effectively disenfranchised by poll taxes, literacy tests, grandfather clauses, and other restrictive requirements, were a neglible factor in the New Deal coalition. However, those blacks outside the South who did vote were converted from their Civil War Republicanism to the New Deal.

Roosevelt's strength in the cities rested on the white working class, a category that comprised most of the poor and many of the relatively recent immigrants, including Jews and such predominantly Catholic groups as Italians, Slavs, and Poles. Some of these had once voted Republican, but during the depression virtually all were led, by economic hardship and perceived interest, into the coalition of the hard-hit.[2]

A third, sometimes neglected, component of the New Deal coalition was its support by middle-class voters. The depression struck the American middle class with the same ferocity as it hit Wall Street brokers and dust bowl tenant farmers, sweeping away jobs, savings, and confidence in the future. In consequence, many middle-class voters supported New Deal efforts to enlist government power in the struggle against unemployment, bank failures, poverty, the dust bowl, and the fluctuations of the business cycle.[3]

[2] Robert R. Alford, *Party and Society: The Anglo-American Democracies* (Chicago: Rand McNally, 1963), pp. 352-53, estimates on the basis of seven surveys conducted from 1936 through 1944 that Democrats regularly received a majority of the working-class votes. Paul Abramson, "Why the Democrats Are No Longer the Majority Party" (a paper delivered at the annual meeting of the American Political Science Association, New Orleans, La., September 4-8, 1973) estimated that from 1936 on, Roosevelt received a majority of the blue-collar votes but received less than half of those of white-collar workers. Abramson estimated that as of 1944 Roosevelt got 60 percent of the blue-collar vote.

[3] Alford, *Party and Society*, reports that Roosevelt won 52 percent of the middle-class vote in 1936 and 50 percent in 1944. Abramson, "Why the Democrats Are No Longer Majority," puts the 1944 election support at 44 percent.

James Sundquist described the Roosevelt coalition this way:

> The New Democratic Party—the New Deal Democratic Party—was issue oriented, working-class based, even more urban centered than before, activist, radical, and wholly devoted to Rooseveltian leadership. Within the party new groups—Italians, Jews, Poles, and all the other new ethnic groups began to contest the entrenched Irish for a share of party leadership and recognition.[4]

This description is accurate, but the New Deal coalition was more inclusive—socially, ethnically, and ideologically—than it suggests.

In the South the Democratic party enjoyed a large majority in all socioeconomic categories; and in the North as well, Roosevelt was supported by one-third to half the voters from business and professional classes. Therefore, although the distinctive class bases of the two parties were accentuated by the New Deal realignment, neither party had a monolithic class base. Still, the Republicans, generally speaking, had better educations, jobs, and incomes than the Democrats; and the popular images of the two parties reflected their composition: Democrats were perceived as being more concerned about the poor, Republicans were perceived as the party of business.

This New Deal realignment which produced new Democratic majorities in the North and the South at the local, state, and national levels dominated American politics from 1932 through World War II and the immediate postwar years until the election of General Eisenhower broke the string of Democratic presidential victories in 1952. It has continued to shape party images and voter loyalties and to influence—but not necessarily to determine—election outcomes down to the present. Whether the patterns of electoral behavior characteristic of the Roosevelt coalition still constitute the norm to which American politics returns after short-term deviations precipitated by such fleeting events as Watergate and Vietnam, or whether these patterns are being altered in some fundamental way, is a central question about the future of American politics.

The Traditional Model of Two-Party Competition. Even though many more Americans have identified with the Democratic than the Republican party since the New Deal realignment, election outcomes since 1948 have demonstrated that neither party can count on a reliable majority in presidential elections. Not only were Dwight

---

[4] Sundquist, *Dynamics*, p. 212.

Eisenhower and Richard Nixon elected for two terms each, but Harry Truman, John Kennedy, and Jimmy Carter won by very narrow margins. Among post World War II Democratic candidates only Lyndon Johnson received a majority of the popular vote. Since neither party can count on a majority, to win they must compete for the support of "switchers," independents and other weak partisans whose votes are up for grabs. Such competition, it is asserted, drives candidates and parties in search of victory inexorably toward the "center" of the political spectrum, that happy hunting ground of the votes out of which majorities are amassed and elections won.

This "spatial model" of political competition, a classic version of which is offered by Anthony Downs in his *Economic Theory of Democracy*,[5] predicts that under conditions of two-party competition, the search for votes will lead each party to deemphasize its distinctive characteristics and positions and to moderate its most controversial demands. The Downsian model of political competition assumes:

(1) that each of the parties will give priority to winning the election and will act "rationally" to maximize its votes;

(2) that an electoral arena can be reasonably assumed to have a "center";

(3) that there exist enough voters capable of being moved from one party to the other to make competition for their votes worthwhile;

(4) that the "floating" votes will be found at the center of the the political spectrum and not at one of its extremes; and

(5) that it will be possible for a party to moderate its positions without losing its partisans with more extreme views.

This model not only purports to explain how victories occur but also how the dynamics of two-party competition drive major parties to behavior that is moderate, pragmatic, and inclusive.[6]

There is a looser version of this model that is closer to the views of working politicians and avoids certain conceptual problems that afflict the more rigorous model. Instead of postulating that parties and politicians will necessarily act in such a way as to maximize their

---

[5] Anthony Downs, *An Economic Theory of Democracy* (New York: Harper & Row, 1957).

[6] Downs would presumably agree with Sartori's observation that two-party regimes themselves nurture the consensus that is a precondition to their persistence. Giovanni Sartori, *Parties and Party Structure*, vol. 1 (New York: Cambridge University Press, 1976), p. 192.

votes, it argues only that parties will behave in this fashion if they want to win. The best statement of this conventional wisdom is that of psephologist Richard Scammon and political demographer Ben Wattenberg, who in their book, *The Real Majority*, argue that parties seeking to win should move toward the center because "it can be safely said that the only extreme that is attractive to the larger majority of American voters is the extreme center."[7] But they understand that candidates and parties may sometimes prefer not to win. Scammon and Wattenberg also understand that various kinds of issues have been involved in recent election contests: some economic, some "social" and cultural, and some political. Nonetheless, they argue, in each election there is a "Voting Issue" which dominates the attention of voters. During the New Deal, it was bread and butter issues, in the late sixties it was "the social issue." To win, they argue, a party needs to preempt the "center" on whatever dimension of ideological conflict is then most salient.

The argument and assumptions of Scammon-Wattenberg in effect set out the norms that have guided the strategy of most successful politicians in this country and in other two-party systems.

"The American Voter" Model of Voting Behavior. The third "base line" against which most discussions of electoral change take place is the description of voting behavior offered by that distinguished team of social scientists who were assembled at the University of Michigan's Survey Research Center in the 1950s: Angus Campbell, Philip Converse, Warren Miller, and Donald Stokes. Their *magnum opus*, *The American Voter*, has shaped research and writing on voting behavior for nearly two decades.[8] Its impact was reinforced by other major studies of the period (among which those of Herbert McClosky, Paul Lazarsfeld et al., and Samuel Stouffer are notable[9]) and also by the steady stream of subsequent studies by the Michigan authors and

---

[7] Richard M. Scammon and Ben J. Wattenberg, *The Real Majority* (New York: Coward-McCann, 1970), p. 21.

[8] Angus Campbell, Philip E. Converse, Warren E. Miller, Donald E. Stokes, *The American Voter* (New York: John Wiley & Sons, 1960).

[9] Herbert McClosky, Paul J. Hoffman, and Rosemary O'Hara, "Issue Conflict and Consensus among Party Leaders and Followers," *American Political Science Review*, vol. 54 (1960); Herbert McClosky, "Consensus and Ideology in American Politics," *American Political Science Review*, vol. 58 (1964); Samuel A. Stouffer, *Communism, Conformity, and Civil Liberties* (Garden City, N.Y.: Doubleday, 1955); Paul F. Lazarsfeld, Bernard R. Berelson, and Hazel Gaudet, *The People's Choice* (New York: Duell, Sloan and Pearce, 1944); Bernard R. Berelson, Paul F. Lazarsfeld, and William McPhee, *Voting* (Chicago, Ill.: University of Chicago Press, 1954).

their collaborators. Still, it was *The American Voter* itself that established the paradigm for later research and reflection.

New, even shocking, as it was when it was originally presented, the conception of voting behavior developed in *The American Voter* has long since become the conventional way of thinking about voters and voting. The "Michigan" model was seminal because it used interviews with a scientifically selected national sample of voters to inquire into previously unexplored psychological dimensions of the voting decision. By focusing on the subjectivities of individuals and relying on survey data, the Michigan authors constructed a model which, in principle, depicted the voter's own conception of the political world, including his beliefs and feelings, his goals and motives, and his relationship to various social and other groups. This focus enabled the authors to develop a paradigm that presents the individual in a social context of his own construction. The result, as almost everyone knows, was a description of voting behavior that conceptualizes voting in terms of candidates, parties, and issues and that emphasizes party identification both as the dominant factor in individual voting decisions and as an anchor of the political system, stabilizing in its effects on the party competition, inhibiting to the emergence of volatile electoral forces.

According to *The American Voter*, attachments to party are formed early and internalized. They serve not only to structure the individual's political world, but also to screen information about that world. Party identification was presented as a major mechanism through which the political system is incorporated into the individual and the individual into the political system.[10] Like all identifications, attachment to party was seen as reinforced by emotion and, once established, difficult to alter.

Apparently, Campbell, Converse, Miller, and Stokes were surprised by the power of party identification and its influence on voting decisions and were also surprised at how little attention most voters paid to politics, at how few voters saw politics in terms of ideological categories or held views that seemed ideologically consistent. They were similarly surprised at how little influence "the issues" had on most voters—much as Samuel Stouffer and his readers had been surprised to discover that, in a period when the nation was frequently described as being hysterical about the "Communist issue," almost no one gave any thought at all to Communist subversion or to Senator Joseph McCarthy or to any related subject, and much as Lazarsfeld

---

[10] It is, of course, not the only such mechanism. National identifications, conceptions of authority, legitimacy, and obligation are also internalized.

and his associates had been surprised by the extent of peer group and reference group influence on voting in Elmira, New York.[11]

We have Converse's word for it that the "common sense view of voting at the time ... was that parties and candidates were attractive or unattractive to voters as a function of issue positions they represented."[12] The authors of *The American Voter* seem further to have believed that "standard democratic theory" required that voting be determined by rational calculation concerning the relations between candidates' and voters' positions on issues. Their findings concerning "the low emotional involvement of the electorate in politics; its slight awareness of public affairs; its failure to think in structured, ideological terms and its pervasive sense of attachment to one or the other of the two major parties"[13] were obviously inconsistent with the "common sense" view (or at least with the authors' conception of the "common sense" view).

Because it confounded widely held expectations, *The American Voter* acquired a reputation for emphasizing the irrational aspects of politics. In fact, it presented voting not as irrational but as nonrational, in the sense that it was seen to be determined generally by party identification rather than by a rational calculus of the relation between voters' views on the one hand and the candidates' and parties' views on the other. If the rationalist expectations of the early researchers sound naive today, it is because their early research into the subjective bases of mass politics wrought a revolution in our expectations on this subject.

These elements—the New Deal, the dynamics of two-party competition, and the Michigan model of voting—can be said with only a bit of oversimplification to constitute the paradigm of "normal politics" with which most professional and semi-professional observers of American politics have approached recent political events.

The Symptoms of Change

No sooner were these conceptions of normal political competition and voting behavior formulated than deviations from them began to be noted. By now, deviations have become so numerous and persistent that more than one observer argues that the time is long overdue when we should revise the generalizations that underlie our expectations concerning partisan alignment, party competition, and voting

---

[11] Stouffer, *Communism*; Lazarsfeld et al., *Voting*.

[12] Fred I. Greenstein and Nelson W. Polsby, *Handbook of Political Science*, vol. 4 (Reading, Mass.: Addison-Wesley Publishing Co., 1975), p. 116.

[13] Campbell et al., *The American Voter*, pp. 116 and 541.

behavior. We look now at some of the recent manifestations of change in each of these patterns.

Whatever Happened to the New Deal Coalition? Whether the Roosevelt coalition still exists as a potential electoral force or a predisposition that can be mobilized by skillful candidates has been put in doubt by the voting behavior of most of its component groups, both regional and socioeconomic. Probably the most dramatic and persistent defection has occurred in the South, but major changes have also taken place in the political habits of the white working class, the professional classes, and the middle class more generally. The consequence, as Verba, Nie, and Petrocik have observed, is a Democratic party that has become "more black, less southern and has developed a larger 'silk-stocking' component" and a Republican electorate that has become "more southern, less black, more Catholic and relatively less of a silk-stocking and Protestant party." [14] As Everett Ladd and Charles Hadley, discussing the elections of 1968 and 1972, observed, "None of the groups of whites prominently associated with the New Deal majority—urban, blue collar, Catholic and southern—were significantly more Democratic than the national electorate, and some actually fell below the meager national standard." [15] Two of these groups—the South and the white working class—are sufficiently crucial to the New Deal coalition to merit special attention.

The South. As early as 1948 there were indications that the New Deal coalition might not outlast the man who served as its catalyst. No region gave Franklin Roosevelt such sweeping support as the "solid South," which in 1944 cast 69 percent of its votes for FDR. However, in the very next presidential election, Harry Truman managed to poll only about 52 percent of the region's total vote, and four states of the previously solid South voted overwhelmingly for Dixiecrat candidate Strom Thurmond. The Democratic presidential candidate continued to poll slightly over half of the region's votes during the next three presidential contests—1952, 1956, and 1960—after which the Democratic total dropped precipitously as more and more Southerners cast their votes for Republican presidential candidates and for George Wallace. Between 1944 and 1964 the South moved from being the region most favorable to Democratic candidates to being less hospitable than any other region.

The trend in party identification followed the declining Democratic electoral fortunes. During the Eisenhower years when "presi-

---

[14] Nie, Verba, and Petrocik, *Changing American Voter*, p. 241.
[15] Ladd with Hadley, *Transformations*, p. 228.

dential Republicans" made their first appearance in significant numbers, the Democratic party identifiers decreased from almost 70 to less than 60 percent of the electorate. Between 1964 and 1976 the percentage of white Southerners who identified with the Democratic party continued to decline. However, as Paul Beck has recently emphasized, "Alterations in the distribution of party identification cannot explain adequately the region's support for Republican presidential candidates. To handle this phenomenon one must turn to voting defections by Democratic identifiers." [16]

It would be farfetched to suggest that Jimmy Carter's success in carrying the states of the South heralds that region's return to the Democratic fold—because Carter's southern origins and evangelical identifications encouraged a sense of regional loyalty that would not be available to Democratic candidates from other areas, because even Carter polled less than half the votes of white Southerners, because on a range of issues opinion in the South continues to be substantially more conservative than that of the dominant wings of the Democratic party, and because long-range trends suggest that a continuing dealignment is underway. Today the Democratic party commands the loyalty of most southern blacks and portions of older white voters. It shows no signs of recouping the affections of most southern whites. The South may not be necessary to Democratic victory, but it was a major component of the Roosevelt coalition.

The working class. No group was more important to the New Deal coalition than the working class, whose well-being was one of the principal goals of Roosevelt's administration. Its identity was always a bit more ambiguous than its role in the New Deal coalition—mainly because class lines have never been clear or firm in the United States and because there has always been a tendency to equate the working class with "working people" and "the poor." Since the depression caused business failures that drove many small businessmen back into the ranks of working class and the unemployed and made almost everyone poor, the notion of the working class was especially capacious during the Roosevelt years. That capacious working class which was an important component of the New Deal coalition was numerous and overwhelmingly white. It voted heavily for Roosevelt and Truman and continued to give a majority of its votes to Democratic candidates until 1968 (except Adlai Stevenson in 1956). Its importance to the Democratic party was reflected in the influence of union leaders among the party's decision makers.

---

[16] Paul Allan Beck, "Partisan Dealignment in the Postwar South," *American Political Science Review*, vol. 71 (June 1977), p. 479.

In 1968, however, Hubert Humphrey, beleaguered by the McCarthy and Wallace challenges, suffered substantial defections from the white working class, who Abramson estimates gave approximately 27 percent of their votes to Humphrey, 30 percent to Nixon, and 10 percent to Wallace (another 27 percent simply failed to turn out) [17] in spite of Humphrey's strong support from labor leaders. In 1972 when the AFL-CIO withheld its endorsement from George McGovern, white working-class defections soared. McGovern failed to win a majority even of the votes of union members and their families.

In 1976, the white working class, like the white South, supported the Democratic candidate, but in much smaller proportions than had once been the case. It should, however, be emphasized that the unreliably Democratic working class of the seventies differs in important ways from that of the New Deal: it is smaller, less poor, and more black. Everett Ladd, among others, has emphasized the political consequences of the affluence that elevated much of the white working class into the middle class. He attributes the decline in its Democratic voting habits to this move up the socioeconomic ladder and to the altered character of the party's elite. [18] Paul Abramson has pointed to the incompatibility of black and white working-class demands as a source of the Democrats' declining support among the latter, emphasizing the fact that black working-class voters have become more Democratic in their voting habits at the same time that the white working class has defected. [19]

The declining capacity of Democratic candidates to attract white workers' support is paralleled by a decreasing tendency of this group to identify with the Democratic party. However, as in the case of the South, declining party identification is not itself an adequate explanation for the uncertain voting habits that we observe. There are also substantial rates of defection among Democratic identifiers.

Once again, it may be that a Democratic candidate can win without the votes of a majority of the white working class (though that has never yet happened), but such a victory would clearly not constitute a renaissance of the Roosevelt coalition.

Other groups. The social composition of the Democratic party and of Democratic majorities has changed in other respects as well. In the period since they have been effectively enfranchised, blacks have become ever more Democratic, and, as that party's loyal support

[17] Abramson, "Why the Democrats."
[18] Ladd with Hadley, *Transformations*, chapters 3 and 4, *passim.*
[19] Abramson, "Why the Democrats."

among whites has been eroded, blacks have come to constitute approximately a fifth of the Democratic presidential electorate.

The political loyalties of religious groups have also been affected. WASPs in and out of the South have become progressively less Democratic, and those in the North have also become less Republican.

The situation of the "white ethnics," a term that is generally applied to Catholics, is similar, but the decline in the Democratic loyalties and voting among this category has been less marked. Nie, Verba, and Petrocik noted some movement out of the Democratic ranks, especially among upper-status Catholics.[20] Ladd and Hadley present data indicating a steady decline in the Catholic tendency to support Democratic presidential candidates.[21] Among Jews, a particularly heavily Democratic group, Democratic party identification and voting have also eroded (see Figure 7-1 and Table 7-1).[22]

Figure 7-1

PERCENTAGE POINT DEVIATION FROM THE DEMOCRATIC PRESIDENTIAL VOTE, SELECTED SOCIAL GROUPS, 1936–1972

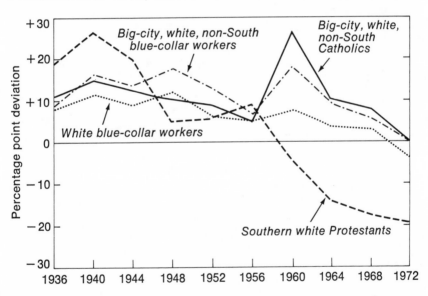

Source: Everett Carll Ladd, Jr. with Charles D. Hadley, *Transformations of the American Party System* (New York: W.W. Norton, 1976), p. 229.

[20] Nie, Verba, and Petrocik, *Changing American Voter*, pp. 229-32.
[21] Ladd with Hadley, *Transformations*, pp. 230-31.
[22] Nie, Verba, and Petrocik, *Changing American Voter*, p. 229.

Table 7-1

PARTY IDENTIFICATION OF SELECTED SOCIAL
GROUPS, 1940–1974

(in percentages)

Social Group	1940	1952	1960	1968	1972	1974
Big-city, white, blue-collar workers outside the South						
Democratic	53	57	62	52	42	47
Republican	21	20	19	21	23	19
Independent	26	23	19	27	36	33
Blue-collar whites						
Democratic	51	53	57	46	39	46
Republican	29	25	26	22	24	21
Independent	20	22	17	32	37	33
Big-city Catholics, outside the South						
Democratic	65	60	71	50	45	51
Republican	13	17	12	22	24	17
Independent	22	23	17	28	32	31
Southern white Protestants						
Democratic	81	73	60	38	35	43
Republican	11	14	22	22	26	24
Independent	8	13	18	39	39	32

Source: Everett Carll Ladd, Jr. with Charles D. Hadley, *Transformations of the American Party System* (New York: W.W. Norton, 1976), p. 231.

The New Deal alignment. To many observers the most striking fact about the erosion of habitual Democratic support among the key groups of the New Deal is how little it has benefited the Republicans. Disaffected Democrats have not transferred their loyalties to the Republicans, but have become independents. Even in the South, where disenchantment with the national Democratic party is strongest, the trend has been less toward "an emerging Republican majority" than toward ever larger numbers of voters without a stable party preference. Similarly, outside the South, Catholics, Jews, and WASPs who no longer identify with the Democratic party have shown little disposition to join the Republican party. Instead they have joined that growing number of Americans who identify with neither party. Summarizing these changes in party attachments, James Sundquist wrote,

> Between the mid-1960s, when the Vietnam, race and social issues rose to their dominant position, and 1972, the Democratic party lost a substantial segment of its former strength to the independents, about five million voters. But so did

the Republican party, about the same number. The loosening of party attachments across the electorate and the movement of masses of voters from party identification to independence has been the most striking development within the party system in the past decade.[23]

Obviously his interpretation is consistent with a restoration of the New Deal alignment. Ladd and Hadley speak, rather, of an inversion of the New Deal class order.[24] Whether the predicted inversion proves a permanent feature of the political scene or whether the New Deal alignment will be restored will be discussed later. For now, I emphasize only that significant shifts away from the New Deal "norm" have, in fact, occurred (see Table 7-2).

The "Abnormal" Pattern of Two-Party Competition. The events of post–World War II politics have raised questions about whether the persistence of the two-party system itself can be assumed. In 1948 and 1968 regional and ideological parties developed, and in 1972 and 1976 there were repeated efforts and threats to establish new parties. Although no third party has emerged on the left since Henry Wallace's effort in 1948, the rumblings on the Democrats' left were taken seriously in 1968 and paved the way for the sweeping party reforms that made possible George McGovern's nomination in 1972. Similarly, third-party talk among new right proponents in 1976 did not result in a schism, but it played a role in the Republicans' selection of a vice-presidential candidate and in the writing of their platform. In sum, though two-party competition is still the norm, it is less taken for granted today than at most times in our history.

Deviations from "normal" patterns of two-party competition also occurred in 1964 and 1972 when first one and then the other party selected a nominee representing a relatively extreme position. In nominating Barry Goldwater in 1964, the Republican party activists who controlled the convention first demonstrated that the search for victory does not necessarily cause a party to compromise differences, accommodate diverse perspectives, or moderate its programs. And in nominating George McGovern eight years later the Democratic convention demonstrated that their party, too, was prepared to defy conventional wisdom.

Having proved, by the nomination of these candidates, that their parties did not necessarily behave in the expected ways, the Goldwater and McGovern supporters went on to challenge the other

---

[23] Sundquist, *Dynamics*, p. 332.
[24] Ladd with Hadley, *Transformations*, pp. 233–46.

Table 7-2
VOTE BY GROUPS IN PRESIDENTIAL ELECTIONS, 1952–1976
(in percentages)

	1952		1956		1960		1964		1968			1972		1976		
	Steven-son	Eisen-hower	Steven-son	Eisen-hower	Ken-nedy	Nixon	John-son	Gold-water	Hum-phrey	Nixon	Wal-lace	McGov-ern	Nixon	Car-ter	Ford	McCar-thy
National	44.6	55.4	42.2	57.8	50.1	49.9	61.3	38.7	43.0	43.4	13.6	38	62	50	48	1
Sex																
Male	47	53	45	55	52	48	60	40	41	43	16	37	63	53	45	1
Female	42	58	39	61	49	51	62	38	45	43	12	38	62	48	51	*
Race																
White	43	57	41	59	49	51	59	41	38	47	15	32	68	46	52	1
Non-white	79	21	61	39	68	32	94	6	85	12	3	87	13	85	15	*
Education																
College	34	66	31	69	39	61	52	48	37	54	9	37	63	42	55	2
High school	45	55	42	58	52	48	62	38	42	43	15	34	66	54	46	*
Grade school	52	48	50	50	55	45	66	34	52	33	15	49	51	58	41	1
Occupa-tion																
Prof. and busi-ness	36	64	32	68	42	58	54	46	34	56	10	31	69	42	56	1
White collar	40	60	37	63	48	52	57	43	41	47	12	36	64	50	48	2
Manual	55	45	50	50	60	40	71	29	50	35	15	43	57	58	41	1

Age (years)																
Under 30	51	49	43	57	54	46	64	36	47	38	15	48	52	53	45	1
30-49	47	53	45	55	54	46	63	37	44	41	15	33	67	48	49	2
50 and older	39	61	39	61	46	54	59	41	41	47	12	36	64	52	48	*
Religion																
Protestants	37	63	37	63	38	62	55	45	35	49	16	30	70	46	53	*
Catholics	56	44	51	49	78	22	76	24	59	33	8	48	52	57	42	1
Politics																
Republicans	8	92	4	96	5	95	20	80	9	86	5	5	95	9	91	*
Democrats	77	23	85	15	84	16	87	13	74	12	14	67	33	82	18	*
Independents	35	65	30	70	43	57	56	44	31	44	25	31	69	38	57	4
Region																
East	45	55	40	60	53	47	68	32	50	43	7	42	58	51	47	1
Midwest	42	58	41	59	48	52	61	39	44	47	9	40	60	48	50	1
South	51	49	49	51	51	49	52	48	31	36	33	29	71	54	45	*
West	42	58	43	57	49	51	60	40	44	49	7	41	59	46	51	1
Members of labor union families	61	39	57	43	65	35	73	27	56	29	15	46	54	63	36	1

* Less than 1 percent.

Note: 1976 results do not include vote for minor party candidates.

Source: *Gallup Opinion Index*, December 1976.

central assumptions of "normal" two-party politics. Both campaigns explicitly rejected the assumption that moderation is the route to victory in a general election. Goldwater and his advisers and supporters remained convinced until near the end that there was in the electorate a "hidden conservative majority" that would rally around the conservative banner. Eight years later, George McGovern and his advisers and followers were equally convinced that independents and weak partisans could be enlisted in a leftward marching "army of the alienated" if only a clear-cut appeal was made to their frustrations. The landslide defeat of each candidate by a more moderate opponent provided some temporarily persuasive information at least about where the voters weren't. However, at the same time that the Goldwater and McGovern experiences proved that the search for victory under conditions of two-party competition does not guarantee that the parties will moderate their images and programs or aggregate diverse interests and perspectives, they also reinforced the argument that parties ought to behave in this fashion if they want to win.

In the process, these two experiences cast light on some related questions. They indicated that, at least for now, floating voters are not potential parts of some "change" constituency but are more attracted to centrist candidates. And they laid to rest, for now, the argument that "independent" voters and "switchers" would not be lost by the adoption of more extreme policy positions (presumably because their votes are not determined by considerations of policy) and the related argument that votes gained by candidates' moderating their positions will be more than offset by votes lost by the defection of more ideologically oriented activists.[25] Despite predictions to the contrary, the experiences of 1964, 1968, 1972, and 1976 indicate that ordinary voters are more likely to defect from an extremist candidate than are activists to defect from a moderate. Hubert Humphrey and Gerald Ford suffered fewer defections from their parties' disgruntled activists than Goldwater and McGovern did from their parties' ordinary voters.[26]

---

[25] A good statement of the argument is Albert O. Hirschman, *Exit, Voice and Loyalty* (Cambridge, Mass.: Harvard University Press, 1970).

[26] Various election studies make these points. The best treatments of each are, I think, those emanating from Michigan's Center for Political Studies: Arthur H. Miller, Warren E. Miller, Alden S. Raine, and Thad A. Brown, "A Majority Party in Disarray: Policy Polarization in the 1972 Election," *American Political Science Review*, vol. 70, no. 3 (September 1976); Arthur H. Miller and Warren E. Miller, "Ideology in the 1972 Election: Myth or Reality—A Rejoinder," *American Political Science Review*, vol. 70, no. 3 (September 1976); Philip E. Converse, Warren E. Miller, Jerrold G. Rusk, Arthur C. Wolfe, "Continuity and Change

But while the experience of the last decade and a half confirms that the conventional wisdom about the functioning of two-party competition still accurately describes the American scene, real and apparent deviations have dramatized the potential for change, have clarified the conditions necessary for the persistence of this pattern of electoral competition, and have indicated the kind of developments that would fundamentally transform the dynamics of electoral competition in America: an intensification and complication of ideological conflict could lead to the rise of third or fourth parties; the deepening of ideological cleavages could make it more difficult for parties to "grow" by compromising diverse perspectives and aggregating diverse interests; the emergence in both parties of an ideological leadership more interested in articulating positions than in winning elections could inhibit the search for victory through moderation; the radicalization of some significant portions of the electorate could increase the attractions of extremism. All of these developments are, in principle, possible; some observers believe that they are also probable, and, perhaps, already in process. For a period in the late sixties and early seventies ideological conflict was exacerbated and complicated; the Democrats' experience in trying to accommodate their McGovernite, Wallacite, and "centrist" factions and the Republicans' experience in accommodating their "liberal" and Reaganite wings made clear the difficulties of aggregation under contemporary conditions; the presence in the Wallacite, McGovernite, and Reaganite factions of numerous activists who gave top priority to "correct" issue positions illustrated the potential destructiveness of party leaders who would rather be right (or left) than President; and the emergence of cross-cutting social and cultural issues more than once complicated the task of finding the "center."

Most important of all, the wide electoral swings from Johnson's landslide in 1964 to Nixon's in 1972 dramatized the "abnormal" behavior of large portions of electorate, whose votes were quite unexpectedly less influenced by party identification than by candidates and issues. These "abnormal landslides," as Ladd has called them, suggested how volatile political competition could become, and this in turn cast doubt on everyone's "normal" expectations.

in American Politics: Parties and Issues in the 1968 Election," *American Political Science Review*, vol. 63, no. 4 (December 1969); Philip E. Converse, Aage R. Clausen, and Warren E. Miller, "Electoral Myth and Reality: The 1964 Election," *American Political Science Review*, vol. 59, no. 2 (June 1965).

Party Identification, Issues and "The American Voter." The intense and widespread interest of political scientists in voting has led them to pay special attention to deviations from the third element of our paradigm of "normal politics": the model of voting behavior originally presented in *The American Voter*. The decisive influence of this study on subsequent research is reflected in the extent to which its findings have served to focus attention on subjects of particular concern to the Michigan group, especially the role of party identification and issues. Continuing concern with these dimensions of voting behavior has enabled us to identify and map changes in the importance of these factors in the voting decision and in their relation to each other.

Party identification. Three important changes have affected the pattern of partisanship: there has been a substantial and continuing decline in the proportion of citizens who identify with the Republican party; there has been a substantial decline in the strength and intensity of attachment to both parties; and there has been a significant increase in the number of voters who describe themselves as "independents." These phenomena are considered by many political scientists to be the most important developments in recent American politics. The fact that some of these trends appear to have been at least temporarily reversed in 1976 and since does not deprive them of their interest or their importance.

In the two decades since *The American Voter* focused attention on party identification, comparative research has confirmed not only its importance in orienting individuals in the political arena and simplifying their choices, but also its role as a stabilizing factor in a democratic political system, one that inhibits the proliferation of parties, discourages the rise of personalist factions and "surge" parties, and encourages and reinforces the institutionalization of political competition. It has become progressively clearer that, in modern nations with far-flung mass electorates, party identification serves to integrate individual citizens into the structure of democratic competition. For these reasons the declining intensity and scope of party identification is viewed not only as intrinsically interesting but also as an indicator of significant systemwide changes.

The strength of partisanship can be measured in various ways: by its durability; by whether a person conceives himself to be a strong partisan; by whether partisan identification affects the evaluation of other persons and issues; and, most important, by whether it determines a person's vote.

The dimensions of this decline are revealed not by responses to a single simple question but by more detailed probing into the intensity, uses, and behavioral correlates of partisanship. Such probing reveals, first, that there has occurred a particularly marked decline in the numbers of strong identifiers (between 1952 and 1976, "strong" Democrats declined from 22 percent to 15 percent of the total electorate, "strong" Republicans from 13 percent to 9 percent); second, that party identifiers have less affection for their party than in the past and are less likely to see party as a basis for evaluating candidates; and, third, that party identification is much less likely to be reflected in voting habits today than in the past.[27] (See Table 7-3 and Figure 7-2.) *The Changing American Voter* summed up these findings with the assertion, "Citizens are less likely to identify with a party, to feel positively about a party, or to be guided in their voting behavior by partisan cues."[28]

The durability of party identification has recently become the focus of a rather intense if sometimes esoteric debate about whether partisanship tends to grow stronger with age (that is, with the length of time it is held, as *The American Voter* reported, or whether the stronger partisanship of older citizens that appeared in the early voting studies was, in fact, an artifact of their generation rather than their age.[29] Certain facts are not disputed: that the old are stronger partisans than the young, that they are more inclined to vote a straight ticket, that their ties to party are more likely to weather periods of realignment, that the strength of partisanship of all age cohorts declined between 1964 and 1968. Most important for the future of the political system is the fact that younger voters (especially those

---

[27] There are various sources for these assertions. Among the studies which have documented the decline of party identification are Nie, Verba, and Petrocik, *Changing American Voter*, especially chap. 4; Arthur H. Miller and Warren E. Miller, "Partisanship and Performance: Rational Choice in the 1976 Presidential Elections," a paper delivered at the 1977 annual meeting of the American Political Science Association, September 1-4, 1977, Washington, D.C.

[28] Nie, Verba, and Petrocik, *Changing American Voter*, p. 57.

[29] Campbell, et al., *American Voter*, pp. 153-60; Philip E. Converse, *The Dynamics of Party Support* (Beverly Hills, Calif.: Sage Publications, 1976); Paul R. Abramson, "Generational Change in American Electoral Behavior," *American Political Science Review*, vol. 68 (March 1974); Paul R. Abramson, "Developing Party Identification: A Further Examination of Life Cycle, Generational and Period Effects," a paper delivered at the annual meeting of the American Political Science Association, Washington, D.C., September 1-4, 1977; Richard A. Brody, "Stability and Change in Party Identification: Presidential to Off-Years," a paper delivered at the annual meeting of the American Political Science Association, Washington, D.C., September 1-4, 1977; Norval D. Glenn and Ted Hefner, "Further Evidence on Aging and Party Identification," *Public Opinion Quarterly*, vol. 36 (Spring 1972).

Table 7-3

PARTY IDENTIFICATION, 1952–1976

(in percentages)

Party Identification	Year												
	'52	'54	'56	'58	'60	'62	'64	'66	'68	'70	'72	'74	'76
Strong Democrat	22	22	21	23	21	23	26	18	20	20	15	17	15
Weak Democrat	25	25	23	24	25	23	25	27	25	23	25	21	25
Independent Democrat	10	9	7	7	8	8	9	9	10	10	11	13	12
Independent Independent	5	7	9	8	8	8	8	12	11	13	13	15	14
Independent Republican	7	6	8	4	7	6	6	7	9	8	11	9	10
Weak Republican	14	14	14	16	13	16	13	15	14	15	13	14	14
Strong Republican	13	13	15	13	14	12	11	10	10	10	10	8	9
Apoliticals: Don't know	4	4	3	5	4	4	2	2	1	1	2	3	1

Note: The survey question was, "Generally speaking, do you usually think of yourself as a Republican, a Democrat, an Independent, or what? (If Republican or Democrat), Would you call yourself a strong (R) (D) or a not very strong (R) (D)? (If Independent), Do you think of yourself as closer to the Republican or Democratic Party?"
Source: Center for Political Studies, University of Michigan.

Figure 7-2

PARTY IDENTIFICATION, 1937–1977

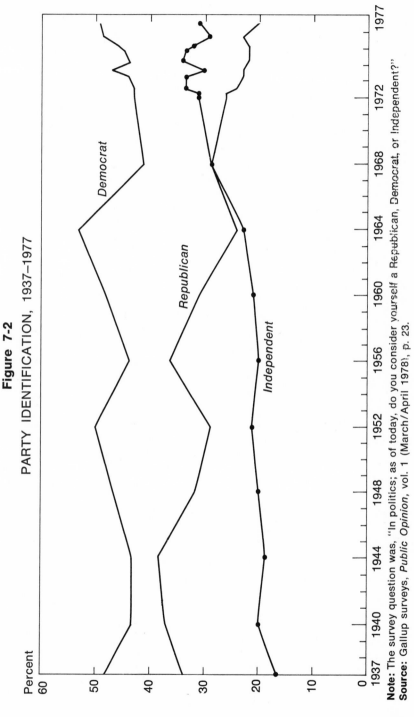

Note: The survey question was, "In politics; as of today, do you consider yourself a Republican, Democrat, or Independent?"
Source: Gallup surveys, *Public Opinion*, vol. 1 (March/April 1978), p. 23.

who have entered the electorate since 1968) apparently have less partisan commitment than did older voters when they were young. Reinforcing this finding is parallel evidence that even young partisans are more negative than other age groups in their evaluation of the parties [30] and are also the most readily disaffected. As Miller and Miller observed,

> On the face of it, the dying generations consisted of staunch partisans who have been and are being replaced by a younger generation much less firmly committed to one or the other two major parties. Without asking why the young are less partisan than the old, the fact of the difference in their levels of partisanship and the fact that one generation is replacing the other provides a first level explanation of why strength of partisanship has declined nationally over the past twenty-four years.[31]

Still, the entire decline in partisanship cannot be accounted for by the predispositions of the younger generation; the data indicate clearly that partisanship has been eroded in all age groups. Richard Brody has presented persuasive evidence that party identification "changes in response to the sorts of electoral and political forces that generally affect political attitudes and behavior," that these changes are more rapid "than life cycle/generational hypotheses would lead us to expect," and that the strength of party identification is less stable (for all generations) than its direction.[32]

An indication that the rise in independents may not be quite what it seems has emerged from analyses by Raymond E. Wolfinger, Richard Brody, and Miller and Miller indicating that those who call themselves independents but who "lean" toward one of the parties do not behave like independents but are *more* partisan than persons who describe themselves as "weak" Republicans or Democrats.[33] If this pattern persists, it suggests that the trend to "inde-

---

[30] Nie, Verba, and Petrocik, *Changing American Voter*, p. 68.

[31] Miller and Miller, "Partisanship and Performance in 1976," p. 24.

[32] Brody, "Stability and Change," p. 52.

[33] Brody, "Stability and Change"; Miller and Miller, "Partisanship and Performance in 1976," p. 20. Commenting on this, Miller and Miller observed, "If, indeed, more than one-third of all voters and more than half of all young voters have rejected the political parties and will henceforth respond to politics as nonpartisans, party support must be greatly weakened and the failure of the two-party system must be very uncertain. If, however, those really outside the party system have only increased from the *ten percent* who were independent Independents or 'a-political' in 1952-56 to *fifteen percent* twenty years later, the change seems less profound."

pendence" may be less important than it at first appeared. But there are other data that make it clear that declining partisanship is not chimerical, but has some very concrete behavioral consequences.

The most dramatic evidence of eroding partisanship has been the appearance in all age groups of a nearly equal tendency to split-ticket voting.[34] Many observers consider the rise of split-ticket voting to be the most important consequence of declining partisanship—and the most impressive testimony to why strong partisanship matters.

The authors of *The Changing American Voter* remind us that in 1956 four out of five Americans who identified with one of the major parties voted for that party's candidate for President, while about 90 percent of identifiers voted for their party's congressional candidate.[35] Since then, election day defections have become progressively more common. (See Table 7-4.) Southern Democrats are especially famous for deserting their party's presidential candidate. Moreover, although defection from the presidential candidate has attracted special notice (as when, in 1972, 42 percent of all Democratic identifiers voted for Richard Nixon), split-ticket voting has grown at all levels of the political system. In fact, Verba, Nie, and Petrocik conclude that "the data for the non-presidential elections are compelling evidence of the weakening of party ties."[36] Closer analysis of these patterns establishes that defection is much less common among persons who think of themselves as "strong" Democrats or Republicans (the group whose numbers have declined most sharply) and that, not surprisingly, defections are rather powerfully related to candidates and issues—a fact most dramatically illustrated in the landslide defeats of Goldwater and McGovern.

Although split-ticket voting was less common among Democrats in 1976 than in 1972 or 1968 and was more common among Republicans (but much more common among Democratic than Republican "leaners"), the 1976 experience does not constitute grounds for concluding that the trend to ticket splitting has been reversed.

In concluding this brief discussion of recent trends in partisanship, we should emphasize: (1) that the patterns of two-party identification of the Eisenhower period were not permanent; (2) that the size of the two parties and the strength of voters' attachment to them have changed, but that (3) they still have a significant hold on the loyalties of Americans (a fact underscored by the inability of a third party to strike roots); (4) that the Republicans have not managed to

---

[34] Nie, Verba, and Petrocik, *Changing American Voter*, pp. 50-55.

[35] Ibid.

[36] Ibid., p. 52.

Table 7-4
DEFECTION RATES OF PARTY IDENTIFIERS, 1952–1976
(in percentages)

Party and Identification	1952	1956	1960	1964	1968	1972	1976
Democrat							
Strong	17	15	9	5	11	26	9
Weak	39	37	28	18	38	52	25
Independent							
Democrat	40	33	15	11	49	44	24
Independent							
Republican	7	6	13	25	19	14	14
Republican							
Strong	1	1	2	10	3	4	3
Weak	6	7	13	43	12	9	22

Note: Entries are percentages of the appropriate category of voter who voted for a presidential candidate other than the candidate of the party with which they identified.
Source: Arthur H. Miller and Warren E. Miller, "Partisanship and Performance: Rational Choice in the 1976 Presidential Elections," a paper presented at the annual meeting of the American Political Science Association, Washington, D.C., Sept. 1-4, 1977.

profit by the disaffection of traditional Democrats in the South and elsewhere, but neither have the Democrats profited by the progressive and continuing decline of Republicans; (5) that, so far, the potential importance of the increased number of independents has been diminished by the tendency of most independents to act like partisans; and (6) that the loosening of partisan ties among the young and the increasingly less effective intergenerational transmission of party identification foreshadow larger changes in voting habits in the future.

Issue Voting. A debate of sorts concerning the influence of issues on electoral behavior has been underway since the posthumous appearance of V. O. Key's short book, *The Responsible Electorate*, presenting the "perverse and unorthodox argument" that "voters are not fools."[37] Though it is not really clear from whom Key was defending the voters, it is clear that he sought to reestablish the proposition that "rational" voting (defined as voting in response to government policies) did take place, that voters do not simply react as members of social aggregates, and that "switchers" are not necessarily either the

[37] V. O. Key, Jr. with the assistance of Milton C. Cummings, Jr., *The Responsible Electorate* (Cambridge, Mass.: Harvard University Press, 1966), p. 7. There is a large literature on issues and voting.

least informed or least admirable voters, but persons who switch to support government policies or outlooks with which they agree. Though the evidence on which Key based his argument (still incomplete at the time of his death) was slim, there has since accumulated impressive data on the impact of issues on voting decisions. Most of these data and analyses do not demonstrate that *The American Voter* was mistaken but show rather that changes have occurred—and that the influence of issues and issue-impregnated candidate images have increased in importance at approximately the same time that party identification has decreased in strength. In the last two decades both the questions and the answers about voters' reactions to issues have been refined and elaborated; so have the measures and analyses with which researchers explore the voters' ideological perceptions and preferences.

Today there is broad consensus among observers that more voters conceive of themselves, parties, candidates, and issues in terms of such broad ideological labels as liberal and conservative and that for many voters these ideological considerations are a significant factor in their voting decision. It has also become clear that the independent effect of issues on election outcomes varies with the nature of the issues, their relation to traditional party alignments, the clarity of the candidates' policy positions, and the nature of the alternatives offered in any given election. Nie, Verba, and Petrocik believe that a "significant and systematic change in the way in which the American public thinks about political matters took place between 1960 and 1964."[38] It was also around 1964 that a precipitous decline in party identification was first noted. It appears, however, that no significant downturn in "ideological thinking" occurred alongside the upturn in partisanship in 1976. Utilizing several indicators, Miller and Miller found only a slight decrease in ideological thinking between 1972 and 1976[39] despite the end of the Vietnam war and the waning of cultural and social conflict. There was an important difference in the impact of issues in the 1972 and 1976 elections, but the difference was that in 1976, when economic issues were once again the most salient, issue preferences were consistent with party attachments, while in 1972 salient social and cultural issues cut across traditional party alignments, dividing the voters in ways unrelated to their normal party loyalties.

---

[38] Nie, Verba, and Petrocik, *Changing American Voter*, p. 147.
[39] Miller and Miller, "Partisanship and Performance in 1976," p. 45.

Summary. These, then, are the principal evidences of changed patterns of voting behavior, briefly delineated. The changes are broad in scope and affect all three dimensions of what had been the relatively stable expectations of political scientists (and others) concerning electoral competition. Little is known about how deep or how permanent these changes will prove to be, and/or what will be their long-range consequences. Some clues are available through a consideration of the principal sources of change, since presumably changes rooted in social structure would be likely to prove more enduring and basic than changes rooted in events. The remainder of this chapter provides an overview of factors thought by some close observers to be causes of recent changes in patterns of electoral behavior.

Sources of Electoral Change

The Electorate. An electorate is variously described as that portion of the population that is legally eligible to vote or as that portion of the population that in fact casts ballots on election day. The former conception emphasizes eligibility, and the latter emphasizes choice. In this discussion I am concerned with the electorate defined in both ways and with the relationship between the two. Whichever way it is defined, the electorate has undergone significant change in recent decades.

The eligible electorate. Population growth and legal and constitutional changes have combined to expand dramatically the number of Americans eligible to vote. Two constitutional amendments expanded the number of eligible voters: the Twenty-fourth Amendment, ratified in 1964, which outlawed the poll tax; and the Twenty-sixth Amendment, ratified in 1971, which lowered the voting age to eighteen. In addition, a series of new laws (the most notable of which was the Voting Rights Act of 1965), court decisions, and government regulatory actions eliminating legal barriers effectively enfranchised the black population. Finally, the proportion of the population eligible to vote has been enlarged by legislation and court decisions liberalizing registration requirements. That the composition of the eligible electorate is relevant to the changes in electoral behavior presently in progress is clear from the fact that nearly half of the young voters identify with no party and from the distinctively Democratic attachment and behavior of black voters.

The voting electorate. The expansion of the electorate affected its composition as well as its size, chiefly by adding to it millions of blacks and young people. The differential turnout of different socio-economic categories also affects the composition of the voting electorate, giving proportionately greater influence to those who vote most regularly. Age, race, education, and occupation are all related to voting habits, and the relations among these factors appear to be quite stable: the young are substantially less likely to vote than the middle aged, the educated are much more likely to vote than the uneducated, white-collar workers are more likely to vote than blue-collar ones, whites are more likely to vote than blacks, and both are more likely to turn out than persons of Spanish origin.

One major change in the voting electorate since 1964 has been the steady decline in turnout. The addition of blacks and young voters contributed to this decline since both these groups have relatively low turnout rates. However, this addition does not account for all the continuing downward trend, which is apparent in all major demographic groups: whites as well as blacks, middle aged as well as young, highly educated as well as uneducated (see Table 7-5).

The fact that turnout has declined during the same period that legal restrictions have been removed and participation has been widely encouraged is both puzzling and disturbing to some observers; Richard Brody discusses the problem at length in the next chapter. Although no one is yet quite certain of its meaning, decreasing turnout has been probed in an effort to determine whether the processes that cause it have relevance for the whole system.

It is interesting that the decline in turnout has not only occurred among all major categories of voters but also that it has persisted through various types of elections: the landslide of 1972 and the exceedingly close elections of 1968 and 1976, contests that featured sharp ideological differences and those that did not. So far turnout has figured importantly in only one theory of American politics—the notion that "alienation" from the system causes potential voters to "tune out and turn off." But this interpretation is belied by the clear-cut evidence that voters who are dissatisfied with the system are neither more nor less likely to vote than those who are satisfied.[40]

Population Migration. The notion that in democratic politics demography is destiny has recently spawned several studies arguing that specified demographic trends would produce, or were producing, specified political transformations. In particular, three demographic

---

[40] Jack Citrin, "Comment: The Political Relevance of Trust in Government," *American Political Science Review*, vol. 68 (September 1974).

Table 7-5

VOTER TURNOUT IN PRESIDENTIAL ELECTIONS BY GROUP CHARACTERISTICS, 1968, 1972, AND 1976

(percent of voting age population reporting they voted)

	Year		
	1968	1972	1976
Male	69.8	64.1	59.6
Female	66.0	62.0	58.8
Age			
18-20		48.3	38.0
21-24	51.0	50.7	45.6
25-34	62.5	59.7	55.4
35-44	70.8	66.3	63.3
45-64	74.9	70.8	68.7
65 and over	65.8	63.5	62.2
Education			
8 yrs. or less	54.5	47.4	44.1
9-11	61.3	52.0	47.2
12	72.5	65.4	59.4
More than 12	81.2	78.8	73.5
Race			
White	69.1	64.5	60.9
Black	57.6	52.1	48.7
Spanish origin	N.A.	37.4	31.8

Source: U.S. Department of Commerce, Bureau of the Census, *Statistical Abstract of the United States* (Washington, D.C., 1977), p. 508.

trends have been persistently or persuasively linked to a changing partisan behavior.

The suburban migration. The movement out of central cities by upwardly mobile voters was linked by Samuel Lubell, Louis Harris, and others to the Republican strength of the Eisenhower era.[41] They argued that as voters with increasing incomes and social status moved from the central city to the suburbs they would abandon the Democratic identifications more appropriate to their previous situations for Republicanism. Though its point of departure was a change in residence, this hypothesis reflected not geographical determinism, but the expectation that observed relations between status, income, and party would prove more compelling than party identification. We

[41] See especially Samuel Lubell, *The Future of American Politics*, rev. ed. (Garden City, N.Y.: Doubleday Anchor Books, 1956).

now know that Democrats who moved to the suburbs tended to take their partisan identifications with them, and also that those who stayed in central cities were as susceptible as the ex-urbanites to the attractions of an Eisenhower or a Nixon. It is less certain, however, whether the growth of the suburbs is associated in any systematic way with the declining strength of party identification. It has been suggested that split-ticket voting and enthusiasm for "nonpartisan" institutions are especially common in the suburbs. If this is the case, increased suburbanization could turn out to be relevant to party decomposition even though it was not a factor in partisan realignment.

The southern migration. Movements into and out of the South have stimulated various projections concerning that region's political evolution. The movement of many poor whites and blacks out of the South and into the cities of the North and West, and the concomitant arrival in the South of Northerners in search of economic opportunity, lower production costs, retirement, and leisure were widely expected to transform southern politics. The emigration of southern blacks presumably removed an important part of the region's "change constituency," and the immigration of Northerners introduced significant numbers of Republicans into this traditionally Democratic area; meanwhile legal changes led to the simultaneous incorporation into the electorate of the region's remaining black population. The political impact of these changes on the composition of the electorate were widely expected to transform the patterns of voting behavior in the South. Kevin Phillips was not alone in his expectation that the "New" South could become the cornerstone of a resurgent Republican party. The minimum expectation of political observers who believe that politics "follows" demographic and social change was that the mobilization of blacks, the immigration of traditional Republicans, and economic development would stimulate the development of two-party competition in the formerly one-party South.

The sun belt migration. The continuing movement out of the North and Northeast and into the "sun belt" is seen as politically momentous by political observers as diverse as Kevin Phillips and Kirkpatrick Sale.[42] Rapid economic development in California and other parts of the South and Southwest, the continuing decline of the older industrial centers, the distinctive characteristics of the work

---

[42] Kirkpatrick Sale regards it as not only momentous but sinister. See his *Power Shift, The Rise of the Southern Rim and Its Challenge to the Eastern Establishment* (New York: Random House, 1975) and Kevin Phillips's more sober *The Emerging Republican Majority* (New Rochelle, N.Y.: Arlington House, 1969).

force in the "new" industries (of which space and computers are prototypes), the rise of the retirement and leisure industries, and the social characteristics of the self-selected internal migrants moving into the sun belt stimulated conservatives and radicals alike to see in that region the foundation of a new conservative majority in American politics. Phillips's *Emerging Republican Majority* predicted, "The upcoming cycle of American politics is likely to match a dominant Republican party based in the heartland, South and California against a minority Democratic party based in the Northeast and the Pacific Northwest (and encompassing southern as well as northern Negroes)."[43] Several years later, after Phillips and other new right activists had virtually abandoned hope for the Republican party, they remained convinced that the sun belt could serve as the geocultural base of a new conservative party.

Socioeconomic Changes. Recently a number of analysts who tend to some variant of social determinism have emphasized the changing occupational structure of the population and of the two parties. Everett Ladd, Kevin Phillips, William Rusher, and Daniel Bell are among those who have made increased affluence and a changing occupational structure the centerpiece of a new theory of American political behavior. Though the term post-industrial society is Daniel Bell's,[44] the construct, as it is linked to politics, owes as much to Bruno Rizzi, Harold Lasswell, Ralf Dahrendorf, and Zbigniew Brzezinski as to Bell.[45] The essential elements of the political version of this theory are the massive growth of higher education; the dramatic increase in the number of persons employed in the "service" and "knowledge" occupations; the emergence of a new elite highly trained in the use of ideas and symbols and skilled in their communication; the progressive accretion of political power by this new "power elite"; and finally, the concomitant shrinking of the economic sectors engaged in the creation of goods and the declining political influence of elites—

---

[43] Phillips, *Emerging Republican Majority*, p. 465.

[44] Daniel Bell, *The Coming of Post Industrial Society: A Venture in Social Forecasting* (New York: Basic Books, 1973).

[45] Bruno Rizzi, *Il Collettivismo Burocratico* (Milan: Sugar Co. Edizione, 1977), originally published in Paris in 1939 as *La Burocratisation du monde*; Harold D. Lasswell and Daniel Lerner, *World Revolutionary Elites* (Cambridge, Mass.: MIT Press, 1965); Ralf Dahrendorf, *Class and Class Society in Industrial Society* (Stanford, Calif.: Stanford University Press, 1959); Zbigniew Brzezinski, *Between Two Ages: America's Role in the Technotronic Era* (New York: Viking Press, 1970). See also, Kevin Phillips, *Mediacracy* (Garden City, N.Y.: Doubleday, 1975); William Rusher, *The Making of the New Majority Party* (New York: Sheed and Ward, Inc., 1975).

notably labor and business leaders—associated with these "older" sectors.

Views about the impact of these new elites on political and electoral behavior vary. "New right" theorists Kevin Phillips and William Rusher believe it has given rise to a class struggle that pits "the knowledge sector" ("nonproducers") against the working and middle classes ("producers"), which in turn will lead to a realignment of the parties reflecting the new social cleavages. Everett Ladd (with Charles Hadley), who has offered the most complete statement of the politics of postindustrial society,[46] predicts the consolidation of new patterns of conflict and new alignments. Politics under conditions of affluence, Ladd argues, will focus on "life style" and the "quality of life" rather than on bread and butter issues and will pit a radicalized privileged class against less economically privileged, more conservative voters. The "abnormal" pattern of party competition and voting behavior described in a previous section of this chapter seems to Ladd persuasive evidence that the transition to postindustrial politics is already far advanced. These hypotheses will be tested (insofar as they are testable) by future developments. For now, they can constitute no more than suggestive and influential efforts to explain the departures from "normal" politics.

"Cross-Cutting" Issues. It is clear that some of the political abnormalities mentioned in the previous section—the decline in party identification, ticket splitting, the Wallace movement, the "abnormal landslides"—resulted from the rise of issues that cut across the New Deal party alignment. That alignment, we know, was based on differences concerning government's role in the economy. But prior to 1964, quite different issues emerged. (See Figure 7-3.) Urban riots, racial politics, Vietnam, and Watergate divided the electorate in new ways.

Many of the new issues involved the legitimacy of American society and government. The southern advocates of "massive resistance" and the northern freedom riders had in common a denial of the legitimacy of existing laws; so, in their different ways, did Daniel Ellsberg and the "plumbers." By the time of the 1968 election, attitudes to the war, the antiwar movement, urban rioters, the police, and the military were linked to each other and to such issues as work, welfare, rock festivals, marijuana, and Mayor Richard Daley. The "social issue," as Scammon and Wattenberg called it,[47] split the culturally conservative (but economically liberal) white working class

---

[46] Ladd with Hadley, *Transformations.*
[47] Scammon and Wattenberg, *Real Majority*, pp. 35-44.

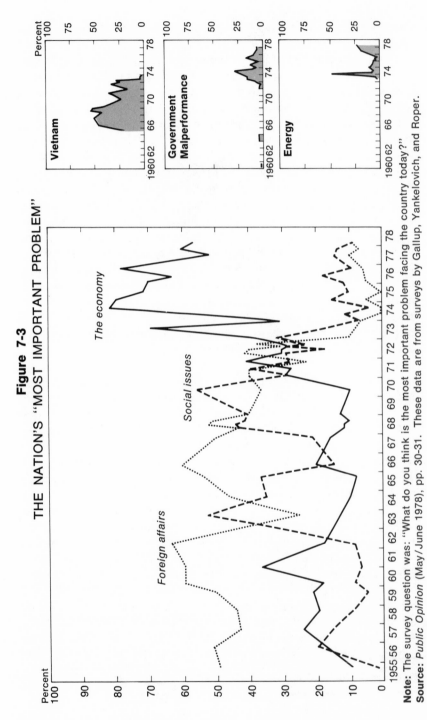

Figure 7-3
THE NATION'S "MOST IMPORTANT PROBLEM"

Note: The survey question was: "What do you think is the most important problem facing the country today?"
Source: *Public Opinion* (May/June 1978), pp. 30-31. These data are from surveys by Gallup, Yankelovich, and Roper.

away from the higher-status programmatic liberals to whom they had been allied since the onset of the New Deal and intensified estrangement of many white Southerners from the National Democratic Party.

The emergence of the new issues constituted another significant departure from the political norm, for in the two decades after World War II no proposition seemed more firmly established than that political conflict in America was limited by consensus on "fundamentals," was concerned with finding pragmatic solutions to practical problems, and was institutionalized. Suddenly, the consensus seemed to have vanished, as familiar welfare state concerns gave way to intransigent moral demands that were as often stated in the streets as through conventional institutional channels.

The power of the new social and cultural issues was apparent in the success of George Wallace, the bitterness of internal Democratic politics from 1967 through 1972, the Nixon landslide, and in the fact that their emergence coincided with increased popular attention to ideology and with the decline of partisanship. But the future of these issues is unclear and will remain so until we have a better understanding of their relationship to historical events like desegregation, the war in Vietnam, and Watergate. If the erosion of cultural consensus preceded and caused racial conflict, resistance to the war, and "Watergate," then related "cross-cutting" issues will doubtless continue to influence American politics; but if the events caused the challenge to legitimacy, then conflict over legitimacy and authority will doubtless recede.

In the 1976 presidential election, economic issues were once again dominant, and social and cultural issues less salient.[48] This may reflect a return to a "normal" preoccupation with bread and butter issues—or the accident of having two culturally conservative candidates confront one another during a time of recession.

Some Very Tentative Conclusions

The events reviewed in this chapter reflect a pattern of limited change with ambiguous implications for the future. In retrospect, 1964 appears to have been the point of origin of the most interesting changes: the decline of party identification, rising concern with issues, decreasing turnout, and declining confidence in government. At the time,

---

[48] Sundquist, *Dynamics*, predicts that the cross-cutting issues of the last decade will not prove lasting (chapters 15, 16, and 17).

as Lyndon Johnson scored his landslide defeat of Barry Goldwater, it did not seem as though the nation was on the brink of a period of significant change. On the contrary, there appeared to be broad consensus on domestic and foreign policy objectives. Barry Goldwater's warnings about the erosion of traditional values and the wages of permissiveness sounded rather like the cries of Chicken Little. Few political observers predicted then that only four years later a substantial majority of voters would desert their normal party and the candidate of that party to support Richard Nixon or George Wallace.

It is important that we know that the trends away from party regularity were already present in 1964. And it is important that we know that no one predicted them in 1964. The knowledge may help us more accurately assess the present. It is entirely possible that a return to "normal" was already underway in 1976, and the fact that this does not seem perfectly clear may reflect only our limitations as observers.

However, there are grounds for believing that we will not quickly return to the norm of pre-Vietnam politics:

- because the youngest voters are the least attached to the two parties;

- because the structure of the parties themselves has been transformed by reform and technology;[49]

- because the society has been so transformed that economic issues are no longer what they once were, unemployment is no longer what it once was, and industry no longer what it once was.

When for many voters the most important economic issues became inflation and taxes rather than unemployment and minimum wages, when the "parties" can be taken over in a single presidential season by a technically sophisticated candidate, when the intergenerational transmission of identifications and values is being continuously weakened, and when governments, public relations firms, direct mail professionals, and specialized pressure groups are progressively assuming the traditional functions of political parties, it is difficult to see how the patterns of behavior characteristic of previous times can be reestablished.

And yet, the Democrats are still the majority party, competition for office is almost always carried out under two—and only two—labels, and a majority of adults still identifies with (or "leans"

---

[49] Jeane Kirkpatrick, *Dismantling the Parties* (Washington, D.C.: American Enterprise Institute, 1978); Ladd with Hadley, *Transformations*.

toward) either the Republican or the Democratic parties. As of 1976 political competition once again appeared to be moderate, limited, pragmatic, and institutionalized, and the American political system seemed, once again, a model of stability.

Obviously evidences of stability are as relevant as the evidence of change to assessing current trends and projecting the future. There are also several theories concerning changing political alignments which might be taken into account. Probably the most influential of these is V. O. Key's theory of "critical" elections. To explain partisan realignment Key called attention to two types of electoral events: "critical elections" in which there occurred a "sharp and durable" realignment [50] and "secular realignments" which were characterized by the long-term, gradual redistribution of voters.[51] In "critical" realignments, voter interest and emotion were said to be high and change in party composition relatively swift; in "secular" realignments, new party alignments were said to develop through the cumulative impact of nearly imperceptible marginal shifts. Key suggested that in fact the two types of political change might prove to be more closely related than they sometimes appeared.

The authors of *The American Voter* distinguished three types of presidential elections relevant to the stability and change of party realignments: *maintaining* elections, in which "the pattern of partisan attachments prevailing in the preceding period persists and is the primary influence on forces governing the vote";[52] *deviating* elections, in which personalities or events alter the outcome of an election without affecting the balance of partisan attachments; and *realigning* elections, in which "popular feeling associated with politics is sufficiently intense that basic partisan commitments of a portion of the electorate change." But while it is relatively easy to relate these stages to events retrospectively, it is very difficult to place the present in these categories.

The owl of Minerva, Hegel noted, flies only in the gathering dusk. That owl presumably knows when the sun is setting. Political observers, on the other hand, find it difficult to be sure even when it is high noon.

---

[50] V. O. Key, "A Theory of Critical Elections," *Journal of Politics*, vol. 17 (1955), pp. 3-18.

[51] V. O. Key, "Secular Realignment and the Party System," *Journal of Politics*, vol. 21 (1959), pp. 198-210.

[52] Campbell et al., *American Voter*, p. 531.

8

The Puzzle of Political Participation in America

Richard A. Brody

On the basis of its ability to provide "opportunities for political oppositions" and of the "inclusiveness" of its political participation, Robert Dahl ranked the United States below the world's top ten "polyarchies" in 1969.[1] Bear in mind that Dahl made this rating after the Civil Rights Act of 1964, the Twenty-fourth Amendment to the Constitution, and the Voting Rights Act of 1965 had together removed whatever residual legality still underlay the disenfranchisement of southern blacks. For Dahl it was enough that systematic and legally sanctioned exclusion from participation in the leadership selection process was, because of the imposition of residency requirements, the lot of the geographically mobile American.[2]

It is pointless to argue with Dahl's ranking. Indeed, as we shall see, there appears to be a legacy of disenfranchisement that survives the elimination of legal bars to participation. Whether we agree with where the United States is placed in his scheme is not important. What is important is that Dahl alerts us to the relevance of context, that is, the situation in which the citizen acts or fails to act. Without this reminder, we are apt to fault the individual when we find, like the authors of *Voting*, that many Americans apparently fail to live up to the expectations of democratic theorists.[3] As we review what is

---

Many of the data used in this study were made available by the Inter-University Consortium for Political and Social Research. Neither the original collectors of the data nor the Consortium bear any responsibility for the analyses presented here.

[1] Robert A. Dahl, *Polyarchy* (New Haven: Yale University Press, 1971), p. 231 ff.

[2] Ibid., p. 246. The 1970 Voting Rights Act and the Court's decision in Dunn v. Blumstein, 405 U.S. 330 (1972), move a fair distance toward eliminating length of residence as a bar to participation.

[3] Bernard R. Berelson, Paul F. Lazarsfeld, and William N. McPhee, *Voting* (Chicago: University of Chicago Press, 1954), p. 307.

known about political participation in the United States over the past two decades, we must examine not only the individual citizen but also the conditions that the citizen encounters when he or she participates politically—whether in the exercise of the franchise, or in demanding that the political system act for the "common good," or in seeking governmental aid on a matter of personal concern.[4]

The picture that emerges from this review is puzzling. The puzzle can be illustrated by an examination of two recent instances of political participation.

The Regulation of Research on Recombinant DNA.[5] After a year of energetic effort and against the expectations of most observers, legislation designed to regulate research on the creation of new life forms via gene splicing is now (1978) stalled in Congress. An examination of this unexpected situation will provide an instance in which to consider the processes of pluralistic participation at work.[6]

Early in 1977, a dozen measures designed to govern research on recombinant DNA and to control the potential hazard to public health posed by such research were introduced into Congress. The two principal bills were those introduced by Senator Edward M. Kennedy, chairman of the Committee on Human Resources, and by Representative Paul Z. Rogers, who heads the Subcommittee on Health of the Committee on Interstate and Foreign Commerce. Senator Kennedy's bill would have established a new national commission to regulate all research on recombinant DNA, fixed the precedent of public control over scientific research by giving a majority of places on the commission to nonscientists, and barred federal preemption of local ordinances controlling research on recombinant DNA. The Rogers bill is more orthodox in its provisions. It gives authority for regulation of this line of research to the secretary of Health, Education, and Welfare, provides for an advisory committee, and permits local ordinances to hold sway only if a special need for local regulation is demonstrated.

Biologists doing research in this area are nearly united in their opposition to the Kennedy bill. Those who believe that congressional action cannot be avoided or who wish to preempt local control prefer

---

[4] Sidney Verba and Norman Nie, *Participation in America* (New York: Harper & Row, 1972), pp. 44-47.

[5] Material for this case examination is drawn from the press, Congressional Quarterly Weekly Reports, and from Barbara J. Culliton, "Recombinant DNA Bills Derailed: Congress Still Trying to Pass a Law," *Science*, vol. 199 (1978), pp. 274-77.

[6] For a concise statement of the theory of pluralistic participation see Nelson W. Polsby, *Community Power and Political Theory* (New Haven: Yale University Press, 1963), pp. 112-38.

the Rogers bill; others believe that if biological researchers are politically involved and scientifically self-disciplined, the present system of control under the guidelines set down by the National Institutes of Health (NIH) in 1976 will be adequate for the future.[7]

If we wish to understand the politics of participation, Polsby advises us in cases such as this (1) to concentrate on outcomes, (2) to begin with the expectation that power will be tied to issues and that the cast of the "powerful" will change from issue to issue, and (3) to expect, because of the fragmentation of American government, that the claims of small intense minorities will receive most attention.[8] In this instance, affected biologists are attempting to exercise "power," that is, to participate in the decision and, by their participation, to affect the outcome. The outcome they seek matches very closely the outcome that they have for the time being obtained[9]—regulation is still in the hands of the scientific community, under the aegis of the National Institutes of Health, and interference from the wider community has been forestalled. An additional indication of the effectiveness of the scientists' participation is found in Senator Kennedy's "temporary" withdrawal of support for his own bill.[10]

This outcome has been achieved not by some pervasive all-purpose power elite but by a collection of initially politically naive individuals possessing a fund of resources that were directly apposite to the matter at hand. The desired outcome ensued when they organized and replaced their naiveté with knowledge of the political system. In other words, political effectiveness came when the scientists stopped believing that they would necessarily be involved in decisions affecting their research and began to pay the price of influence: becoming informed, organizing, and lobbying on their own behalf.[11] Through these means, their resources—first and foremost, their special knowledge and expertise, but also their general standing and reputation for integrity[12]—were converted into political power.

---

[7] See, for example, Philip H. Abelson, "Recombinant DNA Legislation," *Science*, vol. 199 (1978), p. 135.

[8] Polsby, *Community Power*.

[9] Congress at this writing is again working on DNA legislation. Observers are unwilling to forecast the final outcome. See Nicholas Wade, "Congress Set to Grapple Again with Gene Splicing," *Science*, vol. 199 (1978), pp. 1319-22.

[10] Culliton, "Recombinant DNA," p. 277.

[11] Polsby, *Community Power*, pp. 116-17.

[12] The fact that researchers themselves called attention to the problem in the first place, worked with NIH to develop its program of safeguards, and conducted research aimed at making future research safer, apparently successfully countered the tendency of congressmen to discount the advice offered by "special pleaders." See Robert M. Rosenzweig, "An End to Autonomy: Who Pulls the Strings," *Change*, vol. 10, no. 3 (March 1978), pp. 29-34, 62.

This illustration shows the American political system working as it was designed to work: a small intense minority has, by its participation, made a claim upon the system. Those elected to guard the interests of the public at large have responded to this claim while keeping open future options for regulation.[13]

Our second case study gives a different impression. It will help us identify the "puzzle" referred to in the title of this chapter.

America at the Polls, 1976. In the midst of the struggle over the regulation of recombinant DNA, the 1976 election took place. Fifty-three percent of the 150 million Americans old enough to vote took advantage of the opportunity to choose between President Ford and Governor Carter. As Figure 8-1 shows, the rate of participation in 1976 was not the lowest since 1920 [14] or even since World War II. It does, however, represent a more marked departure from the trend established between 1920 and 1960 than any election in this period. Moreover, an even smaller proportion of the electorate took the opportunity to help choose the legislators who would represent them in innumerable matters that directly touch the lives of American citizens (among others, the regulation of DNA research).

Political science has little difficulty accounting for the relationship of participation to outcome in the instance of the regulation of gene-splicing research. It fits comfortably within the framework provided by the theory of pluralistic participatory democracy. But the shrinking level of participation in American national elections confounds our expectations and is at odds with the explanations of turnout offered by available theories of political behavior.

In this chapter I will review the explanations of voting participation developed by political scientists over the past thirty years. I will also consider research on other forms of political participation—electoral and nonelectoral. Paradoxically, political science seems to have a better handle on the less common forms of participation. As the extreme case of the effective mobilization of biological researchers shows, and a review of less exotic modes of participation will also

---

[13] That the system has worked as intended does not preclude intense political conflict among scientists, between them and elements of the public, and among members of Congress who are building careers or simply asserting jurisdictional claims over an area created by novel technology. The Wade, Rosenzweig, and Culliton articles are rich in accounts of this kind of politics.

[14] The 1920 election is chosen as the beginning of the series because the legal extension of the suffrage to all adults was completed then; prior to 1920 and the Nineteenth Amendment, the categorical exclusion of women made the proportion of the adult population participating in elections much lower.

Figure 8-1
OBSERVED AND EXPECTED TURNOUT IN PRESIDENTIAL ELECTIONS, 1920–1976

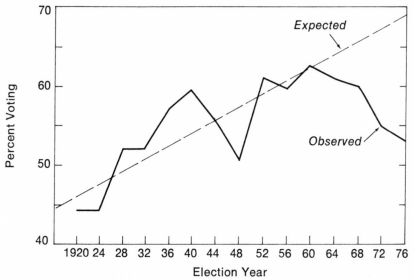

Note: The linear trend 1920-1960 is drawn from a time-series of the actual voting rates in this period. The expected vote curve produced by this regression has the following equation: expected turnout = 44.8% + 1.63% per election (CR^2 = .72).

Source: Bureau of the Census, *Statistical Abstract of the United States*, 1962; Bureau of the Census, *Projections of the Population of Voting Age for States*, Current Population Reports, Series P-25, No. 626, May 1976; Bureau of the Census, *Voting and Registration in the Election of November 1976*, Current Population Reports, Series P-20, No. 322, March 1978. Entries are votes cast as a percent of voting age population.

show, political science explanations of "higher" forms of participation appear to be adequate. However, the explanations that have been successful in informing us about voting participation in any given election give us very little insight into the trends in turnout over the past two decades. It is to a demonstration of this latter proposition that the next section is devoted.

Studies of Participation and Trends in Turnout

Three general emphases—legal context, individual attributes, and the character of the choice situation—dominate research on electoral participation. Studies of the effect of the legal context have emphasized the role played by community-imposed restrictions in reducing the rate of participation.[15] In the United States the only remaining legal barriers to participation are registration regulations. The Fifteenth and Nineteenth Amendments and the Court's holdings in the first eighty years of Fifteenth Amendment cases[16] combined to remove constitutional authority for the categorical exclusion of any class of persons from exercising the franchise in national elections. With the civil rights movement in the 1960s came the Twenty-fourth Amendment, which eliminated the poll tax,[17] and the Voting Rights Act of 1965, which suspended the use of literacy tests to bar blacks from registering.[18] By the mid-1960s the only registration regulations that could help explain state-to-state variations in rates of participation had to do with the permanency of one's registration, the conditions under which one was purged from the voting rolls, residency requirements,[19] the date of the closing of the voting rolls, and a series of arrangements that make it more or less convenient to register to vote.

Research on the effect of registration laws is in complete agreement that the more costly any arrangement is to the potential voter, the more it will reduce the rate of participation. "Cost," in this sense, can mean having to travel out of one's neighborhood to find a registrar, having to register during one's working hours, or having to take steps to register a month or more in advance of the election (before the campaign is in full swing). Estimates of the effects of a given provision differ from study to study because of differences in sampling frame, sample size, the nonlegal variables included in the equation, and the estimation technique, but there is no disagreement on the general proposition that, *ceteris paribus*, registration arrangements affect turnout.

---

[15] See Lester W. Milbrath, "Political Participation in the States," in *Politics in the American States*, ed. Herbert Jacob and Kenneth N. Vines (Boston: Little, Brown, 1965), pp. 25-60; Orley Ashenfelter and Stanley Kelley, Jr., "Determinants of Participation in Presidential Elections," *The Journal of Law and Economics*, vol. 18 (1975), pp. 695-733; and Steven J. Rosenstone and Raymond E. Wolfinger, "The Effect of Registration Laws on Voter Turnout," *American Political Science Review*, vol. 72 (1978), pp. 22-45.

[16] For a case-by-case history of the application of the Fifteenth Amendment, see Edward S. Corwin, ed., *The Constitution of the United States of America: Analysis and Interpretation* (Washington, D.C., 1953), pp. 1183-86.

[17] The Twenty-fourth Amendment bars the poll tax in federal elections; the Court's ruling in Harper v. Virginia State Board of Elections, 383 U.S. 663 (1966), eliminated the tax for any election.

[18] The Voting Rights Act Amendments of 1970 and the extension of 1975 eliminated literacy tests as a prerequisite for registration.

[19] Taken together the Voting Rights Act Amendments of 1970 and the Court's holding in Dunn v. Blumstein, 405 U.S. 330 (1972), mean that the residency requirement is effectively reduced to a thirty-day maximum. See Rosenstone and Wolfinger, "Effect of Registration Laws," p. 24.

The Rosenstone and Wolfinger study, which is based on the most inclusive sampling frame and the largest sample, summarizes the effect of registration provisions on the individual's probability of voting as follows:

> The provision with the largest impact is closing date. Depending upon one's probability of otherwise voting, a 30-day closing date decreased the likelihood of voting by 3 to 9 percentage points. A 50-day closing date (in effect in Arizona and Georgia) lowered the probability of voting by about 17 percent for those with a 40 to 60 percent chance of going to the polls.
>
> Variation in some other provisions also affected turnout. Irregular registration office hours (less than 40 hours a week) lowered by 2 to 4 percentage points the probability that a person would vote. Offices closed on Saturdays and in the evening decreased by 2 to 6 percent the probability of voting. In states that did not allow any form of absentee registration the chances of voting were 2 to 4 percent lower.[20]

Applying these findings to another question, Rosenstone and Wolfinger estimate that, if every state in 1972 had had the most accommodating version of each of these registration provisions, the turnout rate in the McGovern-Nixon election would have been about nine percentage points higher than it was.[21]

The Twenty-fourth Amendment and the voting rights legislation of the mid-1960s, as has been pointed out, abolished the poll tax and literacy test as registration restrictions. Ashenfelter and Kelley estimate that, other things being equal, the elimination of these two provisions would have increased turnout by ten percentage points.[22] Since these provisions were in the main found in southern states, it is in that region that we would expect to observe the effect of their abolition.

Figure 8-2 displays the trend in turnout in presidential elections disaggregated by census region. The dramatic changes in the rate of participation in the South are readily apparent: by 1976, the proportion of southerners exercising the franchise was nearly double that of 1948. While turnout was declining in the rest of the nation, it was increasing in the South. Moreover, the period of rapid increase, 1960 to 1968, coincides with the abolition of the poll tax, the suspension of literacy tests, the civil rights movement, and federal intervention in

---

[20] Ibid., p. 31.
[21] Ibid., p. 33.
[22] Ashenfelter and Kelley, "Determinants of Participation," p. 722.

Figure 8-2
REGIONAL TURNOUT IN PRESIDENTIAL ELECTIONS, 1948–1976

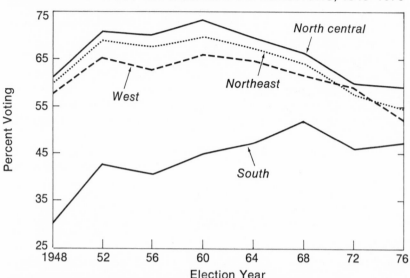

Source: For 1948-56, Richard M. Scammon, ed., *America Votes*, vol. 4 (Pittsburgh: University of Pittsburgh Press, 1962); 1960-72, Bureau of the Census, *Projections of the Population of Voting Age for States*; 1976, Bureau of the Census, *Voting and Registration in the Election of November 1976*. For definitions of the four regions, see Bureau of the Census, *Projections*, Table 4.

the voter registration system. Without question, other factors are also related to this change in southern turnout rates, but it seems reasonable to assert that the substantial reduction in restrictive registration regulation over this period is a direct cause of the increase in participation.

This extremely interesting body of research only serves to deepen our bewilderment about the trend in turnout since 1960. The changes in registration regulations over the past twenty years would lead us to expect higher rather than lower turnout rates. Moreover, the overall changes in the South would also lead us to expect higher rates. Had it not been for these changes, we might be seeing rates of participation even lower than those observed in the last three elections. The legal context helps us understand state-to-state variation in turnout. But the source of the trend across elections evidently lies elsewhere.

The second emphasis in research stresses qualities of the individual voter. In this category one finds studies that examine the role of personal *capacities* (indexed by factors such as education and income), *motivations* (indexed by measures such as political involvement and political efficacy), and *socialized political values* (indexed by measures such as sense of citizen duty and habituation to voting participation).[23]

The effect on turnout of every conceivable individual attribute has been examined at one time or another. Under the rigors of multivariate analysis only education appears to be related to rates of participation across the full range of its variation.[24] Other attributes such as income, age, sex, race, marital status, and occupational category come into play, with each other and with other factors, to sharpen our understanding of the variation in rates of participation in specific population subgroups.

Every investigation has established the link between education (as indexed by years of schooling) and turnout. In 1972, for example, the difference between the rates of participation for the least educated population group (those with four or fewer years of schooling) and those who have had postgraduate education is over fifty percentage points—in the former group 38 percent voted, in the latter 91 percent.[25] Those who had pursued their education beyond high school comprised in 1972 one-fourth of the *potential* electorate but one-third of the *actual* electorate. More generally, those whose education stopped before they completed high school tend to be underrepresented in the actual electorate; those who went on to college tend to be overrepresented; and those who completed high school but did not go on to college comprise about the same proportions of the *potential* and *actual* electorates.

Considered by themselves, income and occupation relate to participation in a manner generally similar to that of education: those with more income and those in higher status occupations are more likely to vote. But both of these attributes are related to education, and the explanatory power of income and occupation independent of education turns out to be very slight. Wolfinger and Rosenstone summarize their finding on income as follows: "Absolute rock-bottom

---

23 The germinal statements in this line of research are found in Angus Campbell, Gerald Gurin, and Warren E. Miller, *The Voter Decides* (Evanston: Row-Peterson, 1954); Angus Campbell, Philip E. Converse, Warren E. Miller, and Donald E. Stokes, *The American Voter* (New York: John Wiley and Sons, 1960); and Berelson, Lazarsfeld, and McPhee, *Voting*. The demographic correlates of turnout are examined in great detail in Raymond E. Wolfinger and Steven J. Rosenstone, "Who Votes?" (mimeo.), paper delivered at the 1977 annual meeting of the American Political Science Association, Washington, D.C., September 1-4, 1977. Estimates of the causal impact of variables from the three areas are found in Richard A. Brody and Paul M. Sniderman, "From Life Space to Polling Place," *British Journal of Political Science*, vol. 7 (1977), pp. 337-60.
24 Wolfinger and Rosenstone, "Who Votes?" pp. 20-32.
25 Ibid., p. 13.

poverty seems to depress turnout somewhat. Beyond that, income doesn't have much predictive power. Above the poverty level, once we know a person's educational attainment, our ability to predict whether he will vote is not substantially improved by knowing how much money he makes."[26] Wolfinger and Rosenstone argue that among the less well educated, certain occupation groups show higher rates of participation because the job itself confers the political skills and interests that otherwise come with higher levels of education.[27] For example, they are able to exploit their large sample to find that farm owners/managers and government employees (especially in high patronage states) participate at a rate beyond that expected on the basis of their educational attainment.[28]

From findings on the relationship of education and occupation to turnout we can conclude that political skills and the motivation that flows from a belief that the outcome matters increase the likelihood that an individual will vote. Political skills and motivation, alone or together, facilitate registration in the face of inconvenient regulations and heighten the meaning of the election for those who are registered.

The analyses of the relationship of education, income, and occupation to the probability of turnout in a given election, however, only increase our puzzlement at the trend in turnout since 1960. Figure 8-3 documents the difficulty: Over the past quarter century, the proportion of the population continuing on to post-secondary education has doubled. In light of this development, and the manifest relationship between education and participation, the steady decline in turnout since 1960 is all the more remarkable.

Other population trends do not decrease our puzzlement. Twenty-five years ago Lipset and his coauthors brought to our attention the nonmonotonic relationship between age and turnout.[29] Lipset presents the finding that rates of participation increase in successive cohorts through the middle-aged group, after which successive cohorts show decreasing rates of participation. The pattern has been replicated in subsequent studies, but the point at which the decline in participation is observed has "progressed" to older and older groups.[30] Explanations

---

[26] Ibid., p. 24. See also, Ashenfelter and Kelley, "Determinants," p. 707.

[27] Ibid., p. 24.

[28] Ibid., pp. 24, 49-56.

[29] Seymour M. Lipset, Paul F. Lazarsfeld, Allen H. Barton, and Joan Linz, "The Psychology of Voting," in Handbook of Social Psychology, ed. Gardner Lindzey, vol. 2. (Reading, Mass.: Addison-Wesley Publishing Co., 1954), p. 1127.

[30] Lipset et al., ibid., peg the downturn at age fifty-five, and Campbell et al., American Voter, p. 494, concur; Verba and Nie, Participation, pp. 138-44, put the breakpoint at age sixty-five; and Wolfinger and Rosenstone, "Who Votes?" p. 34, find age seventy as the key group.

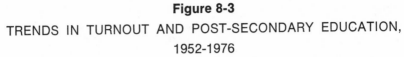

Figure 8-3
TRENDS IN TURNOUT AND POST-SECONDARY EDUCATION, 1952-1976

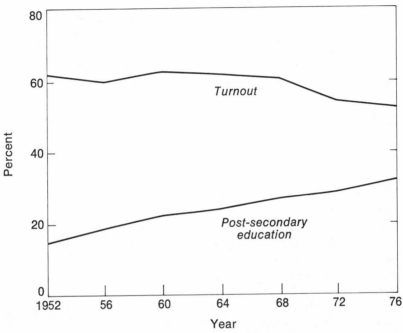

Source: For turnout, see Figure 1; for education data, Codebooks of the American National Election Studies (Institute for Social Research, University of Michigan) for indicated year.

of the decline past middle age have emphasized health and other problems that "slow down" older people. However, unless one is prepared to argue that "slowing down" has set in at progressively later ages over the past quarter century, one has to look to other factors to explain the decline of participation among older cohorts. Verba and Nie look to the educational and income differences between older and younger citizens and conclude that the so-called slowdown really reflects the different distribution of status characteristics at different age levels.[31] Wolfinger and Rosenstone expand our understanding of this phenomenon by showing that education, sex, and marital status are the factors that explain the lower turnout of those seventy years and older.[32] Aging as such does not reduce the proba-

---

[31] Verba and Nie, *Participation*, pp. 144-45.
[32] Wolfinger and Rosenstone, "Who Votes?" pp. 34-42.

bility of voting; it is rather that citizens over the age of seventy are less apt to vote because they are less well educated and more likely to be women and to be without spouses than the rest of the population.

The educational deficit of older cohorts is passing out of the electorate as the individuals who comprise these cohorts are replaced by people born during and after the arrival of mass secondary education in the United States. Presumably the sex differences in life expectancy will not pass away. However, there are reasons for expecting that the differences in the rate of participation observed for men and women seventy and older in 1972 will not persist. To begin with, in 1972 men and women, in the 91 percent of the population below the age of seventy, showed virtually no difference in turnout rate. Moreover, the educational difference between the sexes is passing into history. Finally, there will soon be no woman in the electorate who grew to maturity with the expectation that she would be excluded from voting. Women born in or before 1902—unless they grew up in one of the ten western states that granted women the suffrage before 1917 [33]—were probably past adolescence before their state government granted them the right to vote. Taking all other plausible differences into account, this female cohort was found in 1972 to participate at a rate about four percentage points below that of its male counterpart.[34]

Can we plausibly claim that these women suffered some permanent impairment to their image of themselves as voters? We cannot substantiate the claim with any available data, but it is noteworthy that as this cohort has aged, the point at which the "age/rate of turnout" curve turns down has "aged" as well—fifty-five in 1956, sixty-five in 1967, and seventy in 1972. Investigations of this curve for 1976 should show seventy-four as the age at which substantial differences in the turnout rate of men and women appear. The explanation for the persistence of this deficit is probably habit. Participation is apparently self-reinforcing behavior. We would expect women who grew up without the expectation of voting to have been less likely than men or younger women to participate when the law was changed, and the force of habit would serve to distinguish them from then on.

---

[33] In the order in which they granted women's suffrage these states were: Wyoming (1869), Colorado (1893), Idaho and Utah (1896), Washington (1910), California (1911), Kansas, Nevada, and Oregon (1912), and Montana (1914). The probability that any women alive in 1972 were raised in these states is affected by the fact that they were among the least populated states at the time.

[34] Wolfinger and Rosenstone, "Who Votes?" p. 35.

However, in accounting for the decline in the turnout rate of the total electorate between 1960 and 1976, knowledge of the voting behavior of this group of women is of no help. Their significance as a group within the electorate was decreasing over this period.

The significance of the youth group within the potential electorate has been growing. But this fact, too, will not solve our puzzle. It is true that those younger than middle age participate at rates lower than those middle aged and older. Verba and Nie attribute this to the problem of "starting up" in the community. They expand upon this as follows: "Citizens who have lived for a shorter time in the community are, in general, less politically active. This has several sources: Voting is limited by residence requirements; new residents may not have developed a stake in the community. They may not have developed the affiliational and interpersonal resources for participation and they have other demands on their time." [35] The legal bar to participation by new residents has largely been removed, but the other factors depressing the turnout vote of youth may very well remain. For our purposes, unless one is prepared to argue that these "start up" factors are increasing in potency, they will not help us solve our puzzle.[36] Cannot one argue that "increasing potency" is precisely the case because of the injection of the eighteen to twenty year olds into the electorate by the Twenty-sixth Amendment? This line of argument achieves only limited success. Wolfinger and Rosenstone estimate that no more than one-quarter of the 1968 to 1972 drop in turnout could have come from the enfranchising of the eighteen to twenty age group.[37]

In sum, the demographic changes in the electorate, to the extent they relate to turnout, on balance would lead us to expect higher rather than lower rates of participation. However, these discrepant trends could be reconciled if the *motivations* and *political values* that intervene between one's social attributes and political actions were changing in a fashion that would lead us to predict reduced participation.

It is useful to think of the elements of one's social class and life stage as linked to voting through their connection to intermediary *political motives* and values. Brody and Sniderman depict the causal linkages with the arrow diagram reproduced in Figure 8-4: For 1972,

---

[35] Verba and Nie, *Participation*, p. 145.

[36] Wolfinger and Rosenstone, "Who Votes?" pp. 44-48, demonstrate that education substantially ameliorates, but does not eliminate, the effect of youth. The increase in education of the electorate would, thus, tend to make this contention implausible.

[37] Ibid., p. 48.

Figure 8-4

THE DETERMINANTS OF TURNOUT, 1972

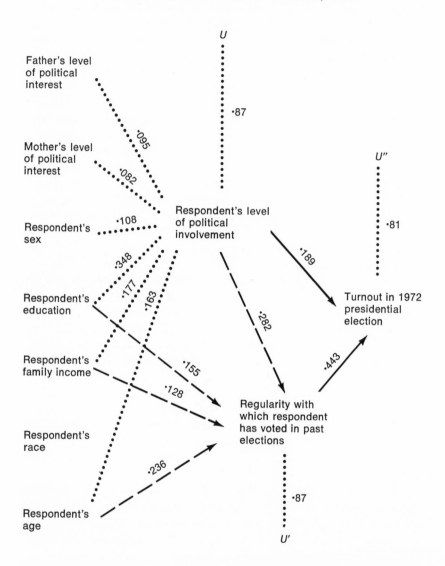

Note: This figure is a path model of turnout for the 1972 election. The entries are path coefficients, which vary between −1 and +1. The arrows indicate direct causal relationships. U, U', and U" represent the factors left out of the model.

Source: Richard A. Brody and Paul M. Sniderman, "From Life Space to Polling Place," *British Journal of Political Science,* vol. 7 (1977), p. 347.

their findings indicate that background attributes have no direct effect on turnout but rather act through their effect upon the individual's level of political involvement and upon the regularity with which the individual has participated in past elections. Of these two factors, "regularity," that is, the habituation of the citizen to voting as a sociopolitical act, is clearly the more powerfully related to the individual's likelihood of voting in the current election.

Following the lead of Campbell, Converse, Miller, and Stokes,[38] Brody and Sniderman measured "involvement" as a composite of the individual's belief that the citizen has a "duty" to vote, his expression of concern over the outcome of the election, his interest in the campaign, his sense of political efficacy, and the strength of his partisan identification. They found that in 1972 "interest in the campaign" was, of the five components, the one most related to the underlying sense of involvement; this was followed by duty, efficacy, and concern about the outcome, which were about equally related. Strength of partisan identification was very weakly related to involvement; it was correlated to the involvement measure only one-fourth as strongly as interest in the campaign.[39]

From the perspective of explaining the decline, this last fact is unfortunate because, as presently measured, the strength of partisan identification has substantially and steadily declined since 1960.[40] Given its relationship to "involvement" and "involvement's" relationship to turnout, the reduction in the aggregate strength of identification with the parties can be at most part of the explanation we are after.

Table 8-1 indicates further that trends in the components of the belief that the citizen has a duty to vote will not help in our search. The American public certainly expresses the belief that citizens should vote in national and local elections irrespective of whether they can affect the outcome; it is only on the linkage between concern for outcome and participation that we observe any significant division of public opinion. But on none of these questions, when we compare the Eisenhower-Kennedy years with more recent elections, do we find that substantial portions of the electorate have forsaken their belief in the duty to vote. Interest in the ongoing campaign gives us essentially the same picture. Figure 8-5 shows that very little change has taken place in expressed interest in the campaign over the last seven elections.

---

[38] *American Voter*, chap. 5.

[39] Brody and Sniderman, "From Life Space," p. 348.

[40] Warren E. Miller and Teresa E. Levitan, *Leadership and Change: Presidential Elections from 1952 to 1976* (Cambridge, Mass.: Winthrop Publishers, Inc., 1976), p. 36.

Table 8-1

BELIEF IN THE CITIZEN'S DUTY TO VOTE, 1952–1976

(in percentages)

Item and Response	Election Year					
	1952	1956	1960	1972	1976
"I'd like to have you tell me whether you agree or disagree with each of these . . . statements."					
"It isn't so important to vote when you know your party doesn't have a chance."/"Disagree"	88.7	90.7	92.5	91.4	91.8
"So many other people vote in the national elections that it doesn't matter much to me whether I vote or not."/"Disagree"	87.7	90.1	92.1	89.9	89.7
"If a person doesn't care how an election comes out he shouldn't vote in it."/"Disagree"	46.0	53.5	55.5	54.1	53.8
"A good many local elections aren't important to bother with."/"Disagree"	82.1	86.1	88.0	86.3	86.1

Note: The percentage bases vary between 1,700 and 2,700 cases. **Source:** American National Election Study (Institute for Social Research, University of Michigan), years indicated.

Figure 8-5

TREND IN INTEREST IN POLITICAL CAMPAIGNS, 1952–1976

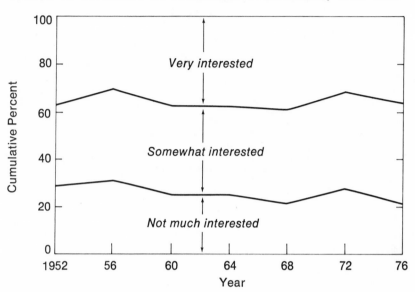

Source: Codebooks for the year indicated, American National Election Study (Institute for Social Research, University of Michigan).

The last two components of the index of political involvement are more helpful. Concern over the outcome of the election varies over a narrow range, but the fraction of the electorate expressing concern— claiming to care a good deal which party wins the election—has declined steadily since 1964. Three of the four measures of "political efficacy" show the same trend. (See Figures 8-6 and 8-7.)

The increased "efficacy" noted on the item which asks respondents if "voting is the only way for people like [them] to have a say in the way government runs things" could represent either an increase in the belief that *even* voting doesn't help or in the belief that other modes of influence are available to the citizen. This item aside, there is clearly an increase in the sense that government is distant and unresponsive to the average citizen. This interpretation is supported by two additional measures which, although they have been gathered only since 1968, show that increasingly large fractions of the potential electorate believe that the link between the vote and public policy is tenuous at best (see Table 8-2).

Figure 8-6
TREND IN CONCERN ABOUT ELECTORAL OUTCOME, 1952–1976

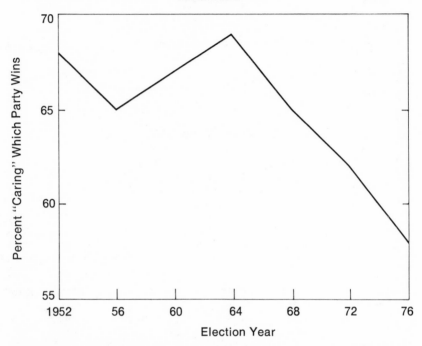

Note: The survey item reads: "Generally speaking would you say that you personally care a good deal which party wins the presidential election this fall or that you don't care very much which party wins." Prior to 1972, more response options were offered; these data combine "care very much" and "care pretty much."

Source: Codebooks for the year indicated; American National Election Study (Institute for Social Research, University of Michigan).

Table 8-2
MEASURES OF POLITICAL EFFICACY, 1968–1976
(in percentages)

	Election Year		
Item/Response	1968	1972	1976
"Generally speaking those we elect to Congress lose touch with the people pretty quickly."/"Disagree"	44.6	32.1	27.9
"Parties are only interested in people's votes but not in their opinions."/"Disagree"	52.4	40.7	36.4

Source: American National Election Study (Institute for Social Research, University of Michigan), codebooks for appropriate years.

Figure 8-7

TRENDS IN POLITICAL EFFICACY, 1952–1976

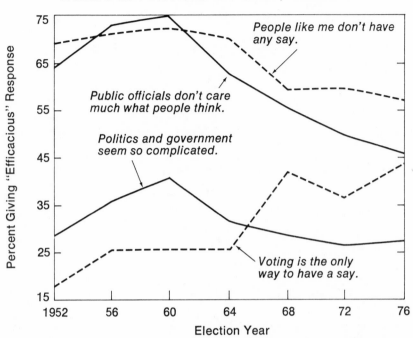

Source: Codebooks for the year indicated; American National Election Study (Institute for Social Research, University of Michigan).

The potential significance of the decrease in elements of political involvement is heightened when we note that habituation to the act of voting was barely less prevalent in 1976 than it was at any time over the past seven presidential elections (see Figure 8-8).

This investigation of motivations and beliefs that are tied to the probability of voting has proved helpful. Some of the attitudes that link background attributes to participation have not changed in a fashion that sheds light on the manifest decline in turnout. Citizens are steadfast in their belief that voting is a citizen's duty, they exhibit no decline in interest in the campaign, and a fairly constant proportion indicate that voting is for them a fully developed habit. However, we have also seen a substantial decline in the belief that participation is politically meaningful, that government is responsive, and that the outcome of the election is a matter of concern to the individual voter. These changes begin to give us an indication that abstention flows

Figure 8-8
TRENDS IN VOTING HABITUATION, 1952–1976

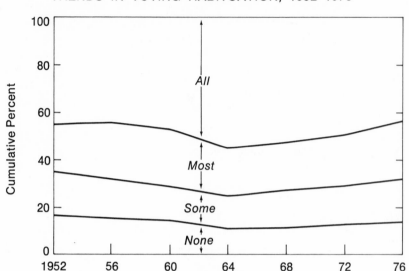

Note: The item reads: "In the elections for president since you have been old enough to vote, would you say you have voted in all of them, most of them, some of them or none of them?"

Source: Codebooks for the year indicated; American National Election Study (Institute for Social Research, University of Michigan).

from the belief—held by an increasingly large segment of the electorate—that voting simply isn't worth the effort.

If this is the case, then we should find it useful to consider carefully the rational basis for abstention. The studies that emphasize elements of the choice situation begin with assumptions of cost and benefit drawn from economic models of choice behavior and look to the voter's perception of the choice situation (as related to the voter's evaluations of the candidates) to explain abstentions from participation.[41]

---

[41] See Anthony Downs, *An Economic Theory of Democracy* (New York: Harper & Row, 1957); Gerald Garvey, "The Theory of Party Equilibrium," *American Political Science Review*, vol. 60 (1966), pp. 29-38; Otto Davis, Melvin Hinich, and Peter Ordeshook, "An Expository Development of a Mathematical Model of the Electoral Process," *American Political Science Review*, vol. 64 (1970), pp. 426-48; Richard A. Brody and Benjamin I. Page, "Indifference, Alienation, and Rational Decisions," *Public Choice*, vol. 15 (1973), pp. 1-17; and William Riker and Peter C. Ordeshook, *An Introduction to Positive Political Theory* (Englewood Cliffs, N.J.: Prentice-Hall, 1973), chaps. 11 and 12.

Treatments of abstention as a response to perceptions of the choice situation begin with the observation that voting is a choice among alternatives. One chooses whether to vote before choosing for whom to vote. It is hypothesized that either of two conditions— "alienation" or "indifference"—reduces the likelihood that the individual will choose to vote. "Indifference" involves the amount of contrast that an individual perceives when he or she considers the available candidates. "Alienation" involves the level of the citizen's evaluation of the candidates, how negative or positive he or she feels about the proffered alternatives.

Under the "indifference-abstention" hypothesis, because expected utility varies with the difference that the outcome would make for the potential voter, those who perceive a great deal of difference in the attractiveness of different candidates will be more apt to vote than those who see little or no difference.

The cost/benefit assumptions of abstention due to "alienation" are more involved. If the voter perceives a difference between the candidates but is negative about the one he likes best, he is said to be "alienated." But we would still expect this citizen to vote unless the cost (in time or effort) of voting outweighed the benefit represented by the perceived difference between the candidates.[42] In other words, the more nearly indifferent is the alienated voter, the more likely he or she is to abstain.

"Indifference" and "alienation" do not exhaust the descriptors of the absolute and relative evaluations of the candidates. Weisberg has used candidate rating scales to identify citizens who are "alienated" in the sense already defined; in addition, he identifies citizens who are "concerned" (who rate one candidate positively and one negatively); those who are "satisfied" (who rate both candidates positively); and those with no or neutral evaluations of the candidates.[43] In Weisberg's scheme, "indifference" can be a further defining characteristic of either "alienation" or "satisfaction"; the concerned cannot be indifferent, and those with no or neutral evaluations are indifferent by definition.[44]

---

[42] Brody and Page, "Indifference," p. 3. Also, see Melvin J. Hinich, "Some Evidence on Non-voting Models in the Spatial Theory of Electoral Competition," (mimeo.), Department of Economics, Virginia Polytechnic Institute, 1977, p. 2.

[43] Herbert F. Weisberg, "Rational Abstention Due to Satisfaction: A Revised Look at the Effects of Candidate Evaluation on Turnout" (mimeo.), paper prepared for delivery at the 1977 annual meeting of the Midwest Political Science Association, Chicago, Illinois, April 21-23, 1977.

[44] Ibid., p. 4.

Weisberg hypothesizes that the rate of rational abstention will be highest among those who are either alienated or satisfied *and* indifferent. Those who are either alienated or satisfied but not indifferent should vote at a rate in between that of those who are indifferent and those who are concerned. Those without opinions or with neutral feelings toward the candidates are expected to abstain at the highest rate, but because "[t]his group would be expected to include a large number of people who are uninvolved in politics and who customarily abstain regardless of who the nominees are," Weisberg does not include them among the rational abstainers.[45]

Weisberg's main findings are displayed in Figure 8-9. They confirm his expectation that concerned citizens will abstain at a rate lower, and citizens with no or neutral opinions will abstain at a rate higher, than the rest of the population. These data do not support the notion that when alienation or satisfaction is augmented by indifference rational abstention will increase. Indeed, the apparent differences between the four middle categories of citizens, in the Weisberg model, cannot be distinguished from sampling variation. Weisberg also tests his hypothesis with data from all of the presidential elections between 1952 and 1972. The 1972 findings are replicated in the aggregate of the six elections.[46]

On the basis of these explorations, Weisberg rejects the notion that rational abstention is a prevalent source of nonvoting. Most citizens, on the basis of their evaluations of the candidates, would be classified as either "concerned" or "satisfied";[47] most nonvoters come from these two groups as well (Figure 8-8 shows that in 1972, 80 percent of nonvoters did; for 1952–1972, 70 percent of nonvoters are classified as either "concerned" or "satisfied"). Added to these facts is the lack of cogency of the notion of indifference, or for that matter of the distinction between satisfaction and alienation.

Taken altogether and in its own terms Weisberg's refutation of the rational abstention hypothesis is quite devastating; but its effect is mitigated by two facts. First, Weisberg's exclusion of citizens with no opinions or neutral opinions from the possibility of rational abstention directly affects his conclusion—and such citizens were one-fifth of the nonvoters in the 1952–1972 aggregate. In addition, by not considering the likelihood of concerned, satisfied, alienated, and neutral citizens' voting irrespective of their reaction to the presidential candidates, Weisberg in effect assumes that, absent differences in

---

[45] Ibid., p. 8.
[46] Weisberg, "Rational Abstentions," p. 14.
[47] In 1972, 85 percent of the CPS/ISR sample fell into these two categories.

Figure 8-9
RATIONAL ABSTENTION IN 1972

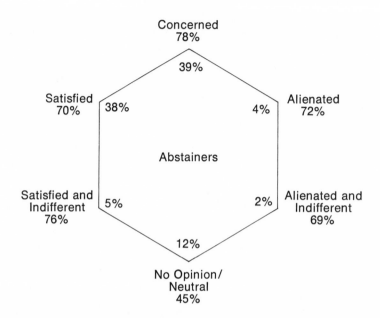

Concerned
78%

Satisfied
70%

Alienated
72%

Abstainers

Satisfied and
Indifferent
76%

Alienated and
Indifferent
69%

No Opinion/
Neutral
45%

Note: Outside the ring are shown the proportions of the electorate in the given categories who voted in 1972; thus, 78 percent of the "concerned" cast ballots. Inside the ring are shown the proportions of the abstainers who fell into the given categories; thus, 39 percent of those who abstained were "concerned." **Source:** Adapted from Weisberg, "Rational Abstention."

candidate evaluations, each of these groups should show the same rate of participation.[48] Careful investigation of the latter assumption raises questions about it, about the former assumption, and, therefore, about the conclusions that rational abstention is not a factor to be considered in the decline in participation.

The model of forces affecting turnout depicted in Figure 8-4 can be used to classify each individual as an "expected" voter or non-voter.[49] This procedure takes account of levels of political involvement, habit, and the sociodemographic factors that indirectly affect

[48] Actually, a lower rate of participation is expected from the group with no or neutral opinions (Weisberg, "Rational Abstention," p. 8), but no provision is made for turnout differentials in the other groups.

[49] Brody and Sniderman, "From Life Space," p. 348.

turnout; it gives us a standard of comparison for the observed rate of participation of, in this case, groups defined on the basis of their evaluations of the candidates. Table 8-3 offers that comparison for the 1972 election. The figures on expected vote indicate that the candidate evaluation groups do differ on the factors predisposing people to vote: It is not only the "no opinion/neutral opinion" group that is differentiated, although as anticipated the gap is greatest here, but the expected turnout of the "satisfied" and "concerned" groups as well. These data support the contention that alienation and indifference combined with alienation reduce participation. They also show that those who offer no opinion or neutral opinions about the candidates participate at a rate very much below that which one would expect on the basis of their education, political involvement, sense of citizen duty, habituation to voting, and all of the other predisposing factors included in the Brody-Sniderman expected vote model. The complete indifference of these citizens to the choices offered to them by the parties reduces their likelihood of voting.

This may provide a clue to the decline in turnout, but it needs to be read with caution for two reasons. First, the measure of participation used in the model is inflated, and the degree of inflation is getting worse.[50] Moreover, the assumption that all of the elements of the Brody-Sniderman model are prior to candidate evaluations is subject to question when we note that concern about outcome and the perception of governmental responsiveness are part of that model. Ongoing research will attempt to settle some of these issues, but, on the basis of what we can now reasonably feel sure about, we cannot go beyond what Brody and Page concluded in their study of the 1968 election: "while neither indifference nor alienation is characteristic of the American public, when they are present they affect political participation."[51]

As a classification of the comparison-of-candidate evaluations, "alienation"—a negative evaluation of the candidate one likes best—cannot be the source of the recent decline in turnout. Over the last

---

[50] The discrepancies (in percentage points) between the proportion of the electorate telling the University of Michigan (cps/src) interviewers that they had voted for President and the figures estimated by the Bureau of the Census for the elections between 1952 and 1976 are the following: 1952, 11.2; 1956, 13.8; 1960, 10.9; 1964, 15.9; 1968, 15.1; 1972, 17.4; and 1976, 18.3. The University of Michigan estimates are drawn from the codebooks for the seven elections; the census estimates are percent of voting age population voting (Current Population Reports, *Population Estimates and Projections*, Series P-25, no. 626, May 1976, table 6).

[51] Brody and Page, "Indifference," p. 7.

Table 8-3
EXPECTED AND OBSERVED RATES OF TURNOUT FOR DIFFERENT CANDIDATE EVALUATION GROUPS, 1972
(in percentages)

	Candidate Evaluation Group					
	Concerned	Satisfied	Satisfied/ indifferent	Alienated	Alienated/ indifferent	No opinion/ neutral
Expected to vote	84.3	76.0	76.7	79.2	77.8	60.0
Actually voted	78.6	69.2	73.0	70.0	68.8	41.2
Difference (in percentage points)	5.7	6.8	3.7	9.2	9.0	18.8

Note: Because of the deletion of cases for which an expected vote could not be computed, the "actually voted" figures differ from those presented in Figure 8-9.

Source: Data derived from applying the Brody-Sniderman model to data from the 1972 University of Michigan American National Election Study.

three elections—those for which we have data [52]—alienation has not been increasing: in 1968, 2.4 percent could not find any candidate that they did not evaluate negatively; the comparable figure in 1972 was 6.2 percent; but in evaluating Ford and Carter only 1.7 percent of the electorate was negative toward both.

The trend in "indifference" is a more promising source of the decline in turnout. Over the past three elections, in which the decline in participation has been sharpest, the proportion of the electorate rating the candidates equally—equally positively, neutrally, or negatively—has risen steadily. In 1968, 8 percent did not rate any candidate more favorably than the others; in 1972 this figure had grown to 10 percent; and in the Ford-Carter pairing one in seven rated the candidates alike.

Two points need to be made about this finding. To begin with, we note that turnout declined about five percentage points between 1968 and 1972 and another two percentage points between 1972 and 1976; a six percentage point increase in indifference cannot explain a seven percentage point decline in participation unless we are (as I am not) willing to assert that each citizen, newly coming to rate the candidates equally, abstained from voting *and* talked other citizens, who were not indifferent, into abstaining as well. More to the point, what do we know when we know that in a summary judgment the candidates came out at the same point? Clearly, this simply transforms the analytic task into the problem of understanding the sources of the ratings of the candidates. Only after that exercise is undertaken will we know whether "indifference" between the candidates is apt to be increasingly important as a root of citizen nonparticipation—presumably as a result of some systemic change in the polity—or whether in the last three elections, for reasons peculiar to each, a slightly larger proportion of the voters than in the previous election was convinced that, since it made no difference who won it was pointless to vote.

If the sources of indifference are not the same from election to election, there is no reason to expect that the rate of participation will not be higher in 1980 than it was in 1976. The condition of legal impediments to participation, and the level of the measures of individual capacity, would lead us to this expectation. With these factors standing as they do, the trend in the rate of participation will depend upon reactions to the candidates proffered by the parties and thus

---

[52] The candidate "feeling thermometers" upon which these statements are based were introduced in 1968. See Herbert F. Weisberg and Jerrold G. Rusk, "Dimensions of Candidate Evaluation," *American Political Science Review*, vol. 64 (1970), pp. 1167-85.

upon the nominees themselves. A discussion of the politics of the candidate-selection process falls within the purview of another chapter in this book; it is sufficient to note here that the playing out of this process, with the electorate as audience, is likely to affect the rate of participation in 1980 and beyond.

Cutting across the line of research, in which attention to participation in presidential elections is the dominant concern, are studies of the variation in rates of participation attributable to the office or the issue being contested and/or the timing of the election in the electoral cycle. An examination of this research gives us a fuller picture of the American citizen as democratic participant.

It is certainly the case that nonpresidential elections show lower rates of participation. This is true of primary elections; the states that had presidential preference primaries in 1976, for example, averaged nearly double their primary election turnout (53 percent versus 29 percent) in the November presidential election.[53] It is true of statewide elections, primary and general.[54] And the electorate for local offices and ballot measures, when a presidential election is not also at stake, is very small.[55]

Moreover, the timing of the election causes variations in participation. For example, turnout for congressional elections held in conjunction with a presidential election is substantially higher—on the average nearly fourteen percentage points higher over the past twenty-one elections—than for midterm congressional elections.[56] This difference in participation in elections for the same office at two different points in time produces the oft-noted saw-tooth pattern to

[53] Austin Ranney, *Participation in American Presidential Nominations, 1976* (Washington, D.C.: American Enterprise Institute, 1977), table 5, p. 25.

[54] Malcolm E. Jewell, "Voting Turnout in State Gubernatorial Primaries," *Western Political Quarterly*, vol. 30 (1977), pp. 236-54; Jae-On Kim, John R. Petrocik, and Steven N. Enokson, "Voter Turnout Among the States," *American Political Science Review*, vol. 69 (1975), pp. 107-23; and Milbrath, "Political Participation."

[55] Jerome M. Clubb and Michael W. Traugott, "National Patterns of Referenda Voting: The 1968 Election," in *People and Politics in Urban Society*, ed. Harlan Hahn (Beverly Hills, Calif.: Sage Publications, 1972), pp. 137-69.

[56] Computed from data in Bureau of the Census, *Population Estimates and Projections*, Series P-25, issued May 1976, table 6, p. 11. In these same data we note that in presidential years over the past eleven elections the roll-off between presidential and congressional turnout has averaged 3.8 percentage points. There is a tendency for the size of the roll-off gap to increase between 1932 and the most recent elections; on the average the gap has been increasing by .2 percentage points per election ($R^2 = .66$ for the linear trend; with $df = N - 2 = 9/9$, the ratio of this slope to its standard error, $b/se_b = 2.5$, is statistically significant with $p < .025$).

the trend in congressional election turnout. Figure 8-10 shows that this pattern is characteristic of the trend lines at both the national and the regional level. There is no reason to believe that congressional elections are special in this regard; if anything, the differential turnout for other offices in presidential and nonpresidential years should be more extreme.[57]

Clearly there is something about a presidential election that brings more people to the polls. Discovering what this "something" is would advance our knowledge of the sources of participation. The trouble is that there are too many "somethings." Since virtually every element of the decision situation is different in a presidential election year—with the probable exception of the body of legal restrictions affecting elections for national office, and the possible exception of the set of socialized political values—disciplined investigation of even small packages of potential explanatory variables will be difficult to carry out.

Figure 8-10

NATIONAL AND REGIONAL TURNOUT IN CONGRESSIONAL ELECTIONS, 1960–1974

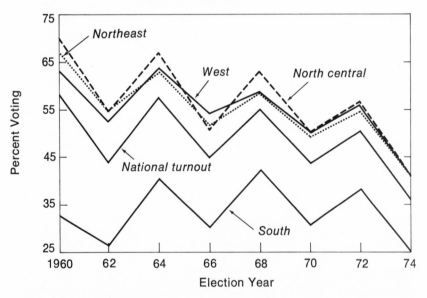

Source: Bureau of the Census, *Projections of the Population of Voting Age for States*, Current Population Reports, Series P-25, No. 626, May 1976.

---

[57] Milbrath, "Political Participation," p. 37.

Trend data on turnout in nonpresidential elections could help us to decide whether the decline in participation in presidential elections reflects a more widespread and general disengagement from political participation or whether the response to the presidency or the presidential candidates has been singular. Alas, I can find no compilation of such trend data for a range of electoral contests. The data in Figure 8-10 raise more questions than they answer: only in 1974 (nationally or regionally) was midterm congressional turnout down. Was this a one-time effect of Watergate, the pardon, and the other events of that eventful period? When we examine participation in the upcoming 1978 elections we will be better able to judge whether the disengagement from politics is widespread and persistent.

Politics One-on-One: Contact as Participation

Our preoccupation with voting as an activity that brings the citizen into contact with the polity should not obscure the fact that there are other ways in which citizens participate. Verba and Nie distinguish two forms of nonelectoral political participation—cooperative activity and citizen-initiated contacts.[58] In each of these two areas of activity we can distinguish between "opinion expression" and the communication of political "demands."[59] Logically four classes of nonelectoral activity can be distinguished: cooperative demand making, cooperative opinion expression, citizen-initiated opinion expression, and citizen-initiated demand making. All of these will be discussed, but the balance of the chapter will concentrate upon citizen-initiated demands upon the political system.

Most of the relevant literature on cooperative demand making falls within the scope of other chapters of this book. To be sure, our glimpse of the biologists' participation in the legislative process—the regulation of research on recombinant DNA—is an instance of cooperative demand making. Indeed we saw in the case of the politics of regulating gene-splicing research that getting organized was a prerequisite to getting results. But as a general rule the processes of "getting organized" and "getting results" are considered separately by political scientists. Getting organized is in the province of those who study interest groups.[60] And ordinarily the results of contact

---

[58] Verba and Nie, *Participation*, pp. 52-53.

[59] Peter K. Eisenger, "The Pattern of Citizen Contacts with Urban Officials," in *People and Politics*, p. 44.

[60] For a comprehensive review of the "interest group" literature, see Robert H. Salisbury, "Interest Groups," in *Handbook of Political Science*, ed. Fred I. Greenstein and Nelson W. Polsby, vol. 4 (Reading, Mass.: Addison-Wesley, 1975), pp. 171-228.

between organized groups of citizens and those who can respond to their demands are treated as part of the legislative process in particular and the policy process in general.[61]

In much the same manner, research on cooperative activity aimed at expressing the policy opinions of organized groups has largely been undertaken to illuminate the success or failure of the mobilization of interests to affect outcomes. The individual's motives for participating in such activities and the consequences for him of doing so have not been of concern to those who study mobilization.[62] In the division of political-science labor, this topic has largely been left unstudied by election experts.

By contrast, many facets of citizen-initiated opinion expression have been subjected to study. The circumstances of the 1960s and early 1970s gave rise to an interest in protest marches and demonstrations as media for the expression of political opinions.[63] Two points are quite clear. Such actions are engaged in by a tiny fraction of the citizenry, and the issue at stake by and large determines the social and ideological composition of the group of protestors. In other words, if we want to account for who is likely to protest we need to look first and foremost to the issue itself. Antinuclear protestors in New Hampshire, farmers picketing the White House for higher price supports, lumbermen driving heavy rigs from Humbolt County to San Francisco and Washington, D.C. to dramatize their demand that more redwoods be made available for timber, do not share a common background in the college sit-ins of the late 1960s. The people burning school buses in Pontiac or Louisville were not burning draft cards five years before. Demonstrations have come from across the entire spectrum of American political opinion and from all social groups.

---

[61] For examples, see James L. Sundquist, *Politics and Policy* (Washington, D.C.: Brookings Institution, 1968), and Raymond A. Bauer, Ithiel de Sola Pool, and Lewis Dexter, *American Business and Public Policy* (New York: Atherton Press, 1963).

[62] For an example to the contrary, see James N. Rosenau, *Citizenship Between Elections* (New York: Free Press, 1974).

[63] For examples of this research, see Sidney Verba and Richard A. Brody, "Participation, Policy Preferences and the War in Vietnam," *Public Opinion Quarterly,* vol. 34 (1970), pp. 325-32; M. Kent Jennings and Gregory B. Markus, "Political Participation and Vietnam War Veterans: A Longitudinal Study," in *The Social Psychology of Military Service,* ed. Nancy L. Goldman and David R. Sigal (Beverly Hills, Calif.: Sage Publications, 1976), pp. 175-200; Lester W. Milbrath, "Individuals and Government," in *Politics in the American States, 2nd Edition,* ed. Herbert Jacob and Kenneth N. Vines (Boston: Little, Brown & Co., 1971), pp. 27-81; and David O. Sears and John B. McConahay, *The Politics of Violence* (Boston: Houghton Mifflin, 1973).

Protestors may share a belief that mass media attention is a pre-requisite for the success of their cause but they share little else. There does not appear to be a cadre of active protestors who move from issue to issue leading (or following) the fashion. Rather, as we might expect from the level of intensity pre-required by such activity, only those deeply and personally affected by an issue (and only a fraction of these) will choose this medium of expression.

Letter writing appears to be a different matter. Figure 8-11 shows that over the period in which smaller and smaller fractions of the eligible electorate were choosing to vote, an increasing fraction of the public was expressing its opinion in writing to public officials. On a given issue, letter writers appear to be more extreme in their

Figure 8-11
TREND IN LETTER WRITING TO PUBLIC OFFICIALS, 1964–1976

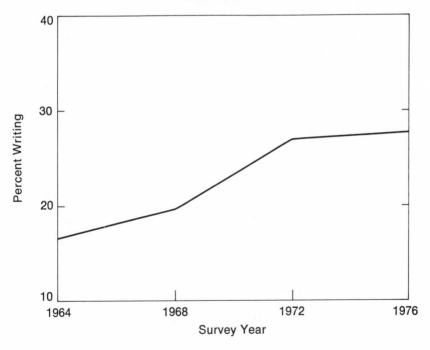

Note: The survey item reads: "Have you ever written any public officials giving them your opinion about something that should be done?"
Source: Codebooks for the year indicated, American National Election Study (Institute for Social Research, University of Michigan).

opinions than the public at large.[64] In the mid-1960s on issues like Vietnam, the power of the federal government, and negotiating with Communist nations, letter writers were more likely to express conservative than liberal opinions.[65] Whether this relationship has persisted in the 1970s is a question that *can* be answered, but I have been unable to find a study that seeks an answer.[66] Not surprisingly, the millions who write to the President and/or to members of Congress each year have more prestigious occupations, higher incomes, and better education than the population at large.[67] Letter writers are also overwhelmingly likely to be politically active in other ways as well.[68]

I have treated letter writing as an instance of opinion expression. Clearly, however, some who use this medium are seeking to affect a policy outcome directly (an "instrumental" motive) and are not simply engaging in "expressive" behavior. The crux of this distinction lies in the factors that intervene between engaging in the activity and deriving satisfaction from it. The "expressive" activity generates its own satisfaction. The letter writer is satisfied simply by writing the letter, by blowing off steam as it were; nothing intervenes between engaging in the activity and obtaining satisfaction. By contrast, the satisfaction obtained from engaging in an "instrumental" activity lies in and depends upon the extent to which the political system responds with the desired policy. Most letters written to public officials would be classified as mixed, but on the whole more expressive than instrumental. *Particularistic, citizen-initiated, demand-making* contact is instrumental political activity in its purest form.

When we examine this mode of political activity we are at the fundamental intersection of the individual and the polity. A brief look at terminology will make it clear why this intersection is fundamental. "Particularistic" is distinguished from "universalistic" and conveys the idea that the benefits sought are for the individual or the primary group to which the individual belongs. Obtaining food

---

[64] Verba and Brody, "Participation," p. 330, and Philip E. Converse, Aage R. Clausen, and Warren E. Miller, "Electoral Myth and Reality: The 1964 Election," *American Political Science Review*, vol. 59 (1965), pp. 321-36.

[65] Converse, Clausen, and Miller, "Electoral Myth."

[66] The relevant data are contained in the readily available national election studies for 1968, 1972, and 1976. Converse, Clausen, and Miller's procedures can be replicated using these data.

[67] Merlin Gustafson, "The President's Mail (Is it Worthwhile to Write to the President?)" *Presidential Studies Quarterly*, vol. 8 (1978), pp. 36-44, and David R. Mayhew, *Congress: The Electoral Connection* (New Haven: Yale University Press, 1974), p. 109.

[68] Rosenau, *Citizenship*, pp. 207-19.

stamps or a zoning variance is a "particularistic" outcome; effecting a change in the food stamp allowance rate or the zoning laws is a "universalistic" outcome. Verba and Nie also refer to particularistic benefits as "personalized" or "parochial."[69] "Citizen-initiated" is distinguished from "coerced" or "government-initiated"; it conveys the notion that the control of the agenda lies with the citizen—the citizen controls the timing and the subject matter of the contact. "Political demands are defined" by Wayne Cornelius "as needs whose satisfaction is felt to depend upon government action, and which are asserted by individuals or groups as specific claims upon the government."[70] Aggressive assertion is not a necessary condition for an action to qualify as a "demand"; the distinction is between a demand for action and the expression of an opinion.

Not all citizen-initiated contacts are particularized in scope. Indeed, it is estimated that fully two-thirds of such acts are related to broad social issues and not to the individual's personal or familial needs.[71] Nor, as we have seen in the example of letters to public officials, do citizen-initiated contacts necessarily involve the making of political demands. But contacts that exhibit these properties are guaranteed to be especially salient to the individual, which is to say that the outcome will be of deep personal concern to the contactor.

This is a relatively new research area for political science. Almost all of the available studies have been published since 1972.[72] Characteristic of new research areas are sharp disagreements on

---

[69] Verba and Nie, Participation, p. 70.

[70] Wayne A. Cornelius, "Urbanization and Political Demand Making: Political Participation Among the Migrant Poor in Latin American Cities," American Political Science Review, vol. 68 (1974), pp. 1125-26.

[71] Verba and Nie, Participation, p. 71.

[72] The exception to this generalization is Gabriel Almond and Harold Lasswell's study of the factors affecting the interaction of relief applicants and relief officials during the 1930s. See Gabriel Almond and Harold D. Lasswell, "Aggressive Behavior by Clients toward Public Relief Administrators," American Political Science Review, vol. 28 (1934), pp. 643-55. And Harold D. Lasswell, The Analysis of Political Behavior (New York: Oxford University Press, 1948), pp. 261-78. The recent studies include Verba and Nie, Participation; Eisenger, "The Pattern of Citizen Contacts"; Herbert Jacob, "Contact with Government Agencies: A Preliminary Analysis of the Distribution of Government Services," Midwest Journal of Political Science, vol. 16 (1972), pp. 123-46; Cornelius, "Urbanization and Political Demand Making"; Daniel Katz, Barbara A. Gutek, Robert L. Kahn, and Eugenia Barton, Bureaucratic Encounters (Ann Arbor: Institute for Social Research, 1975); Brody and Sniderman, "From Life Space"; Paul M. Sniderman and Richard A. Brody, "Coping: The Ethic of Self-Reliance," American Journal of Political Science, vol. 21 (1977), pp. 501-21; and Bryan D. Jones, Saadia Greenberg, Clifford Kaufman, Joseph Drew, "Bureaucratic Responses to Citizen-Initiated Contacts: Environmental Enforcement in Detroit," American Political Science Review, vol. 71 (1977), pp. 148-65.

fundamental questions. For example, Verba and Nie estimate that 15 percent of the American public have contacted public officials to demand particularized benefits.[73] By comparison, Katz and his colleagues find that 58 percent of their national sample have utilized one or more of seven specific governmental services.[74]

The fact that the Katz study came six years after the Verba-Nie study is not a plausible explanation for so massive a difference. More plausible are the differences in their approaches: Katz and his associates ask their respondents, for example, whether they had ever "gotten any help from government officials or agencies [in] finding a job."[75] They repeat the same question for job training, workman's compensation, unemployment compensation, public assistance, hospital/medical care, and retirement benefits.[76] Verba and Nie do not directly probe this form of participation but construct their measure from available items as a way of making sense of their data.[77] Unfortunately we have no other nationwide studies with which to reconcile this disparity.[78] My intuition is that the approach used by Katz and his associates intermixes political participation with routine contact with the end-points of the bureaucratic chain. Such routinized contacts may be to the consumer no more "political" than buying groceries. On the other hand, the pervasiveness of government in the life of the average American probably means that more than the one American in seven found by the Verba-Nie approach has attempted to influence the actions of government on matters which relate to the contactor's personal problems.

Given the disparate estimates of how many Americans participate in this manner, it is not surprising that findings on who participates and on the relationship between this activity and other modes of political behavior differ from study to study as well.[79] Nevertheless there are points of agreement in the studies that help to illuminate the processes of political participation at this fundamental point of con-

---

[73] Verba and Nie, *Participation*, p. 393.

[74] Katz et al., *Bureaucratic Encounters*, p. 20.

[75] Ibid., p. 212.

[76] Ibid., pp. 213-18.

[77] Verba and Nie, *Participation*, p. 393.

[78] The Jacob ("Contact") and Eisinger ("The Pattern of Citizen Contacts") studies are based on samples in Milwaukee, Wisconsin; the Jones et al. ("Bureaucratic Responses") study is based on data from Detroit; and the Brody-Sniderman national data lack a specific probe on whether the respondent made problem-related contacts.

[79] On many points the Katz et al. study is at odds with the rest. The fact that specific programs were studied and that the proportion using government services was at least twice that in any other study obviates any comparison.

tact. There is agreement on what Verba and Nie label the "flow of problems from citizen to government."[80] The nature of the flow informs our expectations about who will choose this form of political participation.

The prerequisites for any governmental response to a citizen's initiative are the perceptions by the citizen that a problem exists, that some arm of government can help to solve it, and, of course, that the relevant arm of government is made aware of it. Upwards of 85 percent have problems or, more precisely, have problems that they are willing to state to survey interviewers.[81] Only a fraction of these citizens—between a quarter and a third[82]—believe that government is relevant to the solution of these problems.

The belief that government is relevant is not uniformly distributed throughout the population. Middle-income citizens are more likely than either lower-income or upper-income citizens to believe that government has a role to play in the solution of their personal problems.[83] This curvilinear relationship stems from the mix of problems associated with income levels and from the association of type of problem with belief in government relevance. Both middle- and lower-income citizens are likely to report suffering financial difficulty, but lower-income citizens tend to stress individual failure and individual responsibility. By contrast, middle-income citizens tend to externalize the source of their economic difficulty and to believe that the wider community has a responsibility to aid in the solution. Above middle income, the curve turns down again, as a result of the belief of upper-income citizens that the "quality of life" problems that they experience most acutely are theirs alone to solve.

Jones and his coauthors point to the simultaneous operation of two principles as the source of the curvilinearity: (1) "The need for . . . governmental services of the particularistic type . . . is inversely related to social well-being"[84] and (2) "Social well-being is directly related to the awareness of government as an instrument for alleviat-

---

[80] Verba and Nie, *Participation*, p. 168. See also Cornelius, "Urbanization and Political Demand Making," p. 1128 and Jones et al., "Bureaucratic Responses," pp. 150-51.

[81] Verba and Nie, *Participation*, p. 168, and Brody and Sniderman, "From Life Space," p. 340.

[82] Verba and Nie, *Participation*, p. 168, and Sniderman and Brody, "Coping," pp. 505-13.

[83] Sniderman and Brody, "Coping," pp. 508-13; Jones et al., "Bureaucratic Responses," pp. 150-52.

[84] Ibid., p. 150.

ing social needs."[85] The resultant of the operation of these two principles is a parabolic curve inflected at the point of intersection of the two lines. Jones, Greenberg, Kaufman, and Drew demonstrate that aggregate demand for governmental services such as rat control and the enforcement of environmental ordinances in Detroit neighborhoods, arrayed according to measures of social well-being, follows the hypothesized pattern. This study and the Sniderman-Brody study taken together suggest that both belief in governmental responsibility and actual contact (at least for services such as these) is most prevalent in the middle levels of American society. These two studies suggest further that a more detailed examination of the differences in the rate of particularistic contacting for black and white Americans — found by Jacob, by Eisinger, and by Verba and Nie[86] — would reveal a group of white Americans at the upper end of the income scale which has a low rate of contacting. The finding of such a dropoff in contacting would suggest the need to take account of motivations as well as skills in framing our explanation of political participation in this area.

The "outcome" of this mode of participation has been studied primarily as "satisfaction" with the contact experience, recalled by the individual. Jacob found that upwards of 80 percent of the Milwaukee residents he studied recalled their contacts with satisfaction.[87] Brody and Sniderman asked those who believed that the government "ought to be helpful" whether it was being helpful. These citizens, who all shared a belief that government had a responsibility to aid them with their most pressing personal concerns, split fifty-fifty in their assessment of governmental performance.[88] We cannot compare this level of satisfaction with Jacob's since Brody and Sniderman lack data on whether these citizens actually made contact and sought assistance.

Bearing in mind the observation that "dissatisfaction may result from a lack of delivery of services because groups of citizens have differential propensities to contact service agencies,"[89] which would argue that a neutral or evenhanded bureaucracy can still give rise to

---

[85] Ibid., p. 151.
[86] Jacob, "Contact," p. 131; Eisinger, "The Pattern of Citizen Contacts," pp. 47-48; and Verba and Nie, *Participation*, pp. 162-68.
[87] Jacob, "Contact," p. 138.
[88] Brody and Sniderman, "From Life Space," p. 354.
[89] Jones et al., "Bureaucratic Responses," p. 149.

dissatisfaction, we note that irrespective of the source of the dissatisfaction it may have consequences. Dissatisfaction with the performance of government with respect to parochial interests has been shown to have effects upon electoral support for incumbents and upon general feelings of political cynicism.[90]

It should not be surprising that perceived performance in the area of a citizen's intense personal concern will relate to vote choice and to feelings of trust in government irrespective of whether help was actually sought. New studies should give us information on whether or not the citizen actually contacted government about a personal problem. With this information we will be able to clarify the links between the personal life of the individual and the individual's actions as a citizen. We will then be able to judge to what extent expectations of assistance are held and get a clearer sense of what Americans believe the scope of government to be.

In the End . . .

This chapter seeks no final answer to the puzzle of political participation in America. We have insufficient information to state with any certainty that the decline in turnout in the presidential elections since 1960 is part of a cynical rejection of politics by the American people. Cynicism has increased and turnout has declined, but other forms of political activity, including activities directly related to the electoral process, have trended upward with the trend in political skills. One has the impression, although good data do not exist, that organizational memberships, in general, and politically relevant interest group memberships, in particular, have also been trending upward. Whether this impression is correct and whether these organizations are successful in mobilizing their membership are questions of central relevance to any judgment about whether or not Americans are turning away from politics.

The picture of participation in America that emerges when we review the available scholarship is confusing because we cannot arrive at any simple conclusions. Is turnout trending downward because Americans are increasingly angry at the political system or because they are satisfied with, if unenthusiastic about, the choices that they are being offered? Does the decline in turnout mean that

---

[90] Brody and Sniderman, "From Life Space," p. 354; Sniderman and Brody, "Coping," p. 515.

political activity in general is declining or that the various modes of participation no longer arise from a common source? The analytic tools that have been developed by scholars working on this subject are broadly applicable and generally helpful but they are also insufficient. Motivation and skill appear to be individual resources pre-required for participation. They serve to distinguish the rates of participation of different groups in American society. They can help us gauge what is necessary in order to overcome the barriers to entering the political system and to distinguish ritualistic, symbolic, and habitual participation from that which is meaningful to the individual and consequential for the polity. We know that motivation can substitute for skill—but we have no idea what the exchange rate is. We know that an individual's skill can be augmented by (or augment) a collective effort. But we know very little about the processes of mobilization and the consequences for the individual of having been mobilized, and nothing about the learning (or unlearning) that takes place in the process. We have seen that "motivation" and "skill" increase our understanding of what is going on in instances of political participation as seemingly diverse as keeping Congress at bay on the regulation of recombinant DNA research and rat control in Detroit. But these two notions do no more than suggest answers to important questions about the decline in turnout between 1960 and 1976.

Much confusion remains in the picture of what I have called "politics one-on-one"—the citizen pressing a personal case with the political system. Could we expect anything else at this stage of development? We lack crucial pieces of research. At this stage we even lack a shared framework in which to place the pieces when we have them.

The confusion that remains in the picture of voting participation, however, does not stem from a lack of pertinent research; we have a superabundance. Nor from the lack of a shared framework; scholars studying turnout, in the main, speak the same language. The confusion in this area stems from the limitations of survey research and the quality of the information it yields. In particular, it stems from the fact that we want answers to newer and much more difficult questions than we have heretofore asked. Accounting for the differential turnout of groups in the society in a given election is more or less routine; we are now challenged to explain what is happening to these groups over time. It is a measure of the success, not the failure, of research on turnout that we now need the solution to a different and more difficult puzzle.

9

The Old States in
a New System

Leon D. Epstein

Discussing state governments in the 1970s raises, more sharply than ever, important questions about the development of American federalism. Are the states being bypassed as a result of increasingly national programs administered directly by national officials or by local officials more or less responsible to Washington? Is policy making even for many state-administered programs so centralized in Washington that state officials are becoming agents, in effect, of the national authority? Or are the states managing their relations with national and local governments, as well as their own institutional arrangements, so as to be effective policymakers for meaningful subnational units?[1]

These questions, empirical though they seem, are not readily answered in straightforward factual terms. Crosscurrents in the federal system often preclude definitive conclusions. And the questions are loaded with normative considerations. Most writers on American federalism have preferences about how powerful state governments should be in relation to national authority. Now as always these preferences mingle with interests whose representatives perceive their substantive policy goals as more readily achieved at one level of government than another. It is hardly realistic to analyze federal relations without an awareness of the political interests seeking to influence the distribution of governmental powers.

An attempt will be made to take these interests into account in this evaluation of the place of the states in the American system. The discussion, however, is organized primarily around state govern-

---

[1] Here and subsequently I use "national" for the government in Washington, trying to reserve "federal" for our intergovernmental system, but I occasionally adopt the customary American usage of "federal" as synonymous with "national."

325

ments themselves. I begin with their evident durability and then examine their activities, intergovernmental relations, institutional modernization, political parties, and innovative capacity. My central concern is to ask what state governments are able to do and what purposes they serve in performing their functions.

Durability

Few believe that a democratic nation so large and diverse as ours should be governed by a single centralized authority and its local agents; but the fifty American states may not seem the ideal units of decentralized authority. Indeed they are not ideal in the sense of being the best or the most rational governmental divisions that we could create from our present area and population. Fifty states are probably too many, and some of them are so small, so poor, or so incoherent geographically as to be handicapped in exercising governmental authority and in mobilizing political participants. We are all familiar with the inherent difficulties faced by states so small in area as Rhode Island, so small in population as Wyoming, or so poor as Mississippi; and we observe that even a state as large and prosperous as New Jersey suffers from an identity problem because much of its population belongs to either the New York or the Philadelphia metropolitan area and so receives its news primarily from daily papers and television stations that are outside New Jersey itself. Perhaps no other heavily populated state is similarly limited with respect to state news, but several states have substantial numbers of people living in places that belong socially and economically, not just for news, to metropolitan centers in adjacent states. Cases in point are much of New Hampshire in relation to Boston; northwestern Indiana in relation to Chicago; northwestern Wisconsin in relation to the twin cities of Minnesota; Kansas City, Kansas, in relation to Kansas City, Missouri; and East St. Louis, Illinois, in relation to St. Louis, Missouri. Markets do not always coincide with states.

Ours is not the only federal order in which historical developments have established states whose size, nature, and boundaries are well short of a rational ideal. It is true that fifty regional governments are a large number compared with only ten in Canada, six in Australia, and ten in West Germany. But Switzerland, despite its much smaller population, has twenty-five regional governing units. Nor is the United States alone in its disparity of state populations. California has sixty-six times as many people as Alaska, but Ontario's population is sixty-nine times as large as Prince Edward Island's, and

326

Switzerland's largest canton has almost eighty-six times the population of the smallest regional unit.

Such resemblances to federal divisions elsewhere do not, it must be granted, make much of a case for our existing states. Nor do these states, or clusters of them, seem as essential as they once did because of a deep and great diversity within the nation. Unlike Canada and Switzerland, whose federalism rests on more durable linguistic differences, the United States is now so nearly homogeneous as to raise questions about the need for entrenched state powers. The effective nationalization of civil rights in the 1960s and 1970s significantly reduced the major regional difference that had for so long sustained the southern attachment to states' rights. Yet important residual cultural differences, evidently greater than Australia's, remain not only between North and South but also between other regions and even between states within a single region.[2] For example, Illinois and Wisconsin sharply differ in the degree to which each tolerates organized corruption.

Certainly our states appear durable enough so that almost nobody proposes to abolish them, or merge them in new and larger regions. The fifty states tend to be accepted, though often regretfully, as elements of a constitutional system that will not be fundamentally altered. Sometimes, however, it is hoped that state powers will decline, or possibly wither away, in favor of revitalized local units as the principal partners of the national government. Robert Dahl spoke in these terms a decade ago. The states, he conceded, were here to stay and therefore to be used for certain purposes, but the city, especially the city of moderate size, was "the better instrument of popular government."[3] Federal grants, he believed, should go directly to cities. In this respect, Dahl's view is like that of many academics and politicians who do not want state governments to draw off money needed by the urban poor. He took an unusual position only in arguing that communities with smaller populations than those of our largest cities, or of enlarged metropolitan areas, should provide the basis for revitalized local government. But, whatever their preferred size, local units are often perceived as alternatives to states as instru-

---

[2] Daniel J. Elazar has written persuasively on the subject of the regional cultures of American states in *American Federalism: A View from the States* (New York: Crowell, 1966), chap. 4. Australia's maintenance of strong states without salient cultural differences is noted in my essay, "The Australian Political System," chap. 1, of *Australia at the Polls: The National Elections of 1975*, ed. Howard R. Penniman (Washington, D.C.: American Enterprise Institute, 1977), pp. 6-9.

[3] Robert A. Dahl, "The City in the Future of Democracy," *American Political Science Review*, vol. 61 (December 1967), pp. 953-970, at p. 968.

ments of decentralized, popularly based authority. They too can be the beneficiaries of the anti-Washington spirit of the 1970s. And, as we shall see, they can benefit materially from the new ways in which Washington distributes its massive revenues.

On the other hand, the states have vigorous intellectual and political defenders.[4] Despite their less-than-ideal size, resources, and boundaries, a case can be made that the fifty states provide the most feasible means for decentralizing authority. Not only does the creation of fewer and more coherent regional governments look unrealistic,[5] but most existing American local governmental units are not impressive substitutes for states. Given their numbers, sizes, resources, and historic boundaries, they are usually even more grossly disadvantaged than the states. Indeed the governmental division between impoverished central cities and more prosperous suburbs, and between urban and adjacent suburban counties, makes it impossible for local government itself to deal satisfactorily with the most pressing social problems. In other words, the governments of cities, counties, and townships are much less likely than states to have "geographic capability"[6]—that is, jurisdictions whose resources provide the basis for dealing with policy-making problems in such areas as education, welfare, and environmental quality. Of course, these disadvantages are reduced when local units are reorganized, as in Indianapolis, so as to have metropolitan city-counties embracing affluent suburbs. A new jurisdiction of this kind can possess a geographic capability more nearly like that of a state; but so far-reaching a reorganization is unusual in the United States. It is difficult to persuade both central cities and suburbs, notably their public officials, that they have something to gain by the submergence of their existing units of government. The limited likelihood of significant new metropolitan governments is itself a reason for turning to the states as instruments of decentralized authority. So is the fact that large areas inevitably remain outside even an enlarged metropolitan jurisdiction.

For some, and perhaps for most, of our states, a more positive case can be made. A number of the largest, California most clearly,

---

[4] Among them are Elazar, *American Federalism*; Ira Sharkansky, *The Maligned States* (New York: McGraw-Hill, 1972); and various contributors to *Publius*, the journal of federalism.

[5] New regional states should be distinguished from the several working examples of interstate collaborative arrangements, including those established by Congress and described by Martha Derthick, *Between State and Nation: Regional Organizations of the United States* (Washington, D.C.: Brookings Institution, 1974).

[6] James Fesler, "The Future of State and Local Government," in *The 50 States and Their Local Governments*, ed. James Fesler (New York: Knopf, 1967), pp. 550-588, at p. 578.

have a geographic capability greater than that of many independent nations, not just greater than that of their local governmental units. And many states even of medium population—Minnesota, Iowa, or Colorado, for example—are also impressively capable from the standpoint of area, resources, and coherence. Only four states (Alaska, Nevada, Vermont, and Wyoming) have fewer than a half million people, and only ten others are below one million.[7] Even some of these relatively small states (Hawaii, for instance) appear to have the wealth and coherence associated with governmental capacity. Nor does comparative poverty, in a large or small state, render self-government meaningless. It may, as Ira Sharkansky has said, just lead to a state's receipt of federal aid in a way analogous to a developing nation's receipt of aid from richer nations.[8] With or without such aid, the economic disparity between American states is nothing like that between nations.

However favorably we view the relative capacity of American states, it can still be acknowledged that a principal asset is their historical existence. They have meaningful traditions to which we are accustomed. Much can be said for using institutions with which citizens are already familiar and with which they identify. There is some such thing as belonging to a state, as to the nation, and it is typical, though not universal, for states to have symbols of pride—their universities, for instance. No doubt, state affairs are often less visible than national or even certain local affairs. But voting turnouts in state elections, while below those in national presidential elections, are higher than in most strictly local elections and fairly substantial by our modest American standards. General comparisons between state and national election turnouts are not feasible because most states hold their gubernatorial elections (and accompanying legislative elections) at the same time as congressional elections or even, in some instances, at the same time as presidential elections. So we do not learn much about the relative voter-interest in state politics from the fact that turnout rates for congressional elections in nonpresidential years are at least fifteen percentage points below presidential turnouts. A more relevant but limited comparison concerns the four states (Kentucky, Mississippi, New Jersey, and Virginia) whose recent gubernatorial elections have been held in odd-numbered years. Each of the four had at least a slightly larger turnout in each gubernatorial

[7] Daniel J. Elazar, "Introduction—The States as Keystones: A Reassessment in the Mid-1970's," *Publius*, vol. 6 (Winter 1976), pp. 3-19.

[8] Ira Sharkansky, *The United States: A Study of a Developing Country* (New York: McKay, 1975).

election held between 1969 and 1975 than in its adjacent congressional election (1970 or 1974). New Jersey, as the only northern state in this category and as a state with previously noted identity problems, is especially significant. Its gubernatorial vote was 2,367,000 in 1969 and 2,122,000 in 1973, while its vote for the House of Representatives was 2,101,000 in 1970 and 2,084,000 in 1974.[9]

Scope of Activities

By most statistical measures of governmental activities, the states have become more rather than less important. Their expenditure increases are impressive. From their own funds (that is, from taxes, license fees, and other revenues that they raised themselves), the fifty states spent almost $86 billion in 1974, or more than three times as much as in 1964, and they are estimated to have spent $92 billion in 1975 and $102 billion in 1976. In contrast to 1964, state expenditures now exceed expenditures of local governments (from their own funds). It is true that state expenditures have not grown as rapidly as the larger expenditures by the national government from its own funds. Even when defense-related expenditures are excluded, the national figure, estimated at $266 billion in 1976, now constitutes a larger proportion of all governmental domestic spending than it did in the 1960s.[10] The relationship is different, however, when we compare the employment totals of Table 9–1 for state, local, and national governments.

Immediately apparent in the table is a large and steady growth in both state and local employment even when federal civilian employment actually declined from its high point in 1967. Moreover, state employment rose at a relatively greater rate than local employment although it is still, in absolute terms, considerably less than half the local total. State employees, it will be noted, are now more numerous than national civilian employees. And state and local employees together are now over four times as numerous as national employees whereas they were only twice as numerous in 1950 and three times

---

[9] Bureau of the Census, U.S. Department of Commerce, *The Statistical Abstract of the United States*, published as *The U.S. Fact Book 1977* (New York: Grosset & Dunlap, 1977), pp. 460, 464, 467.

[10] U.S. Advisory Commission on Intergovernmental Relations, *Significant Features of Fiscal Federalism* (Washington, D.C.: ACIR, June 1976), p. 11. Specifically excluded (as "defense-related" expenditures) from the national figures, so limiting comparisons to the domestic public sector, are expenditures for national defense, international affairs and finance, space research and technology, and the estimated portion of new interest attributable to these functions.

Table 9–1
GOVERNMENT EMPLOYMENT IN THE UNITED STATES,
SELECTED YEARS, 1950–1975
(in thousands)

			Employees		
		Federal civilian	State and local		
Year	Total		Total	State	Local
1950	6,402	2,117	4,285	1,057	3,228
1960	8,808	2,421	6,387	1,527	4,860
1965	10,589	2,588	8,001	2,028	5,973
1967	11,867	2,993	8,874	2,335	6,539
1970	13,028	2,881	10,147	2,755	7,392
1971	13,316	2,872	10,444	2,832	7,612
1972	13,759	2,795	10,964	2,957	8,007
1973	14,139	2,786	11,353	3,013	8,339
1974	14,628	2,874	11,754	3,155	8,599
1975	14,986	2,890	12,097	3,268	8,828

Source: Bureau of the Census, U.S. Department of Commerce, *The Statistical Abstract of the United States*, published as *The U.S. Fact Book 1977* (New York: Grosset & Dunlap, 1977), p. 284.

as numerous in 1965. Making the comparison in this way is not unreasonable. Although state and local governments may in one sense be perceived as alternative agents of decentralized authority, it is nevertheless true that local units are creations and agencies of state governments, much as local governments in a unitary system are creations and agencies of a national government.

In any case, employment by the subnational units of our federal system has been thriving absolutely and relatively. It should be noted that its growth, and the growth by states considered separately, is even greater in employment than in expenditures. One reason is that increasing numbers of state and local employees are engaged in activities at least partly supported by intergovernmental transfers of federal as well as state funds (a subject to be explored at length later). Another reason is that the largest growth in state and local employment has been in education—over half of all state and local employees were in education in 1975. Education is a labor-intensive service, and it as well as certain other state services employ many part-time workers, all of whom are counted in Table 9–1. But limiting the comparison to full-time workers does not dramatically alter the ratio; in 1975, state and local full-time employees totaled 9,410,000 compared with 2,582,000 full-time national employees—still over three and one-half times as many state and local employees.[11] Altogether, then, employment as a measure of governmental activity emphasizes, without unfairly exaggerating, the role of state and local units.

Separating state from local governmental activities is not entirely satisfactory especially when we are looking collectively at all fifty states. Some states finance and control various services, notably education, much more fully than others. Hawaii, to take the extreme example, has assumed the total costs of public education.[12] And other states vary considerably in the degree to which they centralize fiscal responsibility in this and other fields. Nevertheless, totals for all fifty states provide a rough indication of the nature of mainly state activities. Note the employment breakdown in Table 9–2.

Education, it is apparent, constitutes by far the major activity for states as it does for state and local governments together. And since elementary and secondary school employment remains overwhelmingly local, the large numbers of state employees in education reflect mainly the scale of public colleges and universities. In addition, all states have employees engaged in supervisory and regulatory roles relating to elementary and secondary schools. It should also be observed that expenditure totals, in contrast to employment tabulations, would show large state financial aids to local schools. More serious is the absence of public welfare from the employment breakdown of Table 9–2; the fifty states spent $22.5 billion, including considerable federal funds, on public welfare programs in 1974. State employees who, along with more numerous local employees, administer those programs are mingled in Table 9–2 partly with "Health and hospitals" employees and also with the "All other" category. Undoubtedly public welfare must be counted, as are education, health and hospitals, highways, and natural resources, among the leading state activities even though its strictly state employees are not separately tabulated.[13]

Another side of state activity is displayed in the tabulation of the sources of funds shown in Table 9–3. Again all fifty states are presented collectively although they vary substantially in the degree to which they depend on certain taxes—income versus sales taxes, for

---

[11] *U.S. Fact Book 1977*, pp. 251, 284.
[12] *The Book of the States 1976-1977* (Lexington, Ky.: Council of State Governments, 1976), p. 215.
[13] Ibid., pp. 260-261.

Table 9–2

STATE EMPLOYMENT IN THE UNITED STATES, 1975

Activity	Employees	
	In thousands	In percentages
Education	1,400	43
Teachers	(407)	(12)
Health and hospitals	592	18
Highways	275	8
Natural resources	165	5
Financial administration	113	3
Police protection	69	2
All other	654	20
Total	3,268	100 [a]

[a] Rounding of percentages produces total of 99 rather than 100 as shown.
Source: Bureau of the Census, U.S. Department of Commerce, *The Statistical Abstract of the United States*, published as *The U.S. Fact Book 1977* (New York: Grosset & Dunlap, 1977), p. 284.

example. A half-dozen states have no individual income tax at all, and several collect only small amounts from it; five states have no general sales tax. Yet the overall picture is useful in several respects. Clearly the states raise most of their funds from their own taxes, license fees, and related charges. Of these, general sales taxes and individual income taxes are the largest revenue producers. The amounts collected from each have greatly increased since 1960—general sales taxes producing about five times as much revenue, and individual income taxes almost eight times as much in 1974 as in 1960. These increases parallel the rise in money received from the national government; the $31.6 billion shown for 1974 is just under five times as much as the states received from Washington in 1960, and it constitutes 21 percent of all state finance in 1974 in contrast to 18 percent fourteen years earlier. Also worth noting is the large-scale borrowing by state governments. The nearly $8 billion shown for 1974 raised the total states' debt outstanding to over $65 billion, compared with $18.5 billion in 1960.[14]

To these purely quantitative measures of state activities, something should be added to give a fuller sense of the governmental services involved. *The Book of the States* does this biennially in more

---

14 *U.S. Fact Book 1977*, p. 273.

Table 9–3
SOURCES OF U.S. STATE GOVERNMENT FUNDS, 1974

	Amount	
Revenue or Related Item	In millions of dollars	In per-centages
Borrowing	7,959	5
General sales and gross receipts taxes	22,612	15
Motor fuels taxes	8,207	6
Other sales and gross receipts taxes	9,737	7
Licenses	6,055	4
Individual income taxes	17,078	11
Corporation net income taxes	6,015	4
Property taxes	1,301	1
Other taxes	3,202	2
From national government	31,632	21
From local governments	1,538	1
Charges and misc. general revenue	14,950	10
Liquor stores revenue	2,049	1
Insurance trust revenue	16,439	11
Total	148,574	100 [a]

[a] Rounding of percentages produces total of 99 rather than 100 as shown.
Source: Bureau of the Census, U.S. Department of Commerce, *The Statistical Abstract of the United States*, published as *The U.S. Fact Book 1977* (New York: Grosset & Dunlap, 1977), p. 273.

than 200 pages of description. Most recently it presents major state services under seven headings: Education (public schools, post-secondary, and library agencies); Transportation (highways, aviation, mass transit, and automobile insurance); Human Services (health, public assistance, and a host of other programs); Public Protection (criminal justice, prisons, state police, consumer protection, public utility regulation, and the national guard); Housing and Development (including planning); Natural Resources (conservation, outdoor recreation, forestry, agriculture, and energy); and Labor Relations (personnel system, employment relations, and employment security).[15]

A more intimate sense of the broad and numerous activities of state governments may come from looking at a compilation of state statutes. Wisconsin's, for example, is in two volumes totaling 4,443

---

[15] *Book of the States 1976-1977*, pp. 309-556.

large pages of statutes. The contents include state laws in many areas beyond those of the major services already noted. Clearly the states provide most of the laws and regulations under which we live, and these include many enforced by local authorities under state jurisdiction. Indeed the state's statutes establish local governments and prescribe their functions. Among other subjects of state legislation are elections, public lands, animal health, food regulation, workmen's compensation, grain warehouses, barbers, medical societies, funeral directors, oil inspection, bingo control, banks, savings and loan associations, insurance, partnerships, corporations, marriage, contracts, automobiles, trucks, snowmobiles, real estate, landlord-tenant relations, mortgages, and, of course, criminal acts.[16]

In a given session, a state legislature may act in many of these areas as well as maintaining the major state services, which it always affects materially through its crucial budgetary appropriation measures. Again in Wisconsin, the scope of legislation is evident in a summary of the 1975 session. Its more significant enactments included regulation of the amounts that processors should pay to growers of vegetable crops, handgun regulation, compensation for victims of crime, additional state aid to local school districts that establish programs of student transfers to promote integration of minorities, liberalized election registration, creation of a child support and paternity program required under federal law, extension of antidiscrimination legislation to the disabled, liberalization of limits on the sale of contraceptives, liability insurance for physicians and other medical personnel, tightened legal provisions concerning involuntary admissions to mental hospitals, reduction (from three-fourths to two-thirds) of the common council vote necessary to override the veto of a city mayor, standards for open burning of solid waste, regulations for power plant siting, levy limitations on municipalities and counties, and budget limitations on school districts. Altogether the legislative session enacted 432 bills out of 2,357 introduced. Among the seriously considered bills that failed of passage were measures to prohibit the use of public money for abortions, to regulate cable television, to create no-fault motor vehicle insurance, to establish a wetlands protection program, and to revise municipal collective bargaining laws while authorizing a limited right to strike under such laws.[17] The wide range of important public issues is apparent. State activities are surely consequential as well as numerous and expensive.

[16] *Wisconsin Statutes 1973* (Madison: State of Wisconsin, 32nd edition).

[17] Wisconsin Legislative Reference Bureau, *1977 Blue Book* (Madison: State of Wisconsin, 1977), pp. 280-293.

The Local Relationship

The large and expanded scope of state activities is one aspect of the continuing role of the states in the American system. Another important element is the changing relationship of the states to other units of government. Much of this involves the national government, but it is worthwhile first to discuss state-local relations. Constitutionally and conventionally, local units—38,000 general-purpose governments and about 40,000 special-purpose agencies like sanitation or school districts—are instruments in many respects for the administration of state policies. Despite significant home-rule provisions for large cities, local governments have lost ground to state governments. Their services have grown less rapidly than those of the states, as measured by numbers of employees (see Table 9–1), and so have their revenues and expenditures during the 1960–1974 period of enormous increases at all levels. With respect to revenues but not expenditures, the state totals increased so much more in those fourteen years that they were $20 billion higher than the local totals in 1974 ($108 billion compared to $88 billion) whereas the two totals had been about the same in 1960 ($26 billion state and $27 billion local).[18]

More directly revealing of changes in intergovernmental relations is the expansion of state financial aid to local governments. By 1974 such aid totaled $45.6 billion, accounting for 38 percent of all state general expenditures and for about one-third of all local government expenditures (up from about one-quarter in 1960). To be sure, the state governments simultaneously received $31.6 billion from the national government, and some of this was "passed through" to local units as part of the $45.6 billion. For public welfare, highways, and certain miscellaneous functions, the states actually received more from the national government than they distributed to local governments. But for education, which is by far the largest aid category, the states provided $27.1 billion to local units while receiving only $6.7 billion from the national government. State payments to local governments include grants-in-aid, state-collected locally shared taxes, and various other disbursements.[19] Types of payment as well as amounts and functional purposes vary greatly among the states.

There is a notable absence of uniformity in aid for education. No educational aid appears for Hawaii because it administers educa-

---

[18] U.S. Fact Book 1977, p. xx.

[19] Ibid., and Book of the States 1976-1977, pp. 592-593, 596. Citations are to sources used for actual amounts and for my calculations based on those amounts. The presentation does not take into account national dollars going directly to local governments; these large sums will be noted later.

tion as a fully state service. Among the other forty-nine states, all of which distribute some financial aid for local schools, the range is from only $33 per capita in New Hampshire to over $175 per capita in four states.[20] Despite such disparity, there is a fairly broad trend toward greater state fiscal responsibility for elementary and secondary education. Pressure in that direction arises not just from an awareness of general limitations on the capacity of local governments to raise revenues, dependent as they are on property taxes, but also from a realization of the gross inequities between rich and poor local school districts. In the absence of greater federal aid for education generally (as opposed to the many special federal programs), the states become the agencies for equalizing educational opportunities through formulae that, in one way or another, redistribute tax resources. Pressure for state action is legal as well as political; state supreme courts in California and New Jersey have found that school finance resting on vastly unequal property values in local communities is unconstitutional. As state governments respond to judicial and other pressures by using their own tax resources to support local schools, they also impose important new controls on how those schools are managed and particularly on how state money shall be spent.[21] Accordingly, elementary and secondary schools, though long meeting general state standards as to curricula, facilities, and teacher qualifications, may become subject to a greater degree of state supervision. So much can be said even though elementary and secondary schools are still almost everywhere primarily the business of local boards and their administrators.

Higher education is in a different position. The vastly expanded colleges and universities of the last few decades are virtually all state institutions. They even include a few formerly municipal universities, like Wayne State in Detroit. Only the City University of New York remains conspicuous as a public institution outside a state's system, and it totters on the brink. Never, however, have local governments had many colleges or universities. Since the nineteenth century, the states have assumed direct responsibility for most of the public sector of higher education. Although that responsibility is now much greater than in the past, it has increased mainly from the growth of existing state systems rather than from takeovers of local units. Nevertheless the increased expenditure for higher education does contribute to the relatively greater growth of state than of local expenditures. Hence, it affects the changing relationship of state and

---

20 *Book of the States 1976-1977*, p. 593.
21 Ibid., pp. 314-316.

local governments as does the greater state financial aid for a traditionally local service, like elementary and secondary education, and the direct state management of a new service, like highway patrolling or smoke pollution control.

Such developments, altogether, help to account for the increased "centralization" of state-local governmental activities that has been discerned in recent decades. Measures of centralization derive from the distribution, as between state and local units, of financial responsibility, service expenditures, and personnel. Despite variations from state to state—California and New York remain relatively decentralized and a few states occasionally decentralize certain of their functions—the trend is broadly toward state rather than local authority. The trend holds for the fifty states aggregately and for the majority of them separately.[22] There are now more state controls over local policies as well as more state policies for local officials to carry out. Although generally state aids, unlike most federal aids, are distributed for fairly broad purposes, they are often accompanied by administrative and procedural rules established in the state capital. They may not be received any more favorably than are orders and guidelines from Washington.

The National Relationship

However much local officials believe that their authority is thus being eroded by state governments, the consequences do not strike most of us as so fundamental as those associated with increased national power in relation to the states. Perhaps this is because we perceive the states themselves as decentralized agencies, only less so than local units, and because we know that the states have limited fiscal resources compared to the national government and so also a relatively limited capacity for long-run domination. Certainly it is the national government which, for better or worse, ordinarily appears as the main actor in altering the distribution of power in the federal system.

Not all of the national impact derives solely from superior financial power. Obviously many new national policies respond to needs and problems that transcend state boundaries in an increasingly closely knit economic and social community. Some of these policies do not even require large-scale federal funds. A prime example is the

---

[22] G. Ross Stephens, "State Centralization and the Erosion of Local Autonomy," *Journal of Politics*, vol. 36 (February 1974), pp. 44-76; G. Ross Stephens, "Federalism, Federal Aids, and the States," *State Government*, vol. 48 (Winter 1976), pp. 22-26.

U.S. Supreme Court's insistence, especially in the 1960s, that state criminal procedures conform to the requirements of the fourth through eighth amendments to the Constitution. Thus no longer can a state court, any more than a national court, convict an indigent defendant of a criminal offense if the state denies him legal counsel; nor can a state court any longer convict a person on the basis of a confession given without prior police warning of the right to refuse to answer questions.[23] The nationalization of these procedural rights came at about the same time as the more dramatic nationalization of minority civil rights, including desegregation by the federal judiciary and the extension of voting and other rights by congressional enactment. Subsequently, it is true, the national government, legislatively and administratively, moved to enforce certain of the latter rights by requiring that recipients of national funds, including state and local governments, meet "affirmative action" standards, particularly by employing members of racial minorities and women. Such requirements are but the most controversial of conditions accompanying national aid. Their significance is enhanced by the enormous increase in the amount and the variety of the aid given to state and local governments.

Even without any controversial conditions attached to national aid, the level of funding itself has become so high that it must substantially affect intergovernmental relations. The rapid growth of federal grants should be stressed before we observe the recent important changes in how and to whom the grants are distributed. Note in Table 9–4 that total federal aid quadrupled in the decade 1964–1974 and that the amount going to the states alone more than tripled—thus exceeding even the rapid growth in state expenditures mentioned earlier. Note also the sharp increase in the percentage columns, reflecting the growing dependence of state and local governments on federal funds relative to their own revenues.

A more common way to express this growing dependence is to say that by 1974 state and local governments received from the national government over 20 percent of *all* their general revenue (the equivalent of 25 percent of revenue from their own sources), compared with about 10 percent in the 1950s.[24] Although the point is clear either way, the method of Table 9–4 sharpens it in several respects. Table 9–4 shows continued substantial increases in dependence for 1975 and 1976, based on estimates for those years, and

---

[23] C. Herman Pritchett, *The American Constitution* (New York: McGraw-Hill, 1977), p. 482.
[24] *U.S. Fact Book 1977*, p. 265.

Table 9–4
FEDERAL AID IN RELATION TO STATE AND LOCAL REVENUES, 1954, 1964, AND 1969–1976

Fiscal Year	Total Federal Aid to State and Local Governments		Federal Aid to States	
	In billions of dollars	As a percentage of state-local revenues from own sources	In billions of dollars	As a percentage of state general revenues from own sources
1954	3.0	11.4	2.7	21.5
1964	10.1	17.3	9.0	32.1
1969	19.4	20.4	16.9	34.1
1970	23.3	21.4	19.3	33.5
1971	27.1	22.8	22.8	37.1
1972	33.2	24.6	26.8	37.9
1973	41.3	27.3	31.4	39.0
1974	42.9	25.8	31.6	35.5
1975 est.	49.2	27.0	35.5	36.1
1976 est.	59.2	29.5	42.7	40.1

Source: U.S. Advisory Commission on Intergovernmental Relations, *Significant Features of Fiscal Federalism* (Washington, D.C.: ACIR, June 1976), pp. 53 and 55.

it shows that, while states depend more heavily than local governments on federal aid, their dependence has been growing somewhat less rapidly than has that of state and local governments considered together.[25] In other words, federal aid given directly to local governments has increased even more rapidly than that given to state governments. Still, Table 9–4 allows one to infer that by far the largest share of federal aid continues to go to the states; the $42.7 billion shown for 1976 is 72 percent of all federal aid for that year, compared to 81 percent in 1972 and 90 percent in 1954 and 1964. Since 90 percent had been usual from 1946 through the 1960s (and 80 percent from 1920 to 1940), the drop to 72 percent is itself of some significance.[26] Even 72 percent involves a kind of overstate-

[25] Estimates for 1977 show a still greater dependence of state and local governments—their federal funds now constituting about 35 percent of revenues from their own sources. *The Economist* (London), November 12, 1976, p. 45.

[26] Stephens, "Federalism, Federal Aids, and the States," p. 25.

ment. Much of the federal aid included in the amount listed for the states is really pass-through money—funds given to the states for distribution to local units according to federal formulae and standards.[27] For 1976, it is estimated that pass-through funds totaled about $12 billion, well over one-third of all the aid that the states received from the national government. From the standpoint of the local governments, the $12 billion of "indirect" federal aid is in addition to their $14.3 billion of direct federal aid and their $42.5 billion of direct state aid. Altogether these three kinds of aid constitute over three-quarters of the general revenue that local governments raised from their own sources.[28] Together the direct and indirect forms of federal aid remain a good deal less than strictly state aid to local governments, but federal aid to local governments has been growing even more rapidly than state aid.

Consequently, insofar as influence in intergovernmental relations follows from financial dependency, one would expect national power to be increasing more rapidly than state power in relation to local units. At the same time, national power would also be expected to be increasing in relation to the states as a result of the growing dependence of the states on federal aid to finance state activities. Notably in certain fields would one anticipate the results of dependence. Federal aid to state and local governments is greatest and has expanded most rapidly in relation to state and local expenditures in the various areas loosely described as health and welfare.[29] Highway aid is, as it has long been, a large item of federal aid; educational aid, while greatly increased in the last decade, is not so overwhelming in relation to state and local expenditures as is health and welfare aid. In the latter category, federal programs most often appear to transform state and local officials into agents of the national government. But in other less noticed fields, like environmental regulation and community development, federal funds have also become substantial both absolutely and in relation to state and local expenditures.

The degree to which national power follows national funds depends partly on the way in which the funds are distributed. To be sure, the availability of federal money in any form affects the capacity of state and local governments to undertake or maintain their programs. Apart, however, from power in that broad sense, the national government may exercise a great deal more by establishing

---

[27] U.S. Advisory Commission on Intergovernmental Relations, *The States and Intergovernmental Aids* (Washington, D.C.: ACIR, February 1977), p. 23.

[28] U.S. ACIR, *Significant Features*, p. 55.

[29] *U.S. Fact Book 1977*, p. 262.

specific purposes for which its grants can be spent, requiring matching amounts by states or local units, and setting rules for administering nationally supported programs. Until recently, the national government did such particularizing for almost all of its fiscal aid (98 percent in 1966), and in 1976 it still did so for 79 percent of the funds it distributed to state and local governments.[30] Appropriately, the method is called the categorical grant-in-aid, and the national government maintains over 500 "main-line" programs of this type.[31] They support many state and local activities—for example, specific agricultural research projects, mental health facilities, vocational training, and highway maintenance. Each grant is not only enacted for a specific programmatic purpose, but also developed and supervised by functional specialists in the relevant congressional committees and their staffs, as well as in federal administrative agencies. There are specialized administrative counterparts for each program at state and local levels. In this situation, there are some limitations on the policy-making role of the state and local officials who have been elected to exercise general responsibility for their governments.[32] Governors and state legislators, mayors and city councils, often help to obtain categorical-grant funds, and they may, with their staffs, exercise influence over their expenditure, but they are unable, for their own states or cities, to determine the programs for which the funds are supposed to be spent. Happy as elected state and local officials are to have federal funds and skillful as many may have become in stretching expenditure guidelines, they naturally prefer broader grants than those provided by most categorical programs.

New Intergovernmental Relations

Two new types of federal aid go a long way toward meeting the preference of state and particularly of local governmental leaders. The first is the block grant. Developed on a large scale beginning in 1966, it has broad functional scope, allows recipients significant discretion as to particular program expenditures within a broad area, and is distributed according to statutory formulae based mainly on

---

[30] Carl W. Stenberg, "Block Grants: The Middlemen of the Federal Aid System," *Intergovernmental Perspective*, vol. 3 (Spring 1977), pp. 8-13, at p. 8. Periodical published by U.S. ACIR.

[31] William H. Kolberg, "The New Federalism: Regional Councils and Program Coordination Efforts," in *The Administration of the New Federalism* (Washington, D.C.: American Society for Public Administration, 1973), pp. 51-64, at p. 54.

[32] U.S. Advisory Commission on Intergovernmental Relations, *Improving Federal Grants Management* (Washington, D.C.: ACIR, 1977), pp. 7-9.

population but occasionally also on such factors as unemployment, housing overcrowding, or poverty. The five federal block grant enactments are for Partnership for Health, Omnibus Crime Control and Safe Streets, Comprehensive Employment and Training, Housing and Community Development, and Title XX Social Services (for family planning and other services). Three of these require no state or local matching funds. Together, in 1976, the five accounted for 9 percent of all federal aid to state and local governments.[33] The block-grant programs occupy middle ground between the categorical grants and the newest type of federal distribution: general revenue sharing (GRS), which constituted 12 percent of federal aid in 1976.

As its name implies, GRS does not have even the broad programmatic focus of a block grant. Its funds may be spent by state and local governments for a wide variety of programs, new or continuing, and, in effect, just to balance their budgets. The money is distributed virtually without strings, apart from provisions for protecting minorities, and by statutory formulae entitling state and local units to annual allocations according to per capita criteria. Originally enacted in 1972 to distribute funds for five years, GRS was extended without major changes in 1976 for almost four more years. The original annual disbursement was $5.3 billion and the new annual rate is $6.8 billion. The change, however, is not a real increase; adjusted for inflation, the amount in real terms will appreciably decline by 1980. So it will also in relation to other federal aids.[34] Nevertheless the GRS amounts are obviously substantial.

Although GRS, like the block grant, is popular with elected state and local government officials regardless of their liberal or conservative ideologies, it has its critics at various levels. Even in state and local governments, there are specialized administrators, not to mention their interest-group clients, who perceive GRS as a poor substitute for the expansion, or even the maintenance, of particular categorical grant programs. And in national politics, many liberals have feared that GRS is a step away from the redistributional programs of the Great Society, the New Frontier, and the New Deal itself. Indeed, the principal champions of GRS have been conservatives wanting to cut down the influence of the federal bureaucracy and of federally mandated programs. A then congressional Republican, Melvin Laird, first attracted attention to GRS with a proposal in 1958. Although it

---

[33] U.S. Advisory Commission on Intergovernmental Relations, *Block Grants: A Comparative Analysis* (Washington, D.C.: U.S. ACIR, 1977), pp. 6-7.
[34] Richard P. Nathan and Charles F. Adams, Jr., *Revenue Sharing: The Second Round* (Washington, D.C.: Brookings Institution, 1977), p. 171.

was advanced, in different form, by the liberal Walter Heller while he chaired the Council of Economic Advisers in the early 1960s, GRS became almost irrevocably cast as a conservative idea when it was embraced by President Richard Nixon and proclaimed the cornerstone of his New Federalism in 1971.[35] Congress substantially changed Nixon's proposal before enacting GRS in 1972, but it retained the central idea of automatically sharing federal tax revenues with state and local governments. So it also retained the New Federalism conception that would enlarge state and local discretion rather than Washington's. Under Nixon, as liberals feared, that conception was accompanied by efforts to reduce or eliminate various categorical aid programs. Despite such efforts, only occasionally successful, the categorical programs continued to grow in the middle 1970s.

GRS has had another kind of impact on the nature of federal aid. Because roughly two-thirds of its funds are allocated to local governments, it changes the overall distribution of federal funds as between state and local governments, helping to account for the already noted reduction in the states' share during the 1970s. Block grants and certain new categorical grants also go heavily to local units, particularly to large cities, and so also contribute to the diminishing proportion allocated to the states even as the absolute amount of federal aid for the states rises. GRS, however, has been the major single factor in reducing the predominance of the states as recipients of federal aid. Perhaps its importance will diminish since its extension to 1980 involves no enlarged sums in real terms. Regardless, however, of the future impact of GRS itself, its two-to-one distributional formula reflects a recent congressional tendency to favor local governments, sometimes large cities in particular, when developing new aid programs.

The same formula, limiting the states to one-third of appropriated funds, is used (under the rubric of Comprehensive Employment and Training) for the large national program called Countercyclical Aid. Legislated over President Ford's veto in 1976 and funded at $1.25 billion for five quarters, it was extended in 1977, partly in accord with President Carter's proposal, at $2.25 billion for five more quarters through fiscal 1978. The "countercyclical" features of the program are that the funds become available only when national unemployment is above 6 percent (which it has regularly been) and that these funds are distributed to state and local governments in

---

[35] Will S. Myers, "A Legislative History of Revenue Sharing," *Annals of the American Academy of Political and Social Science*, vol. 419 (May 1975), pp. 1-11.

relation to the unemployment levels in their particular jurisdictions.[36] The purpose of the grants is to help state and local governments maintain existing levels of public service—that is, government jobs—without having to raise their taxes during an economic downturn. So the aid resembles GRS not only in its two-thirds allocation to local units but also in its support for already established state and local activities. Understandably a leading congressional opponent of Countercyclical Aid, Representative Jack Brooks, a moderate liberal from Texas, called it a disguised form of GRS.[37] Even more understandably, he did not prevail in Congress. Successfully supporting the 1977 extension were the elected state and local officials whose governmental services were already dependent on Countercyclical Aid as well as GRS, and they had weighty reinforcements from the unions of state and local employees together with their AFL-CIO leaders.

In other words, broad forms of federal aid to state and local governments, like categorical grants as well as any other distribution of funds to public or private clients, tend to produce politically effective expectations that the aid will be continued. Notably, this simple generalization holds when the relevant clients are both numerous and articulate. GRS, like Countercyclical Aid, is a case in point. The very scope of its congressional enactment reflects the building of a large constituency. Rather than being focused as strongly as many liberals would have liked on helping the needy central cities, GRS funds, and specifically the two-thirds earmarked for local governments, have gone to small as well as large units, including townships and affluent suburbs, all qualifying for shares on something close to a per capita basis. The law's complex distributional formulae take need and local revenue raising into account, but floor and ceiling provisions of the act limit the effects of the formulae. Therefore, while big cities and large urban areas, along with poor rural areas, have received the largest amounts of aid per capita, one can conclude, as have the authors of the most detailed study of the distributional effects of GRS, that "the problems of the most troubled central cities are not in any major way ameliorated by general revenue sharing."[38] Substantial redistribution has not been achieved. What has been achieved, however, is support to enact and extend the program. To that end, proponents found it useful to include numerous small local units and to make concessions to the essentially per-capita distributional

---

[36] *Congressional Quarterly Weekly Report*, vol. 25 (May 21, 1977), pp. 974-975.
[37] Ibid.
[38] Nathan and Adams, *Revenue Sharing*, pp. 84, 106, 107.

preference of the more prosperous areas.[39] Even the allotment of one-third of the GRS funds to state governments was a partial concession to the claims of existing units. Satisfying state claims, however, seems less spectacular than Congress's willingness to provide funds for 38,000 local governmental units.

It is no wonder, then, that GRS should have been described as a lobbying triumph for state and especially local governmental officials.[40] These officials, with clientele backers, may once have developed their programs mainly in response to national initiatives in particular areas, but as beneficiaries of federal funds they themselves initiate new demands. Among these demands is that for general funding in addition to continued categorical grants. The extent to which the subnational clients thus coopt federal programs, making them serve state and local rather than national interests, may be open to question. But there can be no doubt about the continued pressure of state and local officials to obtain federal funds. Washington's public sector lobby is a major force. The U.S. Conference of Mayors, the National Governors' Conference, the National Association of Counties, and the Council of State Governments all actively seek to influence national policy, congressional and administrative. Characteristically they are now represented in Washington by permanent headquarters with specialized staffs, although mayors and governors themselves frequently visit the national capital.[41] Sometimes the interests of the several state and local organizations diverge or even conflict. At other times, they plainly have much in common. Together they represent the interests of the numerous employees of state and local governments, many of them unionized or otherwise organized in professional associations (including teachers) that are capable of exerting parallel pressures on Congress. Moreover, they also champion the interests of the more numerous citizens dependent on state and local services.

Public sector lobbying is not a new phenomenon. Cities, counties, and township organizations all operated in state capitals, as they still do, before establishing major Washington activities. But the importance of their lobbying, along with that of state governments, is now greatly enhanced by the possibilities in the national arena. Samuel Beer is right to call attention to the increased scope and

---

[39] Samuel H. Beer, "The Adoption of General Revenue Sharing: A Case Study in Public Sector Politics," *Public Policy*, vol. 24 (Spring 1976), pp. 127-195, at p. 148.
[40] Ibid., pp. 169-171.
[41] Donald M. Haider, *When Governments Come to Washington* (New York: Free Press, 1974).

influence of public-sector lobbying.[42] It represents the growing interests, or, more sharply put, the growing appetites of existing interests. Insofar as their pressure succeeds, as it seems to be doing, in increasing the national government's fiscal responsibility for state and now often directly for local activities, it is hard to describe the process as one of central "encroachment." Perhaps that may be an eventual result, but we cannot be sure how much effective control accompanies federal funds, particularly when distributed as GRS or block grants. Certainly state and local governments, while seeking these funds, want as little national control as possible. At times, however, they may need the funds so desperately that they must risk a lessening of their autonomy.

New York City's well-publicized effort to avoid bankruptcy illustrates how a local government, in this instance the largest and most important, encounters that risk. Having long provided many services, notably higher education and a large portion of welfare expenditures, that are elsewhere more heavily the responsibility of state government, New York City has had expenditures not only far larger than that of any other U.S. city, but also larger than that of any state except California and New York. By the mid-1970s, these expenditures so exceeded city revenues, even with GRS and other federal grants (plus state aids), that the city became heavily dependent on borrowing to finance its annual deficits. It sank deeper into debt than any other city or state. No doubt, this unmanageable situation was aggravated by New York state's relatively decentralized financial arrangements. Also it is probable that New York City was unusually generous, even profligate, in supporting certain services and especially the unionized employees carrying out those services.

Nevertheless, except in degree, New York City's plight was fairly typical of the experience of America's older central cities, almost all of which faced growing public demands while losing more and more of their middle-class taxpayers as well as many manufacturing and commercial enterprises. Cities generally needed and received increased state and national help; New York City needed even more, and needed it more acutely. Its first port of call was New York state. The state's response was to establish a Municipal Assistance Corporation (MAC) to sell bonds, backed by the state, to help finance city expenditures, including those necessary to repay outstanding indebtedness. Accompanying this state financial help was an increased control, partly by MAC direction, of the city's budget. MAC, however, did not find it much easier than had the city to sell

---

[42] Beer, "The Adoption of General Revenue Sharing," pp. 166-171.

bonds at acceptable interest rates; the state's credit was now threatened by its assumption of financial responsibility for the foundering city, whose difficulties remained despite state-imposed restraints on salaries and other municipal expenditures. Although greater than the city's, the state's financial capacity was also limited. By 1975 and 1976 only the national treasury remained to be tapped as a means to avert bankruptcy, and New York City did obtain from a reluctant President and Congress crucial short-term help in the form of $2.3 billion in seasonal loans. The terms involved not just repayment, with interest, but also the city's agreement further to curtail its employment and so its services. The federal loans provided no long-run solution, and in 1978, as they were repaid and as their congressional authorization was expiring, New York City (and New York state) asked for more federal assistance either by way of more seasonal loans or, preferably from the city's standpoint, of U.S. Treasury guarantees for new city and MAC bonds.[43] Whether either would be obtained was uncertain in early 1978, but any additional national loans or fiscal guarantees actually granted would probably be accompanied by considerable federal supervision of city budget balancing and so of many city policies. No one doubts that this would constitute a significant precedent for the national government's assuming a role in relation to American cities that has traditionally belonged to the states.

Institutional Modernization

That New York City, and other cities, turned to the national government can be explained largely in terms of the limited fiscal resources of state governments relative to those of the U.S. Treasury; but other more remediable deficiencies have often appeared to preclude effective state action. Some of these deficiencies remain, but several have been substantially corrected by structural modernization during the last few decades of greatly expanded state activities. Institutional changes were overdue. State legislatures had grossly underrepresented urban areas, their executives were usually weak, and their administrative structures unsystematic. Almost anyone concerned with the revitalization of state governments in the federal system started with recommendations for institutional modernization. So it was for the 1955 Kestnbaum Commission.[44] The same theme, with special emphasis on the need for stronger executive authority,

---

[43] New York Times, January 15, 1978, sec. 4, pp. 1, 6.
[44] Commission on Intergovernmental Relations, A Report to the President (Washington, D.C., 1955), pp. 37-45.

was sounded a decade later by former Governor Terry Sanford in his widely circulated argument for greater and more effective state power. Like many others in the 1960s, Sanford was particularly interested in improving the states' capacity to deal with urban problems.[45] Here, as for various other purposes, the states were viewed as poorly organized for the exercise of power.[46]

Certain organizational difficulties derive from limits imposed by state constitutions, including stipulations of brief gubernatorial terms, short legislative sessions, and division of executive authority among several elected officers. Moreover, several constitutions have limited the financial powers of state governments by outlawing income taxes and setting unrealistically low ceilings for bonded indebtedness. Hence, to modernize, many states have had to amend or even rewrite their constitutions. In fact, during recent decades, they have done so, usually by substantive amendments. For example, in the first half of the 1970s, numerous states changed their constitutions with respect to tax authority, debt limits, legislative capacity, executive strength, and electoral reapportionment procedure.[47] Not all structural rigidities have been thus eliminated. But the constitutional changes have been consequential enough so that, joined with certain other reforms (like merit-system extensions for the civil service), they produce state governments distinctly more modern than those of the 1950s or early 1960s.

Just what should be treated as "modern" among state institutions is often a matter of opinion or even of ideology. From the start, the constitutional structures of most states were in many ways more radically or popularly democratic than the structure of the national government established by the U.S. Constitution of 1787. And they often became more so in the nineteenth and early twentieth centuries. For example, all but thirteen states provide for some form of popular election of their supreme court justices and all but seven for popular election of lower-court judges. Occasionally the election is only to confirm or reject appointees, but more often the election is a straightforward affair using either a partisan or a nonpartisan ballot.[48] These long-established state judicial arrangements are subject to continued efforts by bar associations and other reform groups to substitute gubernatorial appointment from professionally approved lists, but

[45] Terry Sanford, *Storm Over the States* (New York: McGraw-Hill, 1967), p. 142.

[46] Richard H. Leach, *American Federalism* (New York: Norton, 1970), pp. 38, 115-142.

[47] *Book of the States 1976-1977*, p. 165.

[48] Ibid., pp. 98-100.

they are durable features in states usually regarded as modern—Wisconsin and Minnesota, to name just two.

Another example of a constitutional arrangement whose modernity depends on one's viewpoint is the frequent provision for popular referendum not just to amend the state constitution but also to make public policy. Thirty-eight states constitutionally provide for the referendum process (and another state has established it legislatively); twenty-four of these specify "petition of the people" as a basis, and others either constitutionally require a referendum in certain circumstances or allow their legislatures to submit referendum proposals (or use some combination of these two arrangements). Twenty-one states go beyond ordinary referendum provisions and also establish the "initiative," whereby a petition from a given percentage of electors places a proposal on the ballot and so allows a measure to be popularly rather than legislatively enacted.[49] California's initiative is best known and most dramatically used.

Despite these interesting tendencies toward direct rather than representative democracy, state governments have usually seemed more significantly different from the national government because of the constitutionally greater authority given legislatures relative to chief executives. In this respect, state constitutions have been non-Hamiltonian, and most of them remain so. Recent efforts to strengthen the governorship need discussion, but first the constitutionally dominant legislatures command attention. They have changed most sharply in recent decades. Of course, their reapportionment since the early 1960s cannot be attributed to a self-motivated modernization process. Nonetheless, responding though they did to requirements established by the national judiciary, the states now have legislative bodies equitably representing their populations. Indeed, with both houses in the standard bicameral system subject to the one-person-one-vote rule, the states can claim greater equality of popular representation than the national Congress, whose Senate grossly but constitutionally overrepresents the people of small states. Gerrymandering of state legislative districts (and of congressional districts) remains possible, but not the creation or the maintenance of districts vastly different in population totals. Although the U.S. Supreme Court, in the 1970s, retreated a little from its apparent insistence in the late 1960s on rigid mathematical equality between legislative districts, the currently allowable deviations do not substantially alter the basic one-person-one-vote principle.[50] Neither central cities nor

---

[49] Ibid., pp. 216-218.
[50] Pritchett, *The American Constitution*, pp. 60-67.

the now more rapidly growing suburbs will be underrepresented as they had been earlier. Given that accomplishment, thanks largely to the federal courts, state legislatures at least fairly represent the people whose problems they may seek to meet. Ironically, a national agency, imposing its will by way of a uniform principle on the diverse practices of the several states, has thus helped to put the states in a position to be more responsive to the wishes of the majority of their citizens.

In addition to their enforced reapportionment, and perhaps partly as a result of it, state legislatures have modernized in other significant respects. Since the mid-1960s, as Patterson has said, they "have been in the process of changing from largely amateur, part-time representative bodies to professional legislatures."[51] The development is widespread although naturally uneven in that larger states are able to professionalize more fully than smaller states. For example, forty-two states had formal or informal arrangements for annual legislative sessions by the mid-1970s, compared with only twenty in 1962–1963. And generally legislatures now deal with more bills and have longer sessions, higher salaries, streamlined procedures, and larger and better-paid staffs.[52] It is true that only a few large and rich states have raised the salaries of the legislators themselves enough to make full-time service feasible for those needing to earn middle-class incomes, but a trend in this direction is apparent. So is the increased provision of professional staffing of legislative committees, notably finance committees, and of the offices of legislative party leaders and even of other individual legislators.[53] Altogether, these changes should make membership in a state legislature more attractive as a long-term career than it has been in the past, and in fact, for whatever reason, there has been a marked increase in the number of state legislators seeking reelection rather than voluntarily retiring after short-term service.[54] Since incumbents tend to be reelected, turnover has declined and a trend toward professionalism has set in at the state level similar to, though much less pronounced than, the trend in congressional careers.

---

[51] Samuel C. Patterson, "American State Legislatures and Public Policy," chap. 4 in *Politics in the American States*, Herbert Jacob and Kenneth Vines, eds. (Boston: Little, Brown & Co., 1976), p. 143.

[52] Ibid., pp. 143-144.

[53] Alan Rosenthal, "The Consequences of Legislative Staffing," in *Strengthening the States: Essays on Legislative Reform*, ed. by Donald G. Herzberg and Alan Rosenthal (New York: Doubleday, 1971), pp. 73-85.

[54] David Ray, "Voluntary Retirement and Electoral Defeat in Eight State Legislatures," *Journal of Politics*, vol. 38 (May 1976), pp. 426-433.

Paralleling the strengthening of the legislative process are changes to enhance the authority of governors. One change is just to lengthen gubernatorial tenure. By 1972 forty-six governors, compared to only thirty-two in 1960, had four-year terms, and forty-three states, compared to only thirty-one in 1960, allowed a governor a second successive term.[55] No similar broad constitutional change has taken place with respect to the division of executive authority among several elected officers. Almost all states still elect five, six, or seven administrative officers. Thus, typically a governor, unlike the U.S. President, does not have his own appointees (or even necessarily members of his own party) in certain salient political positions—notably the attorney general's. The governor's disadvantage here may be mitigated by legislative removal of functions from a constitutional office like that of the treasurer or the secretary of state, whose duties then become minor. But functions bestowed elsewhere among state agencies have not always been subject to much gubernatorial control. Characteristically a great deal of state administration has been in the hands of relatively autonomous boards and commissions provided by legislatures if not by constitutions. Members of such boards and commissions, while usually appointed by governors (subject to legislative advice and consent), were meant to be, and often have been, essentially independent of gubernatorial control.[56] Longer terms for governors may help achieve such control, but other more direct steps have been taken for the purpose.

Governors have actively fostered administrative reorganizations that establish new administrative departments for broad functional areas (transportation, social services including health, natural resources, urban affairs, and so on). Nineteen states enacted comprehensive executive branch restructuring between the mid-1960s and the mid-1970s.[57] The purpose is not only to have a more coherent grouping of state services but also to make these services more directly responsible to the state's chief elected official. Governors conceive of this development as one that establishes a cabinet of executive officers, like the U.S. President's. Another means for enhancing gubernatorial leadership is executive control of budget making. In thirty-four states the governor has sole responsibility for preparing the budget, and in a majority of these states the governor possesses

[55] Haider, *When Governments*, p. 299.
[56] Deil S. Wright, "Executive Leadership in State Administration," Thad Beyle and J. Oliver Williams, eds., *The American Governor in Behavioral Perspective* (New York: Harper & Row, 1972), pp. 275-288, at p. 282.
[57] *Book of the States 1976-1977*, p. 105.

an item veto.[58] The latter is a potent instrument for influencing final policy outcomes in the appropriation process, and it is noteworthy that while many governors have this instrument the U.S. President does not.

Not all observers of state government are persuaded that gubernatorial power should be further strengthened. In the 1970s some of the opprobrium of the "imperial presidency" may also be associated with a powerful governor. Hence, making legislatures more effective, through their professionalization, seems a useful counter to enhanced executive authority particularly in financial matters. Also, certain traditional state activities are not always viewed as properly subject to direct gubernatorial or even legislative control. Regulatory functions are a case in point, and so is education. State universities in particular cherish a kind of self-governing independence, under a largely autonomous lay board, from legislatures as well as governors. They do not want to be treated as state agencies in the same manner as most other governmental services.[59] Resisting gubernatorial control, mainly through extension of managerial control over expenditures, has become a principal concern of state university administrations.

In addition to the several structural changes in state institutions, there are changes in taxation that also involve modernization. In a sense, that characterization follows from the fact that state revenues have expanded rapidly to match greatly increased state expenditures, and especially from the fact that they have expanded more rapidly than local taxes. These are not just recent trends; from less than 20 percent of all state and local taxes at the turn of the century, state taxes rose to 55 percent of that total by 1972.[60] Inevitably the sharp rise, particularly since the 1960s, means new kinds of levies as well as increases in old rates. Both income and sales taxes, rather than one or the other, have been adopted by most states, although here as in other respects considerable variations exist as to degree and method of reliance on a particular kind of tax. Overall the fifty states rely so heavily on various sales and gross receipts taxes that the effect is highly regressive as compared with that of national taxation (see Table 9–3). Individual income taxes, while high in several states,

---

[58] Sarah McCally Morehouse, "The Governor as Political Leader," chap. 5 in *Politics in the American States*, p. 226.

[59] Leon D. Epstein, *Governing the University: The Campus and the Public Interest* (San Francisco: Jossey-Bass, 1974), chap. 3.

[60] Clara Penniman, "The Politics of Taxation," chap. 11 in *Politics in the American States*, p. 435.

produce only 11 percent of the funds collected by all fifty states.[61] Corporate income taxes add modestly to progressivity, and generally the states have tried to move in a progressive direction by substituting various state taxes for the dependence by local units on property taxes.[62] "Property tax relief" has been, and is likely to continue to be, a popular program. It accompanies efforts to compensate, through state redistributional taxes and expenditures, for the unequal resources of local governments in providing support for education and other services. Thus changes in state taxation are part of a "modernizing" centralization at the state level that has already been emphasized.

Parties and Interest Groups

Modernized or not, state governments are salient as always for political parties and interest groups. Although Washington, more than ever, has become the main arena, where the stakes are immeasurably greater than those of any one state and perhaps greater than those of all the states together, the fifty state capitals are still crucial sites for political mobilization. Most notably, parties are essentially state units that are only loosely federated in national organizations. National preferences may determine voter identification and electoral alignments, but insofar as American parties have regularized memberships, whether ideological or patronage-based, they are organized in state and local units. Unlike the loosely federated national committees, a state party may consist of a fairly large cadre of office-seekers or even of numerous individual activists organized in local branches. Elsewhere, city or county "machines" are independent centers of power, at times dominating a state organization as has Chicago's Democratic party.

Organizing parties basically at subnational levels is a common feature of federal systems. Not just in the United States but wherever there are substantial, constitutionally guaranteed powers at the regional level, parties organize to compete for power at that level. Most evidently in Australia and Canada, as in the United States, regional party organizations are the bases for national party federations. Within these federations, as within the national government itself, the regional parties help to maintain the decentralization that they represent. This is not the same as saying that decentralized parties are, in an original causal sense, responsible for governmental

---

[61] *Book of the States 1976-1977*, pp. 298-299.
[62] Sharkansky, *The Maligned States*, pp. 58-59.

decentralization.[63] After all, regional parties exist in the first place as responses to the existence of significant regional governments. Hence the most that ought to be claimed causally for parties in a federal system is that, once created at subnational levels, they act as preservative agents for an already decentralized governmental system.[64] They do so most sharply when organizations holding regional power do not even belong to one of the two major national party federations, as in Canada, but they function similarly even within the more familiar American pattern in which national and state competition is almost wholly between the same two parties.

The American pattern, however, is not one of uniform two-party competition between roughly equal forces. The absence of strong or meaningful interparty competition is familiar over long periods in several regions. And it remains familiar in most southern states, notably for their legislative bodies, even when they have ceased to be consistently one-party Democratic in presidential elections and in some statewide races. On the other hand, one-party Republican states in the north have almost disappeared without many states' approaching one-party Democratic status. For the post-reapportionment years of 1962–1973, only seven states, all southern and Democratic, were classified as one-party in the most frequently cited tabulation of state party competition. The same tabulation listed thirteen states in the modified one-party Democratic category, seven in the modified one-party Republican, and twenty-three in the two-party competitive.[65] The balance, it can be observed, is decidedly in favor of the Democrats, who improved their position relative to that in a similar 1946–1963 classification. The most recent elections, those of 1974 and 1976, reinforced the 1962–1973 trend. Moreover, these elections also produced Democratic advantages in most of the two-party states. Advantages here may be temporary, but they are worth noting. After the 1976 election, there were twenty-eight states in which the Democrats had majorities in both legislative houses while also holding the governorship. Republicans had comparable power in no more than two states. The remaining states had some form of divided control.[66]

[63] Morton Grodzins, "American Political Parties and the American System," *Western Political Quarterly*, vol. 13 (December 1960), pp. 974-998.

[64] William H. Riker, "Federalism," chap. 2 in *Governmental Institutions and Processes*, vol. 5 of *Handbook of Political Science*, Fred I. Greenstein and Nelson W. Polsby, eds. (Reading, Mass.: Addison-Wesley, 1975), p. 435.

[65] Austin Ranney, "Parties in State Politics," chap. 2 in *Politics in the American States*, pp. 60-61.

[66] Gerald Pomper, *The Election of 1976* (New York: McKay, 1977), pp. 106-114.

Characteristic of more than half of the states in most other recent years, divided control is a likely enough result of two-party competition. It is least frequent in the South, where one-partyism prevails. The association of divided control with two-party competition means that the latter often does not serve to put responsibility on a single party to govern a state. Nor, from the electorate's standpoint, is responsibility meaningfully fixed in a one-party state. For example, Republicans in most southern states are not capable of winning control of both legislative houses and the governorship should voters be dissatisfied with Democratic incumbents. In other words, one-partyism frustrates believers in responsible party government even more surely than do the separation of powers and bicameralism when there is two-party competition. The six southern states that never had divided control between 1946 and 1974 simply did not have meaningful party competition. The other forty-four states had at least one period, and usually more, of divided control.[67] Most Americans, accustomed to that result at the national level as well, remain untroubled about it. In contrast to many political scientists, they may even prefer divided control. At the very least, they are quite willing to tolerate this particular obstacle to responsible party government.

Toleration, if not positive preference, on that count is matched by a persistent and even growing attachment to the consequences of the direct primary as the means of selecting or nominating party candidates. Less than ever before do organized party memberships at state and local levels regularly control nominating processes as a means of helping to ensure the responsibility of subsequently elected officeholders, by holding them to a common program. The decline in the number and effectiveness of patronage machines has not led to the general substitution of ideological or programmatic dues-paying organizations. Sporadically, such organizations arise in a few states, but, like the remaining patronage machines, they must ordinarily compete in direct primaries in order to win control of their party's label. All fifty states now provide, in one way or another, for direct primaries for statewide office, as well as for most other offices.[68] A primary, it is true, is not mandatory everywhere. A half-dozen states make it only an allowable alternative, which parties can (and often do) adopt instead of the convention method, and a few of the states require a primary only when convention or committee choices are challenged by losers who have had substantial support. Even

---

[67] Ranney, "Parties," p. 82.
[68] Book of the States 1976-1977, p. 219.

when these exceptional states are taken into account, final nomination by convention or committee is infrequent. The direct primary is nearly universal.

Moreover, the primary is increasingly "open," in fact if not in form. Under federal judicial interpretations, states can no longer prevent voters from switching their party registrations in the months preceding a given primary. Louisiana has gone still further toward instituting openness. Instead of running first in separate party primaries, all candidates, regardless of their party labels (which appear on the ballot), compete against each other in a single election that can produce a winner by absolute majority; if no candidate wins an absolute majority, a second or runoff election is held between the two top candidates. These two candidates may be of the same party. In that case, the process resembles the old and still-used Democratic runoff primary of other southern states. But Louisiana has reduced the potential number of elections from three (two primaries and one general) to two.[69] In effect, the state combines primary and general elections. Interestingly, it does so in response not to the old pro forma Republican competition in a traditionally Democratic state, but to newly effective Republican candidacies. Whatever the motives of the Louisiana legislators—and most of them are Democrats, who can be suspected of wanting to perpetuate the election of Democratic candidates—the general impact of their new primary law is more compatible with an individualistic, candidate-centered politics than with organized two-party competition.

The same can be said for the much better known and more widespread adoption of the primary election device to choose delegates to Democratic and Republican presidential nominating conventions. In contrast to 1968, when only sixteen states used the presidential primary, twenty-nine had adopted the device by 1976 and thereby elected over two-thirds of the delegates to each national convention. This rapid conversion from the use of the caucus, the state convention, and the party committee, as the means for choosing presidential delegates, turns out to have been the response preferred by most states to the national Democratic party's insistence on reform in delegate selection after 1968.[70] The other option available to the states—and perhaps the one the national party reformers expected them to choose—was to open the older intraparty organiza-

---

[69] Ibid., pp. 206-207.

[70] Austin Ranney, *Curing the Mischiefs of Faction* (Berkeley: University of California Press, 1975), p. 206. See also Ranney's discussion in Chapter 6 of the present volume.

tional procedures. Either way, established state party leaders would have had to share, and probably lose, control over the selection processes. Open caucuses no less than primaries can be captured by candidate-centered, or issue-oriented, enthusiasts. By choosing the more heavily participatory—but also the more regularized—method of presidential candidate selection, namely primaries, most states complied with national party rules in a plainly nonorganizational direction. Even though they, or their state parties, were being forced to use selection procedures that met national party standards, even those relating to primary methods, the states acted on the assumption that loosely identified party voters, not just organized activists, should make the decisive choice of delegates and so of presidential candidates. Insofar as the process was nationalized by the post-1968 reforms, it was at the expense of the already weakened state and local party organizations. But the nationalization itself did not substitute a centrally mobilized party membership for any existing state-level organizations. Rather it simply accelerated the development of candidate-centered organizations, mainly, to be sure, national in character.

Hence, our national parties are still federations of state organizations, be the latter only weakened versions of old machines or newer professionally staffed membership parties. Plainly, parties survive in some form at the state level. Governors and legislators, with only rare exceptions, are elected under Republican and Democratic labels, and both the executive and legislative branches are organized by party. In two-party competitive states, Republican and Democratic legislative caucuses are often fairly cohesive policy-making agencies.[71] Furthermore, governors and legislators act as partisans not just in state affairs but also in national politics. Governors are important figures in presidential campaigns even if they are not so often the leading candidates. They attempt, with some success, to head their state parties and especially their state delegations to national conventions. And legislators no less than governors may act as national partisans when performing the decennial task of drawing congressional district boundaries. Although now prevented by the U.S. Supreme Court from maintaining or creating districts with grossly unequal populations, state governments, when controlled by a given party, may still gerrymander congressional boundaries to maximize the number of House seats that the dominant party can win. It is understandable that nationally oriented Republicans believe it urgent for their party, before 1981, to win at least one house or the governor-

---

[71] Patterson, "American State Legislatures," pp. 178-182.

ship in many of the twenty-eight states that the Democrats fully controlled in 1977. For this purpose, national Republican party leaders, in and out of the Congress, may seek to help their state organizations, just as national Democratic leaders, for similar reasons, will help state Democrats. State party success is relevant to the national party cause.

It is not only parties whose political efforts are still organized significantly at state levels. Interest groups display a similar pattern. Even the major economic interest groups, for whom national policy making is of greatest importance, are often federations of state-based components. If not actually federal in their structure, they ordinarily maintain state organizations. Business, labor, agriculture, doctors, and veterans—just to name the most familiar—are all effectively present in state capitals as they are in Washington. Similarly, the local government officials, only recently mobilized for large-scale national lobbying, have long been major participants in state policy making.

The extent to which these or any other interest groups deliberately concentrate their efforts at state rather than national levels is not clear. No doubt, certain economic groups are so geographically concentrated in their support that they can be much more influential in state than in national politics. Texas oil and gas producers are cases in point. Particular interest groups undoubtedly want the rewards available from favorable Washington decisions, but when the latter are unobtainable, as they may well be, such groups prefer that the national government stay out of their policy-making area and allow outcomes to be determined by state governments, some of which at least may be influenced by the relevant interests. Not all interest groups, however, can accomplish major purposes through state policy making. Dairy farmers, for example, need national action to secure the price support that they regard as crucial. Much the same must hold for any other group seeking large-scale governmental subsidies or, of course, tariff protection. On the other hand, many business interests subject to regulation—utilities and insurance companies, for instance—may have a stake in limiting the national government's role because of their supposed capacity to influence state legislation and administration more advantageously. That capacity varies from state to state not only in accord with the relative concentration of a given group's support but also in accord with the general structure of each state's politics.

Intensive pressure even from small organizations, it is usually thought, can be more effective where parties are weak and uncohesive than where they are strong. The belief is that an interest group, particularly a business group, finds it easier to influence individually a majority of legislators, perhaps through key committee members, than to influence a majority party functioning as a disciplined voting bloc. Yet it is also recognized that certain other interest groups may be so large in certain states that they can be decisive in determining the policies of a major party—as are the United Automobile Workers within Michigan's relatively cohesive Democratic party.[72]

No discussion of state politics should conclude without devoting more attention to the role of the governor. Not only is he as likely now as in the past to be the head of his party in state and in national affairs, but he is increasingly consequential as a policy-making official. His opportunities are surely enhanced by the tendency to lengthen his term and by other constitutional reforms previously reviewed. In addition, a governor in many states can use the electronic media with at least a portion of the effectiveness associated with the U.S. President's performance. Governors too have televised press conferences, as well as other media-provided opportunities to address their constituents, even if less commandingly and dramatically than the President. They thus identify themselves with the state policies and programs which they have initiated and for which they seek support. Furthermore, governors have become visible as their states' principal emissaries to Washington. They are perceived as successfully obtaining federal funds and to some extent, under general revenue sharing and block grants, as the coordinators of the distribution of these funds.[73] They are even said to perform as "federal systems officers," trying to increase their control over the distribution of federal funds within their state governments and so reduce the independent power of bureaucratic specialists.[74] Generally, the degree to which governors can achieve control of this kind is linked to their success in using party as well as the mass-communications media to assert effective political leadership.

Innovation and Diversity

In a nation whose federalism now derives from mainly historical differences between states and regions, rather than from currently

[72] L. Harmon Zeigler and Hendrik van Dalen, "Interest Groups in the States," chap. 3 in *Politics in the American States*, p. 105.

[73] Richard P. Nathan and Associates, "Monitoring the Block Grant Program for Community Development," *Political Science Quarterly*, vol. 92 (Summer 1977), pp. 219-244.

[74] J. Oliver Williams, "Changing Perspectives on the American Governor," in *The American Governor*, pp. 1-5; and Deil S. Wright, "Governors, Grants, and the Intergovernmental System," ibid., pp. 187-193.

salient conflicts like those of Canada's linguistic groups, the continued existence of state governments is often justified by the suggestion that the states respond innovatively to the political desires of their separate constituencies. The suggestion assumes that there are differences between state constituencies and that state governments are able to respond to these differences as the more removed national government cannot. At their best, states might thus be experimental laboratories for new and untried policies subsequently available for adoption, with variations, in other states or nationally. But at the least, state governments are expected to diverge from each other in significant and useful ways.

"Useful" is a crucial qualifying adjective. Thereby certain deviant policies are excluded. Segregation by Jim Crow legislation, so long a striking practice of southern states, is hardly what present-day advocates of federal diversity have in mind. On the other hand, it was precisely the difference that southern states' rights advocates traditionally defended when they resisted national desegregation pressure. As a minority in the nation, southern whites preserved their policy-making dominance, however discriminatory, by invoking the reserved powers of the state governments that they did control. For several decades, this claim appeared to be the most significant aspect of a federally based argument against a more centralized national system.[75] But in the 1970s, with civil rights nationalized at least to the extent of making the South no more discriminatory than the North, the proponents of state powers are associated with different policies. Some policies remain open to criticisms similar to those directed at the old segregation laws. Thus, states that respond to business interests by maintaining legislation unfavorable to unionization—right-to-work laws, for instance—are not universally acclaimed for their divergence from the practice of most industrial states. Instead they fortify the critics of federalism who believe that its principal beneficiaries are now minority economic interests, particularly businesses gaining special advantages from certain more readily influenced state governments. Liberals are happy to seek the overriding of state pro-business legislation by the U.S. Congress or the Supreme Court. So too are liberals concerned with social issues eager to reverse the exercise of state powers to impose capital punishment or prohibit abortions. In contrast, they tend to welcome as properly innovative an environmental success like Wisconsin's enactment of a special cigarette tax to support state parks or Oregon's banning of

---

[75] Riker, "Federalism," declares that "the main effect of federalism since the Civil War has been to perpetuate racism" (p. 154).

throwaway containers. Similarly greeted are broader measures like progressive income taxes, stringent utility regulations, generous welfare measures, and election reforms encouraging larger voter turnouts.

No doubt, states often adopt measures of that kind. Moreover, certain states are pacesetters for others. But the differences should be put in a balanced perspective. Our state governments, in many significant ways, are more strikingly similar than different. Structurally and institutionally, this is surely true despite an unevenness of modernization. The fact that all fifty states maintain the separation of legislative and executive powers, none experimenting with parliamentary-cabinet government, is much more noteworthy than the differences that exist in such matters as length of terms, nature of the gubernatorial veto, and Nebraska's unicameralism. So too is the virtually universal provision for a direct primary more important than the differences between the types of primary used in the several states. The crucial characteristic is candidate selection by substantial numbers of loosely defined "party voters," registered or not, rather than by organized party members. Yet early in the twentieth century the direct primary was an innovation, particularly in Wisconsin, a means of rejecting the then established convention method of nomination. In that light, the subsequent adoption of the direct primary by the other states may be viewed as a triumph (if one likes the direct primary) for the experimental laboratory idea rather than as just another example of the similarity of state institutional practices.

Can an innovation as important as the direct primary be successfully adopted and spread in present circumstances? Working against the possibility is the temptation for late twentieth-century reformers to concentrate on national legislation in ways that were not available seventy years ago when the U.S. Constitution was understood to limit national powers severely. But politically it may still be harder to secure action by a national majority than action in a few states. And because of greater and more highly organized communication between officials, legislative and executive, of the several states, successful state innovations can more readily be copied. An interesting test of possibilities lies in the mundane area of voter registration. Traditionally treated, for constitutional and other reasons, as a subject for state regulation, the field was entered by the national government in the 1960s to ensure that blacks and other ethnic minorities would not be prevented from registering, chiefly in southern states. And there is no doubt that Congress could now constitutionally act to impose a uniform registration system for national elections. Indeed such a system, using social security numbers or postal cards, has been proposed in Congress. The object is to make it simpler and easier for citizens to register and so to vote in larger numbers.

In the absence so far of national registration, some of its objectives have been pursued in the states. Two, Minnesota and Wisconsin, have adopted and used a procedure allowing their citizens to register on election day, at polling places, if they have not registered earlier in the usual way. Their experience with such registration in 1976 has been critically examined, and it is by no means clear that the system will readily be adopted elsewhere.[76] Even if successful in Minnesota and Wisconsin, election-day registration may be thought likelier to encourage fraudulent voting in states whose politics are customarily more corrupt than Minnesota's or Wisconsin's. Nevertheless the innovation surely fits the conception of states as experimental laboratories. Experiments do not have to succeed in order to be useful.

More often than the institutional or procedural matters of the kind just discussed, substantive policies command the attention of those looking for differences between states. The same major services —education, welfare, and highways—exist in all states, but these and other common services may be provided in varying ways and degrees.[77] How much variation is now possible, even if states should have varying preferences, must be considered in light of the pressures for conformity accompanying national programs that finance state services. Probably education, by far the largest field of state expenditure and a still predominantly state and local responsibility, is less subject to these pressures than most state services despite the growth of federal grants and of certain federal requirements. States retain considerable leeway in educational policy making, particularly for the universities and colleges that they, rather than local governments, directly finance and control. Not only have certain states traditionally spent more money than others (as proportions of their per capita incomes) on their universities and colleges, but several have maintained more prestigious research institutions than have other equally rich or richer states. California, Michigan, Wisconsin, and most other midwestern states are thus thought to provide higher quality public university education than New York, New Jersey, and Massachusetts. The difference is no less meaningful if attributed not to the greater virtue of the midwestern and western states but to the fact that they

---

[76] Richard G. Smolka, *Election Day Registration* (Washington, D.C.: American Enterprise Institute, 1977).

[77] *Book of the States 1976-1977*, pp. 260-261.

had fewer well-established, competing private universities when they first developed their state institutions.

More recent responses by all states, including the eastern states, to rising demands for publicly provided higher education may reduce expenditure differences and perhaps qualitative differences also. On the other hand, the greatly expanded networks of colleges and universities obviously increase the significance of the states' responsibilities in a governmental field that remains primarily theirs. Hence, state governments exert a broadened policy-making influence on higher education by their budgetary allocations and by their arrangements for the administration of geographically separate colleges and universities. In the latter area, states have in fact diverged considerably. Some maintain a separate board and administration for each campus, although often linked by a statewide coordinating council; others, notably California, maintain two separate state systems, each with numerous campuses; and still others, like Wisconsin, establish a single board and central administration for all public colleges and universities.[78]

In these and other respects, higher education appears to be exceptional among major policy areas. Not only is it a state rather than a mixed state-local responsibility, but it is still generally supported by state-imposed taxes and fees. Federal grants and contracts, it is true, are large and crucially important (especially for new programs), but they do not provide the basic support of most instructional programs. Although national funding has been accompanied by national influence of many kinds, especially in major research universities, it has not led to Washington's control of higher education in the same way or degree that it has in large segments of the welfare field. There, it is evident, the states are administering an essentially federal program when they distribute Supplementary Security Income. The national government provides most of the funds, and it establishes the minimum standards for assistance and the eligibility criteria.[79] A national system exists even if it apparently operates through fifty units of government. And such a system seems likely to be extended to other welfare programs, like Medicaid and Aid to Dependent Children, in which states now retain greater discretion for developing and administering policies in response to federal mandates. Nor is welfare the only area where, in one way or another, states administer essentially national programs. Environ-

---

[78] Epstein, *Governing the University*, chaps. 3, 4.

[79] Robert Albritton, "Welfare Policy," chap. 9 in *Politics in the American States*, pp. 352, 355-356, 359-360, 368.

mental regulation is another and newer case in point. Until the mid-1960s, such regulation, insofar as it existed, was largely a state affair. But congressional enactment of clean air and water pollution control legislation, particularly in the early 1970s, established federal standards and made state and local governments responsible for much of their enforcement.[80]

In the environmental area, however, there is a policy development that clearly shows a state to have been innovator, experimental laboratory, and model to be followed by other states and possibly by the national government. The innovation here is Oregon's already-noted ban on throwaway containers. Put into effect in 1973, the ban involves a mandatory deposit on all beverage containers. By early 1978, three other states (Vermont, Maine, and Michigan) had adopted a similar policy and so had a dozen cities and counties. The environmentalist group chiefly pressing for such legislation had high hopes for more state and local victories, which would make it easier to obtain national legislation.[81] Plainly the group was working on both fronts, but just as plainly it found it possible to win in states where environmentalism was generally strong and where the beverage industry and its employees were not. In contrast, it was not successful in Wisconsin, which, however strong its environmentalists, has both milk and beer among its major products. Nationally, too, these beverage interests might be more formidable than in many states.

Interesting though the throwaway container case may be, it and most other similar instances of state innovation do not bulk large beside the massive new and expanded programs that depend on Washington and often originate there. Less room for state experiments exists when national standards accompany national dollars, as has been characteristic of all but the recent general revenue sharing and related grants that go mainly to support established state and local services.[82] Innovation in policy making appears to be heavily federal. States are likely to differ in their administrative procedures and (incrementally) in the financial contributions that they add to the national funding. These differences may be fairly large, but, despite considerable academic dispute on this point, the different expenditures appear closely related to the socioeconomic character of particular states (per capita income, industrialization, and urbanization) rather

---

[80] Charles O. Jones, "Regulating the Environment," chap. 10, ibid., pp. 406-408.

[81] *Wisconsin State Journal* (Madison), January 20, 1978, sec. 1, p. 17.

[82] Douglas D. Rose, "National and Local Forces in State Politics: The Implications of Multi-Level Policy Analysis," *American Political Science Review*, vol. 67 (December 1973), pp. 1162-1173.

than to independent qualities of their political systems.[83] Both the actual diversity by way of significant policy making and the capacity of states to develop such diversity are uncertain.

Conclusion

Just as uncertainty characterizes the capacity of the states to achieve significant diversity, so also it characterizes the answers to the general questions with which this chapter began. Nevertheless, there are tentative if partly ambiguous answers. By most measures used in the preceding analysis, the states are thriving within the federal system. Their constitutional durability is in little doubt, their activities are greatly expanded, their capacity and their authority are increasingly more impressive in relation to those of local governments, they are changing their institutional structures so as to be more effective as agencies of government, and they remain important arenas for the decentralized American party system. Although a large portion of the increased scope of state government activities turns out to be promoted and financed by national funds, there is a sense in which expansion on that basis is a mark of success for the states. Given the inherent resource limitations of subnational units relative to those of the national government, the alternatives to state administration of federally sponsored programs are either direct national administration or more national financing of local government activities. In fact, these alternatives have been developed, the latter most decidedly in the 1970s under the distributional formulae used in general revenue sharing and certain block grants. But the states, even under these new programs, are also substantial beneficiaries. And they are still *the* major beneficiaries of the predominant categorical grants-in-aid. It would, therefore, be a drastic overstatement to suggest that state governments are being generally superseded by local governments as administrators of federally financed programs. At most, the states in this respect have lost a little ground to local governments, relatively speaking, while gaining more federal aid in absolute terms.

On the other hand, the intergovernmental relations of the 1960s and 1970s are open to a more pessimistic interpretation concerning

[83] See, for example, Thomas R. Dye's *Politics, Economics, and the Public: Policy Outcomes in the American States* (Chicago: Rand McNally, 1966), an especially influential book among the many able, technical, and occasionally conflicting works published on the subject during the last fifteen years. These works have recently been discussed by Michael S. Lewis-Beck, "The Relative Importance of Socioeconomic and Political Variables for Public Policy," *American Political Science Review*, vol. 71 (June 1977), pp. 559-566.

the long-run role of the states. Despite their continuation as prime beneficiaries of federal aids, the states, like local governments, may be perceived as losing independent policy-making authority because they must, particularly in so many large matters, respond to nationally provided programs and, practically speaking, act as administrative agents for these programs. That perception of declining state authority developed especially from the experience of the 1960s when President Johnson's Great Society seemed to impose national policies both directly and through major new categorical-grant programs. Power, it was said, was shared, but the state's share rested on the permission of the national government. So the pattern was called "permissive federalism" rather than "cooperative federalism," the old term describing the first large-scale grant programs of the 1930s.[84] At the same time, observers of the federal system became aware of the influence of a "professional-bureaucratic complex" of national, state, and local administrators. Members of this complex, reinforced by elected officials, seemed the effective force for the maintenance and expansion of the aid programs.[85] No doubt, they remain consequential in the late 1970s, perhaps even adding to their influence through the increasing development of various district and intrastate "regional" agencies more responsive to federal grants than to elected state or local authorities.

Curiously, however, just as the professional-bureaucratic complex has been studiously observed, its impact must be juxtaposed with that of the recent success of elected state and local officials in obtaining block grants, general revenue sharing, and related federal funds that can be used at the discretion of their governments. The degree to which national funding influences state as well as local policy making could diminish insofar as aid shifts from the categorical to the general. Whether federal aid will thus continue to shift in favor of general-purpose support is a critical unknown in estimating the position of the states in the federal system. Pressures for expanding categorical aid programs have by no means diminished; the professional-bureaucratic complex is itself formidable, as are its numerous clients. It is plain, however, that elected state and local officials have also become

---

[84] Michael D. Reagan, *The New Federalism* (New York: Oxford University Press, 1972), p. 163.

[85] Samuel H. Beer, "Modernization of American Federalism," *Publius,* vol. 3 (Fall 1973), pp. 49-95. No matter whose initiative is most responsible for aid programs, their recent growth suggests so significant a change in governmental relations as to cause a critic to doubt whether there is effective representative control of the actual spending agencies by "the banker governments" (national and state). Edward K. Hamilton, "On Nonconstitutional Management of a Constitutional Problem," *Daedalus,* vol. 107 (Winter 1978), pp. 111-128, at p. 123.

a mighty lobbying force in favor of national grants to maintain their public payrolls. Their success hardly erodes state or local policy-making authority. To be sure, state and local services thus become dependent on national funds. But such services are ordinarily of state and local origin. They did not come into existence only in response to national initiatives.

Perceiving the federal relationship in this comparatively new light suggests that the United States may be moving closer to the established Canadian and Australian patterns in which national tax revenues are distributed to regional governments as a result of regular negotiating sessions between the principal elected officials at each level. For example, in Australia, where the national government has preempted the income-tax field, there is an annual Premiers' Conference at which the executive leaders of each of the country's six states meet to bargain with the national prime minister over the funds that the states will need to carry out their very considerable responsibilities.[86] Canada's process is similar. Note, however, that with only ten provinces to be represented, Canada's conferences of heads of government are as feasible as Australia's. It is harder to imagine the same kind of conference between fifty American governors and the U.S. President. But the conference as such may be less necessary in the American system. Its purpose could be achieved—perhaps it already is—by means of state representation and state and local pressure on Congress, which definitely exercises a financial authority that in Australia and Canada, as in most parliamentary systems, belongs in practice to the executive.

In one way or another, it can be concluded that American state governments remain strong and important elements in the federal system. Supposing only the status quo (as of 1978) with respect to the predominance of categorical grants over general-purpose grants, the states will at the least be principal administrative agents for many expanding federal programs while also maintaining their own activities. That hardly means "independence," but the states have never been literally independent and they cannot become more nearly so in a nation whose problems are increasingly broad in scope. Instead, the states, like their local governments, will almost certainly become increasingly dependent on national financial resources. We do live in

---

[86] Jean Holmes and Campbell Sharman, *The Australian Federal System* (Sydney: Allen & Unwin, 1977), chap. 5. For a review of similar Canadian arrangements, see Howard Cody, "The Evolution of Federal-Provincial Relations: Some Reflections," *The American Review of Canadian Studies*, vol. 7 (Spring 1977), pp. 55-83.

a centralizing if not in a fully centralized federal system.[87] Within that system, diversity in state policy making is possible in some areas. For it to be significant, however, often requires resistance to a national majoritarian interest seeking to impose its preference through Congress or the U.S. Supreme Court. In other words, we would have to tolerate in particular states the legislative success of interests that appear, perhaps temporarily, to be only minority interests in the nation. Such interests are at least as likely to be conservative as liberal, even if they are no longer those of the segregationists who gave "states' rights" a bad name.

---

[87] Riker, "Federalism," suggests that the United States might now fit the category of "partially centralized federalism" (p. 133).

10

The American Poli the Late 1970s: Bui Coalitions in the Sand

Anthony King

The central concern of this volume has been with the changes in the American political system that have occurred since about the time of President John F. Kennedy's election in 1960. Let us in this final chapter first consider the changes that have been described in the nine chapters thus far. We can then go on to consider whether it is reasonable to speak of a "new American political system," and to discuss the most striking features of the new system, insofar as it exists.

The Facts of Change

In the realm of political ideas, two changes stand out. Both affect not merely the outputs of politics but the way in which politics is conducted. The first is the decline of the ideas of the New Deal as the principal organizing themes of American political life. The central idea of the New Deal was a simple one: that the federal government could, and should, solve the country's economic and social problems. To be a liberal was to believe in the efficacy of government, particularly the federal government. To be a conservative was to doubt the capacity of government to solve economic and social problems, and also to oppose the government's acting in ways that infringed upon liberty and diminished individual self-reliance. If some government had to act, conservatives preferred that it be a state or local government; such governments were less powerful, and therefore less threatening, as well as being closer to the people. The point about the ideas of the New Deal was not that they constituted *a* source of political division in America, but that for more than thirty years they constituted *the* source of political division. To know that a politician or aspiring politician was a New Dealer, or alternatively an anti-New ller, was to be able to predict his stands on a wide variety of seemingly discrete political issues: public housing, public power, social security, progressive taxation, the role of labor unions, and so on.[1] Even the other great political issues of the 1930s and 1940s, like race and foreign affairs, came to be discussed to a considerable extent in New Deal terms.

Sometime in the early 1960s the ideas of the New Deal began to lose their organizing capacity; in the late 1970s they have lost it almost completely. Not only has the belief in the efficacy of government generally declined; more to the point, it is now all but impossible to infer a person's views on one range of subjects from his or her views on another range. Someone may be in favor of public housing, but deeply skeptical about the role of labor unions; another person may be in favor of taxing the rich, but at the same time suspicious that "welfare" may be doing what the conservatives always said it would do—namely, deprive the poor of incentives to work. And so on.[2] Moreover, many of the issues of the 1960s and 1970s—women's rights, abortion, drugs, the environment, the question of an amnesty for Vietnam draft dodgers—make little sense in New Deal terms one way or the other. The politics of the 1930s and 1940s resembled a nineteenth century battlefield, with two opposing armies arrayed against each other in more or less close formation; politics today is an altogether messier affair, with large numbers of small detachments engaged over a vast territory, and with individuals and groups frequently changing sides. As a result, the task of political leadership, as we shall see in more detail later, has become a great deal more complicated.

The second outstanding change in the realm of ideas is the altogether new emphasis on the value of participation in politics. In the 1960s it came to be thought good for both the participating individuals and the polity that ordinary men and women should have a direct say not merely in the choice of public office holders but in the

---

[1] This was not true for the average voter, of course. Indeed students of voting behavior were concerned to distinguish between the ordering of opinions that went on among the political elite and the much lower level of ordering that went on among voters. See especially Angus Campbell, Philip E. Converse, Warren E. Miller, and Donald E. Stokes, *The American Voter* (New York: John Wiley, 1960), chap. 10.

[2] This proposition is almost certainly true, yet it is hard to produce solid evidence to support it. Surveys of elite opinion are still relatively uncommon. But see the symposium by sixty-four American intellectuals on the topic "What is a Liberal? Who is a Conservative?" in *Commentary*, vol. 62 (September 1976). Almost all of the contributors agree that the old labels are no longer very useful—indeed that they are often positively misleading.

making of public policy. "Many forces, ideal and material," writes Samuel Beer in Chapter 1 of this volume, "have been reshaping American attitudes toward political action. But the idea of participatory democracy, drawing on old themes of political romanticism, has given a sharp new twist to the democratic values of the American political tradition and to any future public philosophy."[3] More specifically, as Beer shows, the participatory idea influenced the way in which many federal programs were administered in the sixties and seventies and had a powerful impact on the democratizing of the two major political parties. The idea that people can and should participate has undoubtedly played a part, too, in the proliferation of "issue groups" in recent years.

Of the great national trinity of political institutions in the United States, the presidency, Congress, and the Supreme Court, the presidency would seem to have changed most, the Supreme Court least. Since the early 1960s, the rate of turnover among Presidents has increased sharply, to the point where both Presidents and those with whom they do business are forced to operate on the assumption that the man in the White House will not remain resident there for very long.[4] Members of Congress, always divided from the President by profound differences of outlook and interest, now, after Vietnam and Watergate, view the presidency with an almost institutionalized suspicion. Once the rule was, "Other things being equal, if the President wants it, we probably ought to let him have it." Today the rule appears to be, "Other things being equal, if the President wants it, we had better look at it pretty closely." As testament to the new congressional mood, there exists a range of recent statutes, the express purpose of which is to limit the President's power to act autonomously: the War Powers Resolution of 1973, the Impoundment Control Act of 1974, and so on.[5] Television and press journalists are also much more disposed to be critical than they once were. Indeed most of the major changes affecting the President have taken place not within the institution of the presidency itself but within its immediate environment. The dispersal of power in Congress makes it more difficult to transact business with that body; the disappearance

---

[3] See above p. 28.

[4] As Fred I. Greenstein points out, between 1933 and 1961 three presidents, Roosevelt, Truman, and Eisenhower, held office for the equivalent of seven four-year terms. Between 1961 and 1978 five presidents, Kennedy, Johnson, Nixon, Ford, and Carter, held office for scarcely more than four four-year terms. "By the late 1970s," he adds, "the rapid turnover in Presidents had become an important quality of the presidency itself." See above pp. 64-65.

[5] See above pp. 81-82.

of the old party organizations deprives the President of both a valuable restraint and a potential source of strength (the President is "chief of party" no longer).[6] The upshot is that the President is often incapable of responding in terms of concrete achievement to the high expectations that the American people continue to have of him. "Intractability is back."[7]

The best publicized change that has taken place in Congress is the change in the system for the selection of committee chairmen, from a system in which seniority was invariably the deciding criterion, to one in which it is usually the deciding criterion, but not invariably. The significance of the breaches made in the seniority rule in 1975 lies to some extent in the new power possessed by the party caucuses; but it lies to a much greater extent in the way in which power in Congress has thereby been even further dispersed. Congress, always a highly decentralized body, has become even more decentralized. Committee chairmen can no longer be little dictators on their committees because dictators can be toppled; committee chairmen have become noticeably more sensitive to the views of their committee colleagues. At the same time, decentralization has been carried several steps further by the proliferation of subcommittees in both houses of Congress, by the explosion in the size of congressional staffs (from a total of roughly 4,000 persons in the late 1950s to more than 12,000 today) and by the fact that so many more congressmen and senators are now holders of committee and subcommittee chairmanships.[8] The powerful few have become the considerably less powerful many. Congress has also taken steps to make itself more autonomous vis-à-vis the President, through general oversight of the activities of the executive branch, but also through its new budgetary procedures and its larger say, formal and informal, in the making of foreign policy. In Patterson's words, "Congress is far more formidable as a political body today than it was in the quiescent days of the 1950s and early 1960s."[9]

But, if change in at least two of the institutions established by the Constitution has been substantial, it is when we come to look at the country's extra-constitutional political institutions—the political

---

[6] For a number of perceptive comments on the effect of the decline of party on the presidency, see Richard E. Neustadt, "The Constraining of the President: The Presidency after Watergate," *British Journal of Political Science*, vol. 4 (October 1974), pp. 383-97.

[7] The phrase is Greenstein's. See above p. 70.

[8] See the discussion in Samuel C. Patterson's chapter in this volume, especially pp. 160-69.

[9] See above p. 177.

parties, the electorate, and interest and issue groups—that the full facts of change are borne in upon us. The parties, the electorate, and the groups are all differently constituted, and behave in different ways from what was regarded as normal, and was indeed normal, only two decades ago.

With regard to the parties, it is open to ask whether the United States any longer possesses such things, at least for the purposes of nominating and electing Presidents. The parties still exist as makers of rules. They still exist as givers of cues to millions of voters. But they would appear no longer to exist as national organizations or even as temporary coalitions of state and local organizations. Presidential politics has become almost entirely candidate-centered. Changes in the parties' rules have opened up participation in the party to a constantly changing congeries of "issue and candidate enthusiasts."[10] Increasingly, the parties, even at the state and local level, lack continuity of personnel; they therefore increasingly lack even the possibility of strong, stable leadership. The new methods of financing presidential campaigns from the federal Treasury have also had the effect of leaving the organized parties, to the extent that they still exist, as mere bystanders, since money is channelled not via the parties but directly to the individual candidates. Probably most important, the proliferation of presidential primaries (seventeen, accounting for 37.5 percent of the votes cast at the national conventions in 1968; twenty-nine, accounting for 72.6 percent of the votes cast in 1976) means that party leaders can no longer hope to control the awarding of what used to be the most valuable prize in their possession—their party's presidential nomination.[11] The proliferation of primaries also means that, since incumbent Presidents can no longer control their party (there being hardly any party for them to control), they can no longer count on renomination. What nearly happened to Gerald Ford in 1976 could well happen to Jimmy Carter in 1980. The changes in the parties' rules, together with the increase in the number of primaries, have rendered the concept of party "membership," always a somewhat tenuous concept in the United States, virtually meaningless in 1978.[12]

---

[10] See the discussion in Austin Ranney's chapter in this volume, especially pp. 230-36.

[11] See Table 6-1 above, p. 218.

[12] Much has been written about the notion of party membership in the United States. See, in particular, Austin Ranney and Willmoore Kendall, *Democracy and the American Party System* (New York: Harcourt, Brace, 1956), chap. 9, and Leon D. Epstein, *Political Parties in Western Democracies* (New York: Praeger, 1967), chap. 5.

The changes in the electorate, though less dramatic than those that have overtaken the parties, are probably even more disconcerting to anyone who grew accustomed to the relatively orderly electoral politics of the 1950s. From the early 1960s onwards, party identification, especially strong party identification, declined quite sharply, while at the same time the incidence of split-ticket voting increased. By the late 1970s, citizens were considerably less likely than before "to identify with a party, to feel positively about a party, or to be guided in their voting behavior by partisan cues."[13] This widespread loosening of attachments to party was accompanied by a substantial increase in voting on the basis of issues and even ideologies—though many of the issues and ideologies were quite new to the period in question.[14] Not surprisingly under the circumstances, the old New Deal coalition gradually disintegrated, as the South ceased to be a one-party Democratic stronghold and as more and more working-class whites showed a willingness to vote for Republican presidential (and, to a lesser extent, congressional) candidates. Almost the only identifiable group in the nation that defied the general trends was the blacks, who as time went on became more and more solidly Democratic. The loosening of attachments to party (the blacks excepted) was accompanied by a loosening of attachments to the act of voting itself. In the sixties and seventies, legal barriers to voting were gradually levelled, and the electorate came to contain increasingly high proportions of citizens who had received a high-school or even college education. Turnout at elections should have increased. Instead it has tended to decline. Apparently for millions of voters, in an era that emphasizes the value of political participation, turning out to vote has ceased to be worth the effort.[15]

The changes in the parties and the electorate have been well researched. Much is known about them, even if their implications are still not clear. The changes that have taken place in American group politics, however, are considerably harder to grasp. Less is known about them; what is known falls less readily into patterns. Nevertheless, three closely related developments appear to have occurred and have been referred to repeatedly in the pages of this book. The first is the increasing professionalization of policy making in the United States. More and more career officials, in both Washington

[13] Norman H. Nie, Sidney Verba, and John R. Petrocik, *The Changing American Voter* (Cambridge, Mass.: Harvard University Press, 1976), p. 57; quoted by Jeane Kirkpatrick, p. 269 above.

[14] See Kirkpatrick's discussion above, pp. 274-75.

[15] For Richard A. Brody's discussion of why this should be so, see above pp. 299-313.

and the states, are professional men and women or are experts of one sort or another; the same is increasingly true of the staffs of both Congress and the interest groups themselves. The day of the amateur, whether the amateur politician or the amateur administrator, appears to be passing.[16] The second development is the rise in American politics of the "issue group." Issue groups are not new, of course; the anti-slavery organizations of the 1850s were just such groups. But issue groups did not figure as a major, continuing element in American political life until quite recently. The traditional interest groups have not disappeared; instead they have been joined by all manner of committees, organizations, and alliances owing their raison d'être not to considerations of self-interest, even corporate self-interest, but to a disinterested concern with the common weal. Most politically interested Americans can name several such organizations without even stopping to think: Green Peace, Friends of the Earth, Nader's Raiders, Common Cause. There is now a multiplicity of such issue groups, locally as well as in Washington. Few of them existed fifteen years ago.

The third development with regard to the groups is the one captured in Hugh Heclo's phrase, "issue network." In Heclo's view, the spread of what he calls "policy professionals" in federal government departments, in Congress, in the interest groups, and in Washington law firms, together with the rise of issue groups and the continuing proliferation and fragmentation of the groups, has given rise to a quite new, distinctive group life. The character of the new group life is formed in part by the extent in the United States of "indirect administration," of government by remote control, in which the federal government assumes relatively few administrative functions itself but instead acts through intermediary organizations—state and local governments, contractors, consultants, and so on.[17] The outcome is a long-term trend toward specialized policy expertise in the ranks of government, and also the development of a wide range "of specialized subcultures composed of highly knowledgeable policy-watchers."[18] As Heclo points out, the growth of such issue networks makes the task of presidential leadership—indeed of political leadership in general—more difficult, as the language in which the issues

---

[16] Rather surprisingly, the position of the amateur remains strong in one of the very places where one would least expect to find him; see below p. 379.

[17] On the general topic of indirect administration, and also the rise of the policy professional, see Beer, pp. 18-22; Heclo, pp. 105-15; and Epstein, pp. 367-68.

[18] The phrase is Heclo's; see above p. 99. For an analysis written independently of Heclo's, which makes some of the same points, see Richard Rovere, "Affairs of State," *New Yorker*, May 8, 1978, pp. 139-46.

are discussed becomes more and more abstruse and as the networks themselves become relatively impervious to outside interference. The questions that Heclo raises toward the end of his chapter are obviously crucial to the future functioning of the American system, and we shall come back to them later.

These, then, in very summary form are some of the propositions advanced in the previous chapters of this volume. To them we may perhaps add a few footnotes.

One concerns the future, if any, of that redoubtable American institution, "the bandwagon." The idea of a bandwagon was always fairly straightforward. Politicians involved in the nomination of presidential candidates always wanted, other things being equal, to be on the winning side. They wanted to be on the winning side because the winning candidate, especially if he became President, could be counted upon to reward those who had supported him before and at the convention more liberally than those who had not. Hence such phrases as "For Roosevelt Before Chicago."[19] Bandwagons had to do not with music but with politicians' self-interest. (Alternatively, a few might jump on the bandwagon simply for the psychological gratification of identifying themselves with the winner; but this was never what bandwagons were really meant to be about.) If Ranney is right, and if it is no longer politicians, but rather ordinary voters, who determine the outcomes of presidential nominating contests, then bandwagons no longer exist, since millions of rank-and-file voters cannot imagine that they will benefit in any way from having voted for the winning rather than the losing candidate. It is sad to note the passing of a great American institution.[20]

Another possible footnote concerns the Supreme Court. The burden of Heclo's chapter in this volume is that issue networks

---

[19] Franklin Roosevelt and his campaign manager, James A. Farley, made sure that most of the jobs in FDR's first administration went only to those who had been "FRBC." See James MacGregor Burns, *Roosevelt: The Lion and the Fox* (New York: Harcourt, Brace, 1956), p. 150.

[20] The traditional bandwagon should be distinguished from the more modern phenomenon of "momentum." It may be that a candidate capturing delegates at early state conventions, or winning early primaries, may attract more publicity and may thereby be enabled to gather momentum: more voters recognize his name; it becomes easier for him to raise money and build up local organizations; and so on. But this process involves much less calculation on the part of most of the people involved than did decisions in the old days about whether, and when, to jump on bandwagons. No one has so far studied momentum in any detail. McGovern in 1972 seemed to benefit from it. Carter in 1976 seemed to acquire it early in his campaign for the nomination, but then to lose it. Carter finished first in only two (South Dakota and Ohio) of the last seven seriously contested primary elections in 1976. See Martin Schram, *Running for President 1976: The Carter Campaign* (New York: Stein and Day, 1977), Book I.

blanket an increasingly large proportion of the totality of American politics, that the language of issue networks is no longer understood by large portions of the electorate, and that the networks fail to simplify complexity, fail to work toward consensus, fail to induce confidence in political leaders, and fail to take actions that result in closure, the ending of debate in favor of action.[21] If Heclo is right (and he probably is), then the paradoxical consequence is that the Supreme Court has become, in some meaningful sense, one of the most responsive, and even the most accountable, of American political institutions—the last bastion, if Shapiro is to be believed, of the amateur tradition, since the justices can no longer claim to be legal scholars and are certainly not members of any issue network.[22] Indeed all that the issue networks fail to provide the Supreme Court provides in large measure: the simplication (very often) of complex issues, a tendency to work toward consensus, a capacity to induce confidence in the public (and, on the part of the justices, a capacity to appear to be confident in themselves), and a willingness, indeed a need, to come to decisions that, if not exactly final, at any rate achieve closure on the immediate issue at hand. The Supreme Court, despite its legal panoply and jargon, may today be one of the few American political institutions that average men and women imagine that they can understand. One wonders whether the justices would be flattered. One imagines that they might.

Another possible footnote to the previous nine chapters concerns a matter of language. Americans for many years past have been wont to speak of civil servants as "bureaucrats," and of their civil service as "the bureaucracy." The language is that of Max Weber.[23] It implies the existence of large numbers of persons arranged in ordered hierarchies and dealing with the problems of governing in a rational, highly routinized way. On this basis, the term bureaucracy as a description of the federal civil service in Washington ought (except perhaps as a term of affection or nostalgia) to be abandoned forthwith. Washington civil servants may be arranged, more or less, in ordered hierarchies. But they are not routine (or even nonroutine) administrators; they are, in Heclo's phrase, "policy professionals."

---

21 See pp. 119-21 above.

22 On the fact that the justices are no longer legal scholars, see the discussion in Martin Shapiro's chapter above, pp. 209-10. The justices of the Burger court contrive to be amateurs in this sense even though more of them are ex-judges than was the case on the Vinson and Warren courts.

23 Weber's description of the defining characteristics of a bureaucracy can be found in H. H. Gerth and C. Wright Mills, From Max Weber: Essays in Sociology (New York: Oxford University Press, 1946).

They do not administer programs themselves, but rather supervise the administration of programs by others. They are charter members of the issue networks, whose methods are anything but ordered and routinized. Thus, to continue to use the term bureaucrat to describe the men and women who work in Washington is to liken, say, the deputy assistant secretary at the Department of Housing and Urban Development to a counter clerk in the Social Security Administration. Of course the two have something in common: they both work for the government. But at that point the resemblance between them ends. The old-fashioned European terms "civil service" and "public service" at least have the advantage of a certain neutrality.

A final footnote concerns the decline of America's political parties, at least as presidential nominating institutions, and also the possibility, discussed by Ranney, that national presidential primaries might be held at same time in the future.[24] Now it is clear that, if national presidential primaries were to be held, they would effectively replace the present nominating conventions. (Indeed, to a considerable extent the present state primaries have done so already.) But, if the nominating conventions were to be replaced, it would not be clear why there should be nominations at all. After all, the conventions existed historically to pick a winner. Why not allow the electorate to pick the winner? It is going to pick him or her sooner or later anyway. Why not sooner? It is hard to see how this logic can be escaped, and it is interesting to note, as Epstein points out in Chapter 9, that one state has already succumbed to it—Louisiana, where the primary and general elections have already been collapsed into one (or two if a runoff is needed), and where voters of all parties can vote for whomever they like from a range of candidates bearing the labels of all parties.[25] Such a free-for-all, organized on a nationwide basis, would certainly save time and money; and, moreover, as Epstein remarks, the general impact of Louisiana's new law "is more compatible with an individualistic, candidate-centered politics than with organized two-party competition." [26] Of course the adoption of the Louisiana system nationwide would sound the death knell of the national political parties in the United States. But they do not appear to be in very good shape now. Perhaps Louisiana, for the first time in its history, represents the wave of the future.

---

[24] For Ranney's discussion, see above pp. 246-47.
[25] See Epstein, p. 357.
[26] Ibid.

A New Political System?

No one can deny that the political system has changed, and changed considerably. The question is: Does it now deserve to be described as a new system? Novelty, like beauty, of course, is in the eye of the beholder, and in the nature of the case there can be no conclusive answer to this question. Many readers will already have made a mental note that quite a few of the developments described in this volume were already well under way by 1960, and that, as Greenstein comments in Chapter 2 on the presidency, some of the political tendencies of the sixties and seventies simply represent a reversion to the politics of the pre-Kennedy era.[27] If the press gave Nixon a rough time, it was not exactly kind to Truman. If the party leaders in the House of Representatives and the Senate have not been strong figures in the 1960s and 1970s, who but an antiquarian (or someone with a prodigious memory) can name the predecessors of Sam Rayburn and Lyndon Johnson? [28]

All of this is true, and caveats like these must be borne in mind. We must also try to distinguish between changes that are merely short-term, however important they may appear at the time, and changes that are genuinely long-term. Several of the previous chapters have wrestled with this problem.[29] Nevertheless, a strong case can be made out that the changes that have taken place in the American political system are both profound and widespread in their implications—that it is no mere rhetorical exaggeration to describe the system as it now functions as new, certainly in a number of crucial respects.

One way of capturing the extent of change is to compare the way in which the system now works with the accounts of its working contained in the leading textbooks on American politics published fifteen or twenty years ago—late in the Eisenhower era and under

---

[27] Indeed the general thrust of Greenstein's chapter is to suggest that the Ford and Carter presidencies represent not so much something new as a harking back to the period before the "strong" presidencies of Kennedy, Johnson, and Nixon; see especially p. 70 ff.

[28] For readers wishing to test their memories, Sam Rayburn's predecessor as Speaker was William B. Bankhead. There were also two interludes during Rayburn's tenure when the Speaker was the much better known Republican, Joseph W. Martin. Lyndon Johnson's predecessor as Democratic majority leader was Ernest McFarland. His immediate predecessor as majority leader was another well-known Republican, Robert A. Taft.

[29] Greenstein, Patterson, and Kirkpatrick all have a good deal to say about the problem of distinguishing between secular and cyclical phenomena; see especially pp. 61-62, 130-31, and 283-85.

Kennedy. The textbooks were not always right; sometimes they differed among themselves. But, taken as a group, they do convey the common understandings of the time in which they were written; textbooks, after all, are seldom works that seek to be controversial or to strive for effect. Let us therefore examine the textbook account of American politics circa 1960. In particular, let us see what they had to say about three of the institutions and structures covered by the present volume: Congress, the political parties, and interest groups.[30]

In their descriptions of Congress, the textbooks of a generation ago were agreed that power was widely dispersed in both the House of Representatives and the Senate, and that the two political parties' leaders in both bodies were only as strong as circumstances and their own personalities permitted. They were also agreed, however, that, despite this dispersal of power, a limited number of concentrations of power could be detected in both houses—rather as clouds, perhaps stars in the making, can be detected among the interstellar gases. The most important of these concentrations were four in number.

First, there were the standing committees. Everyone agreed that it was in the standing committees that the real work of Congress was done. John Ferguson and Dean McHenry described the committees as " 'little ministries' with enormous power." [31] Woodrow Wilson's characterization of American government as "government by the Standing Committees of Congress" was frequently quoted.[32] Second, if the committees were powerful, their chairmen were almost as powerful, since the committees were largely run by their chairmen. "It is almost impossible," Robert Carr and Marver Bernstein wrote, "to exaggerate the importance of the role played by committee chairmen in the legislative process." [33] Carr and Bernstein went on to set out at length the powers of committee chairmen. "In theory," they concluded, "the manner in which a chairman exercises these powers is

---

[30] The writer should make it clear straight away that the following accounts represent a severe foreshortening of what some of the textbook authors had to say and may do violence to some of the subtlety of their arguments. The aim is not to discuss particular authors, for their own sakes but rather to draw out what a considerable number of textbooks had in common. Also, it goes without saying that what may sound dated and wrong-headed in 1978 or 1979 may well have been—probably was—up-to-date and perfectly sensible in the late fifties or early sixties.

[31] John H. Ferguson and Dean E. McHenry, *The American System of Government*, 6th ed. (New York: McGraw-Hill, 1961), p. 258.

[32] Ibid.

[33] Robert K. Carr, Marver H. Bernstein, Donald H. Morrison, and Joseph E. McLean, *American Democracy in Theory and Practice*, 3d ed. (New York: Holt, Rinehart and Winston, 1961), p. 316.

subject to review and even control by the committee as a whole, but it is a rare committee that ever undertakes to check or rebuke its chairman."[34] Third, it was agreed that the power of committee chairmen owed a good deal to the fact that they were, in practice, irremoveable, since their selection was based not on merit or even popularity but on seniority. More than one textbook reproduced a Herblock cartoon showing elderly members of Congress being selected for committee posts by a man with a long ruler who was engaged in measuring the length of their beards.[35] Finally, it was universally agreed that in the House of Representatives enormous power, for good or ill, was wielded by the Rules Committee, which had for all practical purposes the power to prevent any bill or resolution from ever reaching the House floor. Another Herblock cartoon depicted the Rules Committee preparing itself to bury a number of pending bills in a pit filled with quicklime.[36]

These descriptions of Congress were undoubtedly accurate in their time. Indeed they would have been accurate at almost any time between about the turn of the century and when they were written. But they are not accurate today. Much of the work of Congress is still done in standing committees, of course; it is hard to see how it could be done otherwise. But the individual committees can no longer be regarded as virtually autonomous mini-legislatures. Many important matters, as Patterson shows in the case of energy, fall within the jurisdictions of several committees.[37] Members of committees, moreover, are highly sensitive to the views of their colleagues in the House and Senate, who will ultimately determine whether the bills reported out of the committees will ever reach the statute book. To the extent that committees do still wield autonomous power, their collective power has largely ceased to be coterminous with the individual power of their chairmen; chairmen have to behave much more circumspectly, not least because, although they are unlikely to be removed, the possibility of their removal now exists. The seniority *norm* is certainly not dead; but the seniority *system* is. As for the House Rules Committee, it is of some interest that Patterson in Chapter 4 of this book mentions it only in passing. Henry Clay would

---

[34] Ibid.

[35] Ibid. Also, Ferguson and McHenry, *American System of Government*, p. 259.

[36] Carr and Bernstein, *American Democracy*, p. 330. The same cartoon (one wonders what the textbook writers would have done without Herblock) appears in Peter H. Odegard, Robert K. Carr, Marver H. Bernstein, and Donald H. Morrison, *American Government: Theory, Politics, and Constitutional Foundation* (New York: Holt, Rinehart and Winston, 1961), p. 438.

[37] See above Table 4-7, p. 162.

probably adapt quite readily to the Congress of the late 1970s; Sam Rayburn, not to mention Judge Smith, might find that the place took a bit of getting used to.[38]

One of the most perceptive textbook accounts of the old American party system is to be found in the early editions of Marian Irish and James Prothro's *The Politics of American Democracy*.[39] Irish and Prothro set out, as was the fashion of the time, a list of the "functions" of the two major political parties. The parties existed, first, to give the people a chance, through group action, to influence the direction of public policy; second, to organize public opinion, so that different policy options could be clarified and interested citizens enlightened on the policy choices of the day; third, to moderate the differences that exist between the various interests that make up the electorate ("In order to win majority support, they must avoid taking any extremist position."); fourth, to serve as agencies for the selection of public officials (since the parties controlled nominations); and, fifth, to help overcome the obstacles to government action thrown up in the United States by checks and balances and the separation of powers.[40]

Now Irish and Prothro did not imagine that the Democratic and Republican parties of the 1950s performed all of these functions satisfactorily or all of the time. On the contrary, they pointed out that the parties frequently failed to provide a link between public opinion and public policy, and that they often failed to build bridges between the executive and legislative branches of government. Even so, there probably was in the postwar period a certain rough and ready fit between the functions that the textbooks said that the parties should perform and the functions that they actually did perform. It is hard to see that there is any such fit today; or, if there is a degree of fit, it is altogether looser. Insofar as the people at large are capable of influencing public policy, it would appear to be much more through

---

[38] Sam Rayburn (D.-Tex.) served longer than anyone else as speaker of the House of Representatives, from 1940 to 1947, from 1949 to 1953, and again from 1955 to 1961. Judge Howard Smith was for many years (1954-1966) the wily and autocratic chairman of the House Rules Committee. The two men clashed in 1961 when Rayburn worked with the Kennedy administration to enlarge the membership of the Rules Committttee so as to deprive the members of the conservative coalition on the committee of their slender overall majority. Smith, however, remained much the most powerful figure on the committee. He began the new regime by refusing to provide the new members of the enlarged committee with chairs. For an account of the Rules Committee in its heyday, see James A. Robinson, *The House Rules Committee* (Indianapolis, Ind.: Bobbs-Merrill, 1963).

[39] Marian D. Irish and James W. Prothro, *The Politics of American Democracy*, 2d ed. (Englewood Cliffs, N.J.: Prentice-Hall, 1962).

[40] Ibid., p. 294.

individual candidates, and interest and issue groups, than through the parties. The parties would appear in the late 1970s to do virtually nothing to enlighten citizens on the policy options currently facing the United States. Whether they moderate the differences between the clashing interests that make up the electorate is, we now know, a matter of contingent fact: usually they do; sometimes they do not.[41] As agencies for the selection of public officials, the parties are evidently in a state of secular decline. They were, moreover, never very good at building bridges between the executive and legislative branches; since the presidency of Lyndon Johnson they have hardly performed this function at all.

The same gap between the textbook notions of the late 1950s and the political realities of the late 1970s opens up when we consider the parties' organizations and their role in the selection of presidential candidates. The description that Irish and Prothro provide of party organization circa 1960 is the classic one, traces of which can still be found in the textbooks today. They describe the American parties as "little more than loose coalitions of state and local factions, brought together to conduct presidential campaigns and, if their party wins, to distribute public offices to loyal supporters."[42] They add in the same passage that candidates for Congress "are even more clearly the product of local rather than national machines." They assign great importance, and a good deal of space, to the national nominating conventions, remarking that, "although the party convention has been replaced by the direct primary in nominations for Congress and most state offices, it remains conspicuously alive in the nominations of presidential candidates."[43]

In view of what has happened since, it is worth quoting what Irish and Prothro have to say about the process of choosing convention delegates. They note that the process is complicated by the fact that each state and the District of Columbia has its own system for choosing delegates; and then they go on:

> Most of these complications arose from attempts in the first two decades of this century to extend the direct primary to the nomination of presidential candidates. Reformers rea-

---

[41] See Kirkpatrick's discussion of this subject at pp. 263-67 above. The two clear-cut cases of non-moderation are of course the Republicans' nomination of Barry Goldwater in 1964 and the Democrats' nomination of George McGovern in 1972. Both nominations led to landslide victories for their opponents.

[42] Irish and Prothro, *Politics of American Democracy*, p. 302.

[43] Ibid., p. 367.

soned that, if the national convention could not be eliminated as the state conventions had been, at least the direct election of delegates pledged to a specific candidate would transform the national convention from a decision-making body into a mere recording device. If successful, the movement would have left the national convention with no more discretion in nominating the President than the electoral college has in electing him. By 1916, half the states were using the presidential primary in one form or another, but since then the tide has turned back in favor of the convention. In 1960, only eleven states chose all their convention delegates in primaries; in four states, some delegates were selected in primaries while others were selected by party committees or conventions.[44]

In the late 1970s, the world is different. The tide that appeared to have been stemmed, even turned back, twenty years ago is now in full flood. It has indeed inundated the conventions, which have now become, and are likely to remain, more often than not "mere recording devices" and not "decision-making bodies." Perhaps we should add that Irish and Prothro were not insensitive to the possibility that the old party organizations might be supplanted. Commenting on the gradual decline of the old-style party machine, they observed sadly:

> If developments of this sort really serve to broaden and nationalize the political concerns of Americans, they are probably a wholesome influence. But if they mean simply that the organizational continuity and responsibility of the old party machine are to be replaced by the confusion of recurrent popularity contests, they may well create a new, less easily identifiable "machine" of professional public relations men and their employers.[45]

In these words we can hear a clear pre-echo of Ranney's comments at at the end of Chapter 6 in this volume. Two decades after Irish and Prothro wrote, American electoral politics has largely become what they feared it might: a "confusion of recurrent popularity contests."

Finally, let us see what the textbooks of a generation ago had to say about the politics of American interest groups. The chapter in Carr and Bernstein's *American Democracy in Theory and Practice* was typical.[46] Like almost all of the textbook descriptions, it probably constituted a fairly accurate reflection of the circumstances of the

---

[44] Ibid., p. 369.
[45] Ibid., p. 307.
[46] Carr and Bernstein, *American Democracy*, chap. 9.

time in which it was written. Carr and Bernstein consider what they call "the spectrum of pressure groups." It is a very broad spectrum indeed, comprising "business, labor, agriculture, the professions such as law, medicine, and education, regional, racial, and nationality groups, war veterans—almost every type of group interest or allegiance known to man." [47] The authors' entire discussion is cast in terms of groups that were in some sense self-interested, even if their self-interest was not necessarily economic and even if they often expressed their self-interest in highly ideological language. The environmental, consumer, and other issue groups that figure so largely in the politics of the late 1970s make no appearance in Carr and Bernstein's pages—for the very good reason that, in the early 1960s, they did not exist. Carr and Bernstein also tend to cast their discussion in terms of blocs: "business," "labor," "agriculture," and so on. But, as Heclo points out in Chapter 3, these blocs, always more fragmented in the United States than in many other countries, are today even more fragmented.[48] Indeed some of them, like agriculture and medicine, have been all but pulverized.

When Carr and Bernstein come to discuss the techniques of pressure groups, they categorize them under three headings: controlling the personnel of government, "electioneering"; bringing direct pressure upon government, "lobbying"; and influencing public opinion, "propagandizing." [49] Elsewhere in their text they note, of course, the extremely close relations existing between certain pressure groups and the federal bureaucracy and many of the independent regulatory agencies. What Carr and Bernstein do not pick up—again, because it did not exist and was therefore not there to be picked up—is the 1960s and 1970s' increasing professionalization of both governmental and interest-group politics, and the development of issue networks so porous in their structure that it is sometimes hard to know where government ends and nongovernment begins, who is the person being lobbied, who is the lobbyist. The activities that Carr and Bernstein describe continue to occur; if anything, they are more intense than they were twenty years ago. But they take place in an entirely new context, both structural and intellectual.

---

[47] Ibid., pp. 197-98.

[48] See Heclo's observations at pp. 94-98 above under the heading "All Join In." Heclo remarks that "a key factor in the proliferation of groups is the almost inevitable tendency of successfully enacted policies to unwittingly propagate hybrid interests." He goes on to describe the impact of federal policies relating to medicine and the delivery of medical services on the hitherto monolithic political representation of the medical profession.

[49] Carr and Bernstein, *American Democracy*, pp. 201-5.

It would be tiresome to pursue this kind of analysis through all of the topics covered in this book. And it is certainly the case that some elements in the political system have changed much less than others; the Supreme Court and the fifty states, for example, stand today very much where they did in the postwar period, or at least under Eisenhower. But enough should have been said by now to convince even the most skeptical reader that many elements in the system have changed quite radically in the past twenty years. If the full extent of change is sometimes not noticed, it may be because some of the changes have occurred only rather slowly and because all of them have taken place in a period filled with dramatic events—the assassinations of the Kennedys and Martin Luther King, Jr., urban riots, Vietnam, and Watergate. The events of the moment may have distracted attention from the more enduring institutional developments that were taking place at the same time. We should also note at this stage that many of the changes described in this volume have had a genuinely systemic character: some elements in the system have changed precisely because others have changed. The job of the President, for example, is quite different now from what it was twenty years ago, not primarily because the legal position of the President has changed (though it has), nor primarily because the institutions of the "institutionalized presidency" have changed (though they have), but because of changes in Congress and the parties and because of the emergence of Heclo's "issue networks." The interconnectedness of change has indeed been one of the recurring themes of this volume.

It is one thing, however, to maintain that a substantially new political system has emerged. It is quite another to state what the most important characteristics of the new system are. T.S. Eliot once wrote a book called Notes towards the Definition of Culture. In the remainder of this chapter, I shall attempt some notes, however preliminary, toward the definition of the new American political system.

Building Coalitions in the Sand

If we examine the literature on American politics, there is one word that keeps recurring in all kinds of different contexts. That word is "coalition." American politics is almost universally seen as the politics of coalition building. Thus, writers on Congress refer to the "conservative coalition" between Republicans and southern Democrats. Writers on the electorate refer to the "New Deal coalition" of white southerners, blacks, and the urban working class. Radicals refer to the desirability of building a "poor people's coalition." And so on.

Contenders for presidential nominations are said to need to build winning coalitions. So are Presidents seeking to ensure the passage of legislation in Congress. Even with regard to the Supreme Court, there is talk of "coalition building and bargaining among the justices." [50]

This view of the character of American politics emerges clearly from a passage in one of the best recent textbooks on the subject, Raymond Wolfinger, Martin Shapiro, and Fred Greenstein's *Dynamics of American Politics*.[51] In their chapter on the ideological context of American politics, the authors are refuting the idea that the Founding Fathers were hostile to the principle of majority rule. On the contrary, they say, the Founding Fathers introduced the majority principle in voting in the House of Representatives and Senate as well as throughout the election process. What the framers of the Constitution feared was that the government might fall into the hands of a dominant majority. The authors continue:

> Instead, they wanted a system in which decisions would be made by what have been called majorities of the moment. Such a majority is not a permanent, homogeneous one capable of turning government into the servant of a single interest. It is a coalition of a number of factions that find themselves in momentary agreement on a single specific issue. Having combined to form a voting majority in Congress and gained the cooperation or at least neutrality of the President, this coalition will dissolve again as soon as what it wants becomes law. Having achieved the single purpose that the member groups or factions shared, there is nothing further to hold the coalition together. As new issues arise, new coalitions will form. A group that happened to be in the winning coalition one time may be among the losers the next time.[52]

Coalition building, in other words, is not merely a fairly accurate description of the way in which American politics has in fact operated for the past two hundred years; it is what the Founding Fathers wanted.

Now in one sense the idea of politics as coalition building is perfectly straightforward—so straightforward as to border on the trivial. Obviously, if a majority is to be formed in any political system, a number of discrete individuals or groups must act together, must

---

[50] See Martin Shapiro above, p. 196.

[51] Raymond E. Wolfinger, Martin Shapiro, and Fred I. Greenstein, *Dynamics of American Politics* (Englewood Cliffs, N.J.: Prentice-Hall, 1976).

[52] Ibid., p. 75.

coalesce. The majority of cardinals electing a Pope form a coalition; so does a majority of the Italian electoral college electing a new Italian president. Indeed there is a sense in which all political formations, whatever their character, are, by definition, coalitions. Political parties are coalitions, interest groups are coalitions, even police forces and armies are coalitions. All of them involve a degree of coalescing, of coming together.

But of course this is not what writers on American politics have in mind when they refer to coalition building. Nor is it usually what American politicians are thinking about when they set about trying to form coalitions. The idea of coalition building in their minds is a good deal stronger. It would seem to consist of two elements. The first element is the assumption of the prior existence of a number of distinct political formations—parties, factions, interests, voting blocs, or whatever—out of some of which, ideally a majority, a coalition can be formed. Metaphorically, politicians build coalitions in the same way that children build houses—out of previously existing building blocks. The second element in the idea of coalition building is that the building blocks should have some sort of structure. They should have a degree of internal structure, possibly even a leader or leaders. From the politician's point of view, the ideal coalition partner is, of course, a group led by someone who can always be sure of being able to deliver the votes or support of his followers. It is worth noting that these two elements—previously existing political formations plus internal structure or leadership—are both contained in the dictionary definition of coalition, in the political sense of the word: "a temporary alliance of distinct parties, persons, or states for joint action to achieve a common purpose."[53] Thus, one speaks of a coalition government in France or of the various coalitions of European states against Napoleon.

Coalitions presuppose blocks—or, more precisely, blocs. Yet, if one message emerges from the pages of this book, it is that fewer and fewer cohesive blocs are to be found in the American polity. Certain words have appeared again and again in the preceding pages: "fragmentation," "proliferation," "decentralization," "disintegration," "breaking up." The ideas of the New Deal are no longer the ideas around which American politics is organized; but no new public philosophy has emerged to take their place. Power in Congress is even more widely dispersed than it used to be; the conservative coalition is much less prominent than it was. The old party machines and

---

[53] *Webster's Third International Dictionary of the English Language* (Springfield, Mass.: G. & C. Merriam, 1971), vol. 1, p. 432.

bosses have largely gone; nothing has replaced them. There are far more interest and issue groups than there used to be; the great majority of them lack internal cohesion. Within the federal government in Washington, the old "iron triangles" (coalitions of a sort) have given way to much more amorphous issue networks, to the description of which a simple Euclidian geometry is no longer appropriate. Even among the electorate, the voting blocs of the 1930s and 1940s have been gradually eroded by time; only the blacks remain. To the words suggestive of disintegration, of breaking up, used so frequently in this volume, we should clearly add "atomization." American politics have become, to a high degree, atomized.

To the extent that all this is true, it would seem to follow that the language of coalition building is no longer the most helpful language in which to describe American politics, indeed that it may be positively misleading. American politicians continue to try to create *majorities*; they have no option. But they are no longer, or at least not very often, in the business of building *coalitions*. The materials out of which coalitions might be built simply do not exist. Building coalitions in the United States today is like trying to build coalitions out of sand. It cannot be done.

What would some of the attributes of an atomized politics, a politics of majority creating rather than coalition building, be likely to be? Four attributes, at least, of such a system suggest themselves. The first is the most obvious: leadership becomes more difficult. Not only does each new majority have to be constructed out of new combinations of individuals and groups, but the number of individuals and groups upon whom influence has to be brought to bear becomes larger. Moreover, each individual or group is likely to have his, her, or its own distinctive interests and opinions—each congressman and senator his own views and electoral base, each section of the medical or agricultural worlds its own interests and preoccupations. Most plant managers, if pressed, will admit that they would rather deal with one strong labor union than with a multiplicity of weaker ones. Deals made with large, strong unions, once struck, are likely to be adhered to; leaders of such unions can deliver their members. By contrast, bargaining with a number of smaller, weaker unions is in itself more complicated; and the bargains arrived at are considerably less likely to endure, not least because of interunion rivalry. Modern American Presidents must feel the same way about Congress. As Greenstein points out in Chapter 2, gone are the days when a President can achieve his object merely as the result of telephone conversations with the majority and minority leaders on Capitol Hill.[54]

Second, leadership becomes more difficult partly because an atomized politics is much harder to understand than a politics of coalition, and is also far more unpredictable. To issue complexity is superadded political complexity. The outcomes of campaigns for presidential nominations always depended on a large number of factors (including the views of dozens of bosses and state governors, and hundreds of convention delegates); today they depend on so many factors (including the votes of millions of primary electors) as to be almost wholly unpredictable. It is no disrespect to the President to say that, if Jimmy Carter, an ex–Georgia governor with no national political experience whatever, can win the presidency, then almost anyone can. Likewise, from the President's point of view, Congress must have become a much more mysterious and unpredictable body than in the past. A Truman or a Kennedy, submitting a proposal for national health insurance to Congress, could make some fairly straightforward predictions about its chances of passing. These would be based on congressmen's and senators' known views on similar issues that had arisen in the past, and on the known attitudes of the various voting blocs in Congress toward the New Deal. Comparable predictions are much more difficult to make today. The watchword of Harold Geneen of ITT used to be, "No surprises."[55] Increasingly, the world of politics in the United States contains nothing but surprises.

Third, one of the many things that becomes harder to predict in an atomized politics is what the consequences of one's actions will be. More specifically, it becomes harder for the individual voter to predict what, in terms of public policy, will be the outcome of his or her electoral decision. There comes to be even less connection than there once was between what voters, even the majority of voters, want and what they get. Elected officials may mean to keep their promises. They may try to keep them. But they cannot deliver. A sense of the futility of the voting act almost certainly underlies some of the secular

---

[54] See Greenstein's account (p. 71 above) of the negotiations over the Civil Rights Bill of 1957 between President Eisenhower and the four party leaders of the time, Sam Rayburn, Lyndon Johnson, Joseph Martin, and William Knowland.

[55] On Harold Geneen's managerial methods, see Anthony Sampson, *The Sovereign State: The Secret History of ITT* (London: Hodder and Stoughton, 1973), esp. chap. 6. Of course, even Geneen was surprised from time to time.

decline in electoral turnout reported by Brody in Chapter 8.[56] Likewise, the passage of the now-famous Proposition 13 by California voters in June 1978 may have owed something not just to people's dislike of high property taxes but to their sense that the whole business of government was increasingly remote and hard to understand—that it had simply gotten out of voters' control. Those who supported Proposition 13 seemed to be saying, in a diffuse (even anomic) way, "For God's sake, listen to us!"[57]

Fourth, it seems not entirely fanciful to hypothesize that an atomized politics may share one characteristic with a human crowd—a tendency to move either very sluggishly or with extreme speed. In this connection, the contrast may be suggestive between Congress's handling of the energy question on the one hand, and its abolition of the mandatory retirement age on the other. In the case of energy, the issue was almost universally agreed to be of great importance. It had been on the policy agenda for several years. Yet in the early summer of 1978, more than fifteen months after President Carter had introduced his original energy package, no effective action had been taken. In the case of the mandatory retirement age, the issue was not one that had been widely discussed. If it was on the policy agenda, hardly anyone had noticed the fact. It certainly did not rank with energy as a matter of major national importance. Yet in March 1978 both houses of Congress passed the measure abolishing mandatory retirement—an action unprecedented in any major industrial country—by overwhelming majorities.[58] In the first case, coalition building proved impossible; in the second case, unnecessary. A careful comparison between Congress's handling of these two issues would probably

---

[56] For Brody's analysis of the various explanations that may account for the decline in turnout, see chap. 8, especially pp. 299-313.

[57] Indeed during the campaign Howard Jarvis, the joint author of Proposition 13 and the chief campaigner for it, frequently spoke of the need for the people of California to gain "control of the government again." He did not appear to be talking solely about taxes. For a discussion of the significance of Proposition 13, see "The Big Tax Revolt," Newsweek, June 19, 1978, pp. 18-24. President Carter's pollster, Pat Caddell, was only one of a number of commentators who subsequently read wider significance into the result on Proposition 13. "Taxes are the flashpoint for a lot of other angers," Caddell was quoted as saying (Newsweek, July 10, 1978, p. 27). "People feel unable to get control of government and make it respond. They don't have a handle on getting government to pay attention to them or their problems. And they don't believe they can elect people who make much difference." In short, for many voters Proposition 13 was a form of generalized emotional release as well as a response to a specific grievance.

[58] The legislation, H.R. 5383, was passed by 391–6 in the House and by 62–10 in the Senate. For a brief history of the new act and a summary of its provisions, see Congressional Quarterly Weekly Report, April 1, 1978, pp. 807-8.

throw considerable light on the functioning of an atomized political system.[59]

It is worth noting parenthetically that the proliferation and disintegration of American political structures would not appear to represent the working out in the United States of large social and political forces that are also present in other countries. Many of the sources of atomization appear to be peculiarly American. In Great Britain, by contrast, most of the old political structures survive more or less intact; and the major interest groups, in particular, have recently tended to form themselves into larger, and stronger, units. The talk in Britain is not of atomization but of its near-opposite, the "corporate state."[60] In Europe generally, not just in countries like Sweden and the Netherlands, the trend seems to be toward "centripetal politics" and "concertation."[61] Thus, if American politics has lost some of its former distinguishing features, it has by no means lost its claim to be considered unique.

What of the future? If Humpty-Dumpty has fallen off the wall, can he be put back together again, and, if so, in what form? Much will depend on the pressures to which the American polity is subjected in the coming decades. As Beer points out in Chapter 1, "there is such a thing as equilibrium without purpose. The balance of social forces today tends toward a kind of peace."[62] In the absence of crisis, the fact that a politics of coalition building has given way to a politics of majority creation may not matter greatly; the American polity may continue to function reasonably successfully and without much disturbance, as it did during most of the late nineteenth century. In the event of major crisis, however, whether social, economic, or international, one imagines that new, more stable structures and alignments would develop, possibly even a new public philosophy. Were

---

[59] One would not want to push the comparison very far, but there seem to be a number of parallels between American politics in the late 1970s and the politics of the Fourth Republic in France. In both cases, a tendency toward immobilism contrasted with moments of frantic activity (for example, during the premiership of Mendes-France). In both cases, there were signs that the public found the political process increasingly bewildering and alien. On the Fourth Republic, see Philip M. Williams, *Crisis and Compromise: Politics in the Fourth Republic* (London: Longmans, 1964).

[60] Much has been written about the possibility that Britain is turning into a more or less benign form of corporate state. See, by way of example, Samuel Brittan, *The Economic Contradictions of Democracy* (London: Temple Smith, 1978), and Michael Moran, *The Politics of Industrial Relations: The Industrial Relations Act of 1971* (London: Macmillan, 1977), chap. 8.

[61] See among other things Ghita Ionescu, *Centripetal Politics: Government and the New Centres of Power* (London: Hart-Davis, MacGibbon, 1975).

[62] See above p. 44.

the crisis to be sufficiently severe, and were an atomized polity to prove incapable of dealing with it, the movement might well be back toward a more powerful presidency. The imperial presidency is currently out of fashion; so, even, is an FDR-style presidency. But fashions change. The one American institution that the future may not be able to mend is the political party. Direct primaries mean the end, as they were meant to, of old-fashioned party organization. Since it seems unlikely that primaries will be abolished, it seems unlikely that political parties can ever exist again in the United States as they did in the century and a half up to about 1968. The textbooks used to say that political parties were essential to the functioning of democracy. We may be about to find out whether they were right.

In the 1930s and 1940s, a distinguished American journalist, John Gunther, wrote a series of books on various parts of the world, with titles like *Inside Europe, Inside Asia,* and *Inside U.S.A.* Gunther's method was to visit a country or town and ask its leading figures all sorts of questions. One of his chief questions was, "Who runs this place? Who is in charge?" Suppose that a reborn John Gunther were to visit the United States today and were to ask, "Who runs this place? Who is in charge?" The short answer, despite President Carter's best efforts, would have to be, "No one. Nobody is in charge here." Such an answer need not be a cause for dejection. Things will go on happening; the United States has shown considerable capacity for running itself. New structures and new leadership will almost certainly emerge. In the meantime, even if the American political landscape is largely new, the old, familiar landmarks still stand. If one feels disoriented, one may also take some reassurance. The republic has endured for more than two hundred years; it seems likely to endure for a good deal longer.

CONTRIBUTORS

Samuel H. Beer is Eaton Professor of the Science of Government at Harvard University, and the author of *British Politics in the Collectivist Age*, which won the Woodrow Wilson Award for 1966. He was president of the American Political Science Association in 1977 and served as a member of the McGovern-Fraser Committee on Delegate Selection and Party Structure in 1969–1972.

Richard A. Brody is a professor of political science at Stanford University. A former fellow of the Center for Advanced Study in the Behavioral Sciences, he is currently a member of the Council of the American Political Science Association and of the editorial board of the *American Political Science Review*. His writing includes articles on voting, public opinion, and the personal relevance of politics.

Leon D. Epstein is Bascom Professor of Political Science at the University of Wisconsin-Madison, where he has been a faculty member since 1948. He contributed to AEI's first Australian election volume, and his earlier works include *Politics in Wisconsin, Political Parties in Western Democracies,* and *Governing the University: The Campus and the Public Interest.* In 1978–1979 he was president of the American Political Science Association.

Fred I. Greenstein is Henry Luce Professor of Politics, Law and Society at Princeton University. His writings include *The American Party System and the American People, Children and Politics,* and *Personality and Politics: Problems of Evidence, Inference and Conceptualization.* He is coauthor of the AEI volume *Evolution of the Modern Presidency: A Bibliographical Survey.*

HUGH HECLO is professor of government at Harvard University and a former senior fellow at the Brookings Institution in Washington, D.C. His most recent work deals with problems of public management and appeared as a 1977 Brookings publication, *A Government of Strangers: Executive Politics in Washington.*

ANTHONY KING, an adjunct scholar of the American Enterprise Institute, is professor of government at the University of Essex in England. He is the author of the earlier AEI volume, *Britain Says Yes,* a study of the 1975 Common Market referendum, and comments on elections for the British Broadcasting Corporation and the London *Observer.* Until recently he was editor of the *British Journal of Political Science.*

JEANE J. KIRKPATRICK, a resident scholar at the American Enterprise Institute and Leavey Professor of the Foundations of American Freedom at Georgetown University, was a member of the Democratic National Convention's Commission on Presidential Nomination and Party Structure and of the Credentials Committee of the 1976 Democratic National Convention. She is the author of *The New Presidential Elite, Political Woman,* and *Leader and Vanguard in Mass Society.*

SAMUEL C. PATTERSON is a professor of political science at the University of Iowa. He is the coauthor of *The Legislative Process in the United States, Representatives and Represented: Bases of Public Support for the American Legislatures,* and *Comparing Legislatures;* coeditor of *Comparative Legislative Behavior: Frontiers of Research;* and editor of *American Legislative Behavior.* He also edited the *American Journal of Political Science* from 1970 to 1973.

AUSTIN RANNEY, a former professor of political science at the University of Wisconsin-Madison and a former president of the American Political Science Association, is currently a resident scholar at the American Enterprise Institute and a member of the Democratic National Committee's Commission on Presidential Nomination and Party Structure.

MARTIN SHAPIRO has taught political science at Harvard, Stanford, and a number of University of California campuses. He is now professor of law at the University of California-Berkeley. He has written a number of monographs, texts, and case books on the Supreme Court and contributes to the law reviews in the areas of judicial decision making and comparative law.

INDEX

Taney, Roger: 203
Task forces: 77
Tati, Jacques: 97
"Technocratic takeover": 18–22
Tennessee: 128
Tennessee Valley Authority: 12, 49
Texas: 71, 127, 157, 345
Thurmond, Strom: 258
Time magazine: 50
Title XX Social Services: 343
Tocqueville, Alexis de: 21, 97
Trade and professional associations: 96, 97
Transformations of the American Party System: 251
Truman Doctrine: 56, 68, 175
Truman, Harry: 52, 58, 59–60, 63, 66, 237, 254, 381
    Congress, relationship with: 70, 80
    electoral support: 258, 259
    Korea, American military intervention in: 80, 82
    presidency, characteristics of: 53–57, 77
    See also Fair Deal
Truman Library: 54
Turkey: 24
Turnout, decline in: 277, 290–315, 323–24, 374
Twenty-second Amendment: 64, 66, 80
Twenty-fourth Amendment: 276, 287, 292, 293
Twenty-sixth Amendment: 221, 276, 299

Udall, Morris: 42
United Automobile Workers: 360
United Kingdom: *See* Great Britain
United Nations: 175
United States Government Manual: 51, 58
University of Alabama: 42
U.S. Conference of Mayors: 95, 346
U.S. v. Nixon: 183, 184

Vance, Cyrus: 108, 112
Vandenberg, Arthur: 68
Verba, Sidney: 221–22, 258, 261, 273, 275, 297, 299, 315, 319, 320, 322
Vermont: 136, 329, 365
Vietnam War: 2, 3, 33, 62, 64, 69, 76, 81, 105, 184, 238, 250, 253, 262, 275, 281, 283, 284, 318, 372, 373, 388
Viguerie, Richard: 243
Virginia: 127, 329
Volksgeist: 23

Voting: 287
Voting Rights Act (1965): 31, 276, 287, 292

Wage and Hour Act: *See* Fair Labor Standards Act
Wagner Act: *See* National Labor Relations Act
Wallace, George: 41, 74, 258, 260, 267, 281, 282, 283, 284
Wallace, Henry: 57, 263
Wallop, Malcolm: 135
Wall Street: 252
War Powers Resolution (1973): 81–82, 175, 373
Warren, Earl: 200–207
Washington, D.C.: 385
Washington, George: 46
Washington law firms: 100–101
Watergate: 33, 62, 69, 72, 74, 77, 79, 81, 147, 241, 250, 253, 281, 283, 315, 373, 388
Wattenberg, Ben: 255, 281–82
Wayne State University: 337
Weathermen: 25
Webb, James: 55, 57
Weber, Max: 53, 107, 379
Weisberg, Herbert F.: 307–9
Wesberry v. Sanders: 136, 179
West Executive Avenue: 47
West Virginia: 127
White, Byron: 201, 202, 203
"White House horrors": 79–80
White House Office: 51, 55, 59, 76, 77–80, 83, 112
White, Leonard: 88
White, Theodore H.: 32, 37
Whitman, Ann: 60–61
Wigoda, Paul: 228
Wilson, Woodrow: 53, 382
Winograd commission: 216
Wisconsin: 225, 227, 326, 327, 334, 335, 350, 361, 363, 364, 365
Witcover, Jules: 41
Wolfinger, Raymond E.: 220, 272, 293, 295–96, 297, 299, 389
Woodward, Robert: 75
Wordsworth, William: 22, 23, 43
Working class: 250, 259–60
World War I: *See* First World War
World War II: *See* Second World War
Wright, Jim: 127, 168
Wyoming: 135, 136, 326, 329

Young, Andrew: 42, 122
Young, James: 88

Disc the relationf
int gaps in
down pol life —